SEX AND SEXUALITY

SEX AND SEXUALITY

Volume 1
SEXUALITY TODAY: TRENDS
AND CONTROVERSIES

Edited by Richard D. McAnulty and M. Michele Burnette

PRAEGER PERSPECTIVES

Westport, Connecticut
London

Library of Congress Cataloging-in-Publication Data

Sex and sexuality / edited by Richard D. McAnulty and M. Michele Burnette.
  v. cm.
 Includes bibliographical references and index.
 Contents: v. 1. Sexuality today : trends and controversies—v. 2. Sexual function
and dysfunction—v. 3. Sexual deviation and sexual offenses.
  ISBN 0–275–98581–4 (set : alk. paper)—ISBN 0–275–98582–2 (v. 1 : alk.
paper)—ISBN 0–275–98583–0 (v. 2 : alk. paper)—ISBN 0–275–98584–9
(v. 3 : alk. paper)
  1. Sex. 2. Sex customs. 3. Sexual disorders. 4. Sexual deviation.
I. McAnulty, Richard D. II. Burnette, M. Michele.
HQ21.S4716 2006
306.77—dc22   2006001233

British Library Cataloguing in Publication Data is available.

Library of Congress Catalog Card Number: 2006001233
ISBN: 0–275–98581–4 (set)
   0–275–98582–2 (vol. 1)
   0–275–98583–0 (vol. 2)
   0–275–98584–9 (vol. 3)

First published in 2006

Praeger Publishers, 88 Post Road West, Westport, CT 06881
An imprint of Greenwood Publishing Group, Inc.
www.praeger.com

Printed in the United States of America

The paper used in this book complies with the
Permanent Paper Standard issued by the National
Information Standards Organization (Z39.48–1984).

10 9 8 7 6 5 4 3 2 1

Contents

Preface

We have had many opportunities to teach and interact with both college students and professional audiences about some very important topics and issues in human sexuality in our roles as authors and college professors. When we were approached to write this three-volume set on sex and sexuality, we were intrigued with the idea of having a forum in which to reach a broader audience. That is our goal for this work. With that in mind, we encouraged our contributors to "talk to" a general audience when writing about the topics that were most important to them. The authors we selected to write these chapters represent both established authorities and budding scholars on the various topics in human sexuality. We are confident that they have all helped us accomplish our goal.

To us, few, if any, other topics in the realm of human behavior are more interesting, exciting, or controversial than sex. And we hope that you will agree after reading the chapters from this set. Each chapter stands alone, and you can choose to read as many or as few as you would like—pick the ones that interest you. We hope that you will find this work to be of significant value to you, whether you are in pursuit of a better general understanding of sexuality or are looking for answers to specific questions.

One theme you will find throughout these texts is that human sexual function is affected by a whole host of factors. These factors are biological, sociocultural, and psychological in nature. The scientific study of sexuality is for all practical purposes a "young" field, and we have only touched the surface in an attempt to fully understand how these factors interact and impact sexuality.

Another theme or concern you will find throughout this work is the question whether "scientific" views of sex are biased by social judgments about normal versus abnormal and/or functional versus dysfunctional sexual behavior. U.S. culture, in particular, holds many strong values and prohibitions about sex. In this context, studying and interpreting research on sexuality in an unbiased manner can be a challenge. Many of our authors caution the reader about this concern.

We wish to thank all the researchers and clinicians, past and present, who have contributed to the science of sex. Many of them have contributed chapters to this set, and for that we are grateful. We also thank our colleagues, families, and friends who supported us during the writing and editing process. Finally, we thank "the team" at Praeger Publishers.

Introduction

In the past few years, we have witnessed major developments in our understanding of sex and sexuality. A landmark survey of sexual practices in the United States offered new insights. The theory of evolutionary psychology inspired countless studies on sexual differences between women and men. Discoveries relating to sexual orientation, including possible brain and genetic factors, have emerged. A medication for the treatment of erection problems became a household term. The scandal of sexual molestation by the clergy captivated the media. Pornography in all of its forms became readily available via the Internet. And sex continued to sell.

The topic of sex is fascinating, intriguing, and even disturbing. We are seemingly surrounded by sexual themes. The media bombard us with sex. Sexuality is a fundamental need and a part of our identity. Yet, this basic human need is often misunderstood, and is often controversial, and sometimes problematic.

Volume 1 in *Sex and Sexuality* offers an overview of recent trends and developments in the field. It provides a summary of the sociocultural determinants of sexual practices and of sexual development through the lifespan. Additionally, some of the more sensitive and controversial topics, including pornography and the sex trade, are reviewed. Each chapter entails an analysis of a topic and related issues, a review of relevant and recent findings, a description of explanations for the issues and trends, and a summary that usually includes suggestions for further study and research.

In Chapter 1, Wiederman explores not only methods but also motives for conducting sex research. Challenges include the stigma attached to sex research, possible volunteer bias, and the potential inaccuracies of sex surveys. In Chapter 2, Baumeister and colleagues offer a concise and informative overview of the leading theories of sexuality. They argue that the two leading theoretical camps—social constructionism and evolutionary psychology—approach the status of cults with their respective dogmatic doctrines and dedicated followers. The historical significance of Freudian theory and, more recently, of social exchange theory is addressed. Kilmer and Shahinfar, in Chapter 3, lament the lack of research on sexuality in childhood, which is truly one of the last frontiers in sex research because of enduring taboos. The limited research has been mostly concerned with abnormal sexual development. The authors favor an ecological systems approach, which considers the contribution of such influences as peer culture, family factors, and community structure to sexual development. Adolescent sexuality has been the subject of much discussion and debate. As Rapsey and Murachver note in Chapter 4, adolescence has invariably been viewed as a problematic phase in human development, including sexual development. This flawed depiction of adolescence has hindered research on normal sexual expression during this phase. Although unwanted pregnancies and sexually transmitted diseases first become evident in this age-group, these problems do not affect most teens, nor should they define adolescent sexuality. Drawing from the General Social Surveys (GSS), Smith, in Chapter 5, offers a succinct summary of important social trends in sexual behavior in the United States. The summary traces changes in sexual activity over the past few decades, including changing rates of cohabitation, extramarital relations, gender of sexual partners, frequency of sexual intercourse and of sexual inactivity, and the impact of HIV. Few topics make people more uncomfortable than sexuality in later life. Sharpe criticizes these prejudiced attitudes and their detrimental impact on mature adults in Chapter 6. The limited research confirms that older adults can, and generally do, enjoy sexual intimacy into late life, even as they redefine the meanings of sex and intimacy.

Sexual orientation remains a fascinating if controversial aspect of human sexuality. In Chapter 7, Kauth reviews the growing amount of research on sexual orientation and identity. His comprehensive and objective review focuses on the relevant findings in America and in other cultures, the current sexuality theories, and recent events involving sexual orientation. In Chapter 8, Burnette examines the relevant research on sex and gender, concluding that men and women are more similar than different. Although popular stereotypes about gender are resistant to change, the findings on transgenderism challenge these simplistic notions. Our views about sexuality are highly influenced by such major sociocultural institutions as the family, medicine, religion, and the media. Bay-Cheng's critical examination in Chapter 9 of these influences dissects or "deconstructs" the various messages, thereby highlighting the comparative and arbitrary nature of these "truths" relating to sex and sexuality.

Her analysis challenges many dominant views of sex in the United States, such as the idea that sexual intercourse alone qualifies as "real" sex. In the same vein, Lewis demonstrates in Chapter 10 that our views of race and ethnicity are determined by culture rather than nature. In other words, categories of race are socially created rather than absolute and biologically determined. Here, too, we find racial stereotypes are oversimplifications. For example, contrary to the stereotype of higher levels of sexual activity among African Americans, Lewis finds this group to be more sexually conservative than others.

The sex trade, in all of its forms, remains a highly visible and controversial aspect of sexuality. Chapter 11 by Brown reviews the extensive and conflicting research on pornography, concluding that it is not as innocuous as some have argued. Brown proposes that even nonviolent pornography promotes callous attitudes toward women. Bullough and McAnulty offer an overview of the research on the "world's oldest profession" in Chapter 12. Despite the stigma, the sex trade thrives in most parts of the world. The authors also discuss a group that has largely been ignored in sex research: exotic dancers. Gil-Rivas and Kooyman discuss sexual risk-taking in Chapter 13. Efforts to understand and prevent sexual risk-taking require an examination of the social context, which in turn is influenced by a variety of individual and contextual factors such as characteristics of the individual, aspects of close interpersonal relationships, attitudes, beliefs, cultural norms, and social and economic conditions. Finally, in a thought-provoking thesis, Baumeister and Stillman offer what will be one of the most controversial chapters in the set. Their discussion of erotic plasticity in Chapter 14 proposes that women's sexual responses and feelings are more affected by social, cultural, and situational factors, whereas male sexuality is relatively more shaped by genetic, hormonal, and other biological factors. For example, the authors point out that women are more likely than men to alter the frequency of sexual activity based on situational factors, and they are also more likely to explore sexual variations, such as same-sex experimentation, than men. Although this chapter is unlikely to resolve this debate, it should inspire lively discussion and productive research.

1

Sex Research

Michael Wiederman ◆

Sex research. Wow! What could be more exciting? People are frequently titillated by the notion of someone conducting research on human sexuality. Because the topic is taboo, and sexual activity is exciting, people often assume that sex research must involve many interesting tasks. Sex research may hardly seem like "work."

The truth is that, although research on human sexuality can be intellectually stimulating, it is rarely arousing sexually or in other ways. Why? Sexuality is deeply private, so most research involves asking people about their sexuality. Researchers typically try to provide a setting in which the respondents are most comfortable—usually by gathering information through anonymous surveys. In the end, sex research often involves handing out and gathering printed survey forms. After analyzing and tabulating the responses, the result is a set of numbers and graphs, but hardly anything that resembles sexually stimulating material (except, perhaps, to some mathematicians).

Although the process of conducting most sex research may not be particularly exciting, people are generally interested in the results of the research. It is implied in Western culture that each individual is supposed to experience a robust sex life, consisting of definite interest in sex (but not too much) and varied sexual experience (but not to include certain behaviors or certain types of partners). So how do we know how we, as individuals, stack up against the rest of society? Even though Western culture often seems saturated with sexual images and references to sex, there is surprisingly little serious discussion or presentation of facts. This is where sexuality research comes in, and this is probably why most people are interested in its results. Sex research holds the promise of providing objective information about what other people do and think and feel sexually.

As members of Western culture, we most likely encounter with interest reports of sexuality research. So, better understanding the process of sex research, and the various pitfalls along the way, will help us become more savvy consumers of sex research results. We will know the questions to ask, even if only to ourselves, so that we remain appropriately critical in our evaluation of what we hear and read about "the latest research." The process of sex research begins with the people who conduct the research.

WHO ARE SEX RESEARCHERS?

Frequently, media reports of sex research include the proclamation "Scientists have found . . . ." This phrase conjures images of men dressed in white lab coats peering into microscopes, writing down their observations, and engaging in feverish discussions with colleagues. Indeed, some sex research is supported by grant money, so that the researchers can focus most of their attention on the study. Most sex research, however, is conducted by faculty members at colleges and universities. These professors typically teach psychology, sociology, or anthropology, although some are professors of communication, biology, social work, medicine, nursing, or public health. For these faculty members, sex research is a small part of what they do on a day-to-day basis. They teach, advise students, attend committee meetings, and have families and social lives. This helps to explain why any particular study may take several months or years to complete.

Why do professors study sexuality? In most colleges and universities, there is an expectation that faculty members will remain active researchers in their respective professional fields. Of course that does not explain why some professors choose sexuality research whereas their colleagues do not. Because professors are more or less free to choose the broad areas in which they conduct their research, it would not be the case that some sex researcher was pressured into studying sexuality. Being pressured *not* to study sexuality would be much more likely. So why do it? There most likely is an intellectual interest on the part of each sex researcher, but the answer to "why" may be as varied as sex researchers themselves (see the books by Brannigan, Allgeier, & Allgeier, 2000, and Bullough, Bullough, Fithian, Hartman, & Klein, 1997, for individual accounts of how sex researchers got into the business).

People often assume that if someone studies a particular sexuality topic, it must be because the person experiences a personal problem or obsession with that topic. So, if someone studies the effects of childhood sexual abuse, it must be that the researcher was sexually abused as a child (or, worse, is a child abuser). If a researcher investigates pornography, it must be that he or she is personally drawn to the use of pornography. There are no data on the subject, so it remains speculation as to why researchers choose the research topics they do. Indeed, sometimes it does seem to result from personal experiences, but many times, research topics are simply those that the professional was exposed to in graduate school, or through colleagues, or those that were being funded by grants.

Unfortunately, assumptions about the personal motives of sex researchers often result in sexuality research being stigmatized compared to most other research topics in the social and behavioral sciences. Sex researchers have been known to study nonsexual topics early in their careers, until they have achieved a degree of respectability (and tenure), so that embarking on the study of sexuality does not jeopardize their livelihood. For example, the sex research pioneer William Masters became well respected for his research and clinical work on infertility before deciding he could afford to study sexual behavior. Some sex researchers choose to study nonsexual topics in addition to sexual ones, perhaps as a way to keep from being pigeonholed as "just a sex researcher." Even within sex research, however, some topics (such as childhood sexuality and adult-child sexual contact) are more stigmatized than others. The less socially desirable the topic, the more the research on that topic seems to be stigmatizing for the researcher who seeks to better understand it.

If sex researchers are frequently stigmatized for their choice of research topic, what about people who choose to participate in sex research? Because sexuality is a private topic, who is most likely to volunteer to participate in sex research? What is in it for them?

WHO PARTICIPATES IN SEX RESEARCH?

Since most sex researchers are faculty members in colleges and universities, it is not surprising that many of the results of sex research are based on college student respondents (Dunne, 2002). Perhaps due to stigma, most sex research is not funded by grants, so researchers do not have money to offer as compensation for the time it takes students to participate in the research. Some faculty researchers offer extra credit in their courses for students who participate in research, and some colleges and universities require students in introductory psychology courses to participate in a certain number of research studies as part of the course. Sometimes, research participants are recruited with no obvious incentive or payoff.

Why is it important to consider who participates in sex research? If the research results are used to imply something about people in general, it is important to consider how well the research sample matches the population in general. College students tend to represent a fairly narrow slice of the population: young adults in their late teens and early twenties who are above average in intelligence and motivation. With regard to sexuality, college students have not had very many years to have had sexual and relationship experience, and they may be more open minded compared to people who never attended college. So, when we learn that a study based on college students revealed certain trends, we should ask whether it is likely that those same results would have occurred among research participants from the general public.

Even though college students represent a fairly unique sample compared to the general public, only certain types of college students are usually studied: those who are taking psychology or sociology courses. How might these students differ from those who choose not to take such courses? Students interested in social and behavioral sciences may be more open-minded and introspective compared to students uninterested in those courses. What about the social science students who then decide to participate in sex research? In what ways might they be different from social science students who choose not to participate, or who choose to fulfill their course requirements through participating in research on nonsexual topics? Research comparing students who participate in sex research to those who choose not to has revealed some consistent differences: sex research participants are more likely to be male, open-minded, and adventurous, and to have more liberal sexual attitudes and greater sexual experience (Dunne, 2002).

Even when sex researchers target the general population, not everyone chosen agrees to participate. Even in the most conscientiously conducted studies, perhaps only 70 percent of those contacted end up participating. How might those 30 percent who do not participate differ from the 70 percent who do? Compared to participants, nonparticipants tend to be older, more conservative in their attitudes and values, and more likely to be female. So, when we hear that a certain percentage of people believe such and such or have had some particular sexual experience, chances are this percentage does not accurately reflect what would be found among the population as a whole.

What we have been discussing in this section is the extent to which any particular sample is *representative* of the population the researcher is trying to understand. The ideal is for the sample to be perfectly representative, meaning, the sample perfectly matches the characteristics of the population. In reality this never occurs, mainly because people cannot be forced to participate in research. So, those who choose to do so will probably always differ in some ways from people who choose not to—and this is especially the case when the topic is sexuality. Some people are simply more open to sharing with researchers details of their sexual attitudes and experiences than are others. These people tend to have more open and liberal attitudes about sex.

Perhaps the least representative of samples occurs when participants themselves have to initiate participation. For example, if a magazine publishes a questionnaire, asking readers to complete it and mail it to the magazine, or asks them to go to a Web site and complete a questionnaire, who is most likely to do so? Participation here requires some effort on the part of respondents, and there is no obvious incentive to participate. So the readers most likely to respond are those who find the topic most interesting or most relevant. If the topic is extramarital sex, we can imagine that those readers who have had some experience with it will be the ones most likely to respond to the survey. After all, if a reader does not have any experience with extramarital sex, the reader is liable to assume the survey does not even apply. It is not very interesting to check "no" or "does not apply" for most survey items.

In the end, savvy consumers of sexuality research need to ask how research participants were recruited. The ultimate question is the extent to which the sample is representative of the population. The less representative the sample, the less accurate the results, and the less we should let the results influence us in our own decision making or opinions. These issues are separate from another important set of issues having to do with how variables are measured.

HOW IS SEXUALITY MEASURED?

Researchers cannot study various aspects of sexuality directly. Instead, each aspect of interest has to be measured. This may seem like a straightforward matter, but measurements are always less than perfect, and sometimes quite a bit so. Depending on the variable the researcher wants to study, the primary choices are observation (Moore, 2002), physiological measurement (Janssen, 2002), and verbal reports (Wiederman, 2002). Because sexual activity is private, there is little that can be observed directly. Researchers could, and have, observed flirtation, rejection, and behaviors involved in trying to connect with a potential mate or sex partner (Moore, 2002). When it comes to actual sexual activity, however, few researchers have chosen the observational route. One notable exception was the pioneering research performed by Masters and Johnson (1966, 1970).

Masters and Johnson were pioneers for a variety of reasons, including the fact that they observed people actually engaged in sexual activity. These researchers recruited singles and couples to come into the laboratory and be observed, videotaped, and their physiological reactions measured. Masters and Johnson (1966) used their data to construct a model of how the typical person responds physically during sexual activity. We can imagine how the volunteers for such intrusive research might differ from people who would never consent to engaging in sexual activity under laboratory conditions.

Some sex researchers continue to use physiological measures in their research (Janssen, 2002). They may measure general physiological arousal (blood pressure, respiration, heart rate) or degree of genital arousal in response to certain stimuli (such as photos of nude children compared to nude adults). The measure of penile arousal involves a band placed around the base of the penis. As the penis becomes erect the band is stretched, thus registering the degree of erection. The measure of vaginal arousal involves a plastic device that looks similar to a tampon and is inserted the same way. The device measures the degree of blood flow to the vaginal walls by bouncing light off them and reading how much and how quickly the light is reflected (more blood flow to the vaginal walls results in less light reflected back to the sensor).

One important limitation of these measures of genital arousal is that they indicate a relative degree of arousal, but not an absolute level. That is, the measurements are calibrated according to each research participant's resting baseline. So the researcher can determine how sexually aroused each participant is relative to his or her nonaroused state. However, there is no absolute level of arousal, because each person's body starts at its own baseline level. Another limitation is that there are only certain situations in which researchers are interested in the degree to which people become sexually aroused in response to certain stimuli. In most cases, researchers are interested in sexual experiences and attitudes, and those require self-report measures.

Self-report measures are the primary tools of sex researchers, and they include paper-and-pencil surveys, diaries, and interviews. Self-report measures are all based on the assumption that respondents can and will accurately indicate their experiences and attitudes (Tourangeau, Rips, & Rasinski, 2000). Let us start with the issue of insight. With sexual attitudes, researchers typically assume that respondents have good insight into how they feel and what they believe. That may be true, but even if it is, there is probably variation across respondents in terms of how much insight each respondent has into his or her own attitudes. With sexual experience, if the researcher asks respondents to indicate number of sexual partners, or how often they have engaged in certain sexual behaviors, the accuracy of self-report depends on memory (Sudman, Bradburn, & Schwartz, 1996). Who is most likely to accurately remember his or her experience? Probably those individuals with very little experience will be able to remember most clearly, whereas those with the most experience will have to rely on estimation to come up with an answer.

People who engage regularly in a particular activity do not remember each instance of that activity, so when asked how often it occurs, the respondent will most likely make a quick estimate (Thompson, Skowronski, Larsen, & Betz, 1996). The thinking might go something like, "Well, my partner and I typically have sex twice a week, and there's 52 weeks in a year, so I guess we had sex about 100 times last year." Respondents typically do not spend much time making such calculations, and they are probably influenced by such things as how often the respondent has had sex recently. Perhaps, in reality, the respondent typically has sex once per week, but lately the frequency has been higher, leading the respondent to overestimate the frequency for the entire year. Of course the same thing could happen in the other direction, resulting in an underestimate for the year. Interestingly, when the researcher takes everyone's estimates and calculates the average, the result might be something like 63.4 times per year. The average sounds very precise, but it is important to remember that most of the individual self-reports that went into it were estimates or guesses (and hence round numbers).

Given that human memory is imperfect, even when respondents are completely honest and open, self-reports may not be accurate (Tourangeau et al., 2000). In an attempt to overcome the limitations of memory and estimation, some researchers use diaries to measure sexual behavior (Okami, 2002). Research participants are instructed to complete self-report measures of sexual activity each day, reporting activity experienced since the previous entry twenty-four hours earlier. The idea is that keeping a running report eliminates the need to remember sexual experiences accurately. Of course the diary method has its limitations. For one, it involves more work for research participants, and each participant has to be motivated and conscientious in completing the forms when he or she is supposed to. Many participants may wait until the last minute and complete all of the forms at once, which defeats the purpose of using daily reports. In an attempt to prompt timely reports, researchers typically require respondents to mail one form per day, or to log into a Web site to complete self-report forms, thereby allowing the researcher to track when entries were made.

Another limitation of the diary method is that respondents might feel somewhat self-conscious in reporting their sexual activity. Respondents might have concerns over being embarrassed or appearing a certain way to the researcher. These concerns are lumped together under the concept *social desirability response bias* (Wiederman, 2002). This term refers to the ways self-reports might be biased by people's tendencies to want to appear in a positive light. Intentionally or unintentionally, respondents might distort their responses to appear desirable or typical. An interesting possibility is that social desirability response affects responses differently based on whether the respondent believes less or greater sexual experience is better, or whether conservative versus liberal sexual attitudes are better. So, social desirability response bias may result in males and young respondents reporting greater sexual experience than they have actually had, compared to women and older respondents who may report less sexual experience than they have actually had.

What can researchers do to minimize the effects of social desirability response bias? One major strategy is to ensure that respondents are anonymous, and to make them feel assured that their identity is not connected to their responses. It is hoped that the respondents will then feel free to be completely honest. After all, why not be completely honest when no one will know how you personally responded to the survey questions? The problem is that social desirability response bias may still influence answers in that respondents want to be able to maintain a certain view of themselves in their own eyes as well as in the eyes of others. So, if a respondent has had certain experiences or holds certain attitudes of which he or she is not proud, there may be the tendency to downplay those, even to himself or herself. Reporting certain attitudes or experiences in black and white on a survey may cause some uncomfortable confrontations with the image of oneself the respondent likes to maintain.

As respondents tend to have to estimate certain information about their own experience, and are motivated to appear "normal," even the response choices given to them may influence their answers (Sudman et al., 1996). Suppose a researcher tries to measure how often respondents have engaged in anal sexual intercourse. After the term is defined, respondents may be asked to choose one of five responses given: (a) never, (b) once, (c) twice, (d) 3–10 times, (e) more than 10 times. These choices imply that the researcher does not expect respondents to have engaged in anal sexual intercourse more than a few times (if ever). Notice that the middle response choice is "twice." Many respondents might assume that the middle choice represents the average or typical respondent. The person who has engaged in anal sex numerous times may feel somewhat embarrassed because the response choices imply that his or her experience is extreme and unusual.

Now let us consider another researcher interested in the same variable. This researcher, however, uses the following response choices: (a) never, (b) 1–10 times, (c) 11–25 times, (d) 26–100 times, (e) more than 100 times. What do these response choices imply about what the researcher, the "expert," expects and considers "normal"? Indeed, research indicates that people will report greater levels of sexual experience with response choices like the second set, compared to the first.

Social desirability response bias might be greatest when data are gathered through face-to-face interviews. Respondents might feel most self-conscious here because they have to report their sexual attitudes and experiences to another person directly. Respondents are no longer completely anonymous. So, why would researchers use interviews rather than paper surveys? One advantage is that the interviewer can make sure all questions are answered (none are skipped or left blank) and can clarify any questions the participant might have. With paper surveys there is no way to clarify the questions or the responses, and there will always be some respondents who interpret the words differently than the researcher intended. One compromise involves using portable computers for "interviews." The respondents wear headphones so that the questions can be read to them privately by the computer. If the respondent has questions about the meanings of particular words, he or she can click on those words to pull up a help window. Of course, this format for gathering data probably works best with respondents who are comfortable using computers (such as college students).

So far we have considered self-report in a general way, or as it applies to reporting one's sexual experience. When researchers are interested in some abstract concept, such as "sexual self-esteem," for example, they typically use scales to measure it. These scales simply comprise several questions, all pertaining to the same concept. Respondents might rate how much they agree or disagree with each statement in the scale, and their total across the items makes up their score on the measure. Constructing valid scales involves many issues, most of which are beyond the scope of our presentation here (see Wiederman, 2002). However, it is important to consider the labels and underlying meanings of such scales.

Suppose a researcher constructed a scale consisting of the following five items. For each item, respondents indicate how much they agree or disagree.

1. It seems that most people put too much emphasis on sex.
2. I have never really been a sexual person.
3. Sex is overrated.
4. Most people are more sexual than I am.
5. Sex is not an important part of my life.

It is debatable whether these five items all measure the same concept. For the sake of argument, let us suppose they do. What might you say this scale measures? What if the researcher called it a measure of "sexual depression"? Do you agree? Now suppose that you encountered a description of the researcher's results and learned that "older adults have greater sexual depression than do younger adults." Apparently, older respondents scored higher on this measure than did younger respondents, but does the conclusion seem accurate given the items constituting the scale? Unfortunately, in mass-media descriptions of research results, we never get to examine the measures used in the research. Despite being left in the dark about this important aspect of research, we need to try to determine what the results of the research really mean.

WHAT DO THE RESULTS OF SEX RESEARCH MEAN?

Many times, researchers are interested in explaining causes and effects: What causes someone's sexual orientation, why do some people have more sexual experience than do others, why does sexual abuse affect some people in certain ways and not others? However, the only time researchers can conclude that one thing causes another is when the results are based on a true experiment. In a true experiment, research participants are randomly assigned to groups. In the simplest case, there are two groups: an experimental group and a control group (Whitley, 2002). The experimental group has something done to them differently than the control group. In sex research that might involve being exposed to sexually explicit material, or undergoing some therapy, or being put under stress to see how sexual functioning is affected.

Because research participants are randomly assigned to the groups, it is assumed that the resulting groups are similar in all respects. So, if after the experiment there is some difference between the groups, the researcher can conclude that what the participants were exposed to must have caused the difference. As a simple example, suppose a researcher was interested in the potential effects of being exposed to typical pornographic films on subsequent attitudes toward women. A group of research volunteers would be randomly split into two groups: one would view a certain amount of sexually explicit film whereas the other group would view a comparable amount of nonsexual film. All research participants would then complete some measure of attitudes toward women. The researcher assumes that the two groups were very similar in their attitudes toward women prior to exposure to the films, and so any difference between the groups after exposure to the film must be caused by having viewed the sexually explicit films.

Note that even in this example of a very simple experiment, there are several important assumptions: that the two groups were comparable in their attitudes toward women prior to the experiment; that the sexually explicit films shown during the experiment are similar to pornographic films viewed by people in the real world; and that the measure of attitudes toward women indeed measures accurately such attitudes. If any of these assumptions is false, the conclusion that exposure to sexually explicit film affects people's attitudes toward women in certain ways is flawed. Then there are also the issues of who the research participants were, and whether what the researcher found with those participants is what would be found with people in general.

Even with all of these potential concerns, it is only the results of an experiment that can be used to conclude that one thing caused another. In all other kinds of studies, the researcher can only conclude that one variable is related to another. This may seem to be a small difference, but it is an important one. There are many topics that the researcher cannot study with an experiment, so concluding that one thing caused another in those areas is simply wrong. Important things researchers cannot manipulate include gender differences, sexual orientation, upbringing or past experiences, sexual activity and experiences, whether people are involved in a sexual relationship, and prior sexual attitudes. Since it is impossible to manipulate these things in an experiment, researchers cannot determine directly what causes them. The best they can do is investigate whether the variable is related (correlated) to other variables, and then speculate about what might cause what.

As an example, suppose a researcher interested in the possible effects of exposure to pornography on attitudes toward women asks respondents to report how much pornography the respondent views and to complete a self-report measure of attitudes toward women. It is then possible to correlate the amount of porn reported with scores on the scale measuring attitudes toward women. If the researcher finds a correlation between the two, can the researcher conclude that exposure to pornography affects attitudes toward women? If not, why?

The simplest explanation for why the researcher cannot legitimately conclude that one thing causes or affects another is that the research was not an experiment. When researchers examine correlations among variables, as was the case in this example, it is impossible to determine which variable causes or affects another. So perhaps people with certain attitudes toward women are more likely to seek out and view pornography. This would be an instance of the attitudes affecting the behavior, rather than the other way around. It is also very possible that both viewing pornography and attitudes toward women are influenced by some other variable or set of variables. Perhaps viewing pornography and holding certain attitudes toward women are more likely among people of lower educational background, so it may be that these variables are related to one another simply because both are related to education.

Remember social desirability response bias? It may be that self-reports of pornography use and attitudes toward women are correlated because both are influenced by social desirability response bias. It is probably not socially desirable to admit to viewing pornography and holding certain negative attitudes toward women. So, respondents who more readily admit pornography use probably are not as concerned about appearing in the most favorable light as those respondents who deny it (even though some of these respondents view pornography). Then, when it comes to admitting having negative attitudes toward women, who is most likely to do so? Those respondents who are not concerned about answering in the most socially desirable light are the ones most likely to admit to both pornography use and negative attitudes toward women. If this is the case, there would be a correlation between pornography use and attitudes toward women, perhaps not because one causes the other, but because both are related to social desirability response bias.

Thus far, we have talked about whether there is a difference between the experimental group and the control group, or whether there is a correlation between two variables. Of course there will always be some degree of difference between two groups, or some degree of correlation between two variables. How do researchers determine whether the difference or the correlation is enough to lead to the conclusion that the two groups differ, or that the two variables are related? The answer is that they calculate whether the difference or the correlation is *statistically significant*. This term implies that the difference or the correlation is important, because the word "significant" means important. However, it was an unfortunate choice of words when the term was coined. Statistical significance is unrelated to the importance of a research result.

To understand what is meant by statistical significance, we need to consider the difference between a population and a sample. A researcher is interested in learning about relationships among variables in the population. However, the researcher has access only to samples from the population. When a researcher tests a group difference or a correlation to determine whether it is statistically significant, he or she is testing how likely that result from the sample is if in fact there is absolutely no difference or correlation in the population. So, if a researcher finds a statistically significant group difference or a correlation between two variables, that simply means that it is very unlikely to have occurred in the sample if there was absolutely no such difference or correlation in the population from which the sample was drawn.

Note that statistical significance does not tell us anything about the size of the difference or the correlation, either in the sample or in the population. If a researcher has a relatively large sample (let us say several hundred participants), then even a small group difference or correlation will be statistically significant. In other words, if there is absolutely no group difference or correlation in the population, then it is unlikely that a researcher would find even a small result in a large sample drawn from that population. So, even small results are statistically significant. These are difficult concepts to understand, especially by just reading about them. The ultimate message is that all research results reported to the public are statistically significant, but the term is misleading because whether a research result is statistically significant depends on both the size of the result and the size of the sample upon which it is based.

Without being told how large a group difference exists or how large a correlation is between two variables, it is impossible to judge the strength of the relationship between two things. Taking our earlier example of the potential effects of watching pornographic films on subsequent attitudes toward women, let us say that the researcher found that the experimental group (exposed to the porn) had statistically significant higher scores on the measure of negative attitudes toward women than did the control group (exposed to nonsexual films). The conclusion is that exposure to porn influenced the self-reported attitudes toward women. But to what degree? The difference between the experimental and control groups was statistically significant, so we know that the difference the researcher found is unlikely if indeed there is no difference between the two groups as they exist in the larger population. Still, there is no guarantee that the difference between the groups accurately reflects what exists in the population. Also, we are not told how large the difference is so that we can judge for ourselves whether to be impressed or dismiss the effect as trivial.

WHAT ARE THE CRITICAL QUESTIONS FOR EVALUATING SEX RESEARCH?

Now that we have covered the basics of conducting research on human sexuality, we are armed with the knowledge to critically evaluate the results of sex research as we encounter them. Being critical does not mean simply trying to find fault. As we have seen here, it is easy to point out flaws because all sex research has them. It would be easy to conclude in despair, "Why should anyone waste time and effort conducting sex research that will be inherently imperfect?" The answer is that some knowledge, even imperfect knowledge, is better than none at all. Science is built on the premise that if enough individual researchers add their imperfect pieces to the puzzle, a clearer picture will eventually emerge. As we will see in the next section, not everyone shares the view that sex research is valuable. Still, it will continue. So when you encounter media reports of sex research, asking yourself the following questions will help put the results in a critical context.

1. Who were the researchers? Were they independent faculty members, or were they employees of a group that has a vested interest in certain findings or conclusions?

2. Who was studied? How were the participants recruited, and who would be most likely to agree to participate? Are these participants likely to be different from the general population?

3. How large were the differences or relationships found? You probably will not have access to this information, but if you know there was a large sample, then it is very possible that the statistically significant finding is actually small.

4. Is the report implying that one thing causes another, when in fact the research was not an experiment? This is very common, probably because people naturally tend to think in terms of causal relationships. However, just because two things are statistically related does not mean that one caused the other—even if such a causal relationship obviously makes sense.

WHAT DOES POLITICS HAVE TO DO WITH SEX RESEARCH?

It has been said that love and politics make strange bedfellows. What about politics and sex research? It may not seem like there should be a connection, but there always has been. Sex is a topic of heated debate as values vary across people. Certain laws exist in an attempt to regulate sexuality and indicate what is right and what is wrong. It is the belief that sex research influences people's sexuality that seems to account for much political and social concern about the research.

In many ways, Alfred Kinsey and his colleagues established the beginning of sexuality research in the United States (Kinsey, Pomeroy, & Martin, 1948; Kinsey, Pomeroy, Martin, & Gebhard, 1953). From that point on, some segments of society have expressed concern that the latest sex research will have a detrimental effect on the sexual values and morals of society's members. Although critics may not articulate it explicitly, their concern seems to be that if sex researchers find certain results, those results will promote undesirable sexual behaviors and attitudes within the public. It is not clear how this might happen, but it could be based on the belief that data indicating that certain percentages of individuals engage in certain sexual behaviors legitimizes those behaviors, and may suggest those behaviors to certain individuals who would not have thought of trying them on their own.

A second concern about sex research is that simply asking certain questions of research participants might negatively affect their sexual values. Again, the assumption seems to be that asking about certain sexual activities makes those activities more acceptable, and may suggest them to otherwise innocent research respondents (this is especially the case when the proposed research respondents are young people). Of course, if the same logic were applied to other research topics, there should be similar protests concerning research on the prevalence of smoking, drinking, drug use, gambling, lying, stealing, unhealthy eating, and so forth.

Ironically, the little research conducted on the potential effects of participating in sexuality research has tended to reveal positive effects. Being asked about your sexual beliefs and attitudes may lead to greater clarification of those beliefs. Some individual participants may later think more about what they believe and why. This has been the case in some research on couples and their feelings about each other (Rubin & Mitchell, 1976; Veroff, Hatchett, & Douvan, 1992). With regard to sexual behavior, it seems plausible that someone might report behaviors or frequencies of experiences that the individual is not proud to report. Doing so might prompt the individual to examine his or her choices in the future. It seems less likely that research participants would conclude from their responses that they have not engaged in sex often enough, or have engaged in enough different sexual behaviors, and then decide to "go wild."

CONCLUSION

All research on sexuality is imperfect. Rather than despair, we should be appropriately critical of any sweeping conclusions we encounter in the media regarding "the latest research." Because of the sensitive nature of the topic, the results of sex research are generally of interest to people. At the same time, the sensitive nature of sexuality leads to special problems when researchers decide to study it. Who will agree to participate? How do you gather information or data? How do you measure sexuality? What do the results mean? All attempts to answer these questions raise just as many questions and potential problems as answers. Still, some research conclusions, even imperfect ones, are better than none at all. When many researchers each contribute their own pieces to the overall puzzle, eventually the picture starts to come into view.

REFERENCES

Brannigan, G. R., Allgeier, E. R., & Allgeier, R. (Eds.). (2000). *The sex scientists.* Upper Saddle River, NJ: Prentice-Hall.

Bullough, B., Bullough, V. L., Fithian, M. A., Hartman, W. E., & Klein, R. S. (Eds.). (1997). *Personal stories of "How I got into sex."* Buffalo, NY: Prometheus Books.

Dunne, M. P. (2002). Sampling considerations. In M. W. Wiederman & B. E. Whitley, Jr. (Eds.), *The handbook for conducting research on human sexuality* (pp. 85–112). Mahwah, NJ: Erlbaum.

Janssen, E. (2002). Psychophysiological measurement of sexual arousal. In M. W. Wiederman & B. E. Whitley, Jr. (Eds.), *The handbook for conducting research on human sexuality* (pp. 139–171). Mahwah, NJ: Erlbaum.

Kinsey, A. C., Pomeroy, W. B., & Martin, C. E. (1948). *Sexual behavior in the human male.* Philadelphia: Saunders.

Kinsey, A. C., Pomeroy, W. B., Martin, C. E., & Gebhard, P. H. (1953). *Sexual behavior in the human female*. Philadelphia: Saunders.

Masters, W. H., & Johnson, V. E. (1966). *Human sexual response*. New York: Little, Brown.

Masters, W. H., & Johnson, V. E. (1970). *Human sexual inadequacy*. New York: Little, Brown.

Moore, M. M. (2002). Behavioral observation. In M. W. Wiederman & B. E. Whitley, Jr. (Eds.), *The handbook for conducting research on human sexuality* (pp. 113–137). Mahwah, NJ: Erlbaum.

Okami, P. (2002). Dear diary: A useful but imperfect method. In M. W. Wiederman & B. E. Whitley, Jr. (Eds.), *The handbook for conducting research on human sexuality* (pp. 195–207). Mahwah, NJ: Erlbaum.

Rubin, Z., & Mitchell, C. (1976). Couples research as couples counseling. *American Psychologist, 31*, 17–25.

Sudman, S., Bradburn, N. M., & Schwartz, N. (1996). *Thinking about answers: The application of cognitive processes to survey methodology*. San Francisco: Jossey-Bass.

Thompson, C. P., Skowronski, J. J., Larsen, S. F., & Betz, A. L. (1996). *Autobiographical memory: Remembering what and remembering when*. Mahwah, NJ: Erlbaum.

Tourangeau, R., Rips, L. J., & Rasinski, K. (2000). *The psychology of survey response*. New York: Cambridge University Press.

Veroff, J., Hatchett, S., & Douvan, E. (1992). Consequences of participating in a longitudinal study of marriage. *Public Opinion Quarterly, 56*, 315–327.

Whitley, B. E. (2002). Group comparison research. In M. W. Wiederman & B. E. Whitley, Jr. (Eds.), *The handbook for conducting research on human sexuality* (pp. 223–254). Mahwah, NJ: Erlbaum.

Wiederman, M. W. (2002). Reliability and validity of measurement. In M. W. Wiederman & B. E. Whitley, Jr. (Eds.), *The handbook for conducting research on human sexuality* (pp. 25–50). Mahwah, NJ: Erlbaum.

2

Theories of Human Sexuality

Roy F. Baumeister, Jon K. Maner, and C. Nathan DeWall ◆

The purpose of this chapter is to provide a brief overview of two major and several other theories regarding human sexual behavior. Theorizing is, however, not essential to sexuality research, and indeed the modern research tradition was heavily influenced by the Kinsey approach, which sought to collect information without owing allegiance to any theoretical perspective.

The status of sexuality theory was debated in a special issue of the *Journal of Sex Research* in 1998. The picture that emerged was not pretty. Two main theoretical orientations (constructionist feminism and evolution) dominate the field. Both approach the status of cults, full of loyal and dedicated supporters who self-righteously heap scorn on anyone who disagrees with them (including most members of the other camp). The battle between these major theoretical perspectives leaves little room for the development of smaller, midlevel theories, as prospective younger theorists are pressured to align themselves with one of the two behemoths. Researchers who do not want to sign up for either camp end up reporting their data with little or no theoretical context, and so evidence accumulates in a theoretical vacuum. New ideas are regarded with skepticism, especially by the two main camps, who react mainly by asking whether the ideas fit or conflict with their dogmas. Ideas presented by male researchers are prone to being criticized and discredited by accusations of sexist bias, which presumably invalidates their thinking. As new researchers shy away from hostile reviewers, they suppress their theorizing, and as a result the journals in this field fill up with articles that simply report patterns of data while giving little or no theoretical elaboration (Weis, 1998).

In the long run, however, we see more grounds for optimism regarding theory development in the study of sexuality. Sex remains one of the most broadly interesting spheres of human activity, and the diversity of interest in it is reflected in a wide range of outlets for new ideas, so that no established elite can dominate all outlets or suppress contrary views. After the taboos against discussing or researching sex have been set aside, the field has begun to discover that a wide range of theoretical approaches to human behavior have something to offer to the study of sex. The coming decades promise to be fertile ones for the development of sex theory.

GENERAL PRINCIPLES AND STYLES OF THINKING

Social Constructionist Theory

Social constructionist theories of sex are one part of the broad theoretical orientation that emphasizes the social construction of reality. This is rooted in the assumption that reality and experience are ultimately subjective, and perhaps truth is relative, too. The social constructionist movement in science and philosophy was in some respects a reaction against positivism, which emphasized gaining knowledge of objective reality. To social constructionists, people cannot really grasp objective reality but must instead devise interpretations of it that are at best only partly driven by external facts and are thus inevitably shaped by subjective preconceptions, biases, and the like.

Hence, social constructionists are deeply skeptical of assertions that sex is subject to universal laws rooted in biology and pancultural human nature. Rather, sexual desire and behavior are a product of upbringing, socialization, religion, the media, political influences, and so forth. Constructionist thinkers emphasize historical, cultural, and personal variations. Constructionist icons such as Margaret Mead (1928, 1961) asserted that what might strike some people as immutable facts of sex are in fact culturally relative arrangements. For example, one of her most famous works asserted that sexual possessiveness and jealousy were products of Western culture and were unknown in other contexts such as Samoa, where people accepted sex easily and naturally without encumbering it with the emotional baggage that Eurocentric societies accumulated. (To be sure, other researchers have bitterly disputed Mead's conclusions, and recent works have concluded that sexual jealousy and possessiveness are universal; e.g., Reiss, 1986.)

Most social constructionists concede some role to biology, just as most biologically oriented researchers acknowledge that culture and socialization have some influence. The difference is one of emphasis. Fervent social constructionists accept that sex is somewhat dependent on hormones, genes, the physiology of sexual arousal, and other biological factors, but they think of these as the rather boring universal foundation. Social circumstances, meaningful interpretation, cultural influence, and subjective experience are assumed to be paramount and widely variable. Ultimately, who wants to do what to whom, how many times, and in what position, are a reflection of social and cultural influences, not direct biological promptings.

In terms of science, and even of personal experiences of sex, the social constructionists emphasize that people cannot fully escape from the shaping and biasing influences of their past experiences, especially including culture and socialization and their particular roles in society. Ultimately, it is impossible for people to *fully* understand the views or experiences of someone from a different background (partial understanding is possible). The most famous and familiar instance of this principle is the often repeated assertion that men simply cannot understand women's experiences, feelings, needs, and wishes. The phrase "men just don't get it" became for a time a feminist slogan. This brings up the feminist theory, which, in the area of sexuality, has been the most important and influential version of social constructionism.

Feminist Sexology

It is possible to be a social constructionist without being a feminist, and vice versa, but in practice, and particularly in the practice of theorizing about sex, the two overlap heavily and few thinkers embrace one without the other. The two theoretical approaches are quite compatible. Moreover, in our view, the high-water mark of both approaches coincided: the 1970s saw the flowering of social constructionist approaches, in part swept along in the wake of the hugely popular and influential book by Berger and Luckmann (1967). That same decade also witnessed the triumph of feminism in many spheres, not the least of which was in sexual theory, driven in part by the so-called sexual revolution of the late 1960s and the early 1970s, which by all accounts took the form of sweeping and extensive changes in female sexuality. (Male sexuality changed far less than female sexuality; see Ehrenreich, Hess, & Jacobs, 1986; also Arafat & Yorburg, 1973; Bauman & Wilson, 1974; Birenbaum, 1970; Robinson, Ziss, Ganza, Katz, & Robinson, 1991.) The undeniable fact that sexual attitudes and behaviors, and female sexuality in particular, had changed so radically in such a short period of time created the sense that almost anything was possible, and thereby seemed to prove the constructionist point that sex depended on historical and cultural context. In our view, large parts of sexual theory today are still deeply rooted in the feminist thinking from the 1970s, including such landmark theoretical works as Brownmiller (1975).

Summarizing feminist theory is hampered by disagreements among feminists, some stemming from core contradictions. For example, some feminists seek to assert gender equality in all things, whereas others seek to establish the superiority of women in as many spheres as possible. (Admittedly, both views share a rejection of theories that men are properly or naturally superior to women.) Some feminists embrace the scientific method and seek to use empirical findings to establish gender equality or female superiority, whereas others regard objective science as a sham and assert that the conclusions of research are inevitably biased by the political (and other) views of the researchers, especially in such socially fraught issues as sex. The controversial book *Who Stole Feminism?* (Sommers, 1995) asserted that feminism had changed over time in fundamental ways but was reluctant to admit having changed, particularly because the newer form seeks to benefit from the moral legitimacy of the earlier. In Sommers's account, feminism of the early 1970s promoted gender equality and fairness, advocated questioning of established ideas, and welcomed the support of men. Feminism since the 1980s, in contrast, has promoted female superiority and female gains at the expense of men, opposed questioning of its own entrenched dogmas, and regarded men (with a few exceptions) as irredeemable enemies. Regardless of whether one accepts that particular analysis, the diversity of feminist views is undeniable. We shall summarize several themes as best we can, but it would not be surprising if here or there a self-proclaimed feminist thinker could be found to deviate from each of them.

A major theme of feminism is that sexual attitudes and practices are rooted in the gender roles that each particular culture and historical period have constructed. Feminism is primarily concerned with male and female differences, and, to feminists, sex is just one manifestation of gender. (We use the term "sex" to refer to sexuality and the term "gender" to refer to both the social and biological distinctions between men and women.)

Feminists have then elaborated a variety of implications of that basic assumption. Tiefer (1995) proposed that sexuality is not solely a product of biology, but is socially constructed and frequently negotiated. From the social constructionist perspective, sexuality is not a universal human phenomenon but is instead only a part of social life and identity that can be sexualized or desexualized through its cultural meaning and regulation (Weeks, 1991). Social constructionists believe that sexual authorities create and maintain expectations regarding sexuality only when such expectations will benefit those in power.

Indeed, power is central to feminist thought. Many have asserted that power is a key ingredient to all feminist analyses (e.g., Riger, 1992; Yoder & Kahn, 1992). Feminist thought emphasizes the concept of patriarchy in explaining gender differences and, in particular, women's problems. Patriarchy is the political domination of males over females. Thus, gender relations and women's problems are explained by examining the oppressive and exploitative social structures allegedly set up by men to favor themselves at women's expense.

In the sexual sphere, power and patriarchy remain centrally useful concepts to feminist theory. Rich (1980) asserted that heterosexuality is not a natural state of affairs, but instead is due to the existence of a social structure in which men occupy many of the high-power positions. Brownmiller (1975) helped popularize the view that rape results from a conspiracy by all men to intimidate all women so as to keep men in power. The view that power rather than sex is the motivating force behind rape has become a central principle of feminist sexology (see later section on rape theory). Dworkin (1981) and others have emphasized that human civilization is built on men's ability to rape and abuse women.

In the 1970s, there was an attempt to deny or minimize gender differences in sexuality and to claim that any observed differences were likely due to patriarchal influences such as the so-called double standard, which prohibits women from enjoying sexual activities that are permitted to men. More recent empirical work by feminist scholars has, however, confirmed the existence of large gender differences in sexuality. Across more than 170 studies testing 128,363 participants, Oliver and Hyde (1993) found large gender differences in the incidence of masturbation and in attitudes about casual sex. Men also expressed more positive attitudes toward sexual intercourse in a marriage or committed relationship than women, and women felt more anxious and guilty about sex than men. Thus, there appear to be substantial differences in how men and women express their sexuality privately and with relationship partners.

Feminists argue that these differences in sexuality perpetuate differences between the genders and create male-female conflicts in close relationships. Regarding the large gender difference in masturbation, women having difficulty reaching orgasm during intercourse—also known as *anorgasmia* (Andersen, 1981; Hyde, 1994)—is sometimes attributed to a lack of experience in masturbation, though other factors such as inept male sexual technique and guilt induced by patriarchal socialization may also contribute. Hyde (1996) recommended sexual education that contains specific instructions for female masturbation as part of the curriculum.

Feminists also argue that the large gender difference in attitudes about casual sex sets the stage for male-female conflict, including sexual harassment and date rape. Gender role socialization, including the sexual double standard (i.e., casual sex is fine for men but not for women), defines social norms and expectations for male and female sexual behavior. These differences are rooted in men having more power than women, both physically and institutionally. According to this line of thought, if the power difference could be eliminated, then the difference in attitudes toward casual sex would vanish also. Clearly, this view is fundamentally opposed to evolutionary and biological approaches such as that of Buss and Schmitt (1993), who propose that the different attitudes toward casual sex are innately different and inextricably linked to the different reproductive strategies and the biological constraints on the sex organs. (That is, having sex with more partners increases the likely number of offspring for men but not for women.) In the field of sex, evolutionary theory arose in part as a reaction against feminist and constructionist thinking. The next section turns to evolutionary theory.

Evolutionary Theory

Some of the earliest thinkers in modern psychology (e.g., James, 1890/1950) thought that an evolutionary perspective was essential for a full theory of human social behavior. This sentiment was largely ignored, however, for the better part of the twentieth century. Theorists did not start actively importing ideas from evolutionary theory until about the late 1960s. When this theory did start to become integrated into theories of human behavior, it did so to the greatest extent in the domain of sexuality. This should come as no great surprise—classic Darwinian theory (e.g., 1859/1964, 1871) implies that differential reproductive success is the key to biological evolution. Sexuality was therefore a natural focus for evolutionarily minded scientists, because mating is central to reproductive success. Nevertheless, many evolutionary researchers found themselves accused of being obsessed with sex.

When an evolutionary approach to sexuality started becoming popular, many people were uncomfortable with its implications. To some, such theories took people's sexual identities out of their own hands and put them into the hands of their genes. Many were distressed by the idea that their sex lives—including their most intimate feelings and desires—were determined not by their own hearts and minds, but by human ancestors who had been dead for hundreds of thousands of years. In suggesting that much of human behavior is rooted in biology, evolutionary theory was viewed as a cynical and even oppressive standpoint, as this implied that many harmful behaviors could not be changed or avoided. Some even viewed the evolutionary perspective as a strategic tool designed by the patriarchy to maintain the sociopolitical status quo.

Evolutionary approaches to sexuality draw upon unifying principles of biological adaptation and evolution by natural selection. The fundamental premise is this: organisms possessing adaptive physical and psychological design features tend to reproduce at a greater rate than organisms with less adaptive features. As a result, these features—referred to as "adaptations"—can become characteristic of the species over evolutionary time.

Applied to sex, evolutionary theory seeks to understand the desires and behaviors of modern individuals as the result of ancestral (both human and prehuman) patterns that produced more and better offspring. Evolutionary theorists contend that virtually all aspects of human mating and sexuality—from the excitement of initial romantic attraction, to the day-to-day maintenance of a long-term relationship, to the anger and distress experienced at a relationship's break-up—have been shaped, at least in part, by evolutionary processes (Cosmides & Tooby, 1992; Maner et al., 2003). That is, they have been shaped by the mating-related constraints under which ancestral men and women evolved.

Many studies show, for example, that men and women differ in the traits they look for in their romantic partners, as well as in their willingness to engage in casual sex. Whereas men tend to place a premium on the physical attractiveness and youth of their partners, women favor partners with maturity and high social status (Kenrick & Keefe, 1992; Li, Bailey, Kenrick, & Linsenmeier, 2002). Men are generally quite willing to engage in casual sex, without any prospect of a long-term relationship, whereas women are relatively more inclined to require some level of commitment before agreeing to intercourse (Clarke & Hatfield, 1989; Simpson & Gangestad, 1991).

From an evolutionary perspective, these sex differences reflect stable differences between men's and women's mating strategies—strategies that are attributable to the different constraints that influenced the reproductive success of ancestral males and females (Buss & Schmitt, 1993). Evolutionary theorists such as Trivers (1972) pointed out that throughout evolutionary history, women have experienced a higher level of initial obligatory parental investment than have men. When pregnancy occurs, a female is generally obliged to invest herself for the nine months it takes to incubate the child, at the very minimum, and usually a lot more. Ancestral males, in contrast, had no such obligation (at least not in the biological sense), and therefore may have benefited from mating with as many females as they could in order to maximize their reproductive success. As a result, suggest theories of differential parental investment, women tend to be relatively more selective than men, looking for a high-quality mate who exhibits the interest and ability to invest resources in his mate and offspring. Moreover, women are relatively more inclined to refrain from having sex until their mate has given them signs that he is willing to remain in a long-term monogamous relationship. Although men generally have high standards for long-term partners, they tend not to be as selective when it comes to short-term sex, exhibiting greater and more frequent willingness to mate with a wider range of females.

Evolutionary theorists are quick to point out that, despite criticisms to the contrary (e.g., Lickliter & Honeycutt, 2003), an evolutionary perspective does not imply genetic determinism—the idea that people's behavior is entirely determined at birth by their genes. Modern evolutionary theories readily acknowledge the role of learning and culture, and explore ways in which genes, learning, and culture interact dynamically to produce sexual behavior (e.g., Gangestad & Simpson, 2000; Kenrick et al., 2002; Krebs, 2003).

It is also worth noting that evolutionary theorists do not assume that people consciously consider their reproductive success when pursuing particular mating strategies. On the contrary, they believe that human sexuality has been shaped by natural selection such that people carry on their romantic lives without necessarily considering the reproductive ramifications of their actions. Indeed, the widespread use of birth control illustrates that people—even highly promiscuous ones—are not simply out to increase the number of their offspring.

Psychoanalytic Theory

Sexuality theory was heavily influenced by psychoanalytic theorizing during the first part of the twentieth century, though this influence has progressively diminished. Probably few researchers currently emphasize psychoanalytic theory in their work, though occasional findings may seem relevant. Psychoanalytic theory has its roots in the seminal thinking of Sigmund Freud (1905/1975).

The sex drive was regarded by Freud as one of the two main motivations that underlie all human striving (the other being aggression). Freud interpreted the sex drive very broadly, so as to encompass desires for love, affiliation, and belongingness. He emphasized that the drive could be transformed in many ways, including via symbolic associations. Creative art and philanthropy, for example, were regarded as transformations (sublimations) of the energy from the sex drive, which suggests that symbolically the philanthropist is having sex with the beneficiaries of his largesse.

In Freud's theory of projection, people avoid acknowledging their own socially (or personally) unacceptable desires by perceiving them instead in other people. Applied to homosexuality, this suggests that people who have homosexual desires but are unwilling to accept them tend to overinterpret the behavior of others as indicative of homosexual tendencies, and then they react with strong disapproval, if not vicious aggression, toward those others. In reaction formation, another defense mechanism, the conscious mind transforms a desire into its opposite, so that someone who feels homosexual desires professes to loathe and despise homosexuality. Lab studies have provided some support for these processes (Adams, Wright, & Lohr, 1996).

Freud proposed that people are by nature bisexual and only gradually become socialized into one gender role. The conscious mind resists the socializing pressures that seek to deprive it of half of itself, and the unconscious motivations may retain the opposite gender from that of the conscious self. The much-maligned concept of penis envy has been interpreted as merely a manifestation of this reluctance to lose half of one's bisexual wholeness (Brown, 1966). (Thus, penis envy does not mean that the girl wishes she were a boy, but rather that she is reluctant to lose half her totality.) For anatomical reasons, girls have to realize earlier in life than boys that they are not complete (i.e., limited to being one gender instead of both, and thus shut out from some realms of human experience), and so this transition is more traumatic for them. Later in life, males do envy the female organs and their reproductive powers, but this adjustment is less severe because by the time boys realize they lack these inner organs they will have accepted the social roles of maleness. Little boys equate the vagina with the anus and therefore think they have everything they might need.

If the adjustment to being sexually differentiated is more traumatic for girls, other adjustments are more difficult for boys. Freud proposed that children develop strong sexual and emotional attachments, first to their mothers, and then to the opposite-gender parent. This latter (Oedipal) attachment leads to a desire to marry and possess that parent. The other parent refuses to tolerate this, however, and can use anxiety as a weapon to stifle this blossoming love. With boys, the father's disapproval of the love for the mother takes the form of an implied threat to castrate the boy, and the boy's resulting fear is so strong that the entire pattern of infantile sexuality gets repressed. With girls, the early loves are divided between the two parents and the threat of castration is moot (because the penis is already seemingly gone), so this so-called Oedipal complex is less threatening and its abandonment both less complete and less traumatic.

Freud was among the first to suggest that sexual perversions were natural and acceptable patterns of behavior. He suggested that they had their roots in childhood experiences, including the repression of Oedipal sexuality. He thought that children were not merely bisexual but open to all forms of physical pleasure, a pattern called polymorphous perversity. Severe Oedipal repression in young men stamped out this all-body sexuality and paved the way for perversions. The less complete repression in women leaves their sexuality more diffused all over the body (hence, for example, women's greater desire for foreplay, defined as stimulating sexual arousal by touching parts of the body other than the sex organs).

Oedipal repression is ostensibly followed by a period of latency, in which there is little direct evidence of sexuality. The sex drive returns in force with the physical and psychological changes of adolescence. The adolescent self finds itself unable to cope with the newly strong desires and hence must detach from loving parents so as to find new mates. Still, the quest for adult mates and relationships is regarded as shaped heavily by the Oedipal love and other experiences from childhood.

Social Exchange Theory

Social exchange theory applies economic concepts to behavior (Blau, 1964; Homans, 1950, 1961; Thibaut & Kelley, 1959). It emphasizes analyzing the costs and benefits of social interaction to the individual participants. It assumes that interactions are most common when they are mutually beneficial, in the sense that each party gains more than it loses. Social exchange theory is a style of analysis and therefore may be compatible with other approaches, including both evolutionary and constructionist/feminist approaches.

Social exchange theory does not restrict its purview to monetary costs and benefits; indeed, other rewards can be paramount, including esteem, love, status, prestige, respect, and attention. Once these are recognized, social exchange theorists may invoke economic principles such as market pricing, scarcity, and competition.

Applied to sexual behavior, social exchange theory examines what sex may bring to the potential lovers, including rewards such as pleasure, love, attention, and prestige, as well as costs such as heartbreak, disease, and disgrace (see Sprecher, 1988, 1992). Pregnancy is of course one possible outcome of sex, but whether it operates as a reward or a cost depends on the motives and preferences of the individual.

A recent formulation of a social exchange theory of sex emphasized that sex itself is often a resource that can be traded—specifically, in heterosexual interactions, sex functions as a female resource, and men will offer women other resources in exchange for it (Baumeister & Vohs, 2004; see also Cott, 1978; Symons, 1979). Thus, female sexuality will be treated by cultural systems as having inherent value, whereas male sexuality has no value. In acts of sex, therefore, women give and men take. In order to make the exchange succeed, the men must usually offer the women something else in return, such as love, respect, marriage or other commitments, or, in some cases, cash. In the sexual marketplace, women operate as sellers, and men as buyers.

The greater cultural value attached to female sexuality (than male sexuality) is seen as creating a variety of patterns. Female virginity is more precious and important than male virginity, and women may regard their virginity as a valued gift they give to someone, whereas men do not regard their own virginity with the same positive value. (If anything, some males regard it as a stigmatizing sign of sociosexual incompetence; Sprecher & Regan, 1996). Female virgins are regarded in many cultures as more desirable sex partners than nonvirgins, whereas no such distinction exists for males. Female infidelity is prohibited and punished more severely than male infidelity (e.g., Tannahill, 1980). Social exchange theory sees this difference as stemming from the view that the unfaithful wife is giving away something precious that belongs to the couple. In contrast, the unfaithful male is not giving away something of value (unless the sex is accompanied by other resources, such as if he spends the household's money on a mistress). Marriage is regarded as a contract in which the woman contributes sex and the man contributes money and other resources. Hence, when divorce criteria differ by gender, the woman's but not the man's refusal to have sex is grounds for divorce, whereas the man's but not the woman's refusal to provide money is grounds (Betzig, 1989). Laws such as those regarding statutory rape are seen as necessary to protect female sexuality from men, but protecting male sexuality from women is not regarded as worthy of legislation.

Social exchange theory emphasizes the development of a local sexual marketplace with a more or less standard price for sex, as indicated in norms that dictate how much money, time, commitment, or other resources a man should invest in a relationship before the woman owes him sex. One principle of economic theory is that sellers compete more than buyers (e.g., Becker, 1976), and this would be reflected in women not only seeking to "advertise" their wares with makeup and sexually attractive clothing, but also possibly competing to offer sex at a slightly lower price than other women so as to attract more or better quality male attention.

Seller competition may become especially acute when supply exceeds demand, which in sexual terms entails that there are more eligible women than men in a community. Studies of sex ratio have confirmed that when there are more women than men, the price of sex goes down (so to speak), so that premarital and extramarital sex become more common and the need for men to invest extensive resources is reduced (see Guttentag & Secord, 1983). Such things may happen after a major war, for example, in which many eligible young men are killed. In contrast, a surplus of males relative to females corresponds to demand exceeding supply, and such communities typically have restrictive or prudish sexual norms that permit sex only when the man has invested and committed a great deal, corresponding to a high price for sex.

Economic theory holds that sellers not only compete but also collude more than buyers. In sex, this would entail women working together to manipulate the price of sex. According to social exchange theory, this underlies traditional patterns in many cultures by which girls and women are socialized to restrain their sexual impulses and hold back from sexual activity. Although some feminists and some evolutionary theorists have assumed that cultural constraints on women's sexuality stem from men's attempts to control women, empirical evidence overwhelmingly indicates that women rather than men are the principal sources of pressure on women to restrain their sexuality (for review, see Baumeister & Twenge, 2002). The social exchange theory proposes that a rational strategy for women would be to work together to restrict the supply of sex available to men, in order to drive up the price. "Cheap" women who offer sex without demanding commitment or other resources in return undermine the bargaining position of other women and are therefore punished by the female community with ostracism, bad reputations, and other disincentives.

SPECIFIC SEXUAL PHENOMENA

In this section we touch on some specific sexual phenomena to highlight the differences between the theoretical perspectives noted above and, where relevant, to indicate other directions of theorizing. As mentioned before, the field of sex research has not been hospitable to midlevel theorizing (i.e., developing theories about specific phenomena apart from the grand perspectives of feminism, evolution, and the like), but some theories have been put forward, and in our view theoretical development in this field would benefit from encouraging more of these narrowly focused theories that may be independent of the grand perspectives.

Sexual Desire

Feminist theory saw itself as liberating women from accumulated false stereotypes. Some rebelled against the view that men desire sex more than women do, proposing instead that women's desire for sex is equal to and perhaps greater than men's (e.g., Sherfey, 1966; see also Hyde & DeLamater, 1997). However, a different tradition of feminist thought has emphasized the view of sexual intercourse as inherently coercive. This would seemingly assume that men want sex more than women do (which is why men would use coercion), though it is possible for feminists to propose that men coerce women for political reasons, so equal desire could still result in unequal coercion.

In contrast, evolutionary theory depicts male desire for short-term sex as stronger than that of female (and empirical evidence overwhelmingly supports this; for review, see Buss & Schmitt, 1993; Oliver & Hyde, 1993). In evolutionary perspective, this is because males (unlike females) can reproduce more if they have sex with a greater number of women. Moreover, males must work hard and take risks to get sex (given widespread female reluctance), and so a low sex drive might leave them disinclined to do so. Human females can normally have only one baby per year, and not much sex is required to accomplish that, so there is no biological payoff for high sex drive.

The social exchange theory is based partly on the assumption of greater male sex drive in general, which research findings also support (Baumeister, Catanese, & Vohs, 2001). According to the theory, this is why men will offer women other resources to induce them to have sex. If women wanted sex as much as or more than men did, the basis for the economy might be undercut.

That gender differences in desire for short-term sex will produce different patterns of sexual decision making has recently been proposed by Haselton and Buss (2000; see also Maner et al., 2005). Their "error management theory" is a midlevel theory though nominally linked to evolutionary theory. It proposes that men and women seek to minimize the more costly type of error. Men seek to minimize the chances of missing out on sexual opportunities, so they pursue all chances and interpret ambiguous behavior by women (such as smiling) as indications of sexual interest. Women, in contrast, seek to minimize the chances of having sex with an unreliable or genetically substandard mate, and so they avoid or refuse sexual opportunities and require suitors to furnish ample signs of suitability before engaging in sex.

Theories about prostitution and pornography are shaped by views of sexual desire. Clearly, prostitution and pornography appeal more to men than to women. To the social exchange theorist, these are low-cost substitutes that cater to the excess male desire that women themselves refuse to satisfy. In contrast, feminist theory assumes equality of desire, and so the greater male interest in prostitution and pornography must be attributed to other, nonsexual motives, such as the wish to degrade and exploit women. (For example, Dworkin, 1981, concluded that "[p]ornography is a celebration of rape and injury to women.") Interpreting male interest in pornography and prostitution as an exploitative political strategy has been a contentious feminist stance that has fueled hostile confrontations between men and women.

Rape

Although recent evidence indicates that women occasionally coerce men into unwanted sexual activity (e.g., Anderson & Struckman-Johnson, 1998) and that homosexual coercion also occurs, the bulk of theorizing has focused on explaining why men rape women. In our view, the major grand perspectives have mostly offered sometimes contentious and mostly unhelpful theorizing, and so the development of midlevel theories to explain rape specifically is needed.

Evolutionary theory has proposed that men rape women because it is one biological strategy for passing one's genes into the next generation (Thornhill & Palmer, 2000). In nature, and presumably in human prehistory, most females mated with a few high-status males, and so the other males were left out. Forcing sex on women was the only way that these lower-status males could reproduce, and so males who were sexually aggressive would have been more likely to pass on their genes than nonaggressive males (which is why, presumably, some genetic impulse to rape remains today). Though plausible, this theory runs far beyond the available evidence (as Thornhill and Palmer acknowledge) and leaves unanswered many specific questions in predicting rape.

Feminist theory depicts rape as reflecting the general pattern of male violence toward and oppression of women. A landmark feminist analysis by Brownmiller (1975) asserted, first, that rape reflects a conspiracy by all men (implying that even nonrapist men support rape) to intimidate and subjugate all women. She even claimed that men are socialized to rape. Second, the analysis insisted that the driving force behind rape is power rather than sex. Although a large amount of empirical evidence has discredited this view point by point (for reviews, see Felson, 2002; Palmer, 1988; Tedeschi & Felson, 1994), it remains popular with many feminists, especially those who regard quantitative data collection as merely another male tool to undercut subjective experience and oppress women. In fairness, the feminist view that rape is about power rather than sex may be an accurate depiction of the female victim's experience. Moreover, the feminist methodological insistence that people cannot fully understand the subjectivity of others in different roles entails that female theorists could not possibly understand the motives or actions of male rapists anyway.

Various other theories have begun to be put forward to explain rape. One early view emphasized low social skills, proposing that men who could not obtain sex by charm would resort to rape, but it has been contradicted by actual studies of rapists, which show that they do have skills and in fact often manage to have a higher amount of consensual sex than other men (e.g., Kanin, 1985). A newer theory by Malamuth (1996) is derived from observations of sexually coercive men, and proposes that a combination of hostile masculinity (masculine personality traits plus negative attitudes toward women), grievance (sense of having been victimized by women), and a view of heterosexual relations as inherently antagonistic, if not downright exploitative, is what predisposes some men toward rape. Malamuth's approach is admirably cautious in its scope and carefully grounded in systematic observations.

Using a similar, empirically based approach, Baumeister, Catanese, and Wallace (2002) proposed a narcissistic reactance theory of rape. Reactance theory (Brehm, 1966) proposes that people respond to loss of options by trying to reassert those options, and in regard to sex, some men may respond to a female's refusal of sex (especially when the man regards the refusal as unexpected or illegitimate) by using force to obtain sex. Narcissistic men, who overestimate their entitlements and are comfortable exploiting others to satisfy their own needs, may be most prone to make that kind of cognitive distortion.

Homosexuality

Explaining homosexuality is a difficult challenge for most theories. Evolutionary theory explains modern sexual desire as based on what patterns of ancestral sexual activity produced the most offspring—but homosexual behavior does not produce offspring, so why has evolution not entirely eradicated homosexual activity? Some evolutionary psychologists have speculated that evolution might allow for homosexuality through processes of kin selection (Bobrow & Bailey, 2001). For example, even if a gay man does not reproduce, he might still pass on his genes by helping to support the reproductive success of his close relatives, who carry a large proportion of his genes.

Constructionist theories explain sexual desire as a product of socializing influences of culture and parenting, but most cultures have disapproved of homosexuality. In particular, the Western tradition has condemned homosexuality with religious, social, and legal pressures, as well as informal pressures often extending to severe violence—so again, one might have expected homosexuality to have disappeared from the scene.

The social exchange theory has little to offer regarding homosexuality, beyond the vague speculation that homosexual activity might offer some individuals more rewards than costs. (For example, getting sexual pleasure without the risk of pregnancy might appeal to some individuals, but seemingly such a bargain would be more appealing to women than men, and, in empirical fact, there are more male than female homosexuals.)

The psychoanalytic view suggests that people are born bisexual, and so homosexuality is one possible developmental outcome that should be considered natural, though statistically unusual. More elaborate psychoanalytic approaches, such as emphasizing intrusive mothers and aloof, rejecting fathers, have not been supported by empirical evidence (see Bem, 1996, for critique).

Bem has proposed an intriguing mixture of nature and nurture. He speculates that some children are temperamentally more suited to play with the opposite gender than with their own. He proposes that at adolescence, the "exotic becomes erotic," which is to say that contact with the unfamiliar gender creates arousal that is then labeled as sexual excitement. Boys who grow up playing with boys will find girls different and exciting, but boys who grow up playing with girls will find other boys to be different and exciting. His view is inherently plausible, but evidence for crucial parts of it is not yet available.

The area of homosexuality is one in which midlevel theorizing seems most in need. Undoubtedly, there are correct elements in constructionist, evolutionary, and other approaches, and somehow these must be reconciled with the continued existence of homosexuality.

CONCLUSION

The vagaries of why people enjoy sex, why they enjoy variety, why they make good and bad decisions about sex, and further questions continue to preoccupy the general public as well as a broad realm of thinkers, but most of this thinking remains at the amateur level. The extensive discussion of sexuality indicates that sex remains an interesting topic, and in the long run, one can expect theorizing about sex to continue and even become better.

Offering an exhaustive account of sexual theories would require a tome written by a team of experts, and even they might not have gotten them all. Our project has been to summarize what we see as the major grand perspectives and provide a smattering of more focused, midlevel theories about sexual behavior. Recent decades have seen progress in both, though perhaps not as much as might have been. Our opinion is that the grand theories should be retained but de-emphasized, and especially the hostility between their adherents should not be permitted to restrict the development of midlevel theorizing. That is, the field of sex research would benefit if young and new researchers were encouraged to develop midlevel theories without having to declare allegiance to a grand perspective or justify themselves to devotees of those great camps.

Freudian theory has been criticized for being notoriously elastic and hence resistant to empirical disconfirmation. We think social constructionist, evolutionary, and probably sexual exchange theories are likewise flexible, and so they may be more useful as explanatory frameworks than as sources of competing, testable, and falsifiable hypotheses. The next decade should concentrate on the cultivation of empirically informed midlevel theories, and once several of those have been refined and honed against the sharp edge of data, only then will it be fruitful to revisit the clash of grand perspectives.

REFERENCES

Adams, H. E., Wright, L. W., & Lohr, B. A. (1996). Is homophobia associated with homosexual arousal? *Journal of Abnormal Psychology, 105*, 440–445.

Andersen, B. L. (1981). A comparison of systematic desensitization and directed masturbation in the treatment of primary orgasmic dysfunction in females. *Journal of Consulting and Clinical Psychology, 49*, 568–570.

Anderson, P. B., & Struckman-Johnson, C. (Eds.). (1998). *Sexually aggressive women: Current perspectives and controversies*. New York: Guilford.

Arafat, I. S., & Yorburg, B. (1973). On living together without marriage. *Journal of Sex Research, 13*, 97–106.

Bauman, K. E., & Wilson, R. R. (1974). Sexual behavior of unmarried university students in 1968 and 1972. *Journal of Sex Research, 10*, 327–333.

Baumeister, R. F., Catanese, K. R., & Vohs, K. D. (2001). Is there a gender difference in strength of sex drive? Theoretical views, conceptual distinctions, and a review of relevant evidence. *Personality and Social Psychology Review, 5*, 242–273.

Baumeister, R. F., Catanese, K. R., & Wallace, H. M. (2002). Conquest by force: A narcissistic reactance theory of rape and sexual coercion. *Review of General Psychology, 6*, 92–135.

Baumeister, R. F., & Twenge, J. M. (2002). Cultural suppression of female sexuality. *Review of General Psychology, 6*, 166–203.

Baumeister, R. F., & Vohs, K. D. (2004). Sexual economics: Sex as female resource for social exchange in heterosexual interactions. *Personality and Social Psychology Review, 8*, 339–363.

Becker, G. S. (1976). *The economic approach to human behavior.* Chicago: University of Chicago Press.

Bem, D. J. (1996). Exotic becomes erotic: A developmental theory of sexual orientation. *Psychological Review, 103*, 320–335.

Berger, P. L., & Luckmann, T. (1967). *The social construction of reality: A treatise in the sociology of knowledge.* Garden City, NJ: Anchor.

Betzig, L. (1989). Causes of conjugal dissolution: A cross-cultural study. *Current Anthropology, 30*, 654–676.

Birenbaum, A. (1970). Revolution without the revolution: Sex in contemporary America. *Journal of Sex Research, 6*, 257–267.

Blau, P. N. (1964). *Exchange and power in social life.* New York: Wiley.

Bobrow, D., & Bailey, M. (2001). Is homosexuality maintained via kin selection? *Evolution and Human Behavior, 22*, 361–368.

Brehm, J. W. (1966). *A theory of psychological reactance.* New York: Academic Press.

Brown, N. O. (1966). *Love's body.* Berkeley: University of California Press.

Brownmiller, S. (1975). *Against our will: Men, women, and rape.* New York: Simon and Schuster.

Buss, D. M., & Schmitt, D. (1993). Sexual strategies theory: An evolutionary perspective on human mating. *Psychological Review, 100*, 204–232.

Clarke, R. D., & Hatfield, E. (1989). Gender differences in receptivity to sexual offers. *Journal of Psychology and Human Sexuality, 2*, 39–55.

Cosmides, L., & Tooby, J. (1992). Cognitive adaptations for social exchange. In J. Barkow, L. Cosmides, & J. Tooby (Eds.), *The adapted mind* (pp. 163–228). New York: Oxford University Press.

Cott, N. (1978). Passionlessness: An interpretation of Victorian sexual ideology. *Signs, 4*, 219–236.

Darwin, C. (1859/1964). *On the origin of species.* Cambridge, MA: Harvard University Press.

Darwin, C. (1871). *The descent of man, and selection in relation to sex.* London: John Murray.

Dworkin, A. (1981). *Pornography: Men possessing women.* London: The Women's Press.

Ehrenreich, B., Hess, E., & Jacobs, G. (1986). *Re-making love: The feminization of sex.* Garden City, NJ: Doubleday Anchor.

Felson, R. B. (2002). *Violence and gender reexamined.* Washington, DC: American Psychological Association.

Freud, S. (1905/1975). *Three essays on the theory of sexuality.* New York: Basic Books.

Gangestad, S. W., & Simpson, J. A. (2000). The evolution of human mating: Trade-offs and strategic pluralism. *Behavioral and Brain Sciences, 23*, 573–644.

Guttentag, M., & Secord, P. F. (1983). *Too many women? The sex ratio question.* Beverly Hills, CA: Sage.

Haselton, M., & Buss, D. (2000). Error management theory: A new perspective on biases in cross-sex mind reading. *Journal of Personality and Social Psychology, 78*, 81–91.

Homans, G. C. (1950). *The human group*. New York: Harcourt, Brace, & World.

Homans, G. C. (1961). *Social behavior: Its elementary forms*. New York: Harcourt, Brace, & World.

Hyde, J. S. (1994). *Understanding human sexuality* (5th ed.). New York: McGraw-Hill.

Hyde, J. S. (1996). Where are the gender differences? Where are the gender similarities? In D. M. Buss & N. M. Malamuth (Eds.), *Sex, power, conflict: Evolutionary and feminist perspectives* (pp. 107–118). New York: Oxford University Press.

Hyde, J. S., & DeLamater, J. D. (1997). *Understanding human sexuality* (6th ed.). New York: McGraw-Hill.

James, W. (1890/1950). *The principles of psychology*. New York: Dover.

Kanin, E. J. (1985). Date rapists: Differential sexual socialization and relative deprivation. *Archives of Sexual Behavior, 14*, 219–231.

Kenrick, D. T., & Keefe, R. C. (1992). Age preferences in mates reflect sex differences in human reproductive strategies. *Behavioral and Brain Sciences, 15*, 75–133.

Kenrick, D. T., Maner, J. K., Butner, J., Li, N. P., Becker, D. V., & Schaller, M. (2002). Dynamical evolutionary psychology: Mapping the domains of the new interactionist paradigm. *Personality and Social Psychology Review, 6*, 347–356.

Krebs, D. L. (2003). Fictions and facts about evolutionary approaches to human behavior: Comment on Lickliter and Honeycutt (2003). *Psychological Bulletin, 129*, 842–847.

Li, N. P., Bailey, J. M., Kenrick, D. T., & Linsenmeier, J. A. (2002). The necessities and luxuries of mate preferences: Testing the trade-offs. *Journal of Personality and Social Psychology, 82*, 947–955.

Lickliter, R., & Honeycutt, H. (2003). Developmental dynamics: Toward a biologically plausible evolutionary psychology. *Psychological Bulletin, 129*, 819–835.

Malamuth, N. M. (1996). The confluence model of sexual aggression: Feminist and evolutionary perspectives. In D. Buss & N. Malamuth (Eds.), *Sex, power, conflict* (pp. 269–295). New York: Oxford University Press.

Maner, J. K., Kenrick, D. T., Becker, D. V., Delton, A. W., Hofer, B., Wilbur, C., et al. (2003). Sexually selective cognition: Beauty captures the mind of the beholder. *Journal of Personality and Social Psychology, 85*, 1107–1120.

Maner, J. K., Kenrick, D. T., Becker, D. V., Robertson, T., Hofer, B., Neuberg, S., et al. (2005). Functional projection: How fundamental social motives can bias interpersonal perception. *Journal of Personality and Social Psychology, 88*, 63–78.

Mead, M. (1928). *Coming of age in Samoa*. New York: William Morrow.

Mead, M. (1961). Cultural determinants of sexual behavior. In W. C. Young (Ed.), *Sex and internal secretions* (pp. 1433–1479). Baltimore: Williams and Wilkins.

Oliver, M. B., & Hyde, J. S. (1993). Gender differences in sexuality: A meta-analysis. *Psychological Bulletin, 114*, 29–51.

Palmer, C. T. (1988). Twelve reasons why rape is not sexually motivated: A skeptical examination. *Journal of Sex Research, 25*, 512–530.

Reiss, I. L. (1986). *Journey into sexuality: An exploratory voyage.* Englewood Cliffs, NJ: Prentice-Hall.

Rich, A. (1980). Compulsory heterosexuality and lesbian existence. *Signs, 5,* 631–660.

Riger, S. (1992). Epistemological debates, feminist voices. *American Psychologist, 47,* 730–740.

Robinson, R., Ziss, K., Ganza, B., Katz, S., & Robinson, E. (1991). Twenty years of the sexual revolution, 1965–1985: An update. *Journal of Marriage and the Family, 53,* 216–220.

Sherfey, M. J. (1966). The evolution and nature of female sexuality in relation to psychoanalytic theory. *Journal of the American Psychoanalytic Association, 14,* 28–128.

Simpson, J. A., & Gangestad, S. W. (1991). Individual differences in sociosexuality: Evidence for convergent and discriminant validity. *Journal of Personality and Social Psychology, 60,* 870–883.

Sommers, C. H. (1995). *Who stole feminism? How women have betrayed women.* New York: Simon and Schuster.

Sprecher, S. (1988). Investment model, equity and social support determinants of relationship commitment. *Social Psychology Quarterly, 51,* 318–328.

Sprecher, S. (1992). How men and women expect to feel and behave in response to inequity in close relationships. *Social Psychology Quarterly, 55,* 57–69.

Sprecher, S., & Regan, P. C. (1996). College virgins: How men and women perceive their sexual status. *Journal of Sex Research, 33,* 3–16.

Symons, D. (1979). *The evolution of human sexuality.* Oxford: Oxford University Press.

Tannahill, R. (1980). *Sex in history.* New York: Stein & Day.

Tedeschi, J. T., & Felson, R. B. (1994). *Violence, aggression, and coercive actions.* Washington, DC: American Psychological Association.

Thibaut, J. W., & Kelley, H. H. (1959). *The social psychology of groups.* New York: Wiley.

Thornhill, R., & Palmer, C. T. (2000). *A natural history of rape: Biological bases of sexual coercion.* Cambridge, MA: MIT Press.

Tiefer, L. (1995). *Sex is not a natural act and other essays.* Boulder, CO: Westview Press.

Trivers, R. L. (1972). Parental investment and sexual selection. In B. Campbell (Ed.), *Sexual selection and the descent of man: 1871–1971* (pp. 136–179). Chicago: Aldine.

Weeks, J. (1991). *Against nature: Essays on history, sexuality and identity.* London: Rivers Oram Press.

Weis, D. L. (1998). Conclusion: The state of sexual theory. *Journal of Sex Research, 35,* 100–114.

Yoder, J. D., & Kahn, A. S. (1992). Toward a feminist understanding of women and power. *Psychology of Women Quarterly, 16,* 381–388.

3

Sexuality in Childhood

Ryan P. Kilmer and Ariana Shahinfar ◆

Sexuality in childhood—the very notion seems an oxymoron. Although many parents and caregivers may prefer to believe that sexuality is something that is not awakened in their child until adolescence, sexuality is no different from other areas of human development in that its roots are planted and take hold in childhood. This does not mean, however, that a young child's capacity to experience and express sexuality is equivalent to that of an adult. Perhaps the most useful approach to understanding child sexuality in this context is to regard it as a "normal" aspect of development, encompassing the set of processes and experiences that provide the groundwork for healthy adult sexual functioning. Despite the obvious evolutionary significance of adult sexual behavior, however, child sexual behavior has been the subject of minimal systematic investigation, and little attention has been paid in the research literature to the normal developmental course through which the foundation is laid for mature adult sexuality.

Ironically, the emphasis in the professional literature is (and has been) on difficulties and problems, such as the impact of sexual abuse, "deviations" in sexual development, and gender role confusion in children. As a result, it appears that we know more about what is viewed as "abnormal" than "normal." Some researchers have recently advocated collecting normative data in order to better understand the behaviors of youngsters who have been sexually abused and to distinguish these behaviors from those of others (e.g., Friedrich, Fisher, Broughton, Houston, & Shafran, 1998; Larsson & Svedin, 2002b). In fact, it was not until there was a heightened awareness of sexual abuse (and its impact), brought on largely by the institution of mandatory reporting laws over thirty years ago, that the need for data on the normal bounds of childhood sexual behavior was highlighted to the research community (Heiman, Leiblum, Esquilin, & Pallitto, 1998). Thus, it appears that researchers, professionals, and others made decisions about what was "abnormal" without first identifying and understanding what was "normal." Nonetheless, the need for information on normal sexual development has been recognized, and some investigations have begun to shed light on child sexuality.

One problem with the limited research in this field is that much of the work draws on findings from anecdotes or case studies. Because they may not apply to the majority of children, these methodologies are considered weak for the purpose of providing a representative picture of the normal course of sexual development. Furthermore, some researchers relying on vignettes or individual experiences have made claims that are difficult to validate, couching "results" as normative without evidence that the descriptions are indeed typical. Admittedly, there are numerous impediments to conducting well-controlled research in this area. First, parents are often considered the most qualified reporters regarding children's daily behaviors, yet sexuality involves private behaviors, many of which parents may not have observed. Even when children are old enough to offer self-reports, the private nature of sexuality may make them hesitant to report on such behavior. There are also ethical constraints regarding the nature of research that can be done with children, particularly when considering the societal taboo surrounding sexuality in many cultures.

This cultural bias may also contribute to difficulty in gathering sound data in that survey respondents may balk at the use of the term "sexual" to describe behaviors engaged in by infants and children, particularly within societies that are less open regarding sexuality (e.g., the United States). While some researchers and theorists (e.g., Friedrich et al., 1998; Martinson, 1997) have noted that it is possible to describe aspects of children's sexual behavior using categories with a corresponding adult behavior or presentation (including self-stimulation, sexual interest, exhibitionism, sexual knowledge, and voyeuristic behaviors), there are some key points that differentiate the presentation of such behaviors in children versus adults. It is possible that emphasizing these differences may make the larger discussion of normative childhood sexuality more palatable and, thus, more possible within a greater variety of cultures. Toward this end, Heiman et al. (1998) have suggested that discussion and investigation of child sexuality might be freed if researchers modify the description of the behaviors under study from "sexual" to "self-exploratory."

We would further suggest that there is a meaningful difference between behaviors motivated by curiosity or "scientific" interest and those driven by sexual interest and, importantly, between behaviors that are *pleasurable* and those that are *sexual*. Put another way, although some of the behaviors in which young children engage involve their genitalia, they are not necessarily sexual in nature.

A second useful distinction between adult and child sexuality relates to the fact that an individual's intentions and cognitions serve an important function in determining whether a behavior is sexual per se (Gordon & Schroeder, 1995). For instance, while numerous parental and professional reports describe infants, toddlers, and preschoolers touching their own genitals, this self-stimulation is qualitatively different in meaning, intention, and experience than similar behaviors would be later in the developmental span. For this reason, and as mentioned at the opening of this chapter, we believe that childhood sexuality is more usefully described as the foundation for, rather than an early sign of, adult sexuality.

With appreciation for the still evolving state of the field's current knowledge base regarding child sexuality, this chapter seeks to (a) provide an overview of theoretical frameworks that may prove useful in considering the processes and experiences that underlie the development of child sexuality, (b) summarize current knowledge regarding childhood sexuality from birth to 12 years of age, (c) consider briefly cross-cultural findings to clarify cultural differences in youngsters' sexual behavior, (d) describe selected nonnormative child sexual experiences and outcomes, and (e) discuss recommendations for future research in this area.

THEORIES RELATING TO
CHILDHOOD SEXUALITY

In considering developmental theories of childhood sexuality, the ideas of Sigmund Freud present a natural starting point. Freud's psychosexual theory is, in fact, the only developmental theory that explicitly names sexuality as a central force in driving human growth and behavior. In brief, Freud argued that children pass through five distinct stages of development (oral, anal, phallic, latency, and genital), each of which centers around a specific area of the body that is most sensitive to excitation and sensual pleasure and thus serves as the primary source of satisfaction and gratification. Successful navigation of each stage involves the child being allowed to experience and explore freely the sources of pleasure attached to each phase while carefully balancing desires/ drives ("id"), what the environment will provide or allow, that is, the constraints of reality ("ego"), and the judgments and limitations enforced by social and societal boundaries and mores ("superego"). Failure to navigate one of the phases of psychosexual development (e.g., by obtaining too much or too little gratification) would, according to Freud, result in fixation at a particular stage. In Freud's view, this fixation could very much influence personality traits and even take the form of various psychological problems, but the key element in Freud's thinking is that a child's ability to master sensual pleasure serves as the foundation for growth and development (see Freud & Gay, 1995, for more on Freud's theory and writings).

Several criticisms have been lodged against Freud's psychosexual theory, including that it (a) has no empirical basis, (b) is essentially untestable via current scientific methods and standards, and (c) was primarily developed through retrospective assignment of meaning to childhood experiences among an adult clinical population (as opposed to thorough prospective observation of children's normative development). Another criticism that holds particular relevance to the topic of this chapter is that, as an approach to development, psychosexual theory assumes cultural universality—that is, psychosexual development and the outcomes associated with passage through the various stages are implied to be a universal experience. This issue becomes relevant when addressing the considerable cultural variability in children's sexual behavior and attitudes that has been reported in the literature (see Larsson, Svedin, & Friedrich, 2000). Perhaps the largest problem with relying solely on psychosexual theory in trying to understand the development of childhood sexuality is that it treats sexuality as the force behind development rather than an outgrowth of a complex and comprehensive developmental package. That is, in giving sexual impulses, behaviors, drives, and issues such prominence, this theory does not fully account for the multiple complex processes and systems at play as children grow and develop, nor does it address the interrelationships between sexuality and these other within-child systems as well as the external factors influencing youngsters' development.

Moving beyond Freudian ideas, more modern approaches to developmental theory attempt to account for such factors and underscore the fact that physiological, cognitive, social, and emotional domains of development are intertwined and, in fact, mutually supportive with respect to human growth (see, e.g., Damon & Lerner, 1998). This idea holds true for the development of childhood sexuality as well. As described by Martinson (1997), there is neither a predictable stage sequence nor a universal course of development that is currently thought to independently describe normal sexual development in the child. Rather, normal developmental processes, including various biological and psychological domains, are thought to contribute to the capacities and behaviors that underlie the child's sexual development (Martinson, 1997). Although it is outside the scope of this chapter to review basic theories of normative development, it is important to keep in mind that the development of childhood sexuality reflects overall growth and development. That is, in order to fully understand changes in the sexual behavior and attitudes of children, one must also understand their developing physical, social, emotional, and cognitive capacities. In addition, sexuality is an area of psychological development that is heavily tied to sociological, anthropological, and historical forces and, thus, cannot be entirely understood without reference to such factors (Frayser, 1994; Gordon & Schroeder, 1995; Larsson et al., 2000; Martinson, 1997). In fact, much research suggests that these larger cultural forces contribute to important differences in the development and expression of sexual behavior among children (see Larsson et al.).

Because of the complex interplay of psychological and sociocultural forces in shaping the development of children's sexuality, the most useful theories for explaining such development must necessarily encompass consideration of intraindividual factors (e.g., biological growth, cognitive development) as well as environmental variables (e.g., cultural standards regarding the expression of sexuality). One approach that effectively considers these various levels is ecological systems theory (Bronfenbrenner, 1977, 1979; Bronfenbrenner & Morris, 1998), and the remainder of this section details the application of this approach to the development of children's sexuality. Ecological systems theory builds on transactional models of development, which emphasize that a child's development is impacted in a bidirectional manner, such that influence flows both from parent to child and from child to parent (e.g., Sameroff & Chandler, 1975). This ecological approach goes further, describing development as occurring within the context of various "nested" levels that mutually interact and influence one another, and include not only the individual child and his or her unique social, emotional, physiological, and cognitive developmental trajectory, but also the various environmental influences that transact with him or her.

The ecological systems model is traditionally depicted as a series of concentric circles, with each ring representing a category of influences on the child. In general, more proximal influences (i.e., factors that more directly influence the child himself/herself) make up the inner rings of the model, and more distal influences (i.e., those that influence the child's development through an impact on his or her larger ecology) would constitute the outer rings. At its core, this approach asserts that individual behavior and development are influenced by a variety of factors in both one's proximal (e.g., family milieu, peer group, school personnel) and more distal (e.g., cultural values and beliefs, neighborhood qualities, community characteristics) environments, as well as the interactions and interrelationships between and among the multiple levels of a child's contextual world (for more on ecological theory, see Bronfenbrenner, 1977, 1979; Bronfenbrenner & Morris, 1998).

The ecological systems framework is well suited for considering the development of children's sexuality because, as Friedrich et al. (1998) note, the available findings "affirm the premise that the behavior of children is reflective of the context in which they are raised." Cultures, communities, and the families within these larger contexts exhibit a wide range of variability in their attitudes toward and reactions to children's sexual behaviors, nudity, and other expressions of sexuality, and these differences are thought to affect children's behaviors, thoughts, and outward expressions of their feelings and impulses (Larsson et al., 2000). Utilizing ecological systems theory, the paragraphs that follow provide a brief backdrop for considering childhood sexuality and the multiple influences on the development of the sexual self (see Figure 3.1 for examples of ecological influences).

At the center of the nested levels described by the ecological framework, and arguably most proximal to the child's developing sexuality, is the unique

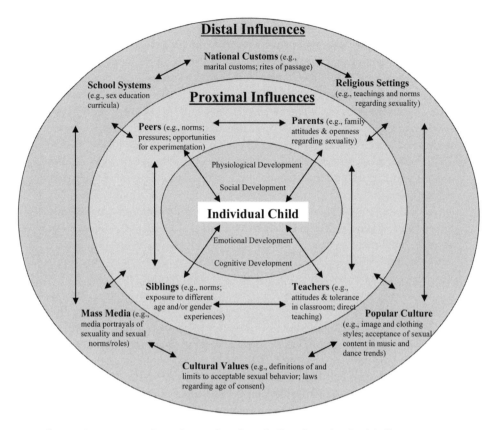

Figure 3.1. Examples of proximal and distal ecological influences on the development of children's sexuality.

social, emotional, physiological, and cognitive developmental trajectory of the individual child. Aspects of intraindividual growth and development, including a child's increasing cognitive capacities and ability to understand thoughts or behaviors as sexual, are relevant to the development of childhood sexuality. Indeed, part of what defines an act as sexual (versus pleasurable) is the understanding of the behavior as such (Gordon & Schroeder, 1995), which develops as a child's cognitive skills develop. Similarly, the child's physiological development provides the necessary backdrop for certain milestones in the development of sexuality, such as the ability to maintain an erection and ejaculate.

Other important proximal influences include those ecological forces that transact directly with the child (e.g., parents, siblings, peers, and teachers). Relevant family factors include how permissive parents are with respect to nudity, sexual television and movie viewing, and opportunities for exposure to adult sexuality—all of which may influence the development of childhood sexual behavior (Friedrich et al., 1992). For example, Friedrich et al. (1998)

found a correlation between openness within the home regarding sexuality and reported child sexual behavior. Other researchers have replicated this finding, identifying an association between an index of family sexuality (including items such as seeing nude adults in the home, bathing with adults, having witnessed intercourse, having nude pictures available in the home, and seeing nudity on television) and sexual behavior scores for youngsters in both U.S. and Swedish samples (Larsson et al., 2000). Although this finding may simply reflect the fact that parents who promote more sexual openness are also more open in reporting their child's sexual behavior, it is also true that a child's behavior is influenced by, and indicative of, the environment in which he or she is raised (Friedrich et al., 1998). Through modeling and the reactions and responses of caregivers and other adults to their acts, statements, and questions, children learn to shape their behaviors, understand which behaviors are viewed as acceptable or not (and which are more appropriate for private settings), and identify the proper language for describing their thoughts, impulses, and behavior (Friedrich & Trane, 2002).

Similarly, the child's peers may play a role in the development and expression of sexual behavior in childhood. Specifically, peers have been found to exert a strong influence on defining norms for each other regarding sexual behavior during preadolescence (Kinsman, Romer, Furstenburg, & Schwarz, 1998), and these influences appear to be stronger than parental social influence in this age-group (Beal, Ausiello, & Perrin, 2001; see also Kinsman, Nyanzi, & Pool, 2000, for an interesting exploration of this idea with an African sample). Additionally, Haugaard and Tilly (1988) found that those undergraduates who made retrospective reports of having experienced a childhood sexual encounter also reported having had more friends as a child, and were more likely to have had a friend in whom they could confide. These findings suggest that the presence of close peers may facilitate childhood sexual exploration by presenting a safe and trusted partner with whom to experiment (Haugaard & Tilly). Peer socialization has also been hypothesized to affect children as young as preschool-age; Friedrich et al. (1998) found that the number of hours spent in day care positively correlated with children's reported sexual behavior. The suggestion is that greater exposure to children from families with other values and experiences may lead to a greater variety of learned sexual behaviors among even very young children.

More distal factors can also have important influences on a child's developing sexuality. For example, ecological systems theory would specifically consider the impact of school programming in the form of sex education on the child's developing sexuality. One theory to explain the cross-cultural differences noted particularly between youngsters growing up in Scandinavian countries and in the United States is that the widespread acceptance and encouragement of sex education in Scandinavia and other Western European countries has a long-standing history, whereas federal standards regarding such education have a more mixed record in the United States (Goldman & Goldman,

1988). For example, the United States has gone from having no federally mandated sex education prior to the 1980s, to the surgeon general calling for sex education as early as the third grade in 1986, at the height of the AIDS crisis (Donovan, 1998). At the time of the writing of this chapter, the debate within the United States regarding sex education centered around whether the current "abstinence-only" approach to sex education favored by the federal government should be changed to an "abstinence plus information on contraception" approach, despite the fact that the United States has a teenage pregnancy rate that is among the highest of any industrialized nation (Singh & Darroch, 2000). As an example of the effect of the educational ecology on children's sexual behavior, the European approach to sexuality education and contraception availability for teenagers has been credited as a central factor in contributing to more rapidly decreasing rates of teenage pregnancy in Western European countries as compared to the United States (Furstenberg, 1998).

Another example of a community influence on the development of children's sexuality that has been noted in the research is the impact of religiosity on sexual behavior and practices. In a retrospective study of childhood sexuality, Haugaard and Tilly (1988) found that in the case of respondents who reported having had a sexual encounter in childhood, the strength of religion in their childhood family was slightly lower than in the case of those respondents who did not report having had a childhood sexual encounter. Of course, this finding could possibly be explained by the emphasis on religion in the childhood family leading to an adult respondent being less likely to report on childhood experiences that involved sexuality, due to shame or guilt. In either case, the point is that religiosity or other cultural frameworks that dictate family attitudes toward sexuality are likely to have an impact on the behaviors a child may engage in or be willing to share through reporting.

Larger sociocultural influences also considered by ecological systems theory include the cultural environment in which the communities and families of developing children reside and function. As described by Frayser (1994, p. 180), "[C]ultural ideas and beliefs can shape the meaning of sexual behavior and define the participants in and limits to that behavior." These cultural messages may exist in the form of laws such as the age at which an individual is able to give consent for participation in intercourse, cultural taboos against incest, and cultural beliefs regarding the age at which children enter adulthood and are ready for sexual initiation and marriage. Cultural messages may also take less organized but equally influential forms, such as how media portrayals treat sexuality and depict gender roles (Ryan, 2000). Ecological theory proposes that these cultural messages are created by communities and influence what messages those communities send to families and children regarding sexuality. Not only are cultural messages regarding sexual behavior available to children through what communities and families teach directly, but they have also become increasingly available through the television, video, and Internet technologies that are ubiquitous in most industrialized nations. It should also be noted that cultural attitudes are not always directly reflected in media expressions of sexuality. For example, the disconnect between the open display of eroticism in the American media and that same society's reluctance to speak openly about private sexual practices has been noted (e.g., Heiman et al., 1998). The effect this mismatch between purported values and media expression has on children's developing sexuality is unclear; however, there is no doubt that cultural messages regarding sexuality are important in shaping children's attitudes toward their developing sexual selves (Frayser, 1994; Goldman & Goldman, 1988; Gordon & Schroeder, 1995; Martinson, 1997).

The transactional influences specified by the ecological systems model described above were presented as a means of organizing the various factors that contribute to the normal development of sexuality in childhood. This model should be kept in mind as we move forward to outline what is currently known.

NORMAL CHILDHOOD SEXUALITY: WHAT WE *THINK* WE KNOW . . .

In beginning a discussion of the current knowledge available regarding the normal development of childhood sexuality, it is important to first offer a definition of the term "normal" within this context. As mentioned earlier, "normal sexuality" is a socially constructed concept that varies considerably both between and within cultures (Frayser, 1994). Some have further suggested that even within these cultural limits, any sexual idea, fantasy, dream, or wish—that is, one that involves thought, not behavior—is considered to be normal (Gordon & Schroeder, 1995). That said, there are some factors that are generally accepted to distinguish normal from abnormal sexual behavior in childhood. Following the thinking developed in the literature on sexual offending, there is consensus among researchers that normal sexual behavior involves (1) consent, (2) equality of partners (for children, this refers to being within five years of one another's age), and (3) a lack of coercion (National Adolescent Perpetrator Network, 1988, 1993). Although these guidelines are meant to provide objective criteria by which the normalcy of sexual behavior may be determined, it should be noted that the interpretation of consent and coercion may be cloudy even within the participating child's mind (Lamb & Coakley, 1993), and that standards regarding age differences may be culturally and historically bound.

Another consideration is that there exist differences in how child sexual behavior is interpreted and reported. For example, most reports regarding these behaviors are provided by mothers or female caregivers. It has been suggested, however, that female and male reporters may hold different standards regarding their views of sexual behaviors—that is, males have been shown to be more liberal in their interpretation and labeling of behavior as sexual (e.g., Heiman et al., 1998). In a study of 307 health care and mental health care professionals, it was found that females rated various child sexual behaviors as more abnormal than did males (Heiman et al.). Similarly, Lamb and Coakley (1993) found in a retrospective study of female undergraduates that those who came from a "restrictive" versus an "open" home were more likely to rate their own childhood sexual encounters as "not normal." These interpretations likely impact the reporting of childhood sexual behavior and thus limit the currently available data.

Recognizing the difficulty in defining normal sexual behavior and the various issues associated with reporting bias, it is safe to say that research on normative child sexual development is in its infancy. What follows is a description of some of the prominent behaviors and processes that are currently thought to constitute normative aspects of childhood sexual development across major age-groups. It is important to note that the findings described below are based on two main sources of information: (1) reports by parents or caretakers based on observed sexual behavior among children, and (2) retrospective reports by adults (usually undergraduate students) regarding their own childhood sexual experiences. Although not directly represented in the current section, data from studies of children who have been brought in for treatment due to concerns about age-inappropriate, sexualized behavior have also yielded information on normal childhood sexuality, if only by offering exclusionary criteria and comparisons. These data are touched upon in a separate section of this chapter and more fully considered in a later volume in this set. Rather than providing definitive answers, the information below is meant to provide a starting point for understanding the normative development of sexuality among children across different age-groups—a knowledge base that is not yet well developed.

Infants and Toddlers (Birth–2 Years)

Infants are born with several capacities consistent with developing into sexual beings. For example, Martinson (1997) presents evidence that one of the earliest systems to develop during the embryonic phase is the skin, and he argues that skin sensitivity and touch are more intimately related to erotic arousal than any of the other senses. Evidence has also been presented that male erections and female vaginal lubrication are present in newborns, thus suggesting that the external genitalia are functional at birth (Martinson, 1997). These capacities indicate that the human newborn possesses several physiologic features that prepare him or her to develop sexually.

The most prominent way in which normal development, including sexual development, is expressed during infancy focuses on the sensory and motor activities that take center stage during this developmental period. Such activities allow infants the capacity to explore both their own bodies and the physical world surrounding them, and to learn from these experiences. This bodily self-exploration naturally includes exploration of the genital area. It has been noted that boys begin genital exploration around six or seven months, while girls generally begin between ten and eleven months (Martinson, 1997). This exploration takes the form of fingering, pleasurable handling, and random exploration and has been noted to disappear in female infants within a few weeks of onset. Male infants, on the other hand, have been noted to continue this behavior as casual play (Martinson, 1997). It should be noted, however, that this self-stimulation is considered to be exploratory and pleasurable rather than masturbatory or sexual in nature (McAnulty & Burnette, 2004). In support of this idea, Martinson (1997, p. 44) notes that "the average infant is not innately motivated and lacks the muscular capacity for the degree of self-stimulation necessary to produce orgasm."

From an anthropologic perspective, Fisher (1989) notes that an important goal of the bodily exploration in which infants engage is to create a map of the body, to which the child will later add significance through transaction with the ecological systems surrounding him or her. This body mapping begins by exploring and then labeling the parts of the body, including genitals. Parents or caretakers have an important role in the child's developing sexuality at this point, as they can either help the child to correctly label or choose to ignore the child's bid for information regarding genitalia. It has been argued that as the infant makes connections between his or her awareness of the body and how adults respond to that awareness, the foundation is being laid for the child's attitude toward his or her body, gender, and sexuality (Frayser, 1994).

As the infant develops further into toddlerhood, genital stimulation takes on a slightly more purposeful note and appears to involve, in addition to manual manipulation of the genitals, the use of objects with which to rub genitals (Levine, 1957). There is also some suggestion that toddlerhood marks the psychological awareness of the genitals and that the sexual behaviors displayed during this period are accompanied by signs of pleasure (Roiphe & Galenson, 1981). In one of the only recent studies of normative child sexual behavior to include toddler-age children, Friedrich et al. (1998) found that 2-year-old children were reported by parents to be relatively sexual (as compared to 10- to 12-year-olds), but that the sexual behaviors displayed by the young children fell within the category of self-stimulation, exhibitionism (i.e., displaying one's genitals), and a lack of personal boundaries rather than behaviors directed toward another individual with sexual intent. Taken together, the available evidence suggests that sexuality in infancy and toddlerhood can best be characterized as prompted by curiosity about one's own and others' bodies.

Preschoolers (3–5 Years)

Although there is a dearth of research on sexuality throughout childhood, the sexual behavior of preschoolers has garnered some attention in the professional literature in recent years. This increase in focus likely reflects two main factors: Parents and guardians often question clinical professionals (pediatricians, psychologists, social workers, etc.) about the appropriateness of their child's observed behaviors at this age, and, perhaps related, the suggestion that certain behaviors may result from sexual abuse or victimization (e.g., see Lindblad, Gustafsson, Larsson, & Lundin, 1995). Such work underscores the clear need to better understand the range of behaviors that may be characterized as "normal."

Although retrospective self-reports have been utilized, more recent studies of preschoolers' sexual behavior have generally involved reporters representing two major domains of a child's functioning—parents (home) and teachers (preschool or day care)—with parental reports being the most widely used method (Friedrich et al., 1998). Overall, early studies suggested that high frequency behaviors included self-stimulating behaviors, attempting to look at people when nude or undressing, and observing the genitals of other children; other more intrusive behaviors, such as masturbating with an object, inserting an object into one's vagina or rectum, or touching an adult's genitals, were considerably more uncommon (see, e.g., Friedrich, Grambsch, Broughton, Kuiper, & Bielke, 1991; Larsson et al., 2000; Lindblad et al., 1995).

In a study that included 574 2- to 5-year-old American children, parents reported that over 60 percent of boys and nearly 45 percent of girls touched their genitals at home, the most commonly reported behavior in this sample (Friedrich et al., 1998). Other common behaviors for both sexes (reported in over 20 percent of children) included standing too close to people, touching or trying to touch their mother's or other women's breasts, and trying to look at people when they are nude or undressing; touching sex parts in public was also a relatively common behavior among boys, reported for 26.5 percent. Behaviors far more rare in this age-group included putting one's mouth on sex parts, trying to have intercourse, asking others to engage in sexual acts, and pretending toys are having sex, all of which were reported in less than 2 percent of both boys and girls.

A comparative study of sexual behavior in preschoolers in the United States found similar results among the 467 3- to 6-year-olds in the sample (Larsson et al., 2000). Parents reported several common behaviors for both boys and girls, including trying to look at people undressing or nude, being shy about undressing, walking around the house without clothes, touching or trying to touch their mother's or other women's breasts, and touching genitals at home. Over one-fifth of girls pretended to be the opposite sex, and boys tended to more commonly touch their genitals in public, show their genitals to adults, and masturbate with their hands. Rare behaviors for both sexes (reported in 2 percent or less) included asking to watch sexually explicit television, asking others to engage in sexual acts, and masturbating with an object; boys also rarely imitated sexual behavior with dolls and put their tongues in others' mouths when kissing.

As might be expected, preschool-age youngsters appear more inclined to engage in sexual behaviors and/or explore sexuality at home than in more structured settings, such as day care or preschool, which generally involve higher levels of monitoring and more specific behavioral rules (see, e.g., Larsson

& Svedin, 2002b). These studies, conducted in Sweden, have suggested that children of both sexes more often walked around indoors without clothes, talked about sex, showed genitals to adults within the family, masturbated or touched their own genitals, and tried to touch other children's genitalia when at home than when at the center. Girls were also significantly more likely to use sexual vocabulary at home, as well as show their genitals to other children, and pretend to be the opposite sex when playing. Larsson and Svedin note that some data suggest that boys do not change their behavior as much between settings, perhaps reflecting socialization pressures on girls. These same researchers denote multiple behaviors common to both home and day care in their sample, including trying to look at other children's genitals, exposure of body and genitals to peers, trying to look at people undressing, and playing "doctor" and other games (e.g., playing "house," including giving birth). More explicit sexual games were very much unusual in both environments studied (Larsson & Svedin, 2002b). This latter finding is supported by the research of Lindblad et al. (1995), who reported that behaviors such as attempting to make an adult touch the child's genitals, using objects against one's own/other children's genitals/ anus, and compulsive masturbation, seemingly without pleasure or to the point that it appeared to cause pain, were very uncommon (reported in 1 percent of youngsters or fewer) in a sample of 251 Swedish preschoolers in day care centers.

Thus, it appears that, as with infants and toddlers, many of the more common behaviors exhibited by preschool-age children fall into two broad categories: (1) self-stimulation and (2) sexual curiosity or exploratory play and behavior. Although the former behavior appears to become less random or accidental as children get older, it is important to keep in mind that it is not necessarily sexual in nature and meaning for preschool-age youngsters. For instance, some authors have reported observations or findings that various means of self-stimulation may serve to release tension or may be associated with other feelings, such as security (see, e.g., Martinson, 1994). Researchers and theorists have also described examples of behavior falling in the second category (i.e., sexual curiosity or exploratory play and behavior), labeling some of them as sexual "rehearsal" play. Among preschoolers, this sexual rehearsal play typically involves exposing themselves to each other and touching one another's genitals, including children of the same and opposite sex (Friedrich et al., 1998; Martinson, 1994), and there is some suggestion that there is more interest in boys' genitals (McAnulty & Burnette, 2004). These often spontaneous behaviors are generally driven by attempts to satisfy curiosity, as opposed to being fueled by sexual interest (e.g., Eisenberg, Murkoff, & Hathaway, 1996), and will manifest in mutual exploration activities such as "playing doctor/nurse" or "I'll show you mine, if you show me yours."

It is difficult to estimate the rates and frequencies of these behaviors, for obvious reasons. However, despite their methodological limitations, some retrospective studies have yielded data regarding sexual rehearsal play and related behaviors. Although the authors note the difficulty in retrospectively catego- rizing experiences by age (thus the possible underestimation of the actual rate of behavior in the younger years), one study involving senior high school students (average age 18.6 years) found that fewer than 10 percent of participants recalled a sexual experience with another child before the age of 6 (Larsson & Svedin, 2002a). This proportion is consistent with findings from cross-cultural research, in which 10 percent of children report sexual rehearsal play before age 6 (Goldman & Goldman, 1988). Despite the lack of specificity regarding its fre- quency and how widely the behavior manifests, sexual rehearsal play has been identified as "universal," at least in the largely Western cultures in which it has been researched (e.g., the United States, England, Canada, Sweden, Australia) (McAnulty & Burnette, 2004, p. 332).

Most children are curious by nature. Both of these major categories of behavior, that is, self-stimulation and sexual rehearsal play, can be viewed as a means by which children learn about sexuality and their bodies, with the learning sometimes happening by accident (via self-exploration), and other times being facilitated by another child telling or showing them. This is consistent with the notion of multiple levels of mutual influence posited by the ecological framework; that is, allowing for individual development and discovery and, as another proximal factor with potential impact, peer influences. Peer influences are self-evident in sex rehearsal play, but, as another case in point, when it comes to self-stimulation, some researchers have noted that boys tend to be more likely than girls to report that a peer explained or showed them how to masturbate (Martinson, 1994). One final common behavior, consistent with this curiosity and desire to make sense of their bodies and their worlds, bears mention as well: children in this age range will also ask questions related to sexual topics, generally focusing on reproduction and childbirth (Larsson & Svedin, 2002b).

Elementary-Age Youngsters (6–10 Years)

Compared to preschoolers, there appears to be less specific attention in the professional literature to the sexual behaviors exhibited by elementary-age children. Nevertheless, one conclusion is clear: in contrast to Freud's theory, in which he argued that youngsters 6 to 12 years old are in a "latency" period during which they essentially lose interest in sexual behavior, children of this age are *not* largely "asexual." They appear to engage in sexual behaviors, though the acts may have different meanings or may take somewhat different forms than in later developmental stages.

As a case in point, one study, described by Ryan (2000), surveyed ele- mentary school teachers about the specific sexual behaviors they had observed in school, as well as which behaviors were most or least frequent. Children rubbing their genitals during class and sexual talk were the most commonly reported behaviors at school, and intrusive behaviors were less frequent. The educators also noted that secrecy and giggling were regularly observed in restrooms and on the playground.

Another study used parental reports of the sexual behaviors of 362 6- to 9-year-old children and identified two behaviors common among both boys and girls (Friedrich et al., 1998). First, as with preschoolers, touching genitals at home was the most frequent behavior reported in this age-group, endorsed by parents for 40 percent of boys and 21 percent of girls. Trying to look at people when they are undressing or nude was the next most common behavior, reported in 20 percent of boys and 21 percent of girls. Several behaviors were rarely endorsed for either sex in this sample, including putting objects in the vagina/rectum, putting mouth on genitals, trying to have intercourse, asking others to do sex acts, undressing other children, and kissing other children.

The researchers noted that items relating to sexually intrusive acts (e.g., touching their mother's or other women's breasts) or self-stimulating behaviors dropped off in observed frequency relative to the younger, preschool-age children they also studied (Friedrich et al., 1998). In fact, they found that the frequency of parent-reported sexual behavior seemed to peak at age 5 and decrease in the years that followed. Importantly, however, they also noted the likelihood that parents are not as aware of their child's behavior at these ages as they may have been at earlier stages when, for example, the child spent less time with peers (Friedrich et al., 1998). Some children in this age band may also have learned that some behaviors were viewed as private in their households and others were perhaps not accepted. Given such socialization factors, they may have been less overt with their behaviors.

In addition, data from retrospective reports of child sexual behavior indicate fairly common engagement in self-stimulatory behaviors as well as sex rehearsal play among school-age children (e.g., Martinson, 1994). In a study involving those from the United States, Canada, England, Australia, and Sweden, 40 percent recalled sex rehearsal play experiences between ages 6 and 9 (McAnulty & Burnette, 2004). Among their sample of senior high school students, Larsson and Svedin (2002a) found that, of the age ranges they studied, several mutual sexual experiences occurred most frequently between 6 and 10 years, including showing one's genitals (28 percent of boys, 23 percent of girls), touching and exploring genitals of the other child (17 percent of boys, 19 percent of girls), and the other child touching the respondent's genitals (17 percent of boys, 19 percent of girls). Other commonly recalled behaviors included simulating intercourse and teasing that involved using sex words, lifting skirts, or peeking in toilet stalls (Larsson & Svedin, 2002a). In another retrospective study, 85 percent of the 128 American female undergraduates surveyed recalled engaging in a childhood sexual game and that the average age of occurrence of the sexual play was 7.5 years (Lamb & Coakley, 1993). The most common experiences reported (29.6 percent) fell within the category of sex rehearsal play (i.e., imitation of adult sex, love scenes, commercialized sexuality, and coercive scenes), followed by playing "doctor," another sexual rehearsal "game" (16.3 percent), exposure (15.3 percent), and experiments in stimulation (14.3 percent). Perhaps most salient to the point regarding the private nature of this play and the difficulty in using parents as sole reporters of sexual behavior in this age band is the finding that for 56 percent of the respondents, no one found out about the game (Lamb & Coakley, 1993). Goldman and Goldman (1988) report a similar finding.

Preadolescents (10–12 Years)

Preadolescence can be considered the bridge period between childhood and adolescence. It is a time during which many changes occur in children—physically, socially, and psychologically. Increased hormone levels propel their bodies toward puberty, while awareness of themselves as sexual beings—and of their peers as potential partners—leads them gradually toward more purposeful engagement in sexual activity and experimentation with partners (Martinson, 1997). Despite the obvious significance of this developmental period in understanding how children move from a simple stimulatory approach to sexuality to a more complex and, indeed, adultlike view of sexuality as a relationship-oriented activity, little is known about normative sexual behavior during this stage.

Part of the reason for the lack of information on preadolescent sexuality has to do with the loss of parents as reliable reporters of their child's more private sexual behaviors at this stage. As Gagnon (1985) described, with reference to obtaining parental report on preadolescent children's experiences with masturbation:

> Three problems emerge with reference to the question about [masturbatory activities of] the child. The first is what opportunities for observation did the parents have; the second is what actual conduct did the parent interpret as masturbation . . . ; and the third is the willingness of the parent to report to the interviewer. All of these . . . will affect to what degree the parental report matches the actual rate of conduct among the children. For these reasons, parental reports cannot be taken as estimates of rates of masturbation on the part of [preadolescent] children. (p. 455)

Parental reports of their preadolescent's sexual behavior suggest that the most frequent activity observed in both preadolescent boys and girls was being "very interested in the opposite sex," with 24.1 percent of boys and 28.7 percent of girls reportedly displaying this interest (Friedrich et al., 1998). This observation by parents matches other information regarding the development of crushes on, and attachments to, individuals outside of the family during preadolescence (Martinson, 1997).

With respect to more private sexual behaviors in preadolescence, however, the information that is available is often dependent on statistics gathered decades ago. For example, Ramsey (as cited in Martinson, 1997) found that masturbation occurred at some point in the sexual histories of most males surveyed, with 29 percent of 10-year-olds, 54 percent of 11-year-olds, and 73 percent of 12-year-olds reporting some engagement in the activity. This finding is notable in that it suggests a pattern of increasing masturbatory behavior as children move from childhood toward adolescence. Ramsey also found that preadolescent boys experienced erections in response to both erotic and nonerotic stimuli, with the nonerotic responses generally tapering off after age 12. Additionally, Kinsey, Pomeroy, and Martin (1948) reported that 20–25 percent of boys had attempted intercourse with a female by age 12. Less information was available then, as it is now, regarding preadolescent female sexuality, possibly due to cultural constraints that discourage girls more than boys from exploring sexuality—a situation that also makes gathering self-reports from girls a more difficult task (Martinson, 1997).

Although fewer data are available regarding normal sexuality among contemporary children, one recent study of children's sexuality found that 20 percent of American boys and girls reported masturbating by age 10, and 50 percent of boys and 25 percent of girls reported masturbating by age 13 (Janus & Janus, 1993). These numbers are supported by another recent Swedish study, in which 6 and 7 percent of boys and girls, respectively, recalled masturbating to orgasm between ages 6 and 10, but nearly 43 percent of boys and more than 20 percent of girls reported such behavior between the ages of 11 and 12 (Larsson & Svedin, 2002a). Taken together with the reports from earlier decades of research, it is safe to say that although the estimates of incidence of masturbation vary by study, culture, and era in which the data were collected, all studies indicate a gradual increase in the behavior throughout preadolescence (McAnulty & Burnette, 2004).

Thus far, we have described self-stimulatory sexual behaviors in preadolescence, but it should be noted that this period of development is also a time during which partnered sexual encounters become more common. In one retrospective study of more than 1,000 American undergraduates, 42 percent of the sample reported having experienced a sexual encounter with another child prior to age 13, with the majority of those experiences involving heterosexual hugging and kissing (Haugaard & Tilly, 1988). In a Swedish study with a similar research design, Larsson and Svedin (2002a) found that 82 percent of those surveyed reported having had a mutual sexual experience before age 13, with hugging, kissing, talking about sex, and viewing pornographic pictures together being the most common behaviors.

It is more difficult to estimate the frequency of experiences involving sexual intercourse during the preadolescent phase. In the Haugaard and Tilly study, 10 percent of the undergraduates surveyed reported having had sexual intercourse before age 13. These·data are consistent with the most recent findings from the Youth Risk Behavior Surveillance (YRBS, a large-scale, representative survey of American adolescents), which indicated that slightly more than 10 percent of males and 4 percent of females (7.4 percent overall) reported initiation of sexual intercourse before age 13 (Centers for Disease Control and Prevention [CDC], 2004). When considering the findings by racial/ethnic category, however, it appears that Hispanic respondents reported nearly double the rates of preadolescent sexual intercourse (8.3 percent) reported by white respondents (4.2 percent), and that black respondents' reports were nearly five times the rate of whites (19 percent). These findings highlight the impact of diverse ecological circumstances on sexual behavior, both with respect to the various ecologies in which different racial/ethnic groups operate, and the different experiences and standards that exist for male versus female children with respect to sexuality and/or the reporting of sexuality. Consistent with this idea, in a large survey of urban, sixth-grade students, Kinsman et al. (1998) found that almost one-third had already initiated sexual intercourse, with those attending a poorer school and living in an area with a high proportion of single-parent families at highest risk for early sexual initiation. It is likely that these relatively high rates may reflect sample-specific issues, as the Kinsman study surveyed only urban children and did not have a sample representative of the broader population.

Overall, the knowledge base regarding preadolescent sexuality suggests that further research on normal sexual practices and behaviors during this phase of development is particularly necessary. Although obvious problems with parental report, ethical constraints regarding self-report, and concern for the validity of reports from both sources of information are issues in this study, its importance toward understanding the transition from childhood to adulthood sexuality is immeasurable.

As we leave behind our summary of the current state of knowledge regarding the normative development of children's sexuality, two points warrant further mention and will be explored briefly in the following sections: First, although we have tried to integrate findings to present a full and balanced picture of the research available regarding children's sexuality, these studies were conducted in several different cultures. Integrating these reports has been useful for the purpose of mapping major trends in the development of children's sexuality, but there are also several cross-cultural findings that are worth noting. A second important point is that normative childhood sexuality has traditionally been understood in the context of nonnormative sexual development, and vice versa. As such, we also offer brief notes to help the reader better distinguish between normative and nonnormative sexual behavior among children.

CROSS-CULTURAL DIFFERENCES: A BRIEF CONSIDERATION

Several authors (see, e.g., Goldman & Goldman, 1982; Martinson, 1994) have discussed differences in sexual knowledge and understanding (e.g., being able to describe intercourse) across cultures. For instance, Goldman and Goldman (1982) interviewed 5- to 15-year-olds from Australia, Sweden,

Canada, England, and the United States, and, in line with other findings in this area, children and youth from the United States were the least well informed. Although some theorists have raised the possibility that such differential knowledge may influence behavior rates as well as what is viewed as normal in a given context, cross-cultural comparisons of sexual behavior have been the focus of little empirical research.

As one key exception, Larsson et al. (2000) used parental reports to examine and compare the sexual behaviors of two samples of 3- to 6-year-old children, one from Sweden and one from the United States (Minnesota). The researchers found that exhibitionistic (e.g., walking around house without clothes), voyeuristic (e.g., trying to look at people undressing), and touching behaviors were most common in both samples. Overall, the preschool-age children from Sweden evidenced higher rates of sexual behavior than those from the United States. Among boys, significant differences were identified for fourteen of the twenty-five behaviors assessed, with Swedish boys exhibiting higher levels for thirteen of the measured behaviors. The differences were somewhat less pronounced among girls; that is, reliable differences were detected on ten behaviors, with Swedish girls displaying higher rates in nine cases. For boys, the behaviors with the largest reported differences (with frequencies varying by 20 percentage points or more) included walking around the house without clothes, talking about sexual acts, using sexual words, touching or trying to touch their mother's or other women's breasts, and touching private parts in public places. Swedish boys exceeded American boys on all but the last behavior. For girls, similar large differences occurred on three items, that is, touching or trying to touch their mother's or other women's breasts, trying to look at others when they are nude or undressing, and talking about sexual acts, all favoring the Swedish youngsters.

In offering interpretations of their findings, Larsson et al. (2000, p. 256) noted that "American children are brought up in a more strict or cautious atmosphere concerning sexual matters, and . . . Swedish children are brought up in a more liberal atmosphere." This possible mechanism of influence, reflecting differences at the familial (e.g., attitudes and values regarding sexuality) as well as sociocultural level (e.g., cultural differences in sexual attitudes, disparate approaches to sexual education), accords well with the tenets of the ecological approach. The researchers also noted that a similar unpublished study comparing Dutch and American preschoolers yielded findings consistent with their own, with higher frequencies of sexual behavior reported in the Dutch sample (Larsson et al.), although cross-cultural findings involving these two groups have been mixed (e.g., Schoentjes, Deboutte, & Friedrich, 1999). Given that Dutch society is among the most open and liberal about sexuality, reported differences in sexual behavior between Dutch and American children may be viewed as providing further support for the notion that larger cultural attitudes about sexuality may influence the behaviors observed. Nevertheless, the literature base is still quite limited in this area, both in number of studies and cultures involved, with the available research largely focusing on Western cultures.

NONNORMATIVE CHILD SEXUAL EXPERIENCES

A full consideration of the impact of nonnormative experiences (e.g., sexual abuse, exposure to inappropriate sexual content) and their emotional and behavioral consequences is beyond the scope of this chapter (for a detailed discussion of the impact of sexual abuse, see Chapter 5, Sexual Assault, in Volume 3 of this set). Although some children who have been sexually abused have no apparent symptoms, studies have consistently identified numerous short- and long-term effects of such abuse (e.g., Browne & Finkelhor, 1986; Finkelhor, 1990; Putnam, 2003). In fact, Kendall-Tackett, Williams, and Finkelhor (1993, p. 173) note that "there is virtually no general domain of symptomatology that has not been associated with a history of sexual abuse," with poor self-esteem, fears, posttraumatic stress disorder, and overly sexualized behaviors among those reported most frequently.

The latter behavioral symptom category is of particular relevance here, since it seemingly reflects behaviors that are atypical, deviating from children's normative developmental trajectories. Indeed, as noted previously, the presence of inappropriate sexual behavior (including content and knowledge not typical for their age) among many abused youngsters (see, e.g., Friedrich, 1993) has led some researchers to emphasize the importance of better understanding what constitutes normal sexual behavior for children across settings (Larsson & Svedin, 2002b). A substantial body of work has assessed the impact of the nonnormative experience of abuse and has attempted to identify the complex processes and pathways that lead to a given outcome.

In their review of forty-five studies, Kendall-Tackett et al. noted that "sexualized" behaviors were the most commonly studied symptom of sexual abuse, and, in his more recent review, Putnam (2003) concluded that sexualized behaviors have been the best-documented outcomes in children who had experienced sexual abuse. This category includes such behaviors as "sexualized play with dolls, putting objects into anuses or vaginas, excessive or public masturbation, seductive behavior, requesting sexual stimulation from adults or other children, and age-inappropriate sexual knowledge" (Kendall-Tackett et al., 1993, p. 165). Findings suggest that developmental level may impact the presentation of such sexualized behavior sequelae; that is, they seem to be more evident among preschoolers and less common in school-age children, perhaps reemerging in different forms (e.g., early pregnancy, promiscuity, sexual aggression) among adolescents (Kendall-Tackett et al.; Putnam). Some researchers (Brilleslijper-Kater, Friedrich, & Corwin, 2004) have noted that age-inappropriate behavior in this domain is more sensitive in differentiating preschool-age victims of sexual abuse than any other age-group.

The actual frequency of such behaviors has varied considerably across studies and has been difficult to determine; however, it is important to note that, across studies, less than half of victims of sexual abuse evidenced sexualized behaviors, and this symptom does not occur only in sexually abused children (Deblinger, McLeer, Atkins, Ralphe, & Foa, 1989; Kendall-Tackett et al., 1993). Friedrich et al. (Brilleslijper-Kater et al., 2004; Friedrich et al., 2001) have noted that age-inappropriate sexual behaviors are also related to a range of factors, including family sexuality, externalizing (i.e., acting out) behavior problems, domestic violence, physical abuse, and life stress. Such findings, particularly when considered in conjunction with the research indicating that a wide range of behaviors occur in normative samples of children (Friedrich et al., 1991; Friedrich et al., 1998), complicate efforts to identify factors that discriminate between sexually abused children and other youngsters. Thus it is critical, as Larsson and Svedin (2002b) emphasize, for professionals working with children and responding to questions about, and reports of, child sexual behavior(s) to be thorough in their information gathering and thoughtful in their interpretation, examining the context in which the sexual behavior occurs, identifying antecedents of the behavior, and noting distress that may be present.

CONCLUSIONS AND FUTURE DIRECTIONS

The literature on normative childhood sexual development is clearly still in its infancy. We are encouraged, however, by the attention that child sexuality has garnered in recent years and note that the continuation of this work is critical, both for professionals working with children and families, and for caregivers, who may have questions and concerns regarding the limits of normal sexual behavior during various stages of children's development. Toward the end of expanding further this important line of study, we offer the following suggestions for future directions for research in this area: First, greater attention needs to be given to the methodologies used to collect data on this important topic. As it stands, much of the information that exists on the topic of normative childhood sexuality has been pieced together from small studies or case reports. When larger-scale studies have been completed (e.g., Kinsey et al., 1948; Kinsey, Pomeroy, Martin, & Gebhard, 1953), the methodologies have been criticized as being less than scientific, and it is likely that the findings are outdated, given the sensitivity of sexual behavior to historical and cultural change. Further, we would encourage the design of prospective, longitudinal studies in order to better understand the pathways that individual children follow toward sexual maturity. Consistent with the early stages of research in any area, the literature on normative sexual development has relied on cross-sectional studies designed to gather initial data on the incidence and prevalence of particular behaviors and experiences. The advantage of moving forward to a longitudinal research design, however, is to allow for better understanding of the antecedents of, and pinpoint the effects of specific ecological influences on, children's developing sexuality. Longitudinal designs also allow for drawing conclusions regarding the effects of particular sexual behaviors or experiences on children's overall development. We would argue that conducting more large-scale, representative studies and utilizing systematic, longitudinal research designs are necessary next steps in bringing the study of normative child sexuality to a position in which a solid picture may be drawn regarding the developmental process behind this area of human behavior.

A second step toward improving the knowledge base available within this area is to expand the study of sexual behaviors and practices to include examination of the context surrounding these behaviors. For example, most studies ask respondents to report on the presence or frequency of particular sexual behaviors. This information, however, may not capture important aspects of the context in which the behavior occurs—that is, whether it was playful, unintentional, uncomfortable, enjoyable, or coercive, to name a few possibilities. In short, most of the methodologies currently used do not allow for investigation of how children *feel* about sexual behaviors in which they have been involved (Lamb & Coakley, 1993). Because a child's feelings regarding a sexual encounter are part of the way in which an experience is labeled as normal versus abusive, it is critical that this information is gathered systematically to the extent that the respondent or observer can offer it.

In a similar vein, information with respect to the environment in which a child is developing is also important in offering a better understanding of those features that contribute to a child's sexual development. For example, data were presented earlier in this chapter regarding racial/ethnic differences in the rates at which adolescent respondents to the YRBS reported having experienced preadolescent sexual intercourse. This information, however, does not help us understand why these differences exist. In keeping with the ecological systems approach, it is likely that these ethnic differences reported reflect larger cultural differences among groups in the areas of peer culture, family factors, and community structure, and some data have begun to emerge in support of this position (e.g., Beal et al., 2001; Kinsman et al., 1998). Without a systematic examination of these factors, however, it is difficult to discern which ecological factors contribute to the reported variations in age at first sexual intercourse and whether these differences are relevant for understanding more global aspects of children's adjustment and adaptation.

A final point that should be addressed in future research is the inclusion of more cross-cultural comparisons among children, those from more widely varying cultures. Although some cross-cultural work has been completed (e.g., among British, Canadian, Scandinavian, Australian, and American samples), it is important to note that all of the cultures included thus far have been of a "Western" orientation. Inclusion of children from other cultures, such as those from Eastern and Southern hemisphere countries, is critical in distinguishing between those features of children's developing sexuality that appear to be universal and those that are culture specific. These cross-cultural comparisons would also offer a more complete picture of distinctions between normal and problematic sexual behavior by presenting a broader picture of the range of behaviors and ecological contexts within which children's sexuality develops (Larsson et al., 2000).

Taken together, these suggestions are intended to help bring the study of normative development of children's sexuality to the next stage—one in which basic data on prevalence of normal sexual behaviors among children are solidly based in systematic research, and where meaningful questions regarding the processes, influences, and outcomes of sexual behaviors in childhood may be addressed through longitudinal study.

REFERENCES

Beal, A. C., Ausiello, J., & Perrin, J. M. (2001). Social influences on health-risk behaviors among minority middle school students. *Journal of Adolescent Health, 28,* 474–480.

Brilleslijper-Kater, S. N., Friedrich, W. N., & Corwin, D. L. (2004). Sexual knowledge and emotional reaction as indicators of sexual abuse in young children: Theory and research challenges. *Child Abuse and Neglect, 28,* 1007–1017.

Bronfenbrenner, U. (1977). Toward an experimental ecology of human development. *American Psychologist, 32,* 513–531.

Bronfenbrenner, U. (1979). *The ecology of human development: Experiments by nature and design.* Cambridge, MA: Harvard University Press.

Bronfenbrenner, U., & Morris, P. A. (1998). The ecology of developmental processes. In W. Damon (Editor-in-Chief) & R. M. Lerner (Ed.), *Handbook of child psychology: Vol. 1. Theoretical models of human development* (5th ed., pp. 993–1028). New York: Wiley.

Browne, A., & Finkelhor, D. (1986). The impact of child sexual abuse: A review of the research. *Psychological Bulletin, 99,* 66–77.

Centers for Disease Control and Prevention. (2004). *Youth risk behavior surveillance—United States, 2003.* Washington, DC: Author.

Damon, W. (Editor-in-Chief), & Lerner, R. M. (Ed.). (1998). *Handbook of child psychology: Vol. 1. Theoretical models of human development* (5th ed.). New York: Wiley.

Deblinger, E., McLeer, S. V., Atkins, M. S., Ralphe, D., & Foa, E. (1989). Post-traumatic stress in sexually abused, physically abused, and nonabused children. *Child Abuse and Neglect, 13,* 403–408.

Donovan, P. (1998). School-based sexuality education: The issues and challenges. *Family Planning Perspectives, 30,* 188–193.

Eisenberg, A., Murkoff, H. E., & Hathaway, S. E. (1996). *What to expect: The toddler years.* New York: Workman.

Finkelhor, D. (1990). Early and long-term effects of child sexual abuse: An update. *Professional Psychology: Research and Practice, 21,* 325–330.

Fisher, H. E. (1989). *Sexual images of the self: The psychology of erotic sensations and illusions.* Hillside, NJ: Lawrence Erlbaum.

Frayser, S. G. (1994). Defining normal childhood sexuality: An anthropological approach. *Annual Review of Sex Research, 5,* 173–217.

Freud, S., & Gay, P. (Ed.). (1995). *The Freud reader.* New York: W.W. Norton.

Friedrich, W. N. (1993). Sexual victimization and sexual behavior in children: A review of recent literature. *Child Abuse and Neglect, 17,* 59–66.

Friedrich, W. N., Fisher, J., Broughton, D., Houston, M., & Shafran, C. R. (1998). Normative sexual behavior in children: A contemporary sample. *Pediatrics, 101,* E9.

Friedrich, W. N., Grambsch, P., Broughton, D., Kuiper, J., & Beilke, R. L. (1991). Normative sexual behavior in children. *Pediatrics, 88,* 456–464.

Friedrich, W. N., Fisher, J., Dittner, C., Acton, R., Berliner, L., Butler, J., et al. (2001). Child Sexual Behavior Inventory: Normative, psychiatric, and sexual abuse comparisons. *Child Maltreatment, 6,* 37–49.

Friedrich, W. N., Grambsch, P., Damon, L., Hewitt, S. K., Koverola, C., Lang, R. A., et al. (1992). Child Sexual Behavior Inventory: Normative and clinical comparisons. *Psychological Assessment, 4,* 303–311.

Friedrich, W. N., & Trane, S. T. (2002). Sexual behavior in children across multiple settings. *Child Abuse and Neglect, 26,* 243–245.

Furstenberg, F. F. (1998). When will teenage childbearing become a problem? The implications of western experience for developing countries, *Studies in Family Planning, 29,* 246–253.

Gagnon, J. (1985). Attitudes and responses of parents to pre-adolescent masturbation. *Archives of Sexual Behavior, 14,* 451–466.

Goldman, J., & Goldman, R. (1988). *Show me yours: Understanding children's sexuality.* New York: Penguin Books.

Goldman, R., & Goldman, J. (1982). *Children's sexual thinking.* London: Routledge and Kegan Paul.

Gordon, B. N., & Schroeder, C. S. (1995). *Sexuality: A developmental approach to problems.* New York: Plenum Press.

Haugaard, J. J., & Tilly, C. (1988). Characteristics predicting children's responses to sexual encounters with other children. *Child Abuse and Neglect, 12,* 209–218.

Heiman, M. L., Leiblum, S., Esquilin, S. C., & Pallitto, L. M. (1998). A comparative survey of beliefs about "normal" childhood sexual behaviors. *Child Abuse and Neglect, 22,* 289–304.

Janus, S. S., & Janus, C. L. (1993). *The Janus Report on sexual behavior.* New York: Wiley.

Kendall-Tackett, K. A., Williams, L. M., & Finkelhor, D. (1993). Impact of sexual abuse on children: A review and synthesis of recent empirical studies. *Psychological Bulletin, 113,* 164–180.

Kinsey, A. C., Pomeroy, W. B., & Martin, C. E. (1948). *Sexual behavior in the human male.* Philadelphia: Saunders.

Kinsey, A. C., Pomeroy, W. B., Martin, C. E., & Gebhard, P. H. (1953). *Sexual behavior in the human female.* Philadelphia: Saunders.

Kinsman, J., Nyanzi, S., & Pool, R. (2000). Socializing influences and the value of sex: The experience of adolescent school girls in rural Masaka, Uganda. *Culture, Health and Sexuality, 2*, 151–166.

Kinsman, S. B., Romer, D., Furstenburg, F. F., & Schwarz, D. F. (1998). Early sexual initiation: The role of peer norms. *Pediatrics, 102*, 1185–1192.

Lamb, S., & Coakley, M. (1993). "Normal" childhood sexual play and games: Differentiating play from abuse. *Child Abuse and Neglect, 17*, 515–526.

Larsson, I., & Svedin, C. G. (2002a). Sexual experiences in childhood: Young adults' recollections. *Archives of Sexual Behavior, 31*, 263–274.

Larsson, I., & Svedin, C. G. (2002b). Teachers' and parents' reports on 3- to 6-year-old children's sexual behavior—A comparison. *Child Abuse and Neglect, 26*, 247–266.

Larsson, I., Svedin, C. G., & Friedrich, W. N. (2000). Differences and similarities in sexual behaviour among pre-schoolers in Sweden and USA. *Nordic Journal of Psychiatry, 54*, 251–257.

Levine, M. I. (1957). Pediatric observations on masturbation in children. *Psychoanalytic Study of the Child, 6*, 117–124.

Lindblad, F., Gustafsson, P. A., Larsson, I., & Lundin, B. (1995). Preschoolers' sexual behavior at daycare centers: An epidemiological study. *Child Abuse and Neglect, 19*, 569–577.

Martinson, F. M. (1994). *The sexual life of children*. Westport, CT: Bergin & Garvey.

Martinson, F. M. (1997). Sexual development in infancy and childhood. In G. Ryan & S. Lane (Eds.), *Juvenile sex offending: Causes, consequences, and correction* (pp. 36–58). Boston: Lexington Books.

McAnulty, R. M., & Burnette, M. M. (2004). *Exploring human sexuality: Making healthy decisions* (2nd ed.). Boston: Pearson Education.

National Adolescent Perpetrator Network. (1988). Preliminary report from the National Task Force on Juvenile Sexual Offending. *Juvenile and Family Court Journal, 39*, 1–67.

National Adolescent Perpetrator Network. (1993). Revised report from the National Task Force on Juvenile Sexual Offending. *Juvenile and Family Court Journal, 44*, 1–120.

Putnam, F. W. (2003). Ten-year research update review: Child sexual abuse. *Journal of the American Academy of Child and Adolescent Psychiatry, 42*, 269–278.

Roiphe, H., & Galenson, E. (1981). *Infantile origins of sexual identity*. New York: International Universities Press.

Ryan, G. (2000). Childhood sexuality: A decade of study. Part I—Research and curriculum development. *Child Abuse and Neglect, 24*, 33–48.

Sameroff, A. J., & Chandler, M. J. (1975). Reproductive risk and the continuum of caretaking casualty. In F. D. Horowitz, M. Hetherington, S. Scarr-Salapatek, & G. Siegel (Eds.), *Review of child development research* (pp. 187–244). Chicago: University of Chicago Press.

Schoentjes, E., Deboutte, D., & Friedrich, W. N. (1999). Child sexual behavior inventory: A Dutch-speaking normative sample. *Pediatrics, 104,* 885–893.

Singh, S., & Darroch, J. E. (2000). Adolescent pregnancy and childbearing: Levels and trends in developed countries. *Family Planning Perspectives, 32,* 14–23.

4

Adolescent Sexuality

Charlene Rapsey and Tamar Murachver ◆

We begin this chapter with an analysis of the ways in which researchers have conceptualized adolescence. We examine how adolescence, and adolescent sexuality in particular, has been depicted as problematic. We then review contemporary theories of adolescence that focus on social, cognitive, and neurological changes. This is followed by a summary of the physical changes involved with puberty. These more general discussions of adolescence then set the stage for an exploration of current understandings of adolescent sexuality. Within this we explore the types of experiences, social settings, and consequences of adolescent sexual behavior. We end with a discussion of education programs and their conflicting goals of controlling adolescent sexuality, while at the same time supposedly helping adolescents become adults with healthy sexual lives.

CONCEPTUALIZATIONS OF ADOLESCENCE

Adolescence refers to the period of time that marks the transition from childhood to adulthood. This span of a decade or more encompasses a period of rapid physical development, the onset of puberty and consequent maturation to full reproductive capacity, substantial social and cognitive developments, and the attainment of the rights and responsibilities of adulthood.

Few periods of development have been reified as adolescence has. Although adolescence marks the transition from childhood to adulthood, with characteristics of both, it is often viewed as a separate entity with its own peculiar characteristics (Lesko, 1996; Rosenblum & Lewis, 2003). A person during this period becomes defined by it—an adolescent—and her or his behavior is interpreted or explained as being caused by this period. Thus, when a 13-year-old daughter storms out of the room, it is "because she is an adolescent." However, if a colleague demonstrates similar behavior, it is not because "she is an adult."

Contemporary ideas about adolescence highlight some key dimensions that supposedly distinguish adolescence from childhood on the one hand and adulthood on the other. During adolescence, sexual awareness, interest, and maturity are established. But rarely today is this coupled with the expectation of making commitments to a lifelong partner or to a family. Thus, part of societal concerns is of controlling adolescent sexuality until careers, income, and housing are adequate to support the responsibilities of a family. In this conceptualization, adolescence is like a holding tank where the emerging adult awaits release into adulthood.

Most societies recognize the adolescent's increased abilities compared to those of childhood. And most cultures begin to insist that individuals during adolescence take greater responsibility for their behavior. This is reflected in the laws and punishments within contemporary societies. Nonetheless, many of the more prevalent ideas about adolescence focus less on the abilities and responsibilities of adolescents and more on adolescence as a problem.

There are a number of variations on the "adolescence-as-problem" conceptualization. Adolescence has often been characterized as a time of substantial turmoil and rebellion. Sometimes, this is explained as the effects of "uncontrolled hormones" when adolescents are at the whim of the new levels of hormones invading their bloodstream. Adolescents are also depicted as extreme and unthinking conformists. According to this view, unlike adults, they are more concerned with fitting in with their peers than with making good choices. Other popular depictions of adolescence focus on heightened conflict with parents and extreme risk taking.

These depictions of adolescence have serious flaws. The "storm and stress" perspective on adolescence was promoted in the twentieth century by G. Stanley Hall (1904). Hall placed human development within an evolutionary framework, and viewed adolescence as the link between more primitive beings and civilized ones. Research over the past few decades has not supported this view of adolescence. Although adolescents might experience more frequent minor conflicts with parents as adolescents come to expect greater influence on choices about their day-to-day lives, most families with adolescent children do not suffer from regular major conflicts (Arnett, 1999; Smetana & Gaines, 1999). Estimates are that only 20–25 percent of adolescents are involved in major conflicts with their parents. The frequency of conflicts decreases from early to late adolescence as children and parents negotiate new boundaries and expectations. It is important to note that changes in the parent-child relationship are driven not only by adolescents, but also by parents, who need to balance protectiveness with the increased granting of autonomy.

Adolescents are often depicted as being unduly influenced by peers—of being conformists. Whereas choices about clothing, hairstyle, and music might be more in line with the choices of peers rather than of parents, most major decisions reflect parental values. Adolescents are not choosing careers, university programs, religious and political values, or ideas about the role of family and society by mainly considering their peers' behavior. In fact, according to Harris (1995), they are likely to choose peers who come from families like their own, and who share similar values to those of their own parents. One of the shortfalls of developmental science is that childhood is extensively studied and then compared to assumed behavior in adulthood. Adolescent conformity to peers is compared to conformity in earlier childhood, with the verdict that adolescents are great conformists. Yet, comparisons with adult populations are rarely provided. It is hard to argue that individuals with only minor responsibilities and very little to lose would conform more to expectations than an older group who have major expectations and responsibilities placed on them by colleagues, employers, and family members. Perhaps adolescents have been viewed as high in conformity, in part, because they have not always conformed to the expectations for adult behavior, which is rarely seen as conformist. In other words, putting on a suit is no less conforming than putting on the right brand of jeans.

Compared to children, adolescents are more likely to take risks. This is partly due to increased opportunity. Adolescents are given permission to drive, to spend time away from adults, and to make some decisions independent from the adults in their lives. They are also relatively free of responsibility for others' well-being. Adolescents also have less experience than older adults. Their decisions might not be guided by the same knowledge or concerns, and they might have fewer social and cognitive skills to deal with awkward situations. Adolescents are more influenced by the perceived benefits of risk-taking behavior than by the perceived risks (Leigh & Stacy, 1993; Parsons, Halkitis, Bimbi, & Borkowski, 2000). This is partly because the benefits are more direct and immediate than are the negative consequences. It means, however, that the adult focus on negative outcomes might not be the best way to motivate and influence adolescents. More importantly, high risk-taking behavior is not necessarily characteristic of the majority of adolescents, even though it is more likely to occur in adolescence than in childhood.

Adolescent sexual behavior is generally perceived of and treated as a problem. Adolescents in Western societies are confronted with a number of conflicting messages. On the one hand, they are immersed in a highly sexualized culture. Sexual images and themes are prevalent in television, movies, music videos and lyrics, and magazines. Sexualized appearances, even for younger children, are promoted through the available clothing choices. On the other hand, especially in North America, adolescents are often told that they are not ready to, or should not, engage in many sexual behaviors. They are like drivers faced with traffic lights where both the green and the red lights are on. And, of course, their bodies are becoming more and more ready for green.

Adolescent sexual behavior need not be a problem, but sometimes it is. Many studies actually define delinquent behavior as including some sexual behaviors (e.g., those involving intercourse). Responsible sexual behavior that cannot result in pregnancy or sexually transmitted disease, is consensual, and is respectful of one's partner might not be a problem, depending on one's viewpoint. As we will show, much of the research on adolescent sexual behavior not only treats it as a problem, but also focuses on the most problematic aspects of sexuality: unwanted pregnancy, sexually transmitted diseases (STDs), and promiscuity. Because of this focus, we know far more about the antecedents and consequences of unprotected adolescent sexual intercourse, and far less about how adolescents develop into healthy adults capable of enjoying their sexuality.

GENERAL THEORIES OF ADOLESCENCE

Psychosocial Explanations

One of the most influential theories of adolescent development describes adolescence as a period of resolving one's identity. Erik Erikson (1959, 1968) theorized that during healthy adolescent development, individuals must question and resolve who they are in terms of their occupation, their political and religious values, and their sexual identity. According to this view, adolescents must "find themselves," and thereafter, they will be ready to launch their lives in the right direction.

Erikson's ideas about identity development during adolescence were developed further by Marcia (1980). Marcia described four stages of identity development that an adolescent could be placed within. The two least mature stages were foreclosure and diffusion, whereas the more mature stages were moratorium and achievement. In foreclosure, the adolescent unquestioningly follows the identity chosen for him or her by influential adults, such as the parents. Adolescents categorized as identity diffused have avoided making a choice or commitment and have given little thought to who they are and the direction they wish to follow. In moratorium, adolescents are in the process of actively searching for and exploring their identity. Finally, adolescents in identity achievement have worked through the process of establishing their identity and have made a commitment toward that end.

The importance of resolving one's identity during adolescence is not taken for granted in more current understandings of adolescent development. Although the concept is not dismissed, a number of findings have questioned whether finding one's identity is a key achievement during adolescence. One problem is that identity crises do not seem to happen all at once. Rather, smaller crises seem to occur when important decisions have to be made. Career directions become critical as an adolescent selects a major at university, and then reappear as an issue years later when the individual seeks employment. Sexual identity emerges as intimate relationships are formed. One other main objection to the identity theory as a key element during adolescence is that research has found that identity moratorium and achievement are often not attained until after the end of the adolescent period (see Kroger, 2003, for a review).

Cognitive Explanations

A number of significant cognitive developments occur during adolescence. Relative to their younger counterparts, adolescents are more able to reason abstractly; consider future, potential outcomes; and reflect on themselves and their own behavior. These abilities in turn impact on adolescents' learning from their environment, their social relations, and their understanding of moral behavior. Reasons for these cognitive advances during adolescence generally focus on one or more of the following: changes in thought as a child enters formal operations (promoted by Piaget, 1952, 1972), changes in information processing (see Siegler, 1998), and advances in metacognition (see Kuhn, 1999).

Compared to children, adolescents are able to think more abstractly. They begin to be able to consider "what would happen if..." and to imagine outcomes they have never experienced. They start to understand more subtle forms of humor and behavior, and can reflect on their thoughts and behaviors to a much greater degree. These changes are reflected in the widening interests adolescents show. These might include politics, questions about morality, and balancing one's obligation to others versus taking care of one's own needs. Whereas adolescents are developing the ability to reason and think in the abstract, most of them lack the general knowledge and experience to apply these abilities faultlessly (Byrnes, 2003). Hence, they might show superb reasoning within a familiar domain, but fail when the area is beyond their knowledge base.

Because adolescents more readily engage in reflective thought, they are able to use metacognitive strategies to a greater extent than younger children can. Reflecting on one's own thoughts and behaviors allows for insights into critical thinking and effective planning. This also allows greater self-regulation. Adolescents show greater ability to monitor their performance, to think about their goals and progress toward them, and to make necessary adaptations.

During adolescence, there is an increased awareness of how oneself and others view the world. Adolescents demonstrate the ability to reflect on their own thoughts and how those thoughts came to be. Similarly, they begin to accept more readily that truths might be relative rather than absolute. This extends into domains such as reasoning about moral issues. Whereas a younger child might believe that a particular behavior is wrong because society accepts it as wrong, an adolescent might consider and appreciate that there could be instances where this might not apply.

Neurological Explanations

There have been a number of exciting advances in the field of neurological development recently. For example, contrary to what was believed only a decade ago, brain development does not stop during adolescence, but continues through to at least the mid- or late-twenties. Most dramatic developments take place in the frontal regions of the cerebral cortex (Giedd et al., 1999). These areas are believed to be critical to abstract thought, the initiation and inhibition of behavior, and other more complex cognitive skills such as advanced planning. The frontal areas are also involved in the regulation of emotion.

Two important neurological developments during adolescence are the decrease in synaptic connections within the prefrontal cortex and the greater connectivity among different brain regions due to increased myelination of nerve fibers (Keating, 2004). Although it might seem counterintuitive, a decrease in synaptic connections between neurons is associated with more efficient neural processing. Brain development after birth is characterized first by a proliferation of synaptic connections, followed by substantial pruning of synapses. The pruning process is guided by experience such that the most used pathways remain and the lesser used ones are removed. During adolescence, the number of synapses in the prefrontal regions in particular declines dramatically, thus increasing the efficiency within this region. In addition, pathways linking different brain regions are made more efficient by the myelination of nerve fibers. Myelin acts as an insulator of neurons and allows faster transmission of nerve impulses.

Recent developments in neuroimaging techniques and their availability are opening up exciting avenues for research. Parallels have been drawn between changes in cognitive abilities during adolescence and neural development. As yet, little research has demonstrated a conclusive link between specific brain changes and consequent cognitive changes or risk-taking behaviors. Nonetheless, interesting patterns of change in both neural processing and behavior across time have been noted. For example, when adults identify the emotional expression in faces, they engage the frontal cortical regions predominantly, as well as a part of the limbic system called the amygdala. Adolescents, on the other hand, respond predominantly within the limbic system—a more primitive region of the brain—and to a lesser degree within the frontal cortex (Baird, Gruber, Cohen, Renshaw, & Yureglun-Todd, 1999). One interpretation of this finding is that adults respond to emotions in a more controlled and rational way compared to adolescents.

PUBERTY

Puberty begins with increased growth and development of secondary characteristics and ends with a fully functional reproductive system. These developments are orchestrated by an elegant cascade of various chemicals produced within the developing child. Even by 8 or 9 years of age, children's bodies are preparing for puberty (Susman & Rogol, 2004). By the end of primary school, many girls will be noticeably in the grips of pubertal change, with the boys soon to follow. Puberty lasts somewhere between two and six years, with a one- to two-year gap in progression on average between girls and boys. Thus, puberty often begins before what is conventionally referred to as adolescence and ends well before adolescence is over.

One of the noticeable features of puberty is the growth spurt. This growth spurt occurs earlier in girls than in boys, and the rate of increase for girls is less than that for boys. For example, the greatest rate of growth for girls is at around 12 years, where they gain approximately 9 cm during the year. Height ceases to increase by around 15 years in girls. Boys, however, reach their highest growth rate at around 14 years, when they gain 10 cm. They begin later, and thus grow for an additional two years on average, and they grow at a greater rate. These two factors account for much of the final height difference between women and men.

Secondary sex features show noticeable changes soon after the increased growth begins. Pubic hair forms, breast buds develop in girls, testicles enlarge in boys, and boys also experience changes to the larynx, which lead to the initial cracking and then lowering of the male voice. Approximately two and a half years after initial breast development, menstruation begins in girls. Spermarche, or first ejaculation, occurs approximately two years after initial testicular enlargement begins in boys. Other changes include increased muscle growth in boys, redistribution of fat in girls and boys, and increases in bone mineral content in both (see Rogol, Roemmich, & Clark, 2002).

A number of psychological factors are associated with puberty. Many of the mechanisms controlling their relationships are not well understood. Pubertal timing is believed to be related to the onset of depressive symptoms in girls (Angold & Worthman, 1993). Antisocial behavior has been linked with puberty, but this might be due to the increased association with older, deviant peers that is likely with early-maturing adolescents (see Susman & Rogol, 2004). Greater moodiness is associated with puberty, but causal links between adolescent moodiness and hormone levels are not particularly strong (Buchanan, Eccles, & Becker, 1992). Greater moodiness might also be influenced by the greater occurrence of negative life events during adolescence (Larson & Ham, 1993).

Timing of puberty is believed to be important, and the effects of timing are different for girls than for boys. Girls who reach puberty earlier than their peers might feel uncomfortable with their changed bodies, particularly the increased body fat in the hips and thighs. They are also susceptible to the influence of older peers. Early-maturing girls might receive attention from older boys and may be encouraged to engage in more deviant behaviors (Caspi, Lynam, Moffitt, & Silva, 1993). Early-maturing boys, on the other hand, tend to feel self-confident and gain status from their more adult-looking bodies.

Secular trends in pubertal timing suggest that nutrition and weight play a role in the onset of puberty (Parent et al., 2003). There has been a general trend over the past century for an earlier age of menarche over time, with similar estimates of earlier puberty for boys. This trend is believed to be due to better nutrition, health care, and living conditions for children. Although it appeared that this trend toward earlier puberty was leveling off, in countries with significant rises in youth obesity rates, menarche continues to occur at even earlier ages.

Researchers have also noted an apparent link between father absence and the onset of daughter puberty. Girls without fathers in the home show earlier onset of menarche compared to those living with fathers in the home. Belsky, Steinberg, and Draper (1991) suggest that father absence increases stress for daughters, which in turn leads to depression, weight gain, and thus, earlier menarche. An alternative explanation is offered by Comings, Muhleman, Johnson, and MacMurray (2002) who argue that the relationship between father absence and daughter's early menarche is genetic. They investigated a particular allele of the AR gene in 121 males and 164 females. In males, this allele was associated with impulsiveness and aggression, and increased number of sexual partners. In females, the allele was associated with father absence, father divorce, and early onset of menarche. These findings do not yet resolve this issue, but they offer another way of understanding the association between father absence and the timing of daughter menarche.

ADOLESCENT SEXUAL EXPERIENCE

Problem of Knowing and Assessing the Facts

Several methodological pitfalls surround the study of adolescent sexuality. One problem is the inconsistency of adolescent self-reports. Lauritsen and Swicegood (1997) compared adults' retrospective reports of their behavior during adolescence with reports given by the same individuals previously, when they were adolescents. They found that 28–32 percent of the reports of age at sexual initiation were inconsistent with those reports given during adolescence. In another study, assessment of answers given over different time periods showed that many youth revised their estimation of the timing of first coitus (Upchurch, Lillard, Aneshensel, & Li, 2002). Specifically, perhaps reflecting social expectations, girls may be more likely to underreport, but boys may be more likely to overreport sexual experience (Siegel, Aten, & Roghmann, 1998). In addition, Hollander (1997) found that, in comparison with their medical records, only 46 percent of participants were able to accurately identify how many STDs they had contracted, and only 76 percent of women accurately reported their pregnancies.

Inconsistencies do not occur randomly, but they occur to different degrees according to gender, age, family variables, and ethnicity. This indicates that participants' answers are affected by more-than-random errors and memory lapses (Lauritsen & Swicegood, 1997; Upchurch et al., 2002). Adolescents may give inconsistent reports regarding coitus, STDs, and pregnancy because they have not understood their own medical treatment, they may wish to give socially desirable answers, they may have misunderstood the question, or they may be reluctant to disclose personal information. Illustrating this reluctance to disclose, another study comparing adult retrospective report with prior adolescent report found no inconsistency for age at first reported coitus, but a significant inconsistency for age at first masturbation (Halpern, Udry, Suchindran, & Campbell, 2000). The authors stated that masturbation, even more so than other behaviors, is a sensitive topic. Adolescents may be reluctant to disclose sensitive information even if they are assured that their reporting is confidential. Furthermore, research suggests that individuals least comfortable with questions about sexuality or with the least amount of sexual experience may decline to participate completely, potentially biasing accounts to a greater degree (Strassberg & Lowe, 1995).

Another factor related to inconsistent reporting includes the language used to ask about sexual behavior. Reluctance by researchers to use explicit or colloquial language may result in varying interpretations by participants. For example, "having sex" may be interpreted in various ways, from coitus, oral sex, the presence of orgasm, through to a variety of individual interpretations (Sanders & Reinisch, 1999; Savin-Williams & Diamond, 2004). Capturing homosexuality may be particularly difficult because attraction, behavior, and labeling can be distinct categories that are often discordant (Diamond, 2000; Friedman et al., 2004). Frequently, researchers conceptualize sex as entailing vaginal/penile penetration. Even if this is clearly communicated to participants, failure to ask about a broader range of behaviors leaves large omissions in our understanding of adolescent sexual experience and the meaning attributed to experiences. It is worth noting that some researchers have begun asking about a wider variety of behaviors and defining what they mean by "to have sex." It is wise to remain aware of potential differences in perception between researchers and participants when conducting and interpreting research. Crucially, researchers must extend their investigations beyond behavior, to attend to the meanings attributed to those behaviors and the social and emotional facets that are an integral part of sexual experience.

Sexual Knowledge

Based on the results of a national survey, Terry-Humen and Manlove (2003) reported that only 26 percent of 13-year-olds were able to state the most effective contraceptive from a choice of withdrawal, condoms, and the contraceptive pill. One-third was unable to identify the condom as the most effective STD prevention method. Very few (8 percent) were able to correctly state the most fertile point in the female fertility cycle. Similarly, adolescents' knowledge about normative behavior is not very accurate, with a tendency to overestimate the sexual behavior of their peers. Results from a sample of 958 12- to 14-year-olds showed that 39 percent of boys and 51 percent of girls endorsed the statement "Most teens your age are having sex," whereas, in reality, only 15 percent of boys and 8 percent of girls in that sample reported that they had had sex (Gomez, Coyle, Gregorich, Marin, & Kirby, 2003).

Sexual Behavior

Masturbation

Despite being a safe and common form of sexual expression, masturbation is still a taboo topic. Research conducted from the 1970s through to the 1990s showed, disconcertingly, that self-stimulation is associated with high degrees of guilt for many people (Davidson & Moore, 1994; Lopresto, Sherman, & Sherman, 1985), and more than any other topic, questions about it made respondents feel very uneasy (Bradburn, Sudman, Blair, & Stocking, 1978; Davidson & Moore; Lopresto et al.). Reflecting this uneasiness, and maintaining it, is the absence of masturbation from media representations of sexuality (Ward, 2003). As a result, masturbation, perhaps more than any other sexual behavior, may be underreported (Halpern, Udry et al., 2000). Furthermore, there has been little research attention on it. With this in mind, the research conducted among U.S. college students showed that 81–86 percent of males and 45–51 percent of females reported ever having masturbated (Leitenberg, Detzer, & Srebnik, 1993; Weinberg, Lottes, & Shaver, 1995). In these studies, males were not only more likely to report having masturbated, but they also reported beginning it at a younger age (an average of 13.5 years versus 14.2 years) and doing so around three times as often as females. In addition, only 15 percent of males but 63 percent of females reported that they had never masturbated by the first time they had sex (Schwartz, 1999). While it may be common sense to contend that self-awareness and self-exploration are healthy aspects of sexual development, research has shown that masturbation is not related to sexual satisfaction, sexual difficulties, or intercourse experience. This suggests that masturbation is neither harmful to, nor necessary for, sexual enjoyment in young adulthood (Leitenberg et al., 1993).

Most researchers argue that males' apparently higher engagement in masturbation is a reflection of society's different expectations for men and women. To support this argument, Weinberg et al. (1995) compared Swedish participants with U.S. students. Sweden has a relatively sexually permissive culture and arguably less of a sexual double standard. Both men and women are encouraged to enjoy their sexuality. Interestingly, overall reported rates of masturbation were higher, and the gap in masturbation experience between males and females was smaller; 99 percent of males reported ever having masturbated, compared to 91 percent of women, although men continued to report a reasonably higher frequency. It is likely that a number of factors contribute to the low rates of masturbation reported by U.S. women; however, perceptions of societal disapproval may be a prominent factor.

Precoital Behaviors

The majority of studies devoted to adolescent sexuality present sex as a dichotomous variable (Whitaker, Miller, & Clark, 2000). Sexual experience is defined as having engaged in vaginal/penile sex, or not. Yet, a much broader range of behaviors and feelings constitute sexual experience. Unfortunately, few studies explore these broader behaviors and feelings or the meanings adolescents attribute to them. As a result, it is possible to give descriptive accounts of some precoital behaviors but difficult to provide any substantive analysis of the relationship between them, their developmental course, how they are interpreted, or how behaviors and cognitions relate to later coitus.

Precoital sexual expression, as with coitus, becomes more common with increasing age. A nationally representative study revealed that 12 percent of virgins and 18 percent of all participants aged 12–14 years had been in a relationship in the last eighteen months that had included "touching under clothes," while 6 percent of virgins and 13 percent of all students reported genital touching within at least one romantic relationship (Bruckner & Bearman, 2003). For older students, another nationally representative study of males found that approximately 40 percent of 15-year-olds and 60 percent of 16-year-olds had precoital sexual experience, such as masturbating or engaging in oral sex (Gates & Sonenstein, 2000). In another study, 35 percent of students in ninth through twelfth grade had engaged in noncoital heterosexual activity in the prior year; specifically, masturbation of a partner (29 percent) and by a partner (31 percent), fellatio with ejaculation (9 percent), and cunnilingus (10 percent). Homosexual masturbation and oral sex were less commonly reported (around 1–2 percent) for different behaviors (Schuster, Bell, & Kanouse, 1996). Retrospective reports by college students of their experiences prior to coitus revealed that most had engaged in kissing and fondling of breasts and genitals, 70 percent of males had performed cunnilingus, and 57 percent of females had performed fellatio at least once; moderate to high engagement in these activities was reported by around one-third of individuals (Schwartz, 1999).

It is difficult to give validated conclusions regarding the relationship of precoital behaviors to coitus, but it appears that they are more likely to be forerunners to coitus than substitution behaviors. Supporting this hypothesis is the finding that teens who postpone coitus also engage in fewer sexual behaviors of any sort (Halpern, Joyner, Udry, & Suchindran, 2000). In addition, there appears to be a reasonably short time frame between engaging in precoital behaviors and engaging in coitus. Specifically, individuals reported activities leading to orgasms with their partners six to eight months before first coitus, and oral sex within one month of first coitus (Weinberg et al., 1995). Yet, there is also evidence to suggest that precoital behaviors may serve to delay sex, at least for a short period. From the limited extant research, it appears that white Americans' sexual behaviors follow a typical progression from extended kissing (necking), through feeling breasts over clothes then without clothes, feeling sex organs over clothes then without clothes, to coitus (Halpern, Joyner, et al., 2000; Smith & Udry, 1985). It seems that black Americans follow a less predictable path, and coitus occurs sooner with fewer preliminary behaviors (Smith & Udry). It is unknown to what degree this finding is a result of ethnicity or social factors and whether it is related to the higher pregnancy rate among black girls. Even if precoital behaviors do not substitute for coitus in the long run, positive aspects of delay may include more time for the relationship to develop and more time to prepare for intercourse. Further research must be undertaken to clarify these issues.

Additional research is needed to investigate the meanings that adolescents attribute to different behaviors. Do adolescents themselves view noncoital sexual behaviors as substitution for, or precursors to, coitus? What are the perceived implications of participating in varying behaviors? Implications to address could include perceived benefits and risks throughout psychological, social, relational, and physiological domains. Researchers are beginning to approach from this angle. For example, it has been reported that adolescents view oral sex as safer, more normative, and more socially acceptable but less pleasurable than coitus (Halpern-Felsher, Cornell, Kropp, & Tschann, 2005). Other issues to address include the varying pressures adolescents feel to engage in different activities, and the extent to which they feel pressured to engage in unwanted sexual activities additional to what they find comfortable. Whereas it is important to ask these questions from the perspectives of pregnancy and disease prevention, the field could benefit from a wider-angle lens that captures the full developmental and experiential aspects of sexuality.

Coitus

In 2003, according to the results of a nation-wide survey (Grunbaum et al., 2004), 46.7 percent of students in grades nine to twelve had had sex. This percentage was highest among black students (67.3 percent), followed by Hispanics (51.4 percent), and white students (41.8 percent). Males were more likely to report having had sex than were females up until twelfth grade, and prevalence increased as students moved through high school. Data for females and males showed that, respectively, 4.2 percent and 10.4 percent had their sexual debut before age 13, 29.9 percent and 37.3 percent in ninth grade, 43 percent and 45.1 percent in tenth grade, 53.1 percent and 53.4 percent in eleventh grade, and 62.3 percent and 60.7 percent in twelfth grade. Altogether, 14.4 percent had had four or more sexual partners, with males (17.5 percent) more likely to report this than females (11.2 percent). Approximately one-third (34.3 percent) of all participants had had sex in the previous three months, indicating that teenagers who have had sex are not necessarily having sex regularly. Of those who had sex in the past three months, in relation to their most recent sexual encounter, 25.4 percent said that they had consumed alcohol or other drugs before and 63 percent had used a condom.

National data collected by Child Trends (National Campaign to Prevent Teen Pregnancy, 2003b) provided more specific details about the circumstances surrounding teenagers' first coital experience. Teenagers aged 16 to 18 years were asked about the first time they had sex; the most likely location was in one partner's family home (56 percent). The most likely time of day was 10 p.m. to 7 a.m. (42 percent), with the next most reported time being between 6 p.m. and 10 p.m. (28 percent).

Sexual Attitudes

Love, curiosity, and desire were the most popular motives given by young (12- to 14-year-old) adolescents for having sex, whereas wanting to avoid AIDS or other diseases was the most common reason for not having sex, followed by not wanting a baby, parent's anger, and feeling they were too young (Gomez, Coyle, Gregorich, Marin, & Kirby, 2003). Teenagers seem to believe that society should encourage them to delay having sex. For example, 90 percent of adolescent boys stated that teenagers should be given a "strong" abstinence message from society (unpublished data cited by the National Campaign to Prevent Teen Pregnancy, 2003a).

"Too Young" versus "Just Right"

Cotton, Mills, Succop, Biro, and Rosenthal (2004) asked adolescent girls how they felt about their readiness to have sex the first time they did. In their sample of predominately (80 percent) African American girls, 14 years was the mean age of first intercourse. The authors reported that 78 percent of the girls said they were "too young" whereas 22 percent said their age had been "just right." Factors associated with a girl reporting her age as "just right" were being younger at the time of interview, being older at the time of first intercourse, endorsing the statement "I was in love," more parental supervision, and a higher level of maternal education. A public opinion poll conducted in 2002 by the National Campaign to Prevent Teen Pregnancy found similar results, with 81 percent of 12- to 14-year-olds and 55 percent of 15- to 19-year-olds stating that they wished they had waited until they were older to have sex (Albert, Brown, & Flanigan, 2003).

Mutual Consent/Coercion

A girl's propensity to regret is likely to be related to the degree she desired intercourse in the first place. Although most girls define the first time they have intercourse as being consensual in that the experience was not forced on them, there is variation in how much they desired sex. Flanigan (2003) asked girls about the "wantedness of sex" in consensual intercourse. She reported that among girls younger than 15, 27 percent rated the wantedness as low, 48 percent as medium, and 26 percent as high. Girls older than 15 were less likely to give a low rating (15 percent) and more likely to give a high rating (42 percent); a similar number (43 percent) reported medium wantedness. This substantial number of girls who were ambivalent, if not reluctant, about participating in first coitus suggests that girls are not being sufficiently equipped to have their desires met. Issues of communication, self-esteem, self-efficacy, subjugation, or pressure of perceived social norms may impact a girl's ability to say and get what she wants in a relationship.

Contraceptive Use

A summary of the trends in contraceptive use by Terry and Manlove (2000) showed that from 1988 to 1995 there was an increase in contraceptive use at first intercourse for all teens who had ever had sex, but among those who were currently sexually active, there was a decline in contraceptive use at last sex. The one exception to this trend was that the contraceptive use of sexually active black females remained stable across the periods. To prevent pregnancy, it is important that adolescents use contraception consistently; unfortunately, the data indicated that 30 to 38 percent of females do not do this, with younger adolescents being the least consistent users.

The factors that determine whether adolescents use contraceptives consistently differ from the factors affecting early sexual debut. Unlike early sexual involvement, contraceptive nonuse does not appear to be associated with other risk factors. In a literature review, Manlove, Ryan, and Franzetta (2004) reported factors specific to the couple that reduce the likelihood of condom use. These included an age gap between partners, physical violence, younger age at first intercourse, and a greater number of partners. They also noted that although having sex early in the relationship increased the likelihood of initial condom use, it reduced likelihood at last intercourse. The impact of relationship type, such as romantic versus casual, has produced contradictory findings. Some studies have found that condoms were more likely to be used in a romantic relationship than in a casual relationship; however, other studies have found the opposite pattern. This discrepancy can be resolved by considering that in longer-term relationships, condoms may be disregarded for other forms of contraception. Discussing contraception with one's partner increases the chances of using it, and females who are more at ease communicating with men in general are more likely to discuss and use contraception.

Individual factors are also associated with condom use, as those who use condoms consistently in one relationship are more likely to do so within other relationships. Characteristics of the individual that decrease the likelihood of condom use included Hispanic ethnicity, low academic achievement, and religiosity. The characteristics that increase the likelihood of condom use included having two biological parents, parents with higher educational attainment, and holding positive attitudes toward contraception. More consistent contraceptive use is associated with hormonal contraceptive methods than with condoms.

CONTEXTS OF SEXUALITY: INTERPERSONAL RELATIONSHIPS

Romantic Relationships

Romantic interests are a defining aspect of adolescence, whether adolescents actually engage in a relationship or participate in fantasy and talk about a person they "like." In one study, 55 percent of all adolescents had been in a romantic relationship in the past eighteen months. The proportion increased with age so that by age 18, 76 percent of adolescents reported having experienced a romantic relationship, and 8 percent reported a "liked" relationship (Carver, Joyner, & Udry, 2003). In another study, with adolescents 14 and younger, 42 percent reported ever having dated. Of those, the majority (40 percent) had only dated 1–3 times (Terry-Humen & Manlove, 2003).

In the Carver et al. (2003) study, approximately half the reported romantic relationships were sexual; again, the proportion increased with the age of the adolescents involved. More relationships involved "touching each other under clothing" (57 percent) than "touching each other's genitals" (52 percent), and 41 percent involved intercourse.

Nonromantic Relationships

Not all sexual involvement occurs within a romantic relationship. A nationally representative sample showed that 14.9 percent of teenagers aged 15 years and older had sex with someone they were not romantically involved with at the time (Manning, Longmore, & Giordano, 2005). The relational context of adolescent sexual experience is important because it affects sexual health behaviors and provides learning experiences and models for later relationships. Specifically, knowing each other as friends before becoming involved in a romantic relationship is related to a lower likelihood of intercourse for males and females (Kaestle & Halpern, 2005). Females are more likely to use a condom if they knew their partner than if they had just met them (Manning, Longmore, & Giordano, 2000), and teenagers who have participated in nonromantic sex are much more likely to do so again (Manning et al., 2005). The implications of nonromantic sexual involvement for attachment, mental health, and later relationship success need to be expanded upon in future research.

Stability of Relationships

Relationships within which first coitus occurs tend to be short. For adolescents younger than 15, 44 percent of their relationships ended within three months. For those 15 years and older, 39 percent of relationships ended within three months (Flanigan, 2003). On the other hand, relationships that include intercourse tend to be more enduring, lasting almost twice as long as platonic relationships. Analyzed at what stage 25 percent, 50 percent, and 75 percent of relationships ended, sexual relationships endured for 5, 11, and 27 months, respectively, whereas relationships that did not include intercourse endured for only 2, 5, and 13 months, respectively (Bruckner & Bearman, 2003).

Age Disparity

The greater the age disparity between a young girl and her partner, the greater the likelihood that they will be sexually involved, that they will not use contraception, and that she will become pregnant (Darroch, Landry, & Oslak, 1999). In adolescents under 14, 8–13 percent of same-age relationships included sex. This doubled when the partner was two years older, increased to 33 percent when the partner was three years older, and was 47 percent when the partner was four or more years older (Albert et al., 2003). Another study replicated this pattern and found that it applied for boys as well. Thirty percent of girls and 73 percent of boys aged 14 years reported sexual involvement when their partner was at least two years older, compared to 13 percent of girls and 29 percent of boys when their partner was within one year of their own age (Marin, Kirby, Hudes, Gomez, & Coyle, 2003).

Early Sexual Debut

The sexual behavior of younger adolescents deserves special attention. The sexual experiences of those 14 and younger seem to be different from those 15 and older, and the negative consequences experienced are greater

(Albert et al., 2003). Despite sexual involvement having different ramifications according to age-group, there is often no breakdown of ages or data collected from adolescents aged 15 and older. Despite increased risk, the proportion of sexually active individuals aged 14 or younger is not declining like that of those in the older age-group, but is instead increasing.

A number of studies have found that younger age at first intercourse is linked to a greater number of sexual partners over time, decreased contraceptive use, increased risk of STDs, increased risk of pregnancy (one in seven sexually experienced 14-year-olds reported having been pregnant), significantly increased likelihood that the sexual attention was unwanted (13–24 percent described it as nonvoluntary) (Marin et al., 2003). Furthermore, younger girls are much more likely to report regret over first sex. In addition, when girls 14 and under give birth, they are at an even greater risk of childbirth complications and of having a baby with a low birth weight (Martin, Hamilton, Ventura, Menacker, & Park, 2002).

Sexual Orientation

Sexual identity development is difficult to study because sexual orientation labels may not accurately represent the experiences of many adolescents (Friedman et al., 2004). Hence, although attention has been given to adolescents who label themselves as gay, lesbian, or bisexual, a large number of factors may affect teenagers' decision to label themselves, including uncertainty about the meaning of their feelings and behaviors, diversity within their experiences of attraction, and fear of negative evaluation. Furthermore, heterosexual, homosexual, and bisexual appear to present as dimensional continuums rather than as distinct categories to which one either does or does not belong. Therefore, the term "sexual minority" includes those youth who experience same-sex attraction, but recognize that they may also experience other-sex attraction, and that their patterns of experience may change over time (Diamond & Savin-Williams, 2003).

Sexual identity development involves interpreting and integrating attractions, behaviors, intimate relationships, fantasy, and labels into a representation of the self. It should not be assumed that the different aspects of sexual identity are stable and/or concordant with each other (Diamond, 2000; Friedman et al., 2004). For example, adolescents who report same-sex attractions do not necessarily participate in same-sex behavior, and adults who identify as gay do not always recall same-sex attractions during adolescence. Experiencing same-sex attraction does not automatically mean that other-sex attraction either does not or has not occurred, or is unimportant, unsatisfying, or unappealing. Most sexual minority youth have been involved with other-sex peers in a variety of ways. As Diamond and Savin-Williams explained, "[I]ndividuals typically experience a diverse array of attractions and behaviors during their adolescent years some of which reflect curiosity and experimentation, some of which reflect social pressure, and some of which reflect an underlying sexual orientation" (2003, p. 395).

Fluidity of attractions and behaviors is particularly true of the experiences of women. This is illustrated by a study of eighty sexual minority women aged between 16 and 23 years, where one-third changed their identity label and half changed their identity more than once (Diamond, 2000). Nevertheless, it appears that men's experiences are not static either, according to the findings of a longitudinal study that comprised men born in New Zealand in 1972/ 1973 and questioned at age 21. The majority (93.2 percent) reported that they had only ever experienced attraction to women, a few (6.5 percent) reported ever being sexually attracted to a man, and a smaller number (4.2 percent) reported current same-sex attraction. Overall, 4.2 percent reported ever having had sex with a man. Of that group, a minority (9.5 percent) reported being only solely attracted to men, and almost half reported that they were now solely attracted to women (Paul, Fitzjohn, Eberhart-Phillips, Herbison, & Dickson, 2000).

A large number of adolescents question aspects of their sexual identity. Much of this uncertainty resolves with time, although a degree of fluidity continues to exist. Unfortunately, wrestling with sexual identity issues is not easy, and sexual minority youth experience a greater number of health risks, including depression, suicide, and substance abuse (Garofalo & Katz, 2001; Savin-Williams, 1994). It is important to remember the "powerful needs for physical affection, emotional security, and simple companionship that underlie *all* adolescents' close relationships," and ensure that adolescents are able to have these needs met safely (Diamond & Savin-Williams, 2003, p. 406).

CONSEQUENCES OF ADOLESCENT SEXUALITY

Pregnancy

Birthrates

Since the 1970s, in industrialized countries worldwide, there has been an overall decline in the childbearing of teenagers aged 15–19 years (Singh & Darroch, 2000). In the United States this decline, particularly in the last decade, has created a degree of optimism—optimism tempered by the fact that the current rate is still one of the highest in the Western world. Decreased adolescent childbearing has occurred in a context of declining fertility for women of all ages, but this trend has generally been more marked among adolescents (Darroch, Singh, & Frost, 2001).

In the United States and several other countries, the decline in birthrates is accompanied by a declining abortion rate. Although abortion trends are less consistent across countries, generally, from 1980 to 2000, there has been a stable or decreasing rate among 15- to 19-year-olds. In the United States, there has been a 31 percent decrease in abortions since the mid-1980s (Darroch & Singh, 1999). Younger adolescents are more likely to seek an abortion. For example, in the United Kingdom in 1997, approximately 50 percent of births were aborted in those under 16, but this figure fell to around 30 percent for those aged between 16 and 19 (Macleod & Weaver, 2003).

Effects for Mother and Child

Bringing a baby into the world is ideally a positive and happily anticipated event. In fact, teenage mothers often share the same positive emotions as adult mothers do around the birth of an infant (Macleod & Weaver, 2003; Milan et al., 2004). Unfortunately, teenage motherhood often occurs in a context that leads to negative consequences for the mother and her child (Felice et al., 1999; LeTourneau, Stewart, & Barnfather, 2004; National Campaign to Prevent Teen Pregnancy, 2002). Whereas, historically, young married women have borne children without attracting societal concern, contemporary society differs significantly from that of even fifty years ago. For young women today, adolescence is more a time to prepare for the future and less a time of marrying and beginning a family. Adolescent parenting can mean a path of narrowed opportunities without the expected acquisition of education and job skills. In addition, adolescent parenting often means single parenting, and while this should not carry stigma, it can carry hardships, including a lack of social and economic support.

Hobcraft and Kiernan (2001) conducted a study in Britain using longitudinal data for over 5,500 women. They described the situations of women at age 33. Controlling for a large number of background variables, they found that the younger a woman was at giving first birth, up until the age of 23, the more likely she was to have experienced a variety of negative outcomes. The experience of an early first birth was a more powerful risk factor than was childhood poverty, although childhood poverty and early first birth together created the worst outcome. Women who gave birth before the age of 20 were most likely to experience single parenting, to be in government-provided housing and receiving financial aid, have no qualifications, smoke cigarettes, have no telephone, be of low income, experience malaise, say life is unsatisfactory, and report moderate or poor health. The authors noted that negative outcomes are unlikely to be the result of the birth of a baby per se, but that early parenting has the potential to limit other opportunities and choices.

While teenage motherhood may be associated with an array of negative outcomes, the relationship is complex. The factors that are said to result from teenage pregnancy are the same factors that put adolescents at increased risk of becoming parents (Bingham & Crockett, 1996; Coley & Chase-Lansdale, 1998). Nevertheless, as discussed by Hoffman (1998), although adolescent parenthood does not, in and of itself, cause disadvantage, nor guarantee that disadvantage will ensue, this does not then mean that efforts to discourage it should be abandoned. As he stated, "Reduction of early parenthood will not eliminate the powerful effects of growing up in poverty and disadvantage. But it represents a potentially productive strategy for widening the pathways out of poverty or, at the very least, not compounding the handicaps imposed by social disadvantage" (p. 243).

Moreover, the results of research investigating the effect of teenage parenthood on the child suggest that children born to adolescent women are at greater risk of being disadvantaged. They are more likely to experience low birth weight, more hospital admissions, neglect, poverty, becoming teenage parents themselves, being disadvantaged on tests of cognitive performance, and doing less well emotionally and socially than children of older mothers (Osofsky, Hann, & Peebles, 1993; Terry-Humen, Manlove, & Moore, 2005).

Effects for Fathers

Substantially more research is directed toward teenage mothers than teenage fathers (Thornberry, Smith, & Howard, 1997). As is the case for adolescent mothers, adolescent fathers are more likely to have encountered greater social disadvantage, including poverty, low educational achievement, and involvement with alcohol and other drugs, petty crime, and violent behavior (Nelson, 2004; Stouthamer-Loeber & Wei, 1998; Thornberry et al.). Unfortunately, it is those factors that may place a man at greater risk of becoming a young father that may also decrease his likelihood of remaining involved with the child (Thornberry et al.). It is unfortunate because there are tremendously beneficial long-term outcomes for children when fathers remain involved and provide quality parenting. Father involvement results in a reduction in family poverty and improved outcomes for children cognitively, behaviorally, and socially (Marsiglio, Amato, Day, & Lamb, 2000; Reid, 2000), and improved psychosocial outcomes for the mother (Gee & Rhodes, 2003; Kalil, Ziol-Guest, & Coley, 2005). More research is needed to investigate the factors that lead to fatherhood and affect continued involvement, and the social and emotional impact of fatherhood on the adolescent boy (Fagan, Barnett, Bernd, & Whiteman, 2003; Marsiglio et al.).

Sexually Transmitted Diseases

Sexually transmitted diseases (STDs) incur high costs. In addition to the immediate negative physical and psychological effects of contracting disease, long-term sequelae can include pelvic inflammatory disease, tubal scarring, ectopic pregnancy, infertility, cancer, and increased mortality (Chesson, Blandford, Gift, Tao, & Irwin, 2004). Adolescents have the highest chance out of all age-groups of contracting an STD (Upchurch, Mason, Kusunoki, Johnson, & Kriechbaum, 2004). For example, 46 percent of all reported cases of *Chlamydia trachomatis* are for girls in the 15- to 19-year age-group (Cothran & White, 2002).

Overall, 25 percent of reported STDs are for adolescents (Weinstock, Berman, & Cates, 2004). This number is particularly alarming when considering that it only applies to the proportion of adolescents who are sexually active and those who seek medical care.

Upchurch et al. (2004) reported that age at first intercourse was the primary predictor of adolescent sexual health. Adolescents who postpone sex tend to have fewer sexual partners, have longer-lasting relationships, and use condoms more consistently (Albert et al., 2003; Flisher & Chalton, 2001). In addition to being at increased risk of disease due to risky behaviors, young women are more physically susceptible to infection. The cervix does not mature fully until late adolescence and until then is less able to resist infection (Joffe, 1997). Furthermore, postponing sexual involvement until late adolescence is particularly important for reducing transmission of those STDs that are not affected by condom use, specifically, those caused by herpes simplex virus, pubic lice, and human papillomavirus (HPV), which leads to cervical cancer (Cothran & White, 2002; Warner et al., 2004; Winer et al., 2003). Although consistently wearing condoms leads to reductions in transmission of most STDs, the aforementioned diseases are contracted through any skin-to-skin contact. Therefore, interventions that lower disease rates need to focus on methods (other than condom use) of reducing risk behaviors, such as delayed sexual debut, STD screening and treatment, and fewer sexual partners.

In addition to interventions that reduce STD transmission, it is crucial to provide, and educate about the necessity of, screening and treatment of STDs. Research to date suggests that adolescents are not being adequately assessed and that professionals and adolescents need to be aware of the importance of regular screening (Fiscus, Ford, & Miller, 2004). It is also important that health practitioners are aware of the possible need to screen for STDs contracted through behaviors other than coitus, such as oral sex (Remez, 2000). Generally, education and media campaigns have focused on vaginal/penile intercourse as being synonymous with sexual behavior (Halpern-Felsher et al., 2005). However, a variety of sexual behaviors outside of this definition still place the young person at risk.

Sexually Transmitted Disease in Developing Countries

The consequence of sexually transmitted disease is particularly devastating in developing countries where HIV/AIDS has become an epidemic. Young women specifically are at a high risk of contracting HIV. The UNAIDS/WHO *AIDS Epidemic Update* reported that in sub-Saharan Africa, 76 percent of infected young people (15–24 years) are female. This report highlights the effect of the social and economic context in determining the sexual health of individuals. An adolescent girl in a developing country commonly has little control over the factors that lead to her becoming infected. She will often marry an older man who has had and may continue to have multiple partners. Cultural expectations that women be sexually naïve result in her holding limited knowledge about the importance of protected sex. In addition, even if she did know about the importance of using a condom, she may have limited power to assert that one be used (UNAIDS/WHO, 2004). As well as the increased incidents of HIV/AIDS, STDs, and unintended pregnancy, adolescents in developing countries also have reduced access to health care. Consequently, there is less opportunity for treatment and there are increased incidents of pregnancy complications, which lead to increased mortality for mother and child.

FACTORS INFLUENCING SEXUAL RISK BEHAVIORS

There are a multitude of cultural, community, family, and individual factors that increase the likelihood of early sexual debut, poor contraceptive use, and adolescent pregnancy. Kirby (2001a) reported more than 100 antecedents from an analysis of over 250 studies. He explained that it is important for educators, policy makers, and parents to be aware of these risk factors so that they can design and implement appropriately targeted interventions and can identify those youth who are most at risk. It is necessary to remember, though, that such a large number of antecedents entails that the contribution of each factor is relatively small. It is also necessary to remember to focus on protective factors, which build resiliency and may attenuate the likelihood of negative outcomes.

Culture

Cultural atmosphere is the broadest and the most inescapable influence on sexual behavior. The media, schools, families, extracurricular clubs, and communities of faith all give messages about appropriate sexual behavior. Out of this melting pot of sources, youth are given contradictory messages. On the one hand, sexuality is glamorized, and on the other, it is prohibited. The media, from movies to magazines, generally depict sexuality in a way that is discordant with reality (Ward, 2003). Equally discordant with reality is the information that depicts only the biophysical aspects and risks of sexual involvement. Adolescents do not merely hear these messages, but they interpret them and choose to accept or disregard them. These choices and interpretations affect adolescent beliefs about what is acceptable and what is normative. These beliefs may be one of the most powerful underlying influences on their sexual behavior (Kirby, 2001b).

Media

Adolescents with unsupervised access to television were more likely to engage in sexual activities (Gruber, Wang, Christensen, Grube, & Fisher,

2005), and adolescents who watched television with more sexual content were more likely to initiate intercourse within the following year (Collins et al., 2004). However, as with most predictors of sexual behavior, the link between media and behavior is not necessarily unilateral. Chapin's (2000) developmental approach to mass media suggests that teenagers actively use the media to find information relevant to their interests and developmental stage. Their interpretation of the media will then also differ accordingly. This theory is consistent with the findings of Brown, Halpern, and L'Engle (2005). They found that pubertal timing influenced girls' likelihood of engaging with media containing sexual content. Early-maturing girls showed more interest in music, magazines, and movies with sexual content and were also more likely to interpret sexual messages as being permissive. Interestingly, late-maturing girls were also more likely to report that they viewed STD- and birth control–related messages. As the authors noted, the rarity of this information in the media suggests that these girls may have been particularly attuned to such information.

Family

Despite the powerful influence of wider community and societal influence, research unequivocally supports the impact of the family (Miller, 1998; Miller, Benson, & Galbraith, 2001; Upchurch, Aneshensel, Sucoff, & Levy-Storms, 1999). This large body of research supports the finding that the most effective way to protect adolescents from disadvantage, including early sexual debut and pregnancy, is a functional and supportive family. Such families have been found to include qualities such as parent-child connectedness, good communication, strong values with expectations for abstinence, parental involvement, awareness and supervision of adolescent activities, high level of maternal education, hereditary influences, and presence of both biological parents in the home (Borawski, Ievers-Landis, Lovegreen, & Trapl, 2003; Di-Lorio, Dudley, Soet, & McCarty, 2004; Ellis et al., 2003; Hutchinson, Jemmott, Jemmott, Braverman, & Fong, 2003; Miller, 1998; Miller et al., 2001; Rose et al., 2005; Sieverding, Adler, Witt, & Ellen, 2005).

Peers

An adolescent's peer group also impacts his or her behavior (Whitaker & Miller, 2000). Adolescents who perceive that their peers are having sex, who have older friends, or who have friends who participate in delinquent activities are more likely to have sex (Bearman & Bruckner, 1999). The importance of social context was exemplified in a study conducted by Bearman and Bruckner (2001). They found that the effectiveness of virginity pledging relied on there being at least some other pledgers within the pledger's school, and differed according to whether the school environment was relatively socially closed or open. Schools whose students primarily formed social groups with peers inside their school were more likely to be affected by the pledge, whereas schools where students formed social groups from diverse contexts were less likely to be affected.

The Individual

There are many studies investigating individual attributes associated with sexual risk behaviors. These include physical maturation; depression and low self-esteem (Longmore, Manning, Giordano, & Rudolph, 2004); low academic aspirations; low community attachment; alcohol and other drug use (Rashad & Kaestner, 2004; Stueve & O'Donnell, 2005); history of abuse; previous pregnancy; and having an older romantic partner, which is associated with greater likelihood of sex, reduced contraceptive use, and higher reports of coercion (Young & d'Arcy, 2005). Individual factors that have been identified as protective include being involved in sports or youth groups, having strong religious beliefs (Whitehead, Wilcox, & Rostosky, 2001), self-efficacy for abstinence (DiLorio et al., 2004), sexual attitudes and knowledge (O'Donnell, Myint, O'Donnell, & Stueve, 2003; Rosengard et al., 2001), and good cognitive ability. The whole picture is complex, however, because these factors interact and are more or less appropriate according to the age, gender, and ethnicity of the individual.

Looking Further

The literature addressing adolescent sexuality has almost exclusively focused on pregnancy and disease. Very little attention has been given to the social and emotional aspects that are integral to sexuality. In one study (Widdice, Cornell, Liang, & Halpern-Felsher, 2005), teenagers were asked their opinions about the risks and benefits of having sex. Along with noting pregnancy and STDs, teenagers noted several social consequences, including negative effect on the relationship, negative emotions such as regret and loss of self-esteem, and parental or peer disapproval. Positive consequences of sexual involvement were predominately social, such as improving the relationship, having fun, and lifting social status. Although pregnancy and STDs are clearly high costs and have therefore been the focus of most interventions, the social and emotional aspects of sexuality should nevertheless be considered in future research.

SEX EDUCATION/PREVENTION

Virtually every North American student in public school will receive some form of sexuality education. Darroch, Landry, and Singh (2000) found that while the content and timing differs, the focus of the curriculum is likely to be on HIV transmission, STDs, and abstinence. Across the United States, 94–95 percent of teachers covered these topics with the majority of teachers reporting that abstinence was the most important message to communicate. This information was most likely to be discussed in the ninth grade. The content of sex education is heavily influenced by the goals of reducing pregnancy and STD transmission, and therefore is directed toward delaying sex debut and declining sexual involvement, as well as encouraging consistent use of condoms (Albert et al., 2003; Flisher & Chalton, 2001).

Franklin and Corcoran (2000) discussed that there has been an evolution in the content of sex education. The first programs developed were knowledge centered, emphasizing the risks and consequences of sexuality. As a reaction to this biological approach, later programs emphasized values, with abstinence promotion and limited discussion of contraception. The impact of HIV/AIDS led to the development of programs independent of previous approaches. Each of these three educational aspects can be seen in the most recently developed sex education programs.

While parents, educators, and policy directors each undoubtedly have adolescent welfare as their goal, there is strong disagreement and controversy surrounding how to best meet this goal (Moran, 2000). Essentially, the argument is centered on values. Traditionally, sexuality was contained within the context of marriage. The sexual revolution questioned this value and instead placed sex within the context of individual fulfillment. Each view offers a different solution to teen pregnancy and STDs; one group advocates abstinence until marriage, the other, contraception. Fear of AIDS further polarized these positions. Although these views are fundamentally dichotomous, there may be more potential for consensus, when determining what messages to convey to young people, than has been attempted so far. We do our young people a disservice by avoiding contentious issues and presenting sexuality in a reductionist manner. This is conveyed by the answer given by one 15-year-old girl who, in answer to the question "What is the main reason some teenagers don't have sex?" wrote, "My choice is to remain abstinent for reasons beyond religion and morals. I know that I am nowhere close to being ready for the consequences that come along with sex. . . . Sex is an act of love, not only an act of pleasure, and, in my opinion, this subject shouldn't be taken so lightly" (cited in Whitehead et al., 2001, pp. 27–28). She included faith, morality, responsibility, pleasure, and relationship and asked for awareness of the magnitude of these issues. This emphasizes that a simple "safe sex" or "true love waits" approach to sexuality is insufficient.

In practice, although sex education is often discussed as being abstinence-only or not, in the United States, sex education exists on a continuum (Kirby, 2001a). Furthermore, the evidence suggests that it is not inconsistent to advocate abstinence and contraception. Kirby (2001b) stated that virtually no study has found that sex education, even when it includes discussion of contraception or condom availability programs, increases rates of sexual activity.

In fact, some studies found that discussion of contraception actually delayed sexual debut and frequency of coitus. Likewise, when contraception is discussed alongside the promotion of abstinence as preferable, contraceptive use does not decrease.

Comprehensive Sex Education

Comprehensive sex education covers contraception, health, and abstinence and has been found in at least seventy studies (Kirby, 2001a; see also Kirby et al., 2004; Speizer, Magnani, & Colvin, 2003) to have some impact on teenage behavior. Nevertheless, as Kirby (2001b) discussed, more research needs to be undertaken before firm conclusions can be drawn. He states that it is clear that there are no "magic bullets." No one approach is single-handedly superior; programs need to target a wide range of antecedents and be open to combining techniques. He outlined the common components of those comprehensive sex education programs that were effective. First, he stated that each component is vital, but one of the most crucial aspects of an effective program is the consistent stressing of abstinence and contraceptive use. Second, he recommended the use of theoretical approaches that have been employed effectively in other health intervention programs. Such programs target specific sexual antecedents and focus on one or more specific sexual behaviors that lead to pregnancy or disease and focus on reducing that behavior. Third, he recommended the presentation of facts about the consequences of sexual involvement, ways to avoid involvement, and ways to protect oneself when one is involved. Fourth, he advocated teaching skills, for instance, hearing examples of and practicing communication, negotiation, and declining unwanted sexual advances. In addition, he suggested addressing the social pressures toward sexual involvement. Fifth, he recommended that program presenters believe in the value of the program, be trained, and use appropriate teaching methods so that participants feel involved and have the ability to personally relate to the material. The material needs to take into account the age, experience, and cultural background of the participants. Finally, he advised against programs of short duration; regardless of the content, they have little measurable effect.

Abstinence-Only Programs

Abstinence-only programs have not been sufficiently studied to justify drawing conclusions about their effectiveness at this stage (Besharov & Gardiner, 1997; Kirby, 2002). In his review of pregnancy prevention programs, Kirby (2001a) stated that only three studies (Kirby, Korpi, Barth, & Cagampang, 1997; Olsen, Weed, Nielsen, & Jensen, 1992; St. Pierre, Mark, Kaltreider, & Aikin, 1995) have evaluated abstinence-only programs in a sufficiently rigorous manner. The findings from those studies suggested that the programs did not impact the sexual behavior or contraceptive use of participants. Yet, as Kirby discussed, there are huge variations in the type of programs that come under abstinence-only education. The above three studies do not reflect the wide range of abstinence programs, some of which may be more effective than others. A program adjunctive to that offered by schools, which is abstinence based, is the virginity pledge. This, perhaps surprisingly, has been found in specific circumstances to effectively delay sexual debut. Bearman and Bruckner (2001) reported that sexually inexperienced young adolescents, in a context where there are enough other pledgers but not too many, are likely to delay intercourse for a substantial period of time. This is consistent with an intention not to have intercourse. However, when they do have intercourse, they are less likely to use contraception but pledge-breakers report no negative effects on self-esteem for breaking the pledge.

Noncurriculum-based Interventions

In addition to curriculum-based sex education, other initiatives have been developed to improve adolescent outcomes. Kirby (2001a) divided interventions into three broad categories based upon whether they target primarily sexual antecedents, nonsexual antecedents, or both. Within each of these broad categories, additional groupings can be made according to the structure of the programs. Programs that target sexual antecedents include curriculum-based programs, community-wide initiatives, sex education for parents and families, and clinic-based programs. Programs that target nonsexual antecedents are broad adolescent development programs that typically include structured preparation time leading to voluntary community service followed by reflection time. The third category of programs includes components of comprehensive health education and adolescent development.

Clinic-based services that provide contraception have been set up in the community and sometimes in schools. Kirby (2001a) explained that clinic-based interventions have not been studied in a comprehensive manner; however, common sense would suggest that contraceptive availability is an important factor dictating contraceptive usage. It does appear that clinic protocols are important. Specifically, providing information about reproductive health, the merits of abstinence, and opportunities for one-to-one discussions were components that facilitated effective service provision. He stated that school-based clinics do not appear to increase contraceptive use overall. Rather, teenagers substituted use of the school-based clinics over the community based clinics. As already stated, studies show that condom availability does not increase sexual activity (e.g. Kirby, 1991; Kisker & Brown, 1996).

Community-wide Interventions

Recognition of the multiple influences on teenage behavior has led to the development of community-wide interventions, including media campaigns through radio, television, posters, and billboards; presentations at large community events; workshops in schools, youth groups, community organizations, health centers, and personal homes; handing out pamphlets and condoms on streets and from door to door; setting up condom vending machines; and so on. The more intensive these initiatives are, the more likely they are to be successful. However, effects have not been found to last beyond the length of the intervention.

Service Learning Programs

Interventions that focus on the nonsexual antecedents of sexual risk taking include adolescent development or service learning programs. Service learning typically involves the adolescent being involved in voluntary community service while receiving input from positive role models during weekly debriefing sessions. In fact, Kirby (2001b) noted that at this stage, the best evidence for effective intervention is current involvement in a service learning program. Positive effects are hypothesized to result from quality time with caring adult role models, self-efficacy resulting from positive social interactions and a belief that they are making a valuable contribution to their communities, and provision of an activity, which means less opportunity to engage in risky activities.

One example of a service learning program is the Reach for Health intervention (O'Donnell et al., 2002). This program involved service in a community setting for three hours each week for thirty weeks. Participants were placed in one or two field placements over each year. At the commencement of the program, participants were given an orientation to the responsibilities and codes of conduct that were required in their placements. Each week, debriefing sessions were held and used to develop critical skills such as communication. The importance of the participants' contribution to the community was emphasized. The youth were required to learn about their organization as well as set personal goals, and they received a jacket and badge to wear. A total of seventy-four health lessons over a two-year period were also included.

Evaluation of the program four years after its commencement found that participants were less likely to report sexual initiation or recent sex compared to the control group that received the health education component only. Those who remained in the program for two years had the best results, but those who remained for one year also had positive results compared to a control group. Among those who had not had sex at the beginning of the project, by the end of the project 80 percent of males in the control group had initiated sex versus 61.5 percent who had been in the program for one year and 50 percent who had completed the full two-year program; among females, the respective figures were 65.2, 48.3, and 39.6 percent.

The most intensive, and therefore expensive, programs focus on sexual and nonsexual antecedents. One example of this type of program is the

Children's Aid Society-Carrera Program. It has been used with at-risk youth and includes the following components:

1. Family life and sex education
2. Academic assessment for specific needs, help with homework, and help with preparation for exams and course entry requirements
3. Work-related activities
4. Self-expression through arts
5. Sports
6. Comprehensive health care

Significant effects were found for girls and included postponement of sexual debut, increased condom use, and reduced pregnancy and birthrates.

Complicating the evaluation of program effectiveness is the fact that different programs may have different success with different groups. For example, different interventions may be more or less appropriate to individuals depending on their gender, ethnicity, sexual experience, at-risk status (e.g., those affected by sexual abuse or substance abusers), and so on (Kirby et al., 2004). The ability to target interventions to specific groups may improve the success of the program.

A consideration that has been missing from intervention research is that sex involves more than the decisions and desires of one individual. The vast majority of intervention research has considered individuals rather than couples. Little attention has been given to the interpersonal aspects of sexuality. Likewise, the physical consequences of sexuality have been emphasized, with the emotional consequences less emphasized. Researchers have only recently attempted to address this imbalance.

Programs in Developing Countries

Education and interventions are vital in developing countries where the life and death consequences of sex are even more pronounced. In the past decade, programs have been developed to address this need. More research needs to be conducted as few programs have been evaluated and most do not measure actual rates of disease. There is unlikely to be one magic answer, but evaluations are important so that the most effective programs can be implemented with long-term success.

Speizer et al. (2003) reviewed forty-one studies of adolescent reproductive health interventions operating in developing countries. Several different types of interventions were included in the review under the categories of school-based programs; mass media; community programs incorporating youth development, peer educators, and education; workplace programs; and health facilities. Interventions generally had a positive impact on knowledge and attitudes, but were less likely to impact on behavior. For each of the various approaches, at least one study found an impact on a behavior. Interventions that aimed to alter multiple behaviors generally did not achieve this goal although they may have succeeded with one behavior or one group of participants, for example, women.

Uganda is one country that, through a consistent countrywide effort, has seen a reduction in the AIDS epidemic (Blum, 2004). The effort, referred to as ABC, includes several tactics: **A**bstinence, **B**e faithful, and **C**ondoms; voluntary counseling and testing; and a focus on reducing mother-to-child transmission. Dramatic reductions in AIDS are accompanied by equally dramatic increases in condom use and abstinence.

Programs in European Countries

The United Kingdom and the Netherlands have large differences in pregnancy rates; moreover, the already low rate in the Netherlands has halved within the last twenty-five years and is one of the lowest among industrialized countries. Lewis and Knijn (2003) compared these countries' approaches in an attempt to understand what processes produce different outcomes in these countries. The reasons given for the higher pregnancy rate in the United Kingdom were social disparity, with women unable to see a life beyond welfare; limited understanding of contraception, sexually transmitted disease, relationships, and parenting; and contradictory messages about sex.

The impact of limited life choices due to social disparity is an issue in the United Kingdom and the United States to a degree that is generally not evident in Western European countries. However, Lewis and Knijn (2003) noted that black women in Amsterdam have a similar pregnancy rate to women in the United Kingdom. This may be because they have more limited life opportunities.

Ignorance of sex and relationship issues was also identified as a contributor to high pregnancy rates. Interestingly, a similar amount of time is devoted to sex education in British and Dutch schools. However, the approaches taken are dissimilar. Lewis and Knijn described the Dutch curriculum as "more explicit, more comprehensive and more coherent" (2003, p. 126). Sexuality education is presented as an integral and normal part of life. This contrasts with the British curriculum, where "[t]he irony is that the greater emphasis . . . on the negative aspects of teenage sex and on prevention continues to feed the often confused and sometimes crude perception of teenagers and the apparent lack of regard, especially on the part of boys, for relationships and for other people" (p. 127). Sexuality in the Netherlands, similar to that of Sweden, emphasizes empathy and responsibility toward one's sexual partner, attitudes that promote responsible sexual behavior.

In addition, continuity in the treatment of sexuality throughout different spheres of society in the Netherlands aids in the presentation of a consistent message about sex. Sexuality is discussed with greater openness, not just in school, but at home and in the media. However, contrary to what has sometimes been assumed, there are strong social expectations regarding acceptable behavior.

Lastly, the different approaches taken by these countries in determining the content of sex education may also contribute to the portrayal of mixed messages and less effective messages. An adversarial approach is used in Britain, but in the Netherlands, there is an attempt to find points of similarity within opposing viewpoints and to reach consensus.

FUTURE DIRECTIONS

In this chapter, we have tried to provide a snapshot of the key issues in and contemporary research on adolescent sexuality. The field of adolescent development is itself going through a period of rapid change. Whereas past research was heavily focused on children under 5 years of age, this focus has shifted, and a greater proportion of research now addresses older children and adolescents. Other changes include new theoretical approaches and methods that view development as integrated systems, combining neurological, biological, cognitive, and social factors, explanations, and applications (see Lerner & Steinberg, 2004).

The study of adolescent sexuality presents some striking contradictions and dilemmas within our society. On the one hand, the period between sexual maturity and the establishment of a family is extending, with the average age of first childbirth reaching into the late twenties and early thirties in many Western countries. In addition, the external, public world we live in has become highly sexualized. And yet, the attitudes reflected within many societies remain ambivalent toward sexual expression, especially by adolescents. Although the lyrics to a popular song might say, "Let's talk about sex," real talk is less forthcoming.

Perhaps it is not sexuality in the media per se that is problematic, but rather it is the way in which sexuality is portrayed and conceptualized in the media. Sex is often presented as something that girls give and boys take, something naughty, something based on physical acts leading to orgasm rather than the shared physical and psychological intimacy created. This might be part of sexual expression, but it is a very limited picture presented. Limited also are the types of people presented as sexual. And this might have serious implications for how adolescents feel about their own bodies and their own sexuality.

We know more about the frequency, contexts, and consequences of adolescent intercourse than we know about how adolescents feel about their sexuality (see Savin-Williams & Diamond, 2004). What factors, for example, predict healthy attitudes toward sexuality during adolescence and into adulthood? What do adolescents think, feel, and know about sexuality, and how does this influence the decisions they make? More importantly, how can

educators and health professionals help adolescents develop positive concep-
tualizations of sexuality and healthy behavior? In most other areas of development, society prepares its young to face the challenges ahead. Perhaps
it is time for our research and practice to reflect this in our approach to sexuality.

Sex and romance can be dangerous. Certain types of relationships and
sexual involvement can lead to a greater likelihood of experiencing lower
academic achievement, serious psychological problems, violence, pregnancy,
and STDs. We cannot forget this. Yet, neither can we forget the beauty of
sexual intimacy. Sexuality has the potential for such impact because it is an
integral and powerful aspect of our humanity, for bad and for good. Yet, it is
not often recognized that the reason sexuality has so much potency for harm is
because it has so much potency for pleasure and fulfillment. It is precisely
because of the powerful and integral nature of sexuality that it is "dangerous."
We should not want to make sexuality "safe" for the same reasons we do not
want to make mountains smaller; however, we must ensure that our young
people are equipped for the journey.

REFERENCES

Albert, B., Brown, S., & Flanigan, C. (Eds.). (2003). *14 and younger: The sexual
behavior of young adolescents*. Washington, DC: National Campaign to
Prevent Teen Pregnancy.

Angold, A., & Worthman, C. W. (1993). Puberty onset of gender differences in
rates of depression: A developmental, epidemiological and neuroendocrine
perspective. *Journal of Affective Disorders, 29*, 145–158.

Arnett, J. J. (1999). Adolescent storm and stress reconsidered. *American Psychologist,
54*, 317–326.

Baird, A. A., Gruber, S. A., Cohen, B. M., Renshaw, R. J., & Yureglun-Todd,
D. A. (1999). FMRI of the amygdala in children and adolescents. *American
Academy of Child and Adolescent Psychiatry, 38*, 195–199.

Bearman, P. S., & Bruckner, H. (1999). *Power in numbers: Peer effects on adolescent
girls' sexual debut and pregnancy*. Washington, DC: National Campaign to
Prevent Teen Pregnancy.

Bearman, P. S., & Bruckner, H. (2001). Promising the future: Virginity pledges
and first intercourse. *American Journal of Sociology, 106*(4), 859.

Belsky, J., Steinberg, L., & Draper, P. (1991). Childhood experience, interpersonal development, and reproductive strategy: An evolutionary theory of
socialization. *Child Development, 62*, 647–670.

Besharov, D. J., & Gardiner, K. N. (1997). Sex education and abstinence: Programs and evaluation. *Children and Youth Services Review, 19*(7), 501–506.

Bingham, C. R., & Crockett, L. J. (1996). Longitudinal adjustment patterns of
boys and girls experiencing early, middle, and late sexual intercourse.
Developmental Psychology, 32, 647–658.

Blum, R. W. (2004). Uganda AIDS prevention: A, B, C and politics. *Journal of Adolescent Health, 34*(5), 428–432.

Borawski, E. A., Ievers-Landis, C. E., Lovegreen, L. D., & Trapl, E. S. (2003). Parental monitoring, negotiated unsupervised time, and parental trust: The role of perceived parenting practices in adolescent health risk behaviors. *Journal of Adolescent Health, 33*(2), 60–70.

Bradburn, N. M., Sudman, S., Blair, E., & Stocking, C. (1978). Question threat and response bias. *Public Opinion Quarterly, 42*(2), 221–234.

Brown, J. D., Halpern, C. T., & L'Engle, K. L. (2005). Mass media as a sexual super peer for early maturing girls. *Journal of Adolescent Health, 36*(5), 420–427.

Bruckner, H., & Bearman, P. S. (2003). Dating behavior and sexual activity of young adolescents. In B. Albert, S. Brown, & C. Flanigan (Eds.), *14 and younger: The sexual behavior of young adolescents* (pp. 31–56). Washington, DC: National Campaign to Prevent Teen Pregnancy.

Buchanan, C. M., Eccles, J. S., & Becker, J. R. (1992). Are adolescents the victims of raging hormones? Evidence for activational effects of hormones on moods and behaviors at adolescence. *Psychological Bulletin, 111*, 62–107.

Byrnes, J. P. (2003). Cognitive development during adolescence. In G. R. Adams & M. D. Berzonsky (Eds.), *Blackwell handbook of adolescence* (pp. 227–246). Malden, MA: Blackwell Publishing.

Carver, K., Joyner, K., & Udry, J. R. (2003). National estimates of adolescent romantic relationships. In P. Florsheim (Ed.), *The development of romantic relationships in adolescence* (pp. 23–56). Mahwah, NJ: Lawrence Erlbaum.

Caspi, A., Lynam, D., Moffitt, T. E., & Silva, P. A. (1993). Unraveling girls' delinquency: Biological, dispositional, and contextual contributions to adolescent misbehavior. *Developmental Psychology, 29*, 19–30.

Chapin, J. R. (2000). Adolescent sex and the mass media: A developmental approach. *Adolescence, 35*(140), 799.

Chesson, H. W., Blandford, J. M., Gift, T. L., Tao, G. Y., & Irwin, K. L. (2004). The estimated direct medical cost of sexually transmitted diseases among American youth, 2000. *Perspectives on Sexual and Reproductive Health, 36*(1), 11–19.

Coley, R. L., & Chase-Lansdale, P. L. (1998). Adolescent pregnancy and parenthood—Recent evidence and future directions. *American Psychologist, 53*(2), 152–166.

Collins, R. L., Elliott, M. N., Berry, S. H., Kanouse, D. E., Kunkel, D., Hunter, S. B., et al. (2004). Watching sex on television predicts adolescent initiation of sexual behavior. *Pediatrics, 114*(3), E280–E289.

Comings, D. E., Muhleman, D., Johnson, J. P., & MacMurray, J. P. (2002). Parent-daughter transmission of the androgen receptor gene as an explanation of the effect of father absence on age of menarche. *Child Development, 73*, 1046–1051.

Cothran, M. M., & White, J. P. (2002). Adolescent behavior and sexually transmitted diseases: The dilemma of human papillomavirus. *Health Care for Women International, 23*(3), 306–319.

Cotton, S., Mills, L., Succop, P. A., Biro, F. M., & Rosenthal, S. L. (2004). Adolescent girls' perceptions of the timing of their sexual initiation: "Too young" or "just right"? *Journal of Adolescent Health, 34*(5), 453–458.

Darroch, J. E., Landry, D. J., & Oslak, S. (1999). Age differences between sexual partners in the United States. *Family Planning Perspectives, 31*(4), 160.

Darroch, J. E., Landry, D. J., & Singh, S. (2000). Changing emphases in sexuality education in U.S. public secondary schools, 1988–1999. *Family Planning Perspectives, 32*(5), 204–211.

Darroch, J. E., & Singh, S. (1999). *Why is teenage pregnancy declining? The roles of abstinence, sexual activity and contraceptive use.* Occasional report. New York: The Alan Guttmacher Institute.

Darroch, J. E., Singh, S., & Frost, J. J. (2001). Differences in teenage pregnancy rates among five developed countries: The roles of sexual activity and contraceptive use. *Family Planning Perspectives, 33*(6), 244–250, 281.

Davidson, J. K., & Moore, N. B. (1994). Masturbation and premarital sexual intercourse among college-women—Making choices for sexual fulfillment. *Journal of Sex and Marital Therapy, 20*(3), 178–199.

Diamond, L. M. (2000). Sexual identity, attractions, and behavior among young sexual-minority women over a 2-year period. *Developmental Psychology, 36*(2), 241–250.

Diamond, L. M., & Savin-Williams, R. C. (2003). The intimate relationships of sexual-minority youths. In G. Adams & M. Berzonsky (Eds.), *Blackwell handbook of adolescence* (pp. 393–411). Malden, MA: Blackwell.

DiLorio, C., Dudley, W. N., Soet, J. E., & McCarty, F. (2004). Sexual possibility situations and sexual behaviors among young adolescents: The moderating role of protective factors. *Journal of Adolescent Health, 35*(6), 528.e11–528.e20.

Ellis, B., Bates, J., Dodge, K., Fergusson, D., Horwood, L., Pettit, G., et al. (2003). Does father absence place daughters at special risk for early sexual activity and teenage pregnancy? *Child Development, 74*, 801–821.

Erikson, E. H. (1959). Identity and the life cycle. *Psychological Issues, 1*, 18–164.

Erikson, E. H. (1968). *Identity, youth, and crisis.* New York: W. W. Norton.

Fagan, J., Barnett, M., Bernd, E., & Whiteman, V. (2003). Prenatal involvement of adolescent fathers. *Fathering, 1*, 283–302.

Felice, M. E., Feinstein, R. A., Fisher, M. M., Kaplan, D. W., Olmedo, L. F., Rome, E. S., et al. (1999). Adolescent pregnancy—current trends and issues: 1998 American Academy of Pediatrics Committee on Adolescence, 1998–1999. *Pediatrics, 103*(2), 516–520.

Fiscus, L. C., Ford, C. A., & Miller, W. C. (2004). Infrequency of sexually transmitted disease screening among sexually experienced US female adolescents. *Perspectives on Sexual and Reproductive Health, 36*(6), 233–238.

Flanigan, C. (2003). Sexual activity among girls under age 15: Findings from the National Survey of Family Growth. In B. Albert, S. Brown, & C. Flanigan (Eds.), *14 and younger: The sexual behavior of young adolescents* (pp. 57–64). Washington, DC: National Campaign to Prevent Teen Pregnancy.

Flisher, A. J., & Chalton, D. O. (2001). Adolescent contraceptive non-use and covariation among risk behaviors. *Journal of Adolescent Health, 28*(3), 235–241.

Franklin, C., & Corcoran, J. (2000). Preventing adolescent pregnancy: A review of programs and practices. *Social Work, 45*(1), 40–52.

Friedman, M. S., Silvestre, A. J., Gold, M. A., Markovic, N., Savin-Williams, R. C., Huggins, J., et al. (2004). Adolescents define sexual orientation and suggest ways to measure it. *Journal of Adolescence, 27*(3), 303–317.

Garofalo, R., & Katz, E. (2001). Health care issues of gay and lesbian youth. *Current Opinion in Pediatrics, 13*(4), 298–302.

Gates, G. J., & Sonenstein, F. L. (2000). Heterosexual genital sexual activity among adolescent males: 1988 and 1995. *Family Planning Perspectives, 32*(6), 295–297, 304.

Gee, C. B., & Rhodes, J. E. (2003). Adolescent mothers' relationship with their children's biological fathers: Social support, social strain, and relationship continuity. *Journal of Family Psychology, 17*(3), 370–383.

Giedd, J., Blumenthal, J., Jeffries, N., Castellanos, F., Liu, H., Zijdenbos, A., et al. (1999). Brain development during childhood and adolescence: A longitudinal MRI study. *Nature Neuroscience, 2*, 861–863.

Gomez, C., Coyle, K. K., Gregorich, S., Marin, B. V., & Kirby, D. (2003). The development of sex-related knowledge, attitudes, perceived norms, and behaviors in a longitudinal cohort of middle school children. In B. Albert, S. Brown, & C. Flanigan (Eds.), *14 and younger: The sexual behavior of young adolescents* (pp. 67–82). Washington, DC: National Campaign to Prevent Teen Pregnancy.

Gruber, E. L., Wang, P. H., Christensen, J. S., Grube, J. W., & Fisher, D. A. (2005). Private television viewing, parental supervision, and sexual and substance use risk behaviors in adolescents. *Journal of Adolescent Health, 36*(2), 107.

Grunbaum, J. A., Kann, L., Kinchen, S., Ross, J., Hawkins, J., Lowry, R., et al. (2004). Youth risk behavior surveillance—United States, 2003 [Abridged]. *Journal of School Health, 74*(8), 307–324.

Hall, G. S. (1904). *Adolescence: Its psychology and its relations to physiology, anthropology, sociology, sex, crime, religion, and education* (Vols. 1 & 2). New York: Appleton.

Halpern, C. T., Joyner, K., Udry, J. R., & Suchindran, C. (2000). Smart teens don't have sex (or kiss much either). *Journal of Adolescent Health, 26*(3), 213–225.

Halpern, C. T., Udry, J. R., Suchindran, C., & Campbell, B. (2000). Adolescent males' willingness to report masturbation. *Journal of Sex Research, 37*(4), 327.

Halpern-Felsher, B. L., Cornell, J. L., Kropp, R. Y., & Tschann, J. M. (2005). Oral versus vaginal sex among adolescents: Perceptions, attitudes, and behavior. *Pediatrics, 115*(4), 845–851.

Harris, J. R. (1995). Where is the child's environment? A group socialization theory of development. *Psychological Review, 102*, 458–489.

Hobcraft, J., & Kiernan, K. (2001). Childhood poverty, early motherhood and adult social exclusion. *British Journal of Sociology, 52*(3), 495–517.

Hoffman, S. (1998). Teenage childbearing is not so bad after all...or is it? A review of the new literature. *Family Planning Perspectives, 30*, 236–244.

Hollander, D. (1997). Take teenagers with a grain of salt. *Family Planning Perspectives, 29*(5), 198.

Hutchinson, M. K., Jemmott, J. B., III, Jemmott, L. S., Braverman, P., & Fong, G. T. (2003). The role of mother-daughter sexual risk communication in reducing sexual risk behaviors among urban adolescent females: A prospective study. *Journal of Adolescent Health, 33*(2), 98–107.

Joffe, A. (1997). Sexually transmitted diseases. In R. Hoekelman (Ed.), *Primary Pediatric Care* (3rd ed., pp. 1577–1593). St. Louis, MO: Mosby.

Kaestle, C. E., & Halpern, C. T. (2005). Sexual activity among adolescents in romantic relationships with friends, acquaintances, or strangers. *Archives of Pediatrics and Adolescent Medicine, 159*(9), 849–853.

Kalil, A., Ziol-Guest, K. M., & Coley, R. L. (2005). Perceptions of father involvement patterns in teenage-mother families: Predictors and links to mothers' psychological adjustment. *Family Relations, 54*(2), 197–211.

Keating, D. P. (2004). Cognitive and brain development. In R. M. Lerner & L. Steinberg (Eds.), *Handbook of adolescent psychology* (2nd ed., pp. 45–84). Hoboken, NJ: John Wiley.

Kirby, D. (1991). School-based clinics—research results and their implications for future-research methods. *Evaluation and Program Planning, 14*(1/2), 35–47.

Kirby, D. (2001a). *Emerging answers: Research findings on programs to reduce teen pregnancy*. Washington, DC: National Campaign to Prevent Teen Pregnancy.

Kirby, D. (2001b). Understanding what works and what doesn't in reducing adolescent sexual risk-taking. *Family Planning Perspectives, 33*(6), 276.

Kirby, D. (2002). *Do abstinence only programs delay the initiation of sex among young people and reduce teen pregnancy?* Washington, DC: National Campaign to Prevent Teen Pregnancy.

Kirby, D., Baumler, E., Coyle, K. K., Basen-Engquist, K., Parcel, G. S., Harrist, R., et al. (2004). The "safer choices" intervention: Its impact on the sexual behaviors of different subgroups of high school students. *Journal of Adolescent Health, 35*(6), 442–452.

Kirby, D., Korpi, M., Barth, R. P., & Cagampang, H. H. (1997). The impact of the postponing sexual involvement curriculum among youths in California. *Family Planning Perspectives, 29*(3), 100–108.

Kisker, E. E., & Brown, R. S. (1996). Do school-based health centers improve adolescents' access to health care, health status, and risk-taking behavior? *Journal of Adolescent Health, 18*(5), 335–343.

Kroger, J. (2003). Identity development during adolescence. In G. R. Adams & M. D. Berzonsky (eds.), *Blackwell handbook of adolescence* (pp. 205–226). Malden, MA: Blackwell Publishing.

Kuhn, D. (1999). Metacognitive development. *Current Directions in Psychological Science, 9,* 178–181.

Larson, R., & Ham, M. (1993). Stress and "storm and stress" in early adolescence: The relationship of negative events with dysphoric affect. *Developmental Psychology, 29,* 130–140.

Lauritsen, J. L., & Swicegood, C. G. (1997). The consistency of self-reported initiation of sexual activity. *Family Planning Perspectives, 29*(5), 215–221.

Leigh, B.C., & Stacy, A.W. (1993). Alcohol outcome expectancies: Scale construction and predictive utility in higher order confirmatory models. *Psychological Assessment, 5,* 216–229.

Leitenberg, H., Detzer, M. J., & Srebnik, D. (1993). Gender differences in masturbation and the relation of masturbation experience in preadolescence and/or early adolescence to sexual behavior and sexual adjustment in young adulthood. *Archives of Sexual Behavior, 22*(2), 87.

Lerner, R. M., & Steinberg, L. (2004). The scientific study of adolescent development: Past, present, and future. In R. M. Lerner & L. Steinberg (Eds.), *Handbook of adolescent psychology* (2nd ed., pp. 1–12). Hoboken, NJ: John Wiley.

Lesko, N. (1996). Denaturalizing adolescence: The politics of contemporary representations. *Youth & Society, 28,* 139–161.

LeTourneau, N. L., Stewart, M. J., & Barnfather, A. K. (2004). Adolescent mothers: Support needs, resources, and support-education interventions. *Journal of Adolescent Health, 35*(6), 509–525.

Lewis, J., & Knijn, T. (2003). Sex education materials in the Netherlands and in England and Wales: A comparison of content, use and teaching practice. *Oxford Review of Education, 29*(1), 113–132.

Longmore, M. A., Manning, W. D., Giordano, P. C., & Rudolph, J. L. (2004). Self-esteem, depressive symptoms, and adolescents' sexual onset. *Social Psychology Quarterly, 67*(3), 279–295.

Lopresto, C. T., Sherman, M. F., & Sherman, N. C. (1985). The effects of a masturbation seminar on high-school males' attitudes, false beliefs, guilt, and behavior. *Journal of Sex Research, 21*(2), 142–156.

Macleod, A. J., & Weaver, S. M. (2003). Teenage pregnancy: Attitudes, social support and adjustment to pregnancy during the antenatal period. *Journal of Reproductive and Infant Psychology, 21*(1), 49–59.

Manlove, B. L., Ryan, S., & Franzetta, K. (2004). Contraceptive use and consistency in US teenagers' most recent sexual relationships. *Perspectives on Sexual and Reproductive Health, 36*(6), 265–275.

Manning, W. D., Longmore, M. A., & Giordano, P. C. (2000). The relationship context of contraceptive use at first intercourse. *Family Planning Perspectives, 32*(3), 104–110.

Manning, W. D., Longmore, M. A., & Giordano, P. C. (2005). Adolescents' involvement in non-romantic sexual activity. *Social Science Research, 34*(2), 384–407.

Marcia, J. E. (1980). Identity in adolescence. In J. Adelson (Ed.), *Handbook of adolescent psychology* (pp. 159–187). New York: Wiley.

Marin, B. V., Kirby, D., Hudes, E., Gomez, C., & Coyle, K. K. (2003). Youth with older boyfriends and girlfriends: Associations with sexual risk. In B. Albert, S. Brown, & C. Flanigan (Eds.), *14 and younger: The sexual behavior of young adolescents*. Washington, DC: National Campaign to Prevent Teen Pregnancy.

Marsiglio, W., Amato, P., Day, R. D., & Lamb, M. E. (2000). Scholarship on fatherhood in the 1990s and beyond. *Journal of Marriage and the Family, 62*(4), 1173.

Martin, J. A., Hamilton, B. E., Ventura, S., Menacker, F., & Park, M. M. (2002). *Births: Final data for 2000*. Retrieved September 19, 2005, from www.cdc.gov/nchs/data/nvsr/nvsr50/nvsr50_05.pdf

Milan, S., Ickovics, J. R., Kershaw, T., Lewis, J., Meade, C., Ethier, K., et al. (2004). Prevalence, course, and predictors of emotional distress in pregnant and parenting adolescents. *Journal of Consulting and Clinical Psychology, 72*(2), 328–340.

Miller, B. C. (1998). *Families matter: A research synthesis of family influences on adolescent pregnancy*. Washington, DC: National Campaign to Prevent Teen Pregnancy.

Miller, B. C., Benson, B., & Galbraith, K. A. (2001). Family relationships and adolescent pregnancy risk: A research synthesis. *Developmental Review, 21*(1), 1–38.

Moran, J. (2000). *Teaching sex: The shaping of adolescence in the 20th century*. Cambridge, MA: Harvard University Press.

National Campaign to Prevent Teen Pregnancy. (2002). *Not just another single issue: Pregnancy prevention's link to other critical social issues*. Washington, DC: Author.

National Campaign to Prevent Teen Pregnancy. (2003a). *The sexual attitudes and behavior of male teens*. Washington, DC: Author.

National Campaign to Prevent Teen Pregnancy. (2003b). *Where and when teens first have sex*. Washington, DC: Author.

Nelson, T. J. (2004). Low-income fathers. *Annual Review of Sociology, 30*, 427–451.

O'Donnell, L., Myint, U. A., O'Donnell, C. R., & Stueve, A. (2003). Long-term influence of sexual norms and attitudes on timing of sexual initiation among urban minority youth. *Journal of School Health, 73*(2), 68–75.

O'Donnell, L., Stueve, A., O'Donnell, C., Duran, R., San Doval, A., Wilson, R. F., et al. (2002). Long-term reductions in sexual initiation and sexual activity among urban middle schoolers in the Reach for Health service learning program. *Journal of Adolescent Health, 31*(1), 93–100.

Olsen, J., Weed, S., Nielsen, A., & Jensen, L. (1992). Student evaluation of sex-education programs advocating abstinence. *Adolescence, 27*(106), 369–380.

Osofsky, J., Hann, D., & Peebles, C. (1993). Adolescent parenthood: Risks and opportunities for mothers and infants. In C. Zeahah (Ed.), *Handbook of infant mental health* (pp. 106–119). New York: Guilford Press.

Parent, A., Teilmann, G., Juul, A., Skakkeback, N. E., Toppari, J., & Bourguignon, J. (2003). The timing of normal puberty and the age limits of sexual precocity: Variations around the world, secular trends, and changes after migration. *Endocrine Reviews, 24*, 668–693.

Parsons, J. T., Halkitis, P. N., Bimbi, D., & Borkowski, T. (2000). Perceptions of the benefits and costs associated with condom use and unprotected sex among late adolescent college students. *Journal of Adolescence, 23,* 377–391.

Paul, C., Fitzjohn, J., Eberhart-Phillips, J., Herbison, P., & Dickson, N. (2000). Sexual abstinence at age 21 in New Zealand: The importance of religion. *Social Science and Medicine, 51*(1), 1–10.

Piaget, J. (1952). *The origins of intelligence in children.* New York: International Universities Press.

Piaget, J. (1972). Intellectual evolution from adolescence to adulthood. *Human Development, 15,* 1–12.

Rashad, I., & Kaestner, R. (2004). Teenage sex, drugs and alcohol use: Problems identifying the cause of risky behaviors. *Journal of Health Economics, 23*(3), 493–503.

Reid, M. (2000). *Kids in trouble.* Auckland: Maxim Institute.

Remez, L. (2000). Oral sex among adolescents: Is it sex or is it abstinence? [Cover story]. *Family Planning Perspectives, 32*(6), 298.

Rogol, A. D., Roemmich, J. N., & Clark, P. A. (2002). Growth at puberty. *Journal of Adolescent Health, 31,* 192–200.

Rose, A., Koo, H. P., Bhaskar, B., Anderson, K., White, G., & Jenkins, R. R. (2005). The influence of primary caregivers on the sexual behavior of early adolescents. *Journal of Adolescent Health, 37*(2), 135–144.

Rosenblum, G. D., & Lewis, M. (2003). Emotional development in adolescence. In G. R. Adams & M. D. Berzonsky (Eds.), *Blackwell handbook of adolescence* (pp. 26–89). Malden, MA: Blackwell Publishing.

Rosengard, C., Adler, N. E., Gurvey, J. E., Dunlop, M. B., Tschann, J. M., Millstein, S. G., et al. (2001). Protective role of health values in adolescents' future intentions to use condoms. *Journal of Adolescent Health, 29*(3), 200–207.

Sanders, S. A., & Reinisch, J. M. (1999). Would you say you "had sex" if . . . ? *Journal of the American Medical Association, 281*(3), 275–277.

Savin-Williams, R. C. (1994). Verbal and physical abuse as stressors in the lives of lesbian, gay male, and bisexual youths: Associations with school problems, running away, substance abuse, prostitution, and suicide. *Journal of Consulting and Clinical Psychology, 62,* 261–269.

Savin-Williams, R. C., & Diamond, L. (2004). Sex. In R. M. Lerner & L. Steinberg (Eds.), *Handbook of adolescent psychology* (2nd ed., pp. 189–231). Hoboken, NJ: John Wiley.

Schuster, M. A., Bell, R. M., & Kanouse, D. E. (1996). The sexual practices of adolescent virgins: Genital sexual activities of high school students who have never had vaginal intercourse. *American Journal of Public Health, 86*(11), 1570.

Schwartz, I. M. (1999). Sexual activity prior to coital initation: A comparison between males and females. *Archives of Sexual Behavior, 28*(1), 63.

Siegel, D. M., Aten, M. J., & Roghmann, K. J. (1998). Self-reported honesty among middle and high school students responding to a sexual behavior questionnaire. *Journal of Adolescent Health, 23*(1), 20–28.

Siegler, R. S. (1998). *Children's thinking* (3rd ed.). Upper Saddle River, NJ: Prentice-Hall.

Sieverding, J. A., Adler, N., Witt, S., & Ellen, J. (2005). The influence of parental monitoring on adolescent sexual initiation. *Archives of Pediatrics and Adolescent Medicine, 159*(8), 724–729.

Singh, S., & Darroch, J. E. (2000). Adolescent pregnancy and childbearing: Levels and trends in developed countries. *Family Planning Perspectives, 32*(1), 14–23.

Smetana, J., & Gaines, C. (1999). Adolescent-parent conflict in middle-class African-American families. *Child Development, 66*, 229–316.

Smith, E. A., & Udry, J. R. (1985). Coital and non-coital sexual behaviors of white and black adolescents. *American Journal of Public Health, 75*(10), 1200.

Speizer, I. S., Magnani, R. J., & Colvin, C. E. (2003). The effectiveness of adolescent reproductive health interventions in developing countries: A review of the evidence. *Journal of Adolescent Health, 33*(5), 324–348.

Stouthamer-Loeber, M., & Wei, E. H. (1998). The precursors of young fatherhood and its effect on delinquency of teenage males. *Journal of Adolescent Health, 22*(1), 56–65.

St. Pierre, T. L., Mark, M. M., Kaltreider, D. L., & Aikin, K. J. (1995). A 27-month evaluation of a sexual-activity prevention program in boys and girls clubs across the nation. *Family Relations, 44*(1), 69–77.

Strassberg, D. S., & Lowe, K. (1995). Volunteer bias in sexuality research. *Archives of Sexual Behavior, 24*(4), 369.

Stueve, A., & O'Donnell, L. N. (2005). Early alcohol initiation and subsequent sexual and alcohol risk behaviors among urban youths. *American Journal of Public Health, 95*(5), 887–893.

Susman, E. J., & Rogol, A. (2004). Puberty and psychological development. In R. M. Lerner & L. Steinberg (Eds.), *Handbook of adolescent psychology* (2nd ed., pp. 45–84). Hoboken, NJ: John Wiley.

Terry, E., & Manlove, J. (2000). *Trends in sexual activity and contraceptive use among teens.* Washington, DC: National Campaign to Prevent Teen Pregnancy.

Terry-Humen, E., & Manlove, B. L. (2003). Dating and sexual experiences among middle school youth: Analyses of the NLSY97. In B. Albert, S. Brown, & C. Flanigan (Eds.), *14 and younger: The sexual behavior of young adolescents* (pp. 17–30). Washington, DC: National Campaign to Prevent Teen Pregnancy.

Terry-Humen, E., Manlove, J., & Moore, K. (2005). *Playing catch-up: How children born to teen mothers fare.* Washington, DC: National Campaign to Prevent Teen Pregnancy.

Thornberry, T. P., Smith, C. A., & Howard, G. J. (1997). Risk factors for teenage fatherhood. *Journal of Marriage and the Family, 59*(3), 505–522.

UNAIDS/WHO. (2004). *AIDS epidemic update, December 2004.* Geneva: Joint United Nations Programme on HIV/AIDS (UN-AIDS) and World Health Organisation (WHO).

Upchurch, D. M., Aneshensel, C. S., Sucoff, C. A., & Levy-Storms, L. (1999). Neighborhood and family contexts of adolescent sexual activity. *Journal of Marriage and the Family, 61*(4), 920–933.

Upchurch, D. M., Lillard, L. A., Aneshensel, C. S., & Li, N. F. (2002). Inconsistencies in reporting the occurrence and timing of first intercourse among adolescents. *Journal of Sex Research, 39*(3), 197.

Upchurch, D. M., Mason, W. M., Kusunoki, Y., Johnson, M., & Kriechbaum, J. (2004). Social and behavioral determinants of self-reported STD among adolescents. *Perspectives on Sexual and Reproductive Health, 36*(6), 276–287.

Ward, L. M. (2003). Understanding the role of entertainment media in the sexual socialization of American youth: A review of empirical research. *Developmental Review, 23*(3), 347–388.

Warner, L., Newman, D. R., Austin, H. D., Kamb, M. L., Douglas, J. M., Malotte, C. K., et al. (2004). Condom effectiveness for reducing transmission of gonorrhea and chlamydia: The importance of assessing partner infection status. *American Journal of Epidemiology, 159*(3), 242.

Weinberg, M. S., Lottes, I. L., & Shaver, F. M. (1995). Swedish or American heterosexual college youth: Who is more permissive? *Archives of Sexual Behavior, 24*(4), 409.

Weinstock, H., Berman, S., & Cates, W., Jr. (2004). Sexually transmitted diseases among American youth: Incidence and prevalence estimates, 2000. *Perspectives on Sexual and Reproductive Health, 36*(1), 6–10.

Whitaker, D. J., & Miller, K. S. (2000). Parent-adolescent discussions about sex and condoms: Impact on peer influences of sexual risk behavior. *Journal of Adolescent Research, 15*(2), 251–273.

Whitaker, D. J., Miller, K. S., & Clark, L. F. (2000). Reconceptualizing adolescent sexual behavior: Beyond did they or didn't they? *Family Planning Perspectives, 32*(3), 111.

Whitehead, B., Wilcox, B., & Rostosky, S. (2001). *Keeping the faith: The role of religion and faith communities in preventing teen pregnancy.* Washington, DC: National Campaign to Prevent Teen Pregnancy.

Widdice, L., Cornell, J., Liang, W., & Halpern-Felsher, B. (2005). Teens tell us the risks and benefits of having sex. *Journal of Adolescent Health, 36,* 107–108.

Winer, R. L., Lee, S.-K., Hughes, J. P., Adam, D. E., Kiviat, N. B., & Koutsky, L. A. (2003). Genital human papillomavirus infection: Incidence and risk factors in a cohort of female university students. *American Journal of Epidemiology, 157*(3), 218.

Young, A. M., & d'Arcy, H. (2005). Older boyfriends of adolescent girls: The cause or a sign of the problem? *Journal of Adolescent Health, 36*(5), 410–419.

5

Sexual Behavior in the United States

Tom W. Smith ◆

INTRODUCTION

Sexual behavior is not only of basic biological importance but also of central social importance. Not only does it perpetuate the human species, but it is also the central behavior around which families are formed and defined, a vital aspect of the psychological well-being of individuals, and a component of a variety of social problems. Among current concerns tied in part to sexual behavior are (1) the familial problems of marital harmony and divorce; (2) criminal problems of rape, incest, child molestation, and prostitution; (3) reproductive problems of infertility, sterility, unwanted and mistimed pregnancies, and abortion; and (4) health problems related to sexually transmitted diseases (STDs).

Moreover, with the coming of human immunodeficiency virus (HIV), the problem of STDs has taken on increasing urgency (Centers for Disease Control and Prevention [CDC], 2004a; Yankauer, 1994). Deaths from acquired immunodeficiency syndrome (AIDS) rose at a rapid pace in the 1980s and early 1990s (CDC, 1995a). By 1992, AIDS had become the number one cause of death among men aged 25 to 44. Cases diagnosed as AIDS peaked in 1993, and rates of AIDS-related deaths peaked in 1995. Both have since declined substantially; cases of AIDS have fallen by more than two-thirds and AIDS-related deaths by over 80 percent since 2001 (CDC, 1998a, 2001; Ventura, Anderson, Martin, & Smith, 1998). Most HIV infections have resulted from sexual behavior, and heterosexual intercourse is an increasingly common mode of transmission (CDC, 1994, 1998a, 2004a).

Because of the importance of sexual behavior in general and of problems related to unsafe sexual activities, we need to arm ourselves with a thorough, scientifically reliable understanding of sexual behavior and to study high-risk behavior (Hewitt & Beverley, 1996). This chapter outlines what is currently known about American sexual behavior. The emphasis will be on general trends and on sociodemographic differences within the following areas:

1. Premarital and adolescent sexual activity, including cohabitation and non-marital births.
2. Adult and general sexual behavior, including extramarital relations, gender of sexual partners, frequency of sexual intercourse, and sexual inactivity.
3. The impact of HIV on sexual behavior, including reported changes in sexual behavior, number of sexual partners, and relationships between sexual partners.

PREMARITAL AND ADOLESCENT SEXUAL ACTIVITY

Premarital sexual intercourse became increasingly common over the last century (Smith, 2003, table 1A; see also Hopkins, 1998; Joyner & Laumann, 2001; Whitbeck, Simons, & Goldberg, 1996). This increase was not merely the result of the so-called sexual revolution of the 1960s. The change was under way for decades prior to the 1960s and has continued since that time. Rates of sex before marriage among men were moderately high even from the beginning (61 percent of men born before 1910 report having had sexual intercourse before marriage) and climbed steadily. Women had relatively low rates of premarital intercourse before that era (only 12 percent of those born before 1910 had premarital sexual intercourse), but their rates grew more rapidly than those of men, and the gap between men and women narrowed significantly over time. By the 1980s (roughly the 1965–1970 birth cohort), women had almost as much sexual experience as men prior to marriage (in 1988, 60 percent of men and 51.5 percent of women aged 15 to 19 had engaged in premarital sex). This increase in premarital sexual experience is confirmed by community studies (Trocki, 1992; Wyatt, Peters, & Guthrie, 1988) and longitudinal panels (Udry, Bauman, & Morris, 1975).

In the early 1990s, the century-long increase in the level of premarital and adolescent sexual activity reached a peak and then declined for the first time in decades (see Abma & Sonenstein, 2000; Bachrach, 1998; Besharov & Gardiner, 1997; Peipert et al., 1997; Singh & Darroch, 1999; Smith, 1998, table 1A; Stossel, 1997). This decrease was greater for males than for females, but both genders showed a leveling off and then some reversal or decline.

With the increase in levels of premarital sexual intercourse came a decrease in the age at first intercourse (see Smith, 2003, table 1B). In 1970, 5 percent of women aged 15 and 32 percent aged 17 were sexually experienced; by 1988, this had grown to 26 percent of 15-year-olds and 51 percent of 17-year-olds (see also Hofferth, Kahn, & Baldwin, 1987; Kahn, Kalsbeek, & Hofferth, 1988). This trend may also have leveled off and possibly reversed to some extent although the evidence is still inconclusive (see Smith, 1998, table 1B).

When the increase in rates of premarital sexual intercourse is coupled with the delayed age at first marriage, the result is an expanded period of sexual activity prior to marriage for the majority of young men and women (Bachrach & Horn, 1987; Ehrhardt & Wasserheit, 1991; Laumann, Gagnon, Michael, & Michaels, 1994). Between 1960 and 2000, the median age at first marriage rose from 22.8 to 26.8 years for men and from 20.3 to 25.1 for women. For women, the average age at first premarital intercourse in 1960 was about 19 (Bachrach & Horn, 1987; Turner, Miller, & Moses, 1989), which meant a short period of premarital sexual activity. In 1990, the average age at first intercourse was 16.9 for women (CDC, 1992a, 1992b, 1995b), meaning an average premarital sexual activity period of 8.2 years. For men, the period of premarital sexual activity now averages 10.7 years (age at first intercourse is 16.1 and first marriage is at 26.8 years).

Along with this wider window of opportunity for sex before marriage, the number of lifetime sexual partners has increased for both men and women (see Smith, 2003, table 1C). Between the pre-1910 birth cohort and the 1940–1949 birth cohort, the percentage of men with two or more premarital sexual partners rose from 49 percent to 73 percent, while for women the increase was from 3 percent to 26 percent. This trend continued until recent years. For example, among sexually experienced women aged 15 to 19 living in metropolitan areas, 38 percent had two or more sexual partners in 1971 compared to 61 percent in 1988. More recently, there is evidence of a slight reversal of this trend. The Youth Risk Behavior Surveillance (YRBS) (CDC, 2004b) reveals that the percentage of male high school students with four or more sexual partners declined from 1989 to 2001, but the trend among females was less clear.

Cohabitation

The rise in premarital and adolescent sexual activity, coupled with delays in marriage, has led to more unmarried people living together. Since 1970, the rate of living together outside of marriage has increased more than sixfold, from 1.1 percent to 7.4 percent of couples (see Bramlett & Mosher, 2002; Smith, 1998, table 2). Similarly, the proportion of single mothers who were cohabiting grew from 2 percent in 1970 to 12 percent in 1995 (London, 1998). While the proportion of cohabiting couples at any one point in time remains relatively small, a large and growing percentage of couples live together at some point in their relationships. Currently, over one-third of adults in their midtwenties to midthirties cohabited before their first marriage, and half of this age-group has cohabited at some point in their lives (see Smith, 1998, table 3A). Cohabitation after a failed first marriage and between subsequent marriages is even more common. According to the General Social Survey (GSS), among those 25 to 44 years old who are in a second marriage, 61 percent cohabited with their new spouse before marriage (Davis, Smith, & Marsden, 2003).

Rates of cohabitation are fairly consistent for both sexes and for most ethnic and racial groups. Higher rates occur among younger adults, the divorced, separated, never married, those living in urban areas, and those who attend church less frequently (see Smith, 1998, table 3B). Cohabitation is usually a short-term arrangement, leading to either marriage or a breakup after about a year (median duration is 1.3 years) (Bumpass & Sweet, 1989; Thomson & Colella, 1992; Thornton, 1988).

Cohabitation has often been characterized as a trial marriage, which is fairly accurate: in 40 percent of cases it leads to marriage within two years, and 60 percent of cohabiting couples eventually marry (Bumpass & Sweet, 1989). However, marriages formed after cohabitation are usually less stable and more likely to end in divorce than marriages not preceded by living together (Axinn & Thornton, 1992; Brown & Booth, 1996; Clarkberg, Stolzenberg, & Waite, 1995; DeMaris & MacDonald, 1993; DeMaris & Rao, 1992; Lillard, Brien, & Waite, n.d.; Popenoe, 1993; Thomson & Colella, 1992). Cohabitation thus does not seem to serve very well the function of a trial marriage (Popenoe).

Unmarried persons who are cohabiting have fewer sexual partners than unmarried individuals who are not, but more sexual partners than married couples (Waite & Joyner, 1996). For example, according to the GSS (Davis et al., 2003), married persons averaged 1.01 partners over the preceding year, the never married who were cohabiting had 1.39 partners, and the noncohabiting never married had 1.67 partners. That fact, along with the temporary nature of most cohabiting relationships, makes living together riskier than marriage when it comes to STDs (Kost & Forrest, 1992; Turner et al., 1989).

Nonmarital Births

With the growing acceptance of sexual activity prior to marriage, the connection between marriage and procreation has also lessened. In the 1960s (and presumably before), when premarital sexual intercourse resulted in conception, it usually resulted in marriage before the child was born (see Driscoll et al., 1999; Smith, 1998, table 4; South, 1999). Since that time, the likelihood of unmarried parents getting married before the birth of their child has steadily fallen. By the 1990s, fewer than 25 percent of women who conceived before marriage got married before the child's birth.

As a result of the higher level of premarital sexual activity and the decline in marriages after a conception but prior to birth, there has been a large increase in out-of-marriage births (Miller & Heaton, 1991; see Smith, 2003, table 5). In 1960, only 5 percent of all births were to unmarried women. This climbed to 14 percent by 1975 and 33 percent by 1994. Then, after over thirty years of increase, the rate leveled off between 1994 and 2000 at approximately 33 percent of all births being to unmarried women.

The trend in the United States has been parallel to that in similar Western and industrialized cultures. While the percent of births to unmarried mothers climbed from 5 percent in 1960 to 33 percent in 1998 in the United States, it rose from 5 percent to 38 percent in Great Britain, from 4 percent to 28 percent in Canada, and from 6 percent to 40 percent in France (Teitler, 2002; U.S. Census Bureau, 2001).

The rate of increase in births to unmarried women has been much greater for whites than for African Americans. For whites, the percent of unmarried births has increased over elevenfold from 2.3 percent of all births in 1960 to 27.1 percent in 2000, while the number for African Americans grew from 21.6 percent in 1960 to 70.4 percent in 1994 (and then down to 68.5 percent by 2000). While the black-to-white ratio has fallen from a little over 9:1 in 1960 to under to 3:1 in 1990s, the gap between African Americans and whites rose from 19 percentage points in 1960 to 44 to 46 percentage points from 1980 to 1996 (with a peak in 1993). The cumulative difference between whites and African Americans is further shown by the fact that by ages 30 to 34, only 23 percent of never-married white women have given birth, while 69 percent of never-married African American women have had a child (Bachu, 1991, 1995; Loomis & Landale, 1994).

While both whites and African Americans have a greater number of births occurring outside of marriage, these increases reflect distinct patterns for these groups (see Smith, 1998, table 5). For whites, the unmarried birth rate (number of births to unmarried women per 1,000 unmarried women aged 15–44) rose throughout the period. It increased more than four times, from 9 in 1960 to 37–39 in 1994–2000. For African Americans, the rate was quite variable over time. It fell from 98 in 1960 to 79 in 1985 before climbing again to 91–93 in 1989–1990. In the early 1990s, this rate declined again, falling to 71.5 in 1999.

In addition, there are many unplanned births in the United States (Abma, Chandra, Mosher, Peterson, & Piccinino, 1997; Williams, 1991). Of women aged 15 to 44 who had a child in 1995, 28 percent reported that they had an unintended birth, and this was 36 percent for women aged 40 to 44. Of those with an unintended birth, 80 percent described the birth as mistimed and 20 percent as unwanted.

In brief, over the last century, premarital sexual activity became more widespread, sexual initiation started at younger ages, the period of premarital sexual activity lengthened, and the number of premarital sexual partners increased. This expansion in premarital sexual activity in turn led to major increases in cohabitation and childbearing among unmarried persons.

During the 1990s, however, a small but historic reversal of some of these trends occurred. The level of premarital and adolescent sexual activity leveled off and, in some aspects, declined, and the proportion of births outside of marriage reached a plateau. These changes are partial rather than across the board (e.g., levels of cohabitation continue to rise) and even those behaviors that have leveled off or reversed are near record-high rates. But even limited changes to a century-long trend are highly notable and potentially important from a public-health perspective.

ADULT AND GENERAL SEXUAL BEHAVIOR

Compared to the amount of information available on premarital and adolescent sexual behavior, there has been little scientifically reliable data on the sexual behavior of adults or of the population in general until recently (Aral, 1994; di Mauro, 1995; Seidman & Rieder, 1994). Moreover, the dearth of representative and credible studies has created a vacuum that has been filled by unrepresentative and sensational misinformation from popular magazines, sex gurus, and others. In this section we review what is known about extramarital relations, sexual orientation, frequency of sexual intercourse, and sexual inactivity.

Extramarital Relations

There are probably more scientifically worthless "facts" on extramarital relations than on any other facet of human behavior. Popular magazines (e.g., *Redbook, Psychology Today, Cosmopolitan*), advice columnists (Dear Abby and Joyce Brothers), pop sexologists (e.g., Morton Hunt and Shere Hite) have all conducted or reported on "studies" of extramarital relations. These studies typically report extremely high levels of extramarital activity (Gibbs, Hamil, & Magruder-Habib, 1991; Reinisch, Sanders, & Ziemba-Davis, 1988; Smith, 1989, 1991b). Hite, for example, reported that 70 percent of women who have been married five or more years "are having sex outside of their marriage" (Smith, 1988). These questionable sources also often claim that extramarital relations have become much more common over time. Joyce Brothers (1990), for example, claimed that 50 percent of married women were having sex outside of marriage, twice the number of the previous generation.

However, representative scientific surveys (Choi, Catania, & Dolcini, 1994; Forste & Tanfer, 1996; Greeley, 1994; Greeley, Michael, & Smith, 1990; Laumann et al., 1994; Leigh, Temple, & Trocki, 1993; Tanfer, 1994; Treas & Giesen, 1996, 2000) indicate that extramarital relations are in fact much less prevalent than claimed (see Smith, 2003, table 6). The best estimates suggest that in a given year, approximately 3 to 4 percent of currently married people have a sexual partner other than their spouse. Over 90 percent of women and over 75 percent of men report being faithful to their spouses throughout their marriage (Laumann et al.).

There is little reliable information on the prevalence of extramarital relations before 1988. Some indirect evidence suggests that extramarital relations may have increased across recent generations. The reported rates in 2002 were 13 percent among those 18 to 29 years old, and 20 percent among those 40 to 49 (see Smith, 2003, table 7). It then falls to 9.5 percent among those 70 and older. Since these are lifetime rates, one would normally expect them either to increase across age-groups or to increase until a plateau is reached (this would be the case if few first-time extramarital relations were started among older adults). The leveling off and then the drop among those 50 and older suggests that members of birth cohorts before about 1940 were less likely to engage in extramarital relations than are spouses from more recent generations (Greeley, 1994; Laumann et al., 1994).

Extramarital relations are apparently more common among younger adults. This is probably a function of younger adults having been married a shorter period of time and the difficulty shifting from a premarital pattern of multiple sexual partners to an exclusive monogamous partnership; related to that trend, recent marriages are more likely to end in divorce than be long-term relationships. The rates of extramarital relations are about twice as high among husbands as among wives (see Smith, 2003, table 7). Extramarital relations are also more common among African Americans, those with lower incomes, those who attend church less frequently, those who have been separated or divorced (including those who have remarried), and those who are unhappy with their marriage. It also may be more frequent among residents of large cities, but the overall relationship with community type is fairly small and somewhat inconsistent. Finally, extramarital relations do not vary significantly by education level.

Same-Sex Sexual Interactions

Few debates have been as contentious as the controversy over the sexual orientation of Americans (Billy, Tanfer, Grady, & Klepinger, 1993; Michaels, 1998; Stokes & McKiran, 1993; Swann, 1993). The gay and lesbian communities have long adopted 10 percent as the proportion of the population that is homosexual. However, a series of recent national studies (see Smith, 1998, table 8A) indicate that only about 2 to 3 percent of sexually active men and 1 to 2 percent of sexually active women identify as gay and lesbian, respectively (see also Anderson & Stall, 2002; Black, Gates, Sanders, & Taylor, 2000; Butler, 2000; Horowitz, Weis, & Laflin, 2001; Sell & Becker, 2001). These national estimates are consistent with figures from local communities in the United States (Blair, 1999; Guterbock, 1993; McQuillan, Ezzati-Rice, Siller, Visscher, & Hurley, 1994; Rogers & Turner, 1991; Trocki, 1992), indirect measurements (Aguilar & Hardy, 1991), and statistics from other comparable countries such as Great Britain, France, Norway, and Denmark (Biggar & Melbye, 1992; Diamond, 1993; Johnson, Wadsworth, Wellings, Bradshaw, & Field, 1992; Melbye & Biggar, 1992; Sandfort, Hubert, Bajos, & Bos, 1998; Spira, Bajos, Bejin, & Beltzer, 1992; Sundet, Magnus, Kvalem, Groennesby, & Bakketeig, 1989; see also Smith, 2003, table 8B).

Rates of same-sex sexual activity increase as the reference period is extended. Recent figures (see Smith, 2003, table 9B) indicate that 3.4 percent of sexually active males have had a male sexual partner in the preceding twelve months, 4.1 percent during the previous five years, and 4.9 percent since age 18 (see also Michael, Laumann, & Gagnon, 1993; Smith, 1991a).[1] As the time frame is lengthened, the percentage of men with exclusively male partners declines. Over the preceding twelve months, 2.8 percent of men identify as gay and 0.6 percent as bisexual; over the last five years, 2.7 percent are gay and 1.4 percent are bisexual; and since age 18, fewer than 1 percent of men identify as gay and 4 percent as bisexual. Most of those who report having both male and female sexual partners since age 18 report only opposite sex partners during the preceding year (Smith, 1991a). Lesbians follow these same patterns.

There is little reliable evidence on whether sexual orientation has changed before the late 1980s. In terms of attitudes, levels of approval of homosexuality declined slightly from 1973 to 1991, but then rose notably during 1992–2000 (Davis et al., 2003; Laumann et al., 1994; Smith, 1994). Studies of male and female homosexuality both in the United States and in Europe regularly find a higher proportion of gay men than lesbians (see Hubert, Bajos, & Sandfort, 1998; Johnson, Wadsworth, Wellings, & Field, 1994; Sandfort et al., 1998; Smith, 1998, tables 8A and 8B; Spira, Bajos, & Ducot, 1994; Wells & Sell, 1990).[2]

Sexual orientation does not vary much across sociodemographic groups (see Smith, 2003, table 9). The most distinctive pattern for both gays and lesbians is that they are less likely to have been married. About 60 percent of those with same-sex partners during the previous twelve months have never been married, compared to the 16 percent of female heterosexuals and 21 percent of male heterosexuals. Second, gays, but not lesbians, are distinctive in congregating in the largest central cities. About 8.8 percent of men in large central cities have had a same-sex partner in the last year, as have 9.6 percent over the last five years and 11.7 percent since age 18. Rates are lowest outside of metropolitan areas. The relative concentration of gay men in large urban centers also occurs in Europe (Johnson et al., 1992; Spira et al., 1992). Lesbians, like gays, are underrepresented in rural areas. Third, more gays and lesbians are found in the lower-income categories, but the relationship is stronger for men than for women. Fourth, race is only weakly related to sexual orientation. Fifth, being gay is unrelated to education, but lifetime lesbian activity appears higher among those with graduate degrees. Sixth, lesbians are more common among younger age-groups. This could indicate an increase in homosexual activity among women across cohorts (see Rogers & Turner, 1991) or it could be a life-cycle effect. Gays show a similar but less pronounced pattern. Finally, lesbians, but not gays, attend church less frequently than heterosexuals. About 4.2 percent of women who rarely attend church have had a female sexual partner in the last year compared to only 1.7 percent of those who attend regularly.

Frequency of Sexual Intercourse

There is some evidence that the frequency of heterosexual intercourse rose from the 1960s to the 1970s (Trussell & Westoff, 1980) and may have declined in the 1980s. Among teenage males aged 17 to 19 living in metro-politan areas, the rate fell from 59.8 times per year in 1979 to 39.0 in 1988 (Sonenstein, Pleck, & Ku, 1991), but among all males aged 17.5 to 19, it rose from 30 to 49 times per year between 1988 and 1991 (Ku et al., 1993). Among unmarried women aged 20 to 29, the rate showed a more modest decline from 59.8 in 1983 to 56.0 in 1988–1993 (Davis et al. 2003; Tanfer & Cubbins, 1992). However, no meaningful change has been occurring among all adults since 1988. On average, adults engage in sexual intercourse about 62 times per year, a little over once a week (see James, 1998; Smith, 2003, table 10A).

The overall adult average is relatively uninformative, however, since the frequency of sexual intercourse varies significantly across sociodemographic groups (see Smith, 2003, table 10B). The factor accounting for most differ-ences in frequency of intercourse is age. Among those aged 18 to 29, the average frequency of intercourse is near 85 times per year. This declines steadily to 63 for those in their forties and to 10.5 for those 70 and older. Among the married, the decline is even more striking, dropping from 110 times per year for those under 30 to 18 for those 70 and older. This pattern applies to both husbands and wives. This age-related pattern is nearly identical to the one reported in the 1988 National Survey of Families and Households (Hughes & Gove, 1992) and is consistent with a large number of other studies (Call, Sprecher, & Schwartz, 1996; Feldman, Goldstein, Hatzichristou, Krane, & McKinlay, 1994; Hawton, Gath, & Day, 1994; Jasso, 1985, 1986; Kahn & Udry, 1986; Laumann et al., 1994; Leigh et al., 1993; National Council on the Aging, 1998; Rao & VandenHeuvel, 1995; Tanfer & Cubbins, 1992; Udry, 1980; Udry, Deven, & Coleman, 1982; Udry & Morris, 1978).

This decline in frequency of sexual intercourse within marriages is ex-plained by several factors. First, the so-called honeymoon effect leads to the highest rates of intercourse among the recently married, and those recently married tend to be younger (Greenblat, 1983; James, 1981, 1998). Second, biological aging increases the likelihood of health problems, including sexual difficulties (Feldman et al., 1994; Leiblum, 1990; Levy, 1992; McKinlay & Feldman, 1992; Morokoff, 1988; Schiavi, 1990, 1992). As a result, even among couples who rate their marriages as very happy (Davis, Smith, &

Marsden, 2003) and those who say they are still "in love" (Greeley, 1991), frequency of intercourse declines with age. Third, some research indicates that the quality of sexual activity declines with marital duration which might reduce the frequency (Liu, 2003).

Marital status also influences sexual activity (see Smith, 2003, table 10B; Wade & DeLamater, 2002). Frequency of sexual intercourse is greatest among married couples (with those remarried slightly exceeding those in their first marriage probably because of the honeymoon effect). The never married and divorced have lower rates, probably because of less continuous and convenient availability of a partner. The widowed have by far the lowest rates, a function of their age as well as lack of a partner. The higher rates of intercourse among married persons compared to unmarried persons are even more apparent when age is taken into consideration. Sexual activity is 25 to 30 percent higher among the married compared to the nonmarried at various ages. Among the married, intercourse is more frequent among those who have happier marriages (Smith, 1991a; Waite & Joyner, 1996). Interestingly, one national survey reported that the highest frequency of intercourse occurred among cohabiting couples (Laumann et al., 1994), perhaps due to the fact that most of those relationships are relatively new.

Husbands and wives generally closely agree on the frequency of intercourse, whether reporting jointly or separately (Bachrach, Evans, Ellison, & Stolley, 1992; Smith, 1992a, 1992b). However, unmarried men and women differ considerably, with men reporting more sexual activity than women do (Bachrach et al.); this statistical anomaly holds up even after accounting for the greater number of widowed women in the population.

A multivariate analysis indicates that higher rates of sexual intercourse are separately and independently related to (a) being younger, (b) having been married less than three years, and (c) rating one's marriage as happy. It is unrelated to gender when controlling for these other factors (Davis et al., 2003).

Frequency of sexual activity also decreases as church attendance increases. While this is somewhat related to the fact that church attendance increases with age, there is still a decline controlling for age. There are few differences in intercourse frequency across racial/ethnic groups, community type, education level, or income. When these factors do seem to affect frequency of intercourse, it can usually be explained by age and/or marital status. Likewise, frequency does not vary if one or both partners are employed (Hyde, DeLamater, & Durik, 2001).

Sexual Inactivity

Sexual inactivity can take three distinct forms: (1) the period prior to first sexual intercourse, (2) periods of extended inactivity after first intercourse and prior to last intercourse, and (3) a period of inactivity after last intercourse. The first has been dealt with above in the discussion of premarital sexual relations. The latter two are discussed here, although it is difficult to distinguish between them.

Sexual inactivity appears to have modestly declined since the early 1980s (see Smith, 2003, table 11). For women of childbearing age and all adults, the proportion not engaging in sex over extended periods (three to twelve months) has decreased in the late 1980s and early 1990s. However, sexual inactivity has increased since 1996.

For adults, there is a U-shaped curve with sexual inactivity most frequent among the youngest and the oldest. Sexual inactivity among the elderly is fairly common and is a function of aging, poor health, and unavailability of a partner. As we saw in the section on frequency of sexual intercourse, sexual activity decreases markedly with age even when a partner is available, perhaps due to habituation or health problems. Higher rates of sexual inactivity are due to a decline in frequency of sexual intercourse among those remaining sexually active and also an increase in the percentage of sexually inactive persons. Among those over 70 years old, 61 percent are not currently sexually active. In this age-group, sexual abstinence occurs in 33 percent of married persons; for unmarried adults, it is closer to 90 percent (see Smith, 1998, table 11).

Sexual inactivity is much less common among younger adults. Among married young adults aged 18 to 49, only 1.0 to 2.4 percent are completely sexually inactive. Virtually every case of sexual inactivity in this age-group is associated with health problems and relationship dissatisfaction (Smith, 1992a; see also Donnelly, 1993; Edwards & Booth, 1976). While 6 percent of married couples of all ages were sexually inactive over the preceding year (Davis et al., 2003), as many as 16 percent of married couples have not engaged in sexual intercourse in the previous four weeks (Donnelly; see also Dolcini et al., 1993). Sexual abstinence is much higher among the nonmarried, ranging between 15 percent and 28 percent for those under 50.

Most other sociodemographic differences are small and merely reflect underlying differences in age and/or marital status, but sexual inactivity is lower in households with higher incomes. While there have been significant increases in all aspects of premarital and adolescent sexual activity, there is little evidence of similar trends in adult sexual behavior. Moreover, adult sexual behavior appears to be more restrained and traditional than it has commonly been portrayed.

THE IMPACT OF HIV ON SEXUAL BEHAVIOR

AIDS is a potentially deadly and infectious disease that is mainly transmitted through tainted blood products, sexual intercourse, and the sharing of needles by users of illicit injection drugs. With the safeguarding of the blood supply, current transmission usually occurs through sexual activity or the sharing of needles with an HIV-positive individual. The only means of restricting the spread of the virus is to adopt safer sexual practices and injection drug use behaviors.

On the one hand, the long latency period of HIV greatly complicates matters since infected people are often not aware of the fact and can transmit the virus to others. On the other hand, since the mid-1980s over 90 percent of the public have known that HIV is spread by sexual intercourse, and knowledge about HIV in general has grown over time (CDC, 1998b, 2000; Herek, Capitanio, & Widaman, 2002; Rogers, Singer, & Imperio, 1993; Singer, Rogers, & Corcoran, 1987).[3] Given the existence of widespread, if imperfect, knowledge about the role of sexual intercourse in spreading HIV, the question arises whether sexual behavior has been modified in light of the known risk.

Overall Changes in Sexual Behavior

A number of studies have asked people whether they have changed their sexual behavior because of HIV (see Smith, 2003, table 12) or have taken steps to avoid exposure to HIV (see Smith, 2003, table 13). Early surveys in 1986–1987 showed that only about 7 to 11 percent of adults reported any precautionary behavior change. At that time, these rates of behavior change were commonly seen as indicating that people were either not informed about the risk of HIV or were not reacting responsibly to these risks. But recent studies on sexual orientation, extramarital relations, and sexual abstinence (see Smith, 2003, tables 6, 9, and 11) indicate that the number of people at risk was in fact smaller than initially feared. And if relatively fewer people were engaged in risky sexual behavior, it would be understandable that few reported altering their behavior. This was directly supported by a 1987 Gallup question in which 68 percent reported they had not changed their behavior because they were not at risk. Likewise, the low level of behavior change among the married (3 to 12 percent) compared to the nonmarried (17.5 to 51 percent) reflects the lower level of risky behavior among married people (see Smith, 2003, table 12). Similarly, more change has been reported by higher-risk groups such as younger adults and some persons from minority groups.[4]

Of the individuals reporting a change in sexual behavior because of the concern about HIV, about 45 to 50 percent report reducing their number of sexual partners—including having only one partner and getting married—20 to 35 percent cite the use of condoms, 17 to 30 percent indicate they have sex less frequently or abstain completely, 10 to 30 percent say they are restricting their partners to people they know well, and fewer than 10 percent of women report they have stopped having sex with bisexual men or injection drug users. Overall, adults report having made behavior changes to reduce their exposure to HIV. Monogamy and/or limiting the number of sexual partners is mentioned by about 20 percent, 10 to 12 percent report using condoms, and 5 to 7 percent practice abstinence (see Smith, 1998, table 13).

Reports of HIV-related behavior change have risen somewhat over time, apparently indicating that risky sexual behaviors are increasingly being modified (see Smith, 2003, table 12) and that more people are taking precautions to avoid exposure to HIV (see Smith, 2003, table 13; see also Feinleib & Michael, 1998). However, since these questions have not often been asked after 1993, it is unknown if this trend continues. Moreover, because of the nature of retrospective questions on behavior change, the accuracy of these trends may be questionable at times. Time series monitoring of the relevant risk behaviors is needed to accurately track behavior changes. We therefore consider what changes have occurred in sexual behaviors that relate to risk of HIV infection—sexual activity among men who have sex with men, number of partners, and familiarity between partners.[5]

Behavior Change among Men Who Have Sex with Men

By the time HIV was identified, its mode of transmission via sexual intercourse documented, and tests for HIV infection developed, the disease was already widespread among the population of men who have sex with men (MSM), especially in San Francisco and New York City. Combined efforts by gay community organizations and public health officials led to the rapid dissemination of knowledge about HIV and the adoption of safer sex practices by MSM. The result was "a dramatic decline in risk practices for HIV transmission. . . . gay men have reduced the number of sex partners, have fewer anonymous sexual encounters, have switched from shorter to longer term relationships, and engaged in less anal intercourse or consistently used condoms" (Ehrhardt, Yingling, & Warne, 1991). More recently, however, there has been little further increase in safer sex practices among MSM and even some backsliding among those who have tired of the diligence and restrictions required by safer sexual practices—among some minority groups, and among younger MSM who did not experience firsthand the toll of the epidemic (Carballo-Dieguez & Dolezal, 1996; Catania, Stone, Binson, & Dolcini, 1995; CDC, 2005a; Ehrhardt, 1992; Ehrhardt et al., 1991; Goldbaum, Yu, & Wood, 1996; Kalichman, 1996; Osmond et al., 1994; Ostrow, Beltran, & Joseph, 1994). As a result, sexual intercourse among MSM remains the most frequent mode for the transmission of HIV in the United States (CDC, 2005a; 2005b).

Changes in Number of Partners

While the overall number of sexual partners among all adults has not diminished in recent years (Smith, 2003, table 14), some change has been occurring among teenagers and young adults (Smith, 2003, table 1C). Among young males, the number of partners was probably rising for most of the century until the early 1990s. However, the evidence is somewhat mixed for the 1980s. The mean number of lifetime partners among sexually active males aged 17–19 in metropolitan areas fell from 7.3 to 6.0 between 1979 and 1988, while among sexually active males aged 17.5 to 19, the mean number of sexual partners in the last twelve months rose from 2.0 in 1988 to 2.8 in 1991 (Ku et al., 1993). During the 1990s, there appeared to be a decline in number of sexual partners. The percentage of male high school students with a lifetime total of four or more partners declined from 31 percent in 1989 to 14 percent in 2001 (see Smith, 1998, table 1C). For young females, there was less clear evidence of a decline in number of partners from the 1990s. The YRBS data (CDC, 2004b) indicate year-to-year fluctuation rather than any definite trend. The GSS shows a decline from the late 1980s to early 1990s to the mid-1990s in the number of sexual partners among those aged 18 to 24, but no further decrease and even possibly a partial increase in the late 1990s and into the twenty-first century.

Despite reductions in number of partners among teenagers and young adults, many youths are still at risk of HIV and other STDs because of having multiple partners and other risky sexual behaviors (Anderson & Dahlberg, 1992; Beckman, Harvey, & Tiersky, 1996; Ku, Sonenstein, & Pleck, 1994; Leigh et al., 1993; Luster & Small, 1994; Smith, 1991a; Trocki, 1992; Tubman, Windle, & Windle, 1996).

Whether the reported decline in number of partners among teenagers and young adults will translate into a lower number of lifetime sexual partners is unknown. If it does, it will reverse a trend that began several generations ago. We can see evidence of that increase in the number of sexual partners since age 18 (see Smith, 2003, table 14). The increase in the number of sexual partners from ages 18 to 29 to ages 40 to 59 mostly represents the accumulation of partners over a person's lifetime. The sharp drop in cumulative partners for those 60 and older occurs because this age-group represents a generation that came to age before the peak in premarital sexual activity. That is, they had fewer premarital partners, married relatively early in life, and, as a result, accumulated fewer lifetime sexual partners than subsequent generations.

Among adults, having multiple sexual partners during the previous year and during the last five years is most strongly associated with being young, unmarried, and male. It is also higher among African Americans (Bakken & Winter, 2002), residents of large central cities, those with low incomes and less education, and infrequent church attenders. The adult lifetime figures show a similar pattern except that there is no relationship between income or race and number of sexual partners, and the less educated have fewer partners than the better educated. The reversal of the education relationship results from earlier cohorts with less education having fewer partners than more recent and better educated cohorts.

Multiple partners are thus found in two main social niches: young un-married adults and adolescents who have not yet "settled down," and among disadvantaged segments of society in general, including inner-city minorities, who also tend to lead less stable and less conventional lifestyles (Ford & Norris, 1995; Wagstaff et al., 1995).

Changes in Relationship to Sexual Partners

STDs and other risks increase not only with one's number of sexual partners, but also with the nature of the relationship between partners. When it comes to STDs, one "sleeps not only with a partner, but with all of that partner's partners." Intimate committed relationships are associated with (but do not guarantee) mutual monogamy, while casual relationships come with little expectation of exclusivity.

The trends in relationships are mixed and depend on the measure and data set being examined. For example, according to GSS findings, there has been no change in the nature of the relationship between sexual partners for most adults and persons under 40 between 1988 and 2002 (see Smith, 2003, table 15A). Most people are engaged in close and presumably mutually monogamous relationships with their spouses or cohabiting partners; however, each year, 3 to 4 percent of sexual partners involve casual relationships, which can range from one-night stands to prostitutes. Another 4 to 5 percent involve sexual partners with whom the person has a superficial relationship (neighbors, coworkers, and long-term acquaintances). Between 1996 and 2002, there was statistically significant variation in whether one was in an ongoing relationship with one's most recent sexual partner, but no clear trend (see Smith, 2003, table 15A). Finally, across birth cohorts of women, the relationship with one's first sexual partner has become more casual over time (see Smith, 2003, table 15C). Among women born between 1951 and 1955, 32 percent were engaged or married to their first sexual partner, 51 percent were "going steady," 16 percent were less closely involved, and 1 percent were no longer with that person. For those born between 1976 and 1980, 4 percent were engaged or married to their first sexual partner, 73 percent were "going steady" with that person, and 23 percent were less connected.

Casual relationships are most prevalent among young unmarried males. They are also more common among African Americans, residents of large central cities, and those with lower incomes. Similarly, having the last sexual encounter with someone with whom one did not have an "ongoing rela-tionship" is more common among men, African Americans, the young, the never married, city residents, those with lower incomes, the less educated, and infrequent church attenders (see Smith, 2003, table 15). One-night stands are equally common for African American and white males, but less frequent for African American females than for white females (Tanfer, 1994). In general, we see that those sociodemographic groups with a high number of lifetime partners also tend to have casual sexual relationships.

SUMMARY

Over the past century, the bonds between marriage and sexual activity have been unraveling. A majority of young men and women have engaged in premarital sexual intercourse, they have become sexually active at earlier ages, and they have accumulated more lifetime sexual partners. While premarital and adolescent sexual activity has increased for both men and women, the most significant changes have been in the sexual behavior of women. The higher rates of sexual behavior parallel a rise in cohabitation and a surge in nonmarital births, and they have contributed to a variety of public health and social welfare problems (Besharov & Gardiner, 1997).

Rather than being an isolated phenomenon, these changes in sexual behavior, living together, and childbearing have been part of broader social changes toward an individualistic rather than a family-centered society (Glenn, 1987; Popenoe, 1993; Smith, 1999). These sexual and relationship trends also mirror the changing roles in society for women (Firebaugh, 1990; Simon & Landis, 1989). Moreover, there are signs of similar shifts in other postindustrial societies. As such, the changes in American premarital and adolescent sexual behavior may result from the development of advanced economies, welfare states, and liberal governments in general rather than from any special situation peculiar to North America.

These trends have recently slowed and, in a few aspects, have shown signs of reversing. First, the increase in premarital and adolescent sexual activity has slowed and waned to some extent. Second, the number of nonmarital births has leveled off (albeit at near record levels). Third, condom use has more than doubled over the last twenty years and apparently continues to increase. Although there have not been decreases in every form of risky sexual behavior in all segments of the population, these changing trends are notable and may reflect an underlying shift in social values.

While marriage is no longer the entry point into sexual activity for most Americans, it remains an important regulator of sexual behavior, and thus may serve as a barrier to STDs. Since most married people tend to be monogamous, marriage limits one's total number of sexual partners and reduces the spread of HIV and other STDs. However, marriage may be less of a barrier than it used to be. Extramarital relations seem to be more prevalent among younger married adults relative to older generations. Yet, there has been no change in disapproval of extramarital relations over the years (Davis et al., 2003; Smith, 1990, 1994). Overall, though, extramarital relations have not increased since 1988, and marital infidelity is less common than suggested by popular culture.

Of course, marriages themselves are also not as enduring as they were in the past. The two-and-a-half-fold increase in divorce rates from the 1960s to the early 1980s and its continuation at historically high levels to this day suggest that approximately half of all recent marriages will end in divorce (Smith, 1999). For most divorced people this means accumulating new sexual partners, especially for those under 50 (Stack & Gundlach, 1992).

Sexual behavior is strongly influenced by age. In general, sexual activity diminishes with age as evidenced by a declining number of sexual partners, less extramarital sex, a reduced frequency of sexual intercourse, and higher rates of sexual abstinence. Cohabitation rates and nonmarital births also decline with age.

There are also significant differences in sexual behavior between whites and African Americans (Bowser, 1992; Brewster, 1994; Brunswick et al., 1993; Kilmarx et al., 1997; Peterson, Catania, Dolcini, & Faigeles, 1993; Quadagno, Sly, Harrison, Eberstein, & Soler, 1998; Reitman et al., 1996; Smith, 1999; Sterk-Elifson, 1992; but see Wyatt, 1989). On average, African Americans become sexually active at an earlier age, accumulate more lifetime sexual partners, have more casual partners, are less likely to marry, have shorter-term marriages, and have many more children born outside of marriage.

Sexual behavior also varies by community type. Residents of large central cities have more sexual partners, casual partners (including prostitutes), and extramarital relations than those living in rural areas. In addition, probably due to selective migration, gay men congregate in large cities. Since sexual and injection-drug risk behaviors are more common in large cities as is the prevalence of HIV, the chances of becoming infected are especially high in these areas (Catania et al., 1992).

Finally, religion exercises a restraint on sexual behavior for some persons (Brewster, Cooksey, Guilkey, & Rindfuss, 1998; Goldscheider & Mosher, 1991; Hogan, Sun, & Cornwell, 1998; Seidman, Mosher, & Aral, 1992; Stack & Gundlach, 1992; Tanfer & Schoorl, 1992; Thornton & Camburn, 1989). Those who attend church regularly are less likely to become sexually active, to have multiple and casual partners, and to have extramarital relations. Church attendance, like rural residence, imposes a restrictive influence on sexual behavior.

Despite the potentially deadly nature of HIV and the widespread knowledge of risk factors, its impact on sexual behavior has been relatively limited. The largest changes occurred among men who have sex with men in large metropolitan centers who adopted considerably safer sexual practices. But the resurgence in new cases of HIV infection suggests some complacency and underestimation of risk in recent years (CDC, 2005a).

Among the heterosexual population, the largest change has been the increased use of condoms. However, condom use is still inconsistent and haphazard. The small reductions in the number of partners among adolescents and youths may represent improved safer sex practices in response to the HIV epidemic. However, those changes have not been universal: most people still have numerous sexual partners, many of which involve casual relationships. It also remains to be seen if reductions in numbers of sexual partners will be temporary or long term; only long-term changes would result in reductions in numbers of lifetime sexual partners. Continuing patterns of multiple sexual partnerships combined with inconsistent condom use mean that many adolescents and adults remain vulnerable to HIV and other STDs (Anderson & Dahlberg, 1992; Dolcini et al., 1993; Smith, 1991b). In addition, the level of nonmarried births is still at record levels and the percent of unplanned births remains high.

In sum, contemporary patterns of sexual behavior remain a source of considerable public policy concern relating to HIV and other STDs, unintended childbearing, and many other public health and social problems.

NOTES

1. It is generally believed that including adolescent behavior would further increase these rates, but firm numerical estimates are not available. For some indication of this, see Billy et al., 1993, and Faulkner and Cranston, 1998. However, other surveys of young adult and teenage sexual orientation do not confirm this trend (Ku, Sonenstein, & Pleck, 1993). Spanning the lower and higher estimates, Turner et al. (1998) found that among males aged 15–19 in 1995, 1.5 percent reported homosexual relations on a paper self-completion questionnaire, but 5.5 percent did so on an audio-computer-assisted self-completion questionnaire.

2. A notable exception is a 1991 U.S. sample of men aged 20–39 and women aged 20–37, which found that 2.3 percent of men and 4.1 percent of women had a same-sex partner in the last ten years (Tanfer, 1994). This anomalous finding may have resulted from the question format, which used a five-point scale ranging from exclusively heterosexual to exclusively homosexual.

3. On knowledge among adolescents, see Kann et al., 1998.

4. On the relation of HIV-related risk behaviors and perceptions of risks, see Holtzman, Bland, Lansky, and Mack, 2001, and on the positive relationship between risky behavior and testing for HIV, see Anderson, Carey, and Taveras, 2000.

5. One sexual risk factor not discussed is type of sexual activity (e.g., vaginal, anal, and oral intercourse). On the comparative risk of these behaviors, see Susser, Desvarieux, and Wittkowski, 1998.

REFERENCES

Abma, J. C., Chandra, A., Mosher, W., Peterson, L., & Piccinino, L. (1997). *Fertility, family planning, and women's health: New data from the 1995 National Survey of Family Growth.* Vital and Health Statistics, Series 23. Hyattsville, MD: U.S. Department of Health and Human Services.

Abma, J. C., & Sonenstein, F. L. (2000). *Sexual activity and contraceptive practices among teenagers in the United States, 1988 and 1995.* Vital and Health Statistics, Series 23. Hyattsville, MD: U.S. Department of Health and Human Services.

Aguilar, S., & Hardy, A. M. (1993). AIDS knowledge and attitudes for 1991: Data from the National Health Survey. *Advance Data, 225,* 1–20.

Anderson, J. E., Carey, J. W., & Taveras, S. (2000). HIV testing among the general U.S. population and persons at increased risk: Information from national surveys, 1987–1996. *American Journal of Public Health, 90,* 1089–1095.

Anderson, J. E., & Dahlberg, L. L. (1992). High-risk sexual behavior in the general population: Results from a national survey, 1988–1990. *Sexually Transmitted Diseases, 19,* 320–325.

Anderson, J. E., & Stall, R. (2002). Increased reporting of male-to-male sexual activity in a national survey. *Sexually Transmitted Diseases, 29,* 643–646.

Aral, S. O. (1994). Sexual behavior in sexually transmitted disease research. *Sexually Transmitted Diseases, 21,* S59–S64.

Axinn, W. G., & Thornton, A. (1992). The relationship between cohabitation and divorce: Selectivity or causal influence? *Demography, 29,* 357–374.

Bachrach, C. A. (1998, May). *Assessing new survey findings.* Paper presented to the American Enterprise Institute Panel on Teenage Sexual Activity and Contraceptive Use: An Update. Washington, DC.

Bachrach, C. A., Evans, V. J., Ellison, S. A., & Stolley, K. S. (1992, May). *What price do we pay for single sex fertility surveys?* Paper presented to the Population Association of America, Denver, CO.

Bachrach, C. A., & Horn, M. (1987, July). *Married and unmarried couples: United States, 1982.* Vital and Health Statistics, Series 23, No. 15. Hyattsville, MD: U.S. Department of Health and Human Services.

Bachu, A. (1991). Fertility of American women: June 1990. *Current Population Reports,* Series P-20, No. 454. Washington, DC: U.S. Government Printing Office.

Bachu, A. (1995). Fertility of American women: June 1994. *Current Population Reports,* Series P-20, No. 482. Washington, DC: U.S. Government Printing Office.

Bakken, R. J., & Winter, M. (2002). Family characteristics and sexual behaviors among black men in the United States. *Family Planning Perspectives, 34,* 252–258.

Beckman, L. J., Harvey, S. M., & Tiersky, L. A. (1996). Attitudes about condoms and condom use among college students. *Journal of American College Health, 44,* 243–249.

Besharov, D., & Gardiner, K. N. (1997). Trends in teen sexual behavior. *Children and Youth Services Review, 19,* 341–368.

Biggar, R. J., & Melbye, M. (1992). Responses to anonymous questionnaires concerning sexual behavior: A method to examine potential biases. *American Journal of Public Health, 82,* 1506–1512.

Billy, J. O. G., Tanfer, K., Grady, W. R., & Klepinger, D. H. (1993). The sexual behavior of men in the United States. *Family Planning Perspectives, 25*, 52–60.

Black, D., Gates, G., Sanders, S., & Taylor, L. (2000). Demographics of the gay and lesbian population in the United States: Evidence from available systematic data sources. *Demography, 37*, 139–154.

Blair, J. (1999). A probability sample of gay urban males: The use of two-phase adaptive sampling. *Journal of Sex Research, 36*, 39–44.

Bowser, B. P. (1992, May). *African American male sexuality through the early life course.* Paper presented to the MacArthur Foundation Research Network on Successful Mid-Life Development, New York.

Bramlett, M. D., & Mosher, W. D. (2002). *Cohabitation, marriage, divorce, and remarriage in the United States.* Vital and Health Statistics, Series 23, No. 22, 1–93. Hyattsville, MD: U.S. Department of Health and Human Services.

Brewster, K. L. (1994). Race differences in sexual activity among adolescent women: The role of neighborhood characteristics. *American Sociological Review, 59*, 408–424.

Brewster, K. L., Cooksey, E. C., Guilkey, D. K., & Rindfuss, R. R. (1998). The changing impact of religion on the sexual and contraceptive behavior of adolescent women in the United States. *Journal of Marriage and the Family, 60*, 493–504.

Brothers, J. (1990, February 18). Why Wives Have Affairs. *Parade*, 4–6.

Brown, S. L., & Booth, A. (1996). Cohabitation versus marriage: A comparison of relationship quality. *Journal of Marriage and the Family, 58*, 668–678.

Brunswick, A. F., Aidala, A., Dobkin, J., Howard, J., Titus, S. P., & Banaszak-Holl, J. (1993). HIV-1 seroprevalence and risk behaviors in an urban African-American community cohort. *American Journal of Public Health, 83*, 1390–1394.

Bumpass, L. L., & Sweet, J. (1989). National estimates of cohabitation. *Demography, 26*, 615–626.

Butler, A. C. (2000). Trends in same-gender sexual partnering, 1988–1998. *Journal of Sex Research, 37*, 333–343.

Call, V., Sprecher, S., & Schwartz, P. (1996). The incidence and frequency of marital sex in a national sample. *Journal of Marriage and the Family, 57*, 609–634.

Carballo-Dieguez, A., & Dolezal, C. (1996). HIV risk behaviors and obstacles to condom use among Puerto Rican men in New York City who have sex with men. *American Journal of Public Health, 86*, 1619–1622.

Catania, J. A., Coates, T. J., Stall, R., Turner, H. A., Peterson, J., Hearst, N., et al. (1992). Prevalence of AIDS-related risk factors and condom use in United States. *Science, 258*, 1101–1106.

Catania, J. A., Stone, V., Binson, D., & Dolcini, M. M. (1995). Changes in condom use among heterosexuals in wave 3 of the AMEN survey. *Journal of Sex Research, 32*, 193–200.

Centers for Disease Control and Prevention. (1992a). Selected behaviors that increase risk for HIV infection among high school students—United States, 1990. *Morbidity and Mortality Weekly Report, 47*, 231, 237–240.

Centers for Disease Control and Prevention. (1992b). Sexual behavior among high school students—United States, 1990. *Morbidity and Mortality Weekly Report, 40,* 885–888.

Centers for Disease Control and Prevention. (1994). Heterosexually acquired AIDS—United States, 1993. *Morbidity and Mortality Weekly Report, 43,* 155–160.

Centers for Disease Control and Prevention. (1995a). First 500,000 AIDS cases—United States. *Morbidity and Mortality Weekly Report, 44,* 850–853.

Centers for Disease Control and Prevention. (1995b). Trends in sexual risk taking among high school students—United States, 1990, 1991, and 1993. *Morbidity and Mortality Weekly Report, 447,* 124–125, 131–132.

Centers for Disease Control and Prevention. (1998a). *Trends in the HIV and AIDS epidemic, 1998.* Atlanta, GA: U.S. Department of Health and Human Services.

Centers for Disease Control and Prevention. (1998b). Youth risk behavior surveillance—United States, 1997. *Morbidity and Mortality Weekly Report, 47,* 1–89.

Centers for Disease Control and Prevention. (2000). HIV-related knowledge and stigma—United States, 2000. *Morbidity and Mortality Weekly Report, 50,* 1062–1064.

Centers for Disease Control and Prevention. (2001). *Year-end edition HIV/AIDS surveillance report.* Atlanta, GA: U.S. Department of Health and Human Services.

Centers for Disease Control and Prevention. (2004a). *HIV/AIDS Surveillance Report, 2003* (Vol. 15). Atlanta, GA: U.S. Department of Health and Human Services.

Centers for Disease Control and Prevention. (2004b). *Youth risk behavior surveillance—United States, 2003.* Atlanta, GA: U.S. Department of Health and Human Services.

Centers for Disease Control and Prevention. (2005a). *HIV/AIDS among men who have sex with men.* Atlanta, GA: U.S. Department of Health and Human Services.

Centers for Disease Control and Prevention. (2005b). *HIV/AIDS Surveillance Report, 2004* (Vol. 16). Atlanta, GA: U.S. Department of Health and Human Services.

Choi, K. H., Catania, J. A., & Dolcini, N. M. (1994). Extramarital sex and HIV risk behavior among US adults: Results from the National AIDS Behavioral Survey. *American Journal of Public Health, 84,* 2003–2007.

Clarkberg, M., Stolzenberg, R. M., & Waite, L. J. (1995). Attitudes, values, and entrance into cohabitational versus marital unions. *Social Forces, 74,* 609–634.

Davis, J. A., Smith, T. W., & Marsden, P. V. (2003). *General Social Surveys, 1972–2002: Cumulative codebook.* Chicago: National Opinion Research Council.

DeMaris, A., & MacDonald, W. (1993). Premarital cohabitation and marital instability: A test of the unconventionality hypothesis. *Journal of Marriage and the Family, 55,* 399–407.

DeMaris, A., & Rao, K. V. (1992). Premarital cohabitation and subsequent marital stability in the United States: A reassessment. *Journal of Marriage and the Family, 54,* 178–190.

Diamond, M. (1993). Homosexuality and bisexuality in different populations. *Archives of Sexual Behavior, 22,* 291–310.

di Mauro, D. (1995). *Sexual research in the United States: An assessment of the social and behavioral sciences.* New York: Social Science Research Council.

Dolcini, M. M., Catania, J. A., Coates, T. J., Stall, R., Hudes, E. S., Gagnon, J. H., et al. (1993). Demographic characteristics of heterosexuals with multiple partners: The National AIDS Behavior Surveys. *Family Planning Perspectives, 25,* 208–214.

Donnelly, D. A. (1993). Sexually inactive marriage. *Journal of Sex Research, 30,* 171–179.

Driscoll, A. K., Hearn, G. K., Evans, V. J., Moore, K. A., Sugland, B. W., & Call, V. (1999). Nonmarital childbearing among adult women. *Journal of Marriage and the Family, 61,* 178–187.

Edwards, J. N., & Booth, A. (1976). The cessation of marital intercourse. *American Journal of Psychiatry, 133,* 1333–1336.

Ehrhardt, A. A., & Wasserheit, J. N. (1991). Age, gender, and sexual risk behaviors for sexually transmitted diseases in the United States. In J. N. Wasserheit, S. O. Aral, K. K. Holmes, & P. J. Hitchcock (Eds.), *Research issues in human behavior and sexually transmitted diseases in the AIDS era* (pp. 97–121). Washington, DC: American Society for Microbiology.

Ehrhardt, A. A., Yingling, S., & Warne, P. A. (1991). Sexual behavior in the era of AIDS: What has changed in the United States? *Annual Review of Sex Research, 2,* 25–47.

Faulkner, A. H., & Cranston, K. (1998). Correlates of same-sex sexual behavior in a random sample of Massachusetts high school students. *American Journal of Public Health, 88,* 262–266.

Feinleib, J. A., & Michael, R. T. (1998). Reported changes in sexual behavior in response to AIDS in the United States. *Preventive Medicine, 27,* 400–411.

Feldman, H. A., Goldstein, I., Hatzichristou, D. G., Krane, R. J., & McKinlay, J. B. (1994). Impotence and its medical and psychosocial correlates in men aged 40–70: Results of the Massachusetts Male Aging Study. *Journal of Urology, 151,* 54–61.

Firebaugh, G. (1990, May). *Components of change in gender role attitudes, 1972–1988.* Paper presented to the Population Association of America, Toronto, Canada.

Ford, K., & Norris, A. E. (1995). Factors related to condom use with casual partners among urban African-American and Hispanic males. *AIDS Education and Prevention, 7,* 494–503.

Forste, R., & Tanfer, K. (1996). Sexual exclusivity among dating, cohabiting, and married women. *Journal of Marriage and the Family, 58,* 594–600.

Gibbs, D. A., Hamil, D. N., & Magruder-Habib, K. (1991). Populations at increased risk of HIV infection: Current knowledge and limitations. *Journal of Acquired Immune Deficiency Syndromes, 1*, 881–889.

Glenn, N. (1987). Social trends in the United States: Evidence from sample surveys. *Public Opinion Quarterly, 51*, S109–S126.

Goldbaum, G. M., Yu, T., & Wood, R. W. (1996). Changes at a human immunodeficiency testing clinic in the prevalence of unsafe sexual behavior among men who have sex with men. *Sexually Transmitted Diseases, 23*, 109–114.

Goldscheider, C., & Mosher, W. D. (1991). Patterns of contraceptive use in the United States: The importance of religious factors. *Studies in Family Planning, 22*, 102–115.

Greeley, A. M. (1991). *Faithful attraction: Discovering intimacy, love, and fidelity in American marriage.* New York: Tor Books.

Greeley, A. M. (1994). Marital infidelity. *Society, 31*, 9–13.

Greeley, A. M., Michael, R. T., & Smith, T. W. (1990). A most monogamous people: Americans and their sexual partners. *Society, 27*, 36–42.

Greenblat, C. S. (1983). The salience of sexuality in the early years of marriage. *Journal of Marriage and the Family, 45*, 289–299.

Guterbock, T. B. (1993, March 10). *Charlottesville/Albemarle County Survey, 1991.* Unpublished figures.

Hawton, K., Gath, D., & Day, A. (1994). Sexual function in a community sample of middle-aged women with partners: Effects of age, marital, socioeconomic, psychiatric, gynecological, and menopausal factors. *Archives of Sexual Behavior, 23*, 375–395.

Herek, G. M., Capitanio, J. P., & Widaman, K. F. (2002). HIV-related stigma and knowledge in the United States: Prevalence and trends, 1991–1999. *American Journal of Public Health, 92*, 371–377.

Hewitt, C., & Beverley, J. R. (1996). The spread of HIV into the general population of the USA: A simulation. *Population Research and Policy Review, 15*, 311–325.

Hofferth, S. L., Kahn, J. R., & Baldwin, W. (1987). Premarital sexual activity among U.S. teenage women over the past three decades. *Family Planning Perspectives, 19*, 46–53.

Hogan, D. P., Sun, R., & Cornwell, G. (1998, August). *Cohort difference, family structure, and adolescent sexual activity.* Paper presented to the American Sociological Association, San Francisco, CA.

Holtzman, D., Bland, S. D., Lansky, A., & Mack, K. A. (2001). HIV-related behaviors and perceptions among adults in 25 states: 1997 Behavioral Risk Factor Surveillance System. *American Journal of Public Health, 91*, 1882–1888.

Hopkins, K. W. (1998). *An explanation for the trends in American teenagers' premarital coital behavior and attitudes between 1960 and 1990.* Unpublished doctoral dissertation, University of Minnesota.

Horowitz, S. M., Weis, D. L., & Laflin, M. T. (2001). Differences between sexual orientation behavior groups and social background, quality of life, and health behaviors. *Journal of Sex Research, 38*, 205–218.

Hubert, M., Bajos, N., & Sandfort, T. (Eds.). (1998). *Sexual behaviour and HIV/AIDS in Europe.* London: University College London Press.

Hughes, M., & Gove, W. R. (1992, May). *Sexual behavior and psychological well-being over the life course.* Paper presented to the MacArthur Foundation Research Network on Successful Mid-Life Development, New York.

Hyde, J. S., DeLamater, J. D., & Durik, A. M. (2001). Sexuality and the dual-earner couple, part II: Beyond the baby years. *Journal of Sex Research, 38*, 10–23.

James, W. H. (1981). The honeymoon effect on marital coitus. *Journal of Sex Research, 17*, 114–123.

James, W. H. (1998). Coital frequency among married and cohabiting couples in the United States. *Journal of Biosocial Science, 30*, 131–132.

Jasso, G. (1985). Marital coital frequency and the passage of time: Estimating the separation effects of spouses' ages and marital duration, birth, and marriage cohorts, and period influences. *American Sociological Review, 50*, 224–241.

Jasso, G. (1986). Is it outlier deletion or is it sample truncation? Notes of science and sexuality. *American Sociological Review, 51*, 738–742.

Johnson, A. M., Wadsworth, J., Wellings, K., Bradshaw, S., & Field, J. (1992). Sexual lifestyles and HIV risk. *Nature, 360*, 410–412.

Johnson, A. M., Wadsworth, J., Wellings, K., & Field, J. (1994). *Sexual attitudes and lifestyles.* Oxford: Blackwell Scientific.

Joyner, K., & Laumann, E. O. (2001). Teenage sex and the sexual revolution. In E. O. Laumann & R. T. Michael (Eds.), *Sex, love, and health in America: Private choices and public policies* (pp. 41–71). Chicago: University of Chicago Press.

Kahn, J. R., Kalsbeek, W. D., & Hofferth, S. L. (1988). National estimates of teenage sexual activity: Evaluating the comparability of three national surveys. *Demography, 25*, 189–204.

Kahn, J. R., & Udry, J. R. (1986). Marital coital frequency: Unnoticed outliers and unspecified interactions lead to erroneous conclusions. *American Sociological Review, 51*, 734–737.

Kalichman, S. C. (1996). Continued sexual risk behavior among HIV-seropositive, drug-using men—Atlanta, Washington, DC, and San Juan, Puerto Rico. *Morbidity and Mortality Weekly Report, 45*, 151–152.

Kilmarx, P. H., Zaidi, A. A., Thomas, J. C., Nakashima, A. K., St. Louis, M. E., Flock, M. L., et al. (1997). Sociodemographic factors and the variation in syphilis rates among U.S. counties, 1984 through 1993: An ecological analysis. *American Journal of Public Health, 87*, 1937–1943.

Kost, K., & Forrest, J. D. (1992). American women's sexual behavior and exposure to risk of sexually transmitted diseases. *Family Planning Perspectives, 24*, 244–254.

Ku, L., Sonenstein, F. L., & Pleck, J. H. (1993). Young men's risk behaviors for HIV infection and sexually transmitted diseases, 1988 through 1991. *American Journal of Public Health, 83*, 1609–1615.

Ku, L., Sonenstein, F. L., & Pleck, J. H. (1994). The dynamics of young men's condom use during and across relationships. *Family Planning Perspectives, 26*, 246–251.

Laumann, E. O., Gagnon, J. H., Michael, R. T., & Michaels, S. (1994). *The social organization of sexuality: Sexual practices in the United States.* Chicago: University of Chicago Press.

Leiblum, S. R. (1990). Sexuality and the midlife woman. *Psychology of Women Quarterly, 14*, 495–508.

Leigh, B. C., Temple, M. T., & Trocki, K. F. (1993). The sexual behavior of U.S. adults: Results from a national survey. *American Journal of Public Health, 83*, 1400–1408.

Levy, J. A. (1992, May). *Sex and sexuality in later life stages.* Paper presented to the MacArthur Foundation Research Network on Successful Mid-Life Development, New York.

Lillard, L. A., Brien, M. J., & Waite, L. J. (n.d.). *Premarital cohabitation and subsequent marital dissolution: A matter of self-selection?* Unpublished paper.

Liu, C. (2003). Does quality of marital sex decline with duration? *Archives of Sexual Behavior, 32*, 55–60.

London, R. A. (1998). Trends in single mothers' living arrangements from 1970 to 1995: Correcting the current population survey. *Demography, 35*, 125–131.

Loomis, L. S., & Landale, N. S. (1994). Nonmarital cohabitation and childbearing among black and white American women. *Journal of Marriage and the Family, 56*, 949–962.

Luster, T., & Small, S. A. (1994). Factors associated with sexual risk-taking behaviors among adolescents. *Journal of Marriage and the Family, 56*, 622–632.

McKinlay, J. B., & Feldman, H. A. (1992, May). *Changes in sexual activity and interest in the normally aging male: Results from the Massachusetts Male Aging Study.* Paper presented at the MacArthur Foundation Research Network on Successful Mid-Life Development, New York.

McQuillan, G. M., Ezzati-Rice, T. M., Siller, A. B., Visscher, W., & Hurley, P. (1994). Risk behavior and correlates of risk for HIV infection in the Dallas County Household HIV Survey. *American Journal of Public Health, 84*, 747–753.

Melbye, M., & Biggar, R. J. (1992). Interactions between persons at risk for AIDS and the general population in Denmark. *American Journal of Epidemiology, 135*, 593–602.

Michael, R. T., Laumann, E. O., & Gagnon, J. H. (1993, February). *The number of sexual partners in the U.S.* Unpublished paper.

Michaels, S. K. (1998). *Queer counts: The sociological construction of homosexuality via survey research.* Unpublished doctoral dissertation, University of Chicago.

Miller, B. C., & Heaton, T. B. (1991). Age at first sexual intercourse and the timing of marriage and childbirth. *Journal of Marriage and the Family, 53,* 719–732.

Morokoff, P. J. (1988). Sexuality in perimenopausal and post-menopausal women. *Psychology of Women Quarterly, 12,* 489–511.

National Council on the Aging (1998). *Healthy sexuality and vital aging: A study by the National Council on the Aging.* Washington, DC: Author.

Osmond, D. H., Page, K., Wiley, J., Garret, K., Sheppard, H. W., Moss, A. R., et al. (1994). HIV infection in homosexual and bisexual men 18 to 29 years of age: The San Francisco Young Men's Health Study. *American Journal of Public Health, 84,* 1933–1937.

Ostrow, D. G., Beltran, E., & Joseph, J. (1994). Sexual behavior research on a cohort of gay men, 1984–1990: Can we predict how men will respond to interventions? *Archives of Sexual Behavior, 25,* 531–552.

Peipert, J. F., Domagalski, L., Boardman, L., Daamen, M., McCormack, W. M., & Zinner, S. H. (1997). Sexual behavior and contraceptive use: Changes from 1975 to 1995 in college women. *Journal of Reproductive Medicine, 42,* 651–657.

Peterson, J. L., Catania, J. A., Dolcini, M. M., & Faigeles, B. (1993). Multiple sexual partners among blacks in high-risk cities. *Family Planning Perspectives, 25,* 263–267.

Popenoe, D. (1993). American family decline, 1960–1990: A review and appraisal. *Journal of Marriage and the Family, 55,* 527–555.

Quadagno, D., Sly, D. F., Harrison, D. F., Eberstein, I. W., & Soler, H. R. (1998). Ethnic differences in sexual decisions and sexual behavior. *Archives of Sexual Behavior, 27,* 57–75.

Rao, K. V., & VandenHeuvel, A. (1995). Coital frequency among married and cohabiting couples in the United States. *Journal of Biosocial Science, 27,* 135–150.

Reinisch, J. M., Sanders, S. A., & Ziemba-Davis, M. (1988). The study of sexual behavior in relation to the transmission of human immunodeficiency virus: Caveats and recommendations. *American Psychologist, 43,* 921–927.

Reitman, D., St. Lawrence, J. S., Jefferson, K. W., Alleyne, E., Brasfield, T. L., & Shirley, A. (1996). Predictors of African American adolescents' condom use and HIV risk behavior. *AIDS Education and Prevention, 8,* 499–515.

Rogers, S. M., & Turner, C. F. (1991). Male-male sexual contact in the U.S.A.: Findings from five sample surveys, 1970–1990. *Journal of Sex Research, 28,* 491–519.

Rogers, T. F., Singer, E., & Imperio, J. (1993). AIDS—An update. *Public Opinion Quarterly, 57,* 92–114.

Sandfort, T. G. M., Hubert, M. C., Bajos, N., & Bos, H. (1998). Sexual behaviour and HIV risk: Common patterns and differences between European countries. In M. C. Hubert, N. Bajos, & T. G. M. Sandfort (Eds.), *Sexual behaviour and HIV/AIDS in Europe* (pp. 403–426). London: University College London Press.

Schiavi, R. C. (1990). Sexuality and aging in men. *Annals of Sex Research, 1*, 227–249.

Schiavi, R. C. (1992, May). *Impact of chronic disease and medication on sexual functioning.* Paper presented to the MacArthur Foundation Research Network on Successful Mid-Life Development, New York.

Seidman, S. N., Mosher, W. D., & Aral, S. O. (1992). Women with multiple sexual partners: United States, 1988. *American Journal of Public Health, 82*, 1388–1394.

Seidman, S. N., & Rieder, R. O. (1994). A review of sexual behavior in the United States. *American Journal of Psychiatry, 151*, 330–341.

Sell, R., & Becker, J. B. (2001). Sexual orientation data collection and progress toward Healthy People 2010. *American Journal of Public Health, 91*, 876–882.

Simon, R. J., & Landis, J. M. (1989). Women's and men's attitudes about a woman's place and role. *Public Opinion Quarterly, 53*, 265–276.

Singer, E., Rogers, T. F., & Corcoran, M. (1987). AIDS. *Public Opinion Quarterly, 51*, 580–595.

Singh, S., & Darroch, J. E. (1999). Trends in sexual activity among adolescent American women, 1982–1995. *Family Planning Perspectives, 31*, 212–219.

Smith, T. W. (1988). Hite vs. Abby in methodological messes. *AAPOR News, 15*, 3–4.

Smith, T. W. (1989). Sex counts: A methodological critique of Hite's *Women in Love*. In C. F. Turner, H. G. Miller, & L. E. Moses (Eds.), *AIDS: Sexual behavior and intravenous drug use* (pp. 537–457). Washington, DC: National Academy of Sciences Press.

Smith, T. W. (1990). The Sexual Revolution? *Public Opinion Quarterly, 54*, 415–435.

Smith, T. W. (1991a). Adult sexual behavior in 1989: Number of partners, frequency of intercourse, and risk of AIDS. *Family Planning Perspectives, 23*, 102–107.

Smith, T. W. (1991b). A critique of the Kinsey Institute/Roper Organization National Sex Knowledge Survey. *Public Opinion Quarterly, 55*, 449–457.

Smith, T. W. (1992a). Discrepancies between men and women in reporting number of sexual partners: A summary from four countries. *Social Biology, 39*, 203–211.

Smith, T. W. (1992b). A methodological analysis of the sexual behavior questions on the General Social Surveys. *Journal of Official Statistics, 8*, 309–326.

Smith, T. W. (1994). Attitudes towards sexual permissiveness: Trends, correlates, and behavioral connections. In A. Rossi (Ed.), *Sexuality across the lifecourse* (pp. 63–97). Chicago: University of Chicago Press.

Smith, T. W. (1998). *American sexual behavior: Trends, socio-demographic differences, and risk behavior.* GSS Topical Report. Chicago: National Opinion Research Council. Retrieved September 9, 2005, from www.norc.uchicago.edu/library/sexual.pdf

Smith, T. W. (1999). *The emerging 21st century American family* (GSS Social Change Report No. 42). Chicago: National Opinion Research Council.

Smith, T. W. (2003). *American sexual behavior: Trends, socio-demographic differences, and risk behavior.* GSS Topical Report. Chicago: National Opinion Research Council.

Sonenstein, F. L., Pleck, J. H., & Ku, L. C. (1991). Levels of sexual activity among adolescent males in the United States. *Family Planning Perspectives, 23,* 162–167.

South, S. J. (1999). Historical changes and life course variation in the determinants of premarital childbearing. *Journal of Marriage and the Family, 61,* 753–763.

Spira, A., Bajos, N., Bejin, A., Beltzer, N., Bozon, M., Ducot, B., et al. (1992). AIDS and sexual behaviour in France. *Nature, 360,* 407–409.

Spira, A., Bajos, N., & Ducot, B. (1994). Trends in sexual behavior. *Sexually Transmitted Diseases, 21,* S14–S18.

Stack, S., & Gundlach, J. H. (1992). Divorce and sex. *Archives of Sexual Behavior, 21,* 359–367.

Sterk-Elifson, C. (1992, May). *Sexuality among black American women.* Paper presented to the MacArthur Foundation Research Network on Successful Mid-Life Development, New York.

Stokes, J. P., & McKiran, D. J. (1993). Estimating the prevalence of homosexual behavior. *Family Planning Perspectives, 25,* 184–185.

Stossel, S. (1997). The Sexual Counterrevolution. *American Prospect, 33,* 74–82.

Sundet, J. M., Magnus, P., Kvalem, I. L., Groennesby, J. K., & Bakketeig, L. S. (1989). Number of sexual partners and the use of condoms in the heterosexual population of Norway—relevance to HIV-infection. *Health Policy, 13,* 159–167.

Susser, E., Desvarieux, M., & Wittkowski, K. M. (1998). Reporting sexual risk behavior for HIV: A practical risk index and a method for improving risk indices. *American Journal of Public Health, 88,* 671–674.

Swann, K. (1993, March/April). Percentage gay. *Bad Subjects, 5,* 1–3.

Tanfer, K. (1994). Sex and disease. *Sexually Transmitted Diseases, 21,* S65–S72.

Tanfer, K., & Cubbins, L. A. (1992). Coital frequency among single women: Normative constraints and situational opportunities. *Journal of Sex Research, 29,* 221–250.

Tanfer, K., & Schoorl, J. J. (1992). Premarital sexual careers and partner change. *Archives of Sexual Behavior, 21,* 45–68.

Teitler, J. O. (2002). Trends in youth sexual initiation and fertility in developed countries, 1960–1995. *Annals of AAPSS, 580,* 134–152.

Thomson, E., & Colella, U. (1992). Cohabitation and marital stability: Quality or commitment? *Journal of Marriage and the Family, 54,* 259–267.

Thornton, A. (1988). Cohabitation and marriage in the 1980s. *Demography, 25,* 497–508.

Thornton, A., & Camburn, D. (1989). Religious participation and adolescent sexual behavior and attitudes. *Journal of Marriage and the Family, 51,* 641–653.

Treas, J., & Giesen, D. (1996, August). *Sex, gender, and rational choice: Determinant of infidelity among married and cohabiting couples.* Paper presented to the American Sociological Association, New York.

Treas, J., & Giesen, D. (2000). Sexual infidelity among married and cohabitating Americans. *Journal of Marriage and the Family, 62,* 48–60.

Trocki, K. (1992). Patterns of sexuality and risky sexuality in the general population of a California county. *Journal of Sex Research, 29,* 85–94.

Trussell, J., & Westoff, C. F. (1980). Contraceptive practice and trends in coital frequency. *Family Planning Perspectives, 12,* 246–249.

Tubman, J. G., Windle, M., & Windle, R. C. (1996). Cumulative sexual intercourse patterns among middle adolescents: Problem behavior precursors and concurrent health risk behaviors. *Journal of Adolescent Health, 18,* 182–191.

Turner, C. F., Ku, L., Rogers, S. M., Lindberg, L. D., Pleck, J. H., & Sonenstein, F. L. (1998). *Adolescent sexual behavior, drug use, and violence: Increased reporting with computer survey technology. Science, 280,* 867–873.

Turner, C. F., Miller, H. G., & Moses, L. E. (Eds.). (1989). *AIDS: Sexual behaviors and intravenous drug use.* Washington, DC: National Academy Press.

Udry, J. R. (1980). Changes in the frequency of marital intercourse from panel data. *Archives of Sexual Behavior, 9,* 319–325.

Udry, J. R., Bauman, K. E., & Morris, N. (1975). Changes in premarital coital experience of recent decade-of-birth cohorts of urban American women. *Journal of Marriage and the Family, 37,* 783–787.

Udry, J. R., Deven, F. R., & Coleman, S. J. (1982). A cross-national comparison of the relative influence of male and female age on the frequency of marital intercourse. *Journal of Biosocial Science, 14,* 1–6.

Udry, J. R., & Morris, N. M. (1978). Relative contribution of male and female age to the frequency of marital intercourse. *Social Biology, 25,* 128–134.

U.S. Census Bureau. (2001). *Statistical abstract of the United States, 2001.* Washington, DC: U.S. Government Printing Office.

Ventura, S. J., Anderson, R. N., Martin, J. A., & Smith, B. L. (1998). *Births and deaths: Preliminary data for 1997.* National vital statistics reports, 47 (4). Hyattsville, MD: National Center for Health Statistics.

Wade, L. D., & DeLamater, J. D. (2002). Relationship dissolution as a life stage transition: Effects on sexual attitudes and behaviors. *Journal of Marriage and the Family, 64,* 898–914.

Wagstaff, D. A., Kelly, J. A., Perry, M. J., Sikkema, K. J., Solomon, L. J., Heckman, T. G., et al. (1995). Multiple partners, risky partners, and HIV risk among low-income urban women. *Family Planning Perspectives, 27,* 241–245.

Waite, L. J., & Joyner, K. (1996, December). *Men's and women's general happiness and sexual satisfaction in marriage, cohabitation, and single living.* Paper presented to the Population Research Center's Demography Workshop, Chicago, IL.

Wells, J. A., & Sell, R. L. (1990). *Project HOPE's international survey of AIDS educational messages and behavior change: France, the United Kingdom and the United States.* Chevy Chase, MD: Project HOPE.

Whitbeck, L. B., Simons, R. L., & Goldberg, E. (1996). Adolescent sexual intercourse. In R. L. Simons (Ed.), *Understanding differences between divorced and intact families: Stress, interaction, and child outcome* (pp. 144–156). Thousand Oaks, CA: Sage.

Williams, L. B. (1991). Determinants of unintended childbearing among never-married women in the United States: 1973–1988. *Family Planning Perspectives, 23,* 212–215, 221.

Wyatt, G. E. (1989). Reexamining factors predicting Afro-American and white American women's age at first coitus. *Archives of Sexual Behavior, 18,* 271–298.

Wyatt, G. E., Peters, S. D., & Guthrie, D. (1988). "Kinsey revisited, part I: Comparisons of sexual socialization and sexual behavior in white women over 33 years." *Archives of Sexual Behavior, 17,* 201–239.

Yankauer, A. (1994). Sexually transmitted diseases: A neglected public health priority. *American Journal of Public Health, 84,* 1894–1897.

6

Later Life Sexuality

Thomasina H. Sharpe ◆

SEXUALITY IN LATER LIFE

The subject of sexuality triggers awkwardness and discomfort in many people. The topic of older adults' sexuality evokes even more discomfort, if not disgust. Although sexuality is a fundamental need across the life span, society typically ignores the sexual needs and concerns of older adults. The older population of the United States is growing at an unprecedented rate. In 2003, persons 65 and older accounted for 12.4 percent of the population. By 2030, that number will rise to 20 percent or higher (U.S. Census Bureau, 2001). The so-called baby boomer generation (the cohort of people born between 1946 and 1964) will increasingly present many challenges to views of sexuality in late life.

There are signs that the growing population of older persons will force society to reconsider its views of aging. Being able to live in one's own home is important to most adults, and older adults are no exception (Novelli, 2002). "Aging in place," as it is called, is especially important to baby boomers, who are challenging many existing views of aging. Not only do they intend to stay in their own homes, they also intend to maintain their current lifestyles into advancing age. They expect to remain healthy well into their seventies and eighties (Lenahan, 2004). This generation, which came of age during the sexual revolution of the 1960s, seems determined to retain its sexual life as well.

Today, adults are living longer, healthier, and wealthier lives than their parents. And they expect to have healthy sexual lives too (American Association of Retired Persons [AARP], 1999, 2005). Most older adults view sex as essential to a successful relationship, and for many it is important to overall quality of life. Marketing executives certainly have realized that sex sells not only to young adults: aging baby boomers are interested in sex (see Katz & Marshall, 2003). Magazines put steamy pictures of graying models on their covers and announce, "Sixty Is the New Thirty!" Beer ads feature elders drinking and necking on the sofa only to be caught by their shocked and much older parents. *A Round-Heeled Woman*, a memoir, follows the sexual exploits of a 66-year-old woman on a quest to have "a lot of sex with a man I like," becoming a best seller (Juska, 2003). Television news shows and newspapers lead with headlines that tout the results of the latest surveys such as those by the Association of Reproductive Health Professionals, the National Council on the Aging, and the Kaiser Family Foundation, which show that people are maintaining satisfying sex lives well into their eighties and even nineties (Sexuality Education and Information Council of the United States [SIECUS], 2002). Yet, despite this budding awareness that older adults are sexual beings, there is little information on sexuality in late life.

Late life is a stage of development like any other across the life span. Aging brings with it many challenges similar to those faced in childhood or adolescence. Sexuality, sexual behavior, intimacy, and relationships are fundamental human needs, whether we are 14 or 84. This chapter will address some of the unique tasks that we face as we age and how they affect our sexuality.

First, it is important to define some of the terms related to sexuality and aging. *Sexual behavior* is any form of physical intimacy that may be motivated by the desire to reproduce or to enjoy sexual gratification. *Sexual desire* is the need for sexual intimacy. *Sexuality* is often used as the general term for the feelings and behaviors of a human being concerning sex (Carroll & Wolpe, 1996). Sexuality encompasses both sexual behaviors and sexual desire. Sexual development occurs through distinct stages, each with its own tasks, challenges, and outcomes. To understand what this means in later life, it is helpful to examine sexual development at the earlier stages, beginning with childhood.

Sexuality and sexual behavior in very young children are mainly based on curiosity. Preadolescents have little physical or mental investment in sexuality. Most of their energy is devoted to forming a sense of identity as part of a community, collecting information and myths about sexuality from friends, school, and family, as well as forming a sense of morality they will use later in their sexual lives. Along with the striking changes of puberty, adolescents begin to revise their individual identities to include sexuality and sexual development. In Western cultures, adolescence provides opportunities to experiment with intimacy, the freedom to explore one's own maturing body, and the chance to master skills useful in the transition to adulthood. During this passage, the young adult moves from dependence to independence. Unlike the curious explorations of childhood, adolescent sexual behavior becomes more expressive and more goal directed. Adolescents and young adults begin to form emotional bonds in their quest for intimacy. Most young adults plan to find a committed relationship, usually with the intention of having children. This focus may change at midlife as couples rediscover the importance of intimacy. Sexual activity in older individuals is primarily motivated by the desire for intimacy, sharing, and pleasure (Hillman, 2000; Stone, Wyman, & Salisbury, 1999).

Interest in the study of aging (gerontology) is growing. Unfortunately, little is actually known about healthy sexual development in late life. There are many reasons for this lack of knowledge. First, statistics about what is "normal" and what is "average" can be misleading. For example, the Association of Reproductive Health Professionals (ARHP) study (2002) reported that 52 percent of men 50 to 59 years of age, 26 percent of those 60 to 69, and 27 percent 70 years and older engaged in some form of sexual activity more than once a week. These statistics may provide a benchmark, but they only offer a glimpse at normal sexual development in these age-groups.

Second, a review of the literature will quickly reveal that most textbooks and articles ignore the subject of sexuality in the elderly population. If it is discussed, the emphasis is on dysfunction or disease rather than on healthy sexual development. In addition, most of what is written on sexuality in older adults is based on the Classic Triad. The Classic Triad consists of the seminal work of Alfred Kinsey, Masters and Johnson, and Eric Pfeiffer (Fogel & Lauver, 1990). Kinsey's investigations into sexual behavior shattered many common myths about sexual activities practiced by older men and women (Kinsey, Pomeroy, & Martin, 1948; Kinsey, Pomeroy, Martin, & Gebhard, 1953). The pioneering research of Masters and Johnson (1966) has formed the basis of most teaching on the normal age-related changes in sexual functioning. Likewise, the Duke Longitudinal Studies reported by Pfeiffer (Pfeiffer, Verwoerdt, & Wang, 1968; Pfeiffer & Davis, 1972) represented a significant piece of research on aging since it allowed for observations of individual changes over time.

Although the Classic Triad opened discussion of sexuality and aging, there are significant limitations to these projects. In most cases, the samples of older adults were very small and not representative of the older population as a whole. For example, older people were administered only a portion of the total survey instrument in the classic Kinsey studies and were excluded completely toward the end of the fieldwork (Rossi, 1994). The studies of both Kinsey and Masters and Johnson were hindered by the small sample size. Kinsey surveyed only 126 men and 56 women over the age of 60, and they were completely excluded from the follow-up surveys. Masters and Johnson (1966) observed only thirty-one men and women over age 60 and only nine of their participants were over 70 years of age. Consequently, caution must be used when applying the findings from these small samples to the general older population (Rossi, 1994).

Similarly, the cultural and social changes that have occurred over the last thirty to sixty years since these studies were conducted are too significant to ignore. Improvements in health and advanced longevity each challenge the relevance of these studies to today's older adults. For example, the average woman now lives to be 82 and, thus, she can be expected to live one-third of her life post-menopausal (Kingsberg, 2002). Simply stated, one-fourth of a woman's sexual life will be experienced in her later years. Given that fact, it is remarkable that there has been so little research on sexual development in older adults.

Finally, the elderly are a more varied group than most people believe. In fact, the definition of "aged" continues to change as medical advances improve the quality of life and longevity. The definition of "late life" tends to be reserved for persons over the age of 65, historically, the age of retirement. Yet, the growing numbers of 70-, 80-, and even 90-year-olds in our population means that late life is a period that can span thirty years or more. We must remember that the differences between people in their sixties and those in their eighties are often greater than those between 20- and 60-year-olds. The differences between a healthy 65-year-old and his 90-year-old parent who suffers from dementia can be more extreme than the differences between a teenager and her 43-year-old mother. In fact, our definition of late life means that two living generations of the same family could be included in the same category, and hence they could be facing some of the very same challenges, including those relating to sexual development.

WHAT IS "OLD"?

When discussing late life, it is important to determine what is "old." Obviously, like beauty, "old" is in the eyes of the beholder. In other words, "old" is highly subjective. People in their eighties may not consider themselves old. In fact, many adults in later life do not consider themselves old because they feel healthy and maintain active lives. They have fallen prey to stereotypes of the elderly as decrepit or infirm and, therefore, believe that as long as they "feel" young and remain active they are not old.

We must consider that how we define old has very real ramifications for policy formation, public perceptions, and for individuals' self-concept (Calasanti & Slevin, 2001). For our purposes, we will use *chronological age* as our criterion and define *later life* as the period after age 65 until death. But this too can be a biased and flawed definition because age identification is made up of more than chronological age or the number of years since a person's birth. It also is made up of how old one feels as compared to one's peers, known as *subjective age,* and one's assessment of one's own status in relation to the ideal for one's age-group, or *functional age* (Calasanti & Slevin). It is important to note that as life expectancy is extended and our knowledge of what is "normal development" for this stage grows, it may become necessary to divide later life into further stages.

THEORIES OF DEVELOPMENT AND AGING

Sexuality in later life is a culmination of all of the developmental processes an individual has experienced up to that point. This stage is generally marked by a stable sense of self-identity. Most changes that do occur tend to take place subtly and gradually, even those that follow momentous life events, such as the loss of a spouse. Most individuals continue to see themselves as basically the same person they have always been (Schuster & Ashburn, 1992). This is also true of a person's sexuality. Yet, theorists have viewed normal development in the elderly in different ways.

Cummings and Henry first described the disengagement theory in 1961. They maintained that in old age, the individual and the society mutually withdraw from one another in four steps. The first begins in late middle age, when traditional roles, such as worker and parent, become less relevant or less important and as one's social circle begins to shrink as friends die or move away. In the second step, people anticipate, adjust to, and participate in this narrowing of the social sphere by giving up many of the roles they have played and by accepting this disengagement. Third, as people become less role centered, their style of interaction changes from an active to a passive one. Finally, because of this more passive style of interaction, older people are less likely to be chosen for new roles, and, therefore, they are likely to disengage further. This theory proposes that the elderly voluntarily participate in the disengagement process and that by old-old age, people prefer to be withdrawn from most social interactions, avoiding the noisy bustle and insistent demands of the younger person's world (Berger & Thompson, 1998; Cummings & Henry, 1961).

Disengagement theory has been highly controversial due to its assumption that this withdrawal is not only universal but also voluntary. But the most unfortunate aspect of the theory is that it reinforces many ageist stereotypes. Palmore (1999) argued that it perpetuated discrimination in everything from forced retirement to socially sterile nursing homes based on the premise that the elderly, after all, want to withdraw.

An opposing theory is the activity theory, which proposes that people age most successfully when they participate fully in daily activities, that is, by keeping busy (Lemon, Bengtson, & Peterson, 1972). According to this theory, remaining active and adopting numerous roles in life promote satisfaction and longevity. But this theory too has fallen out of favor. Yet, many of the elderly continue to believe that activity is the key to successful aging, so much so that gerontologists have dubbed this philosophy "the busy ethic" (Ekerdt, 1986).

The argument against activity theory is that it is not the absolute number of roles or activities an elder engages in that predicts satisfaction but how close the level of activity is to one's individual preference (Lomranz, Bergman, Eyal, & Shmotkin, 1988). This is the general basis of the continuity theory, which states that each person deals with late adulthood in much the same way that he or she coped with earlier periods of life (Atchley, 1989). The continuity theory is a primarily sociologically oriented theory that uses the concept of continuity of socialization and the idea of stages of life. Each stage builds upon the next, and to understand a person's response to aging you must examine the complex interrelationships among the biological, psychological, and social changes in his or her life and previous behavior patterns (Cox, 2005).

Controversy surrounding the disengagement and activity theories has also led many gerontologists to turn to developmental psychology theories to explain the adjustments of advancing age (Cox, 2005). Sigmund Freud (1949) emphasized sexual function in the overall development of humans. Freud believed that early sexual development had important and lasting effects. He emphasized the earliest developmental stages as the most important and believed that development culminates in adulthood with the final or genital phase. On the other hand, Erikson (1984) proposed eight stages that continued throughout the life span. He stated that late life was a time for reflecting on one's own life and its significance. He described the developmental task of old age as *integrity versus despair.* Ego integrity involves an acceptance of the way one has lived and continues to live one's life. It is also the assessment that one remains in control of one's own life. Erikson defines the failure to master this stage as ego despair. Ego despair is a state of conflict about the way one has lived and continues to live one's life. It is the subjective experience of dissatisfaction, disappointment, or disgust about the course of one's life, together with the conviction that if given another chance one would have chosen a different course. The individual struggles with despair and, therefore, fears death and the loss of meaning (Schuster & Ashburn, 1992).

Continuity theory and Erikson's psychosocial theory of development seem most useful in understanding sexuality in late life. Older persons believe sexuality is a vital part of their lives, much like it was in their early adulthood. If they have successfully mastered a sense of ego integrity, they are more likely to accept their sexuality and continue to feel in control. A sense of satisfaction with one's past sexual experience seems to be an important predictor of a person's satisfaction with sexuality in late life. The frequency of sexual activity decreases with age, but sexual satisfaction does not (AARP, 2005; ARHP, 2002; Avis, 2000; Kingsberg, 2002; Laumann, Paik, & Rosen, 1999; Schuster & Ashburn, 1992; SIECUS, 2002).

In fact, older adults often find that some aspects of their sexual lives improve with age. There are, of course, inevitable physical changes with advanced age. Older individuals also find that they are not immune to the effects of societal and peer attitudes on what is acceptable sexual behavior. Ageism affects many people, including older persons themselves.

SEXUAL PHYSIOLOGY IN LATER LIFE

> There seems to be no physiologic reason why the frequency of sexual expression found satisfactory for the younger women should not be carried over into the postmenopausal years. (Masters & Johnson, 1966, p. 246)

> There is every reason to believe that maintained regularity of sexual expression coupled with adequate physical well-being and healthy mental orientation to the aging process will combine to provide a sexually stimulative climate within a marriage. This climate will, in turn, improve sexual tension and provide a capacity for sexual performance that frequently may extend to and beyond the 80-year age level. (Masters & Johnson, 1966, p. 270)

When discussing aging and sexual physiology in late life, most articles and texts adhere closely to the observations of Masters and Johnson (1966). They concentrated on senescence or the weakening and decline in the body, as well as the sexual response cycle and the changes in individuals over the age of 40. The sexual response cycle consists of four phases: drive or desire, arousal, release or orgasm, and resolution, which includes the refractory period in men. In the presence of desire, a person experiences the drive to engage in sexual behavior. Effective sexual stimulation, whether psychological or physical, triggers erotic arousal or excitement. The plateau phase, a period of sustained arousal, follows. Continued effective sexual stimulation leads to orgasm, followed by resolution, during which organs and tissues return to their resting state. The pattern of changes throughout the sexual response cycle applies to both sexes with the exception of the resolution phase. Following orgasm, men experience a refractory period during which they are unable to respond to further stimulation until an obligatory period of rest has occurred (for a review, see Trudel, Turgeon, & Piché, 2000).

Drive or desire remains fairly stable in both men and women throughout life. Multiple studies, including those by Avis (2000), Laumann et al. (1999), as well as surveys by the National Council on the Aging, AARP (1999, 2005), and ARHP (2002), have shown that frequency of sexual activity may decrease but satisfaction and desire do not (Kingsberg, 2002; Schuster & Ashburn, 1992).

Arousal is the phase most affected by aging. In women, the decline and eventual cessation of estrogen production during menopause may lead to atrophy of urogenital tissues and an overall decrease in genital vasocongestion and lubrication during arousal. Both sexes may experience a prolonged arousal phase, which may require more direct genital stimulation (Demeter, 1998; Masters & Johnson, 1966; Miller, Versi, & Resnik, 1999).

Orgasm tends to be the phase least affected by aging, especially in women. Men may need sustained direct stimulation and additional time to reach orgasm.

They also tend to have decreased volume of ejaculate and less forceful ejaculation. Women retain their ability to achieve orgasm. Some women may experience pain during orgasm that is associated with the orgasmic contractions of the uterus and vagina becoming less rhythmic and coordinated (Demeter, 1998; Masters & Johnson, 1966; Miller et al., 1999). Yet, despite this change, older persons report that their orgasms are as satisfying as ever. For those who have problems achieving orgasm, it is likely to be related to medications, illness, or previous problems with orgasm. In other words, aging alone does not interfere with the ability to have an orgasm.

The refractory period is the phase most affected in older men. The resolution phase right after orgasm becomes shorter with advanced age: in other words, men return to the non-aroused state more quickly with advanced age. But the time that it takes a man to regroup, the refractory period, is prolonged as it can take anywhere from twelve to twenty-four hours or longer before he can achieve another orgasm (Milsten & Slowinski, 1999). Women tend not to have a refractory period and, therefore, are less affected by aging during this phase. A woman who is multiorgasmic will remain so in late life (Beers & Berkow, 2000; Demeter, 1998; Masters & Johnson, 1966; Miller et al., 1999).

In women, other changes that occur with aging include shortening and narrowing of the vagina, as well as changes in the chemistry of the vagina; decreased acidic secretions increase the risk of vaginal infections (Trudel et al., 2000). Cystitis, or bladder infection, is more common in older women. Decreased estrogen levels may also lead to a decrease in clitoral size, incontinence, and a graying and thinning of pubic hair. Estrogen replacement therapy prevents or reduces many of these problems. However, estrogen replacement may also increase the risk of some cancers and heart attacks in women with heart disease and therefore must be used with caution. Women who remain sexually active have fewer problems maintaining their sexual activity and genital health. Some of the declines in sexual functioning that are more common in older persons are related to illness, medication side-effects, or even sexual inactivity rather than to aging per se (Beers & Berkow, 2000; Demeter, 1998; Miller et al., 1999).

Normal physical changes in older men include decreased production of testosterone, which levels off around age 60. Likewise, the testicles decrease in size and firmness, sperm production is reduced, and the prostate increases in size. In addition, men may notice that preejaculatory fluid is reduced. Erections may be less durable and less firm. Men do not experience an equivalent of menopause, and they often remain fertile throughout life. Although sexual dysfunction is not a part of aging, erectile dysfunction is a common concern for many older men. The incidence of erectile dysfunction does increase with age, but aging per se is not the cause. Medical conditions and medications are usually responsible for the increased rate of erectile dysfunction in older men (Laumann et al., 1999). Stress and emotional problems also can affect erectile functioning. For example, the widower's syndrome refers to temporary erectile dysfunction experienced by some men who remarry following the death of their first wives. This is more likely to occur if the former wife's prolonged illness demanded sexual abstinence (Rossi, 1994).

In the book *Fifty—Midlife in Perspective*, Katchadourian (1987) points out that these age-related physical changes are not abnormalities and do not preclude an enjoyment of sex at midlife and beyond. Some individuals, however, do have difficulty accepting these normal age-related changes in sexual functioning. Sexual dysfunction specifically refers to recurring and persistent problems with sexual desire, performance, or satisfaction. One of the most common forms of sexual dysfunction is the inhibition of sexual desire, evident by a continuous and overall lack of sexual interest. Disorders of sexual excitement may result in problems with erection in men and vaginal lubrication in women. Difficulties with orgasm in the male typically take the form of premature ejaculation and sometimes of failure to ejaculate. Women may experience undue delay or inability to reach orgasm despite normal sexual arousal and adequate erotic stimulation. Painful intercourse, which is rare in men, is common among women. It is typically caused by spasm of the musculature surrounding the vaginal opening, which may be due to psychological factors or various forms of pelvic pathology (Katchadourian).

Sexual dysfunction usually arises from multiple causes, including psychological, physiological, physical, and interpersonal components. In late life, sexual dysfunction can be viewed from three different perspectives (Katchadourian, 1987). First, the normal physiological changes that occur may be misperceived as evidence of sexual failure. For example, a softer penis or a drier vagina is seen as a sign of impotence or loss of sexual desire. Second, sexual dysfunction can result from physical illness. And third, since sexual intercourse entails an interaction between two individuals, sexual dysfunction often reflects disturbances in a couple's relationship, which may or may not be related to sexual issues.

These documented age-related changes in sexual functioning are based on studies of a small number of men and women. What is becoming increasingly clear is that aging alone does not usually cause sexual problems. For example, menopause has a small effect on women's sexual functioning (Avis, 2000). Conditions such as heart disease, stroke, diabetes, depression, and alcohol abuse have a much greater impact on sexual functioning than does aging (Tallis, Fillit, & Brocklehurst, 1998).

It is also important to realize that sexual intercourse is not the only sexual outlet for people of any age. Older adults enjoy sexual fantasy and masturbation. Abstinence is also a legitimate choice for some individuals. Increasingly, the Internet is increasingly being used as a resource for older adults for finding information, meeting other people, or even as a safe outlet for sexual needs (Adams, Oye, & Parker, 2003).

SOCIETY AND LATER LIFE SEXUALITY

Societal expectations often have more of an impact on sexuality in late life than actual physiological changes do. Many of the common views and stereotypes of aging profoundly influence older adults and their sexual attitudes. According to the sociological view of the normative timetables of the life course, sexual interest should begin in midadolescence and reach full expression during midadulthood, coinciding with the height of fertility and physical attractiveness. Therefore, sex is believed to be the prerogative of youth (Booth, 1990). This view partly arises from traditional values that equate sexuality with procreation. Because pregnancy and childbirth are not part of the older person's experience, it is assumed that they should not need or want sex (Rossi, 1994). This attitude is a reflection of the larger problem of ageism.

Robert Butler, the first director of the National Institute on Aging, coined the term *ageism* to describe the process of systematic stereotyping and discrimination of older adults (Butler, 1969; Robinson, 1994). He equated ageism with racism and sexism and defined it as simply "not wanting to have all those ugly old people around" (Butler, 1975). By the nineteenth century, there is clear evidence of contempt for the aged along with the development of a cult of youth in literature, the emergence of derogatory terms such as "fogey" and "geezer," and the introduction of mandatory retirement policies. By this time, people increasingly associated advanced age with helplessness, illness, and "senility" (Calasanti & Slevin, 2001; Haber, 1983). Fischer (1977) attributes the decline in the status of older people to two important factors: the growth of the population due to increased life expectancies and birth rates, and the radical expansion of the ideas of equality and liberty that were seen as the "new world order." Older persons had the misfortune of belonging to the old world order, and they were seen as reminders of what the new order hoped to avoid: dependence, disease, failure, and death (Calasanti & Slevin, 2001; Cole, 1992).

Ageism is a cultural phenomenon whose acceptance is widespread as it cuts across all social classes, age-groups, and regions (Kart, 1989). Many of the stereotypes of aging are particularly negative with respect to sexuality. Depictions of older adults as sickly, senile, unattractive, impotent, and asexual have a powerful influence on all people, including older persons. Myths and stereotypes of older persons are pervasive; they are perpetuated in the mass media as well as in literature. But ageist attitudes toward sexuality were not born out of a vacuum as they have a long history.

In reviewing perceptions and attitudes from the Middle Ages, Covey (1989) found that although little had been written about elderly sexuality, what did exist was overwhelmingly negative. A double standard was also revealed that painted older men's participation in sexual activity as comical or pathetic, whereas older women's participation in sex was viewed as unnatural and evil. For example, older men were thought to have no capacity for sexual relations, and those who were able to maintain active sex lives were believed to have exceptional qualities that helped them gain social status and even increase their life span. In contrast, older women were thought to be able to have sex in later years only if they were able to trick a man into going to bed with them, a feat so abhorrent that it required the aid of witchcraft. Bullough (1976) revealed that medieval religious prohibitions mirrored popular beliefs about sexuality in the elderly. At the core is the belief that sexual intercourse was intended for procreation only. This doctrine promoted the belief that older adults who had sex were engaged in a "sin against nature." Thus, we can trace clichés of "wicked witches" and "dirty old men" to distant history (Covey, 1989; Hillman, 2000).

In contemporary Western cultures, we equate aging with dying, and we view older adults as defective or decrepit. This view is fortunately not universal. Many cultures prize and admire the characteristics of old age. In a groundbreaking study of more than 106 cultures, Winn and Newton (1982) described many of the beliefs about sexuality in late life as stereotypes. In fact, most cultures they studied had favorable views of sexuality and aging: fewer than 3 percent have prohibitions against sex for older adults. The vast majority of older adults, 70 percent of men and 84 percent of women, enjoyed active sexual lives. In many Eastern and Middle Eastern cultures, men who were as old as 100 continued to engage in sexual relations. Many cultures did not view a loss of sexual functioning as an inevitable part of aging. For example, some African cultures attribute erectile problems to such unnatural phenomena as illness or witchcraft (Winn & Newton).

In the majority of these traditional cultures, menopause is not associated with changes in older women's level of sexual activity: it is simply a phase in a woman's life. In certain African and Asian cultures, an older woman's physical attractiveness is unrelated to her sexual status: older women are considered as sexually desirable as younger women. In addition, although a double standard operates with regard to elderly sexuality, it is in the opposite direction: older women are more likely to engage in sexual relations and are often described as becoming less sexually inhibited and more sexually adventuresome with age. In certain South American and Eastern cultures, older women even serve as sex educators for sexually inexperienced young men (Winn & Newton, 1982). An ancient Turkish proverb illustrates the positive sexual attitudes espoused by many traditional and preindustrial cultures: "Young love is from earth, while late love is from heaven" (Hillman, 2000).

Health care providers, unfortunately, are not exempt from ageist attitudes. Even physicians often assume that sexuality is unimportant in late life (Butler, 1975). The American health care system also perpetuates ageism by focusing on acute care and cure rather than on chronic care, which some older adults need. It is also done covertly by denying or limiting services, by not including aging issues in training materials or educational offerings for providers, and by not requiring training in geriatrics in medical schools even though older adults constitute a significant proportion of their future patients. But ageism is not the only obstacle to a healthy expression of sexuality for older adults. Some of the other barriers include lack of a partner, sexual dysfunction, attitudes of adult children, altered body image, previous attitudes toward sex, attitudes of peers, religious prohibitions against sex outside of marriage, depression, lack of autonomy of choice, lack of privacy, marital conflict, and libido mismatch. As Judith Levy (1994) noted in *Sexuality Across the Life Course*:

> [A]lthough negative influences of ageism are an important variable that potentially can dampen sexual interest, meeting the rigors and demands of daily life also shapes older people's sexual drives. Engaging in sex at any age requires an investment of time, psychosocial involvement and energy. Like individuals of other age groups, older people's sexual drives may decline or die under the pressures of mental or physical fatigue, preoccupation with business interests, overindulgence in food or drink, physical illness and fear of sexual failure. (p. 291)

In the Duke Longitudinal Studies, Verwoerdt et al. (Pfeiffer et al., 1968; Verwoerdt, Pfeiffer, & Wang, 1969) found that sexual interest did not decline with age in their sample of men and women aged 64 to 94. In fact, sexual interest can persist indefinitely. They also found that patterns of sexual behavior in the later years correlate with those of younger years. Individuals who enjoyed an active sexual life in their younger years usually retained their sexual interest in the later years. Unfortunately, older persons are not immune to ageism, which they may internalize. Older adults may feel shame and embarrassment about having sexual interests (Brogan, 1996; Trudel et al., 2000).

Nontraditional Relationships among Older Adults

Due in part to the sexual revolution and the gay rights movement, older adults are becoming more open about their involvement in nontraditional romantic relationships including gay, lesbian, and cohabiting heterosexual relationships (Hillman, 2000). Alternative sexual lifestyles can present new and unique challenges at all stages of life, and this can be especially difficult for older adults. Many of the obstacles faced by all aging adults, such as institutionalization, lack of or loss of a partner, ageist attitudes from the community or adult children, and loneliness apply to those in unconventional relationships too. Research by Kelly (1977) shows that although many of these individuals do enjoy stable relationships in later life, they still have to face the fears of losing a partner or of having to live in an assisted-living arrangement (Burnside, 1988). These challenges are magnified by the prejudice and bias against alternative sexual lifestyles. Older same-sex or unmarried couples may be required to live in separate rooms in nursing homes, or one partner may be denied the visits usually reserved for family members. They may lack the family or social support offered to traditional heterosexual couples upon the loss or death of a spouse. In a culture that values youth and beauty, many gay men struggle to accept their changing physical appearance. Controversy also persists among clinicians and researchers regarding various issues such as the adoption of gay or bisexual identities later in life, particularly among women, and the impact of affairs within the context of long-term marriage (Hillman, 2000).

Many of these fears or myths are simply extensions of ageist attitudes. Sex, which supposedly only concerns young people, is just as important for aging gay and lesbian couples as it is for their heterosexual counterparts. Biases against same-sex relationships, premarital sex, or extramarital sex are shaped by cultural norms and values. Interestingly, several researchers have theorized that older adults who have experienced societal prejudice when they were younger may actually be more resistant to internalization of ageism later in life. It seems the experience of "coming out" may teach individuals skills useful in dealing with ageism or perhaps inoculate them against myths about aging (Berger, 1995; Francher & Henkin, 1973; Friend, 1990; Kimmel, 1978).

McDougall (1993) found that developmental and demographic changes associated with aging may actually work to the advantage of older gay men and lesbians. It is much more socially acceptable for two older men or women to live together as roommates than it is for younger same-sex couples. In fact, society seems to recognize that people, including older adults, want and need companionship. This belief, coupled with the ageist assumptions that older adults do not engage in sex and the invisibility of older gays and lesbians as a group, allows older same-sex couples to live together without causing any undue distress or homophobic anxiety among their heterosexual neighbors. Likewise, society is less likely to label physical contact among older adults of the same sex as inappropriate since it is not viewed as sexual in nature (Hillman, 2000; McDougall, 1993).

Older Institutionalized Adults

In the eyes of society, there is perhaps no place that is more asexual than a nursing home or assisted-living facility. Abbink (1983) noted that intimacy is a need "which is manifest from conception to death and it does not decrease in intensity or significance through adulthood." It is maintained not only by sexual intercourse, but also by touching, stroking, patting, hugging, and kissing, as well as emotionally by the sharing of joy, sorrow, affection, ideas, and values (Abbink). Yet, society seems to believe that institutionalized adults somehow lose the need for intimacy. Therefore, intimacy needs among the institutionalized aged require special attention.

Older institutionalized adults suffer from isolation and sensory deprivation, which probably intensify their need for physical contact. Stiffl (1984) suggests that these individuals require sexuality as part of their spiritual and emotional well-being rather than separating it out. She points out the importance of understanding that all meaningful sexual relationships are not heterosexual; accepting masturbation as an expression of sexuality; providing touch along with "feeling" objects to handle, fondle, and hold; using live pets to provide sensory stimulation; encouraging the use of music (romantic, sentimental, sensuous, and erotic) in nursing homes; and encouraging the opportunity for sexes to meet, mingle, and spend time together without structuring the trysting time or place too rigidly (Stiffl; Burnside, 1988).

Staff attitudes and institutional barriers against sexual expression are not the only factors affecting sexual expression in nursing-home residents. Illness, dementia, lack of privacy, and medications continue to be negative factors. Elderly people in nursing homes are also limited in their sexual opportunities by their own attitudes. Although sexual activity outside of marriage is widely accepted now, this was not the case during 1920–1940, when these elderly were developing a sense of morals. Also, the inequality in the ratio of men to women in these institutions effectively deprives lone elderly women of an opportunity to maintain an active sex life.

THE OLDEST OF THE OLD AND SEXUALITY

In their book, *The Oldest of the Old in Everyday Life,* Ruth Dunkle, Beverly Roberts, and Marie Haug (2001) discuss how the oldest adults perceive themselves and how they cope with change and stress. The authors studied "very old" adults, those 85 years of age and older. There is very little research on what is the fastest growing segment of the U.S. population. Most of these oldest adults are women, who often have health problems, and are more apt to be institutionalized, all of which can significantly impact their sexuality. Lack of partners, illness, medication, isolation, and lack of privacy all are obstacles to sexuality in older persons. The oldest adults are more likely to have lost their spouses and to have a shrinking network of friends, which limits opportunities for sexual expression and intimacy (Dunkle et al., 2001).

Satisfactory marital and sexual relationships are important to quality of life from early adulthood throughout life. Whereas young adults often form social friendships in the workplace, the oldest of the old turn to social clubs, church groups, political organizations, and senior centers for social support. However, the oldest women have fewer opportunities for sexual relationships because of the gender imbalance in this age-group. There are two women for every man among adults 80 years of age and older (U.S. Census Bureau, 2001). The gap increases in older age-groups.

Contrary to popular stereotypes, unmarried and widowed older women miss having a sexual relationship. They report that the gender imbalance detracts from their quality of life. The need for a healthy sexual partner remains important for most adults in all age-groups. It is especially challenging for many of the oldest of the old (Dunkle et al., 2001).

SEXUALITY AND DEMENTIA

Dementia involves more than declining mental abilities. The cost of dementia, especially Alzheimer's disease, on the individual, the partner, the family, and society is quite high. Sexual functioning during the early to moderate stages of Alzheimer's disease is often not spared; the individual may experience problems with orgasm, erectile dysfunction, and impaired sex drive. As dementia progresses, inhibitions may be compromised, which can introduce many problems for patients and their partners. In the later stages of dementia, patients may fail to recognize their lifelong partners.

Partners of patients with dementia struggle with the progressive changes in their relationships, including the loss of intimacy and sexual fulfillment. Caregiving is often stressful and demanding, which can add to the loss of intimacy. For many couples, dementia may cause reversals in roles and affect every aspect of their relationship (Lenahan, 2004).

There are basic guidelines that caregivers and providers can use to determine if a patient with dementia is able to consent to sexual activity. Several factors to consider include degree of mental impairment, lifelong sex values and practices, the ability to initiate and decline sexual overtures, and overall physical health (Galindo, 1995). Without a doubt, the sexual needs of adults with dementia and their partners pose significant challenges (see Ehrenfeld, Bronner, Tabak, Alpert, & Bergman, 1999).

SEXUALITY AND END OF LIFE

Later life sexuality has received little attention. Sexuality at the end of life, however, has been virtually ignored. Recent studies suggest that sexual expression can serve as a form of communication and intimacy that should be considered in the overall care plans of individuals receiving hospice (Hordern, 2003; Stausmire, 2004). Health care providers should encourage an open discussion of sexual needs of adults who may be near the end of their lives. Couples who previously enjoyed active sexual lives should be reassured that they can participate in various forms of intimacy to the extent that their health permits (Lenahan, 2004).

CONCLUSIONS

Sexuality is a fundamental need for adults of all ages. Older adults usually retain an interest in sexual intimacy, and they view it as an important part of rewarding relationships (AARP, 2005). Unfortunately, negative views of aging and common stereotypes are detrimental to sexual enjoyment later in life. A growing body of research reveals that older adults are able to enjoy sexual fulfillment if they are physically and psychologically healthy and if they have a partner (Trudel et al., 2000). The sexual problems that are more prevalent in older populations are not products of aging per se: they are due to factors such as medications or illnesses. There are predictable changes in sexual functioning with advancing age, but none of these preclude sexual activity although they may require some adjustments.

The sexual needs of the growing segment of the population have been largely neglected. Similarly, the needs of the oldest adults, those living in institutions, and those suffering from health problems, including dementia, are only beginning to be understood. More research is needed to address these needs and to combat the negative stereotypes and myths about sexuality and aging.

REFERENCES

Abbink, C. (1983). Adult development and the impact of disruption. In S. Lewis & I. Collier (Eds.), *Medical-surgical nursing: Assessment and management of clinical problems* (pp. 14–31). New York: McGraw-Hill.

Adams, M. S., Oye, J., & Parker, T. S. (2003). Sexuality of older adults and the Internet: From sex education to cybersex. *Sexual and Relationship Therapy, 18*, 405–415.

American Association of Retired Persons. (1999). *Modern maturity sexuality study*. Washington, DC: Author.

American Association of Retired Persons. (2005). *Sexuality at midlife and beyond: 2004 update of attitudes and behaviors*. Washington, DC: Author.

Association of Reproductive Health Professionals. (2002). Sexuality in middle and later life. Retrieved October 10, 2003, from www.siecus.org/pubs/fact/fact0018.html

Atchley, R. C. (1989). A continuity theory of normal aging. *Gerontologist, 29*(2), 183–190.

Avis, N. E. (2000). Is there an association between menopause status and sexual functioning? *Menopause, 7*(5), 286–288.

Beers, M. H., & Berkow, R. (2000). Sexuality. Retrieved October 10, 2003, from www.merck.com/mrkshared/mm_geriatrics/sec14/ch114.jsp

Berger, K. S., & Thompson, R. A. (1998). *The developing person through the lifespan* (4th ed.). New York: Worth.

Berger, R. M. (1995). *Gay and gray: The older homosexual man* (2nd ed.). New York: Haworth Press.

Booth, B. (1990). Does it really matter at that age? *Nursing Times, 86*, 51–52.

Brogan, M. (1996). The sexual needs of elderly people: Addressing the issue. *Nursing Standard, 10*, 42–45.

Bullough, V. L. (1976). *Sex, society, and history*. New York: Science History.

Burnside, I. M. (1988). *Nursing and the aged: A self care approach* (3rd ed.). New York: McGraw-Hill.

Butler, R. N. (1969). Age-ism: Another form of bigotry. *Gerontologist, 9*, 243–246.

Butler, R. N. (1975). Psychiatry and the elderly: An overview [Abstract]. *American Journal of Psychiatry, 132*, 893–900.

Calasanti, T. M., & Slevin, K. F. (2001). *Gender, social inequalities, and aging.* Walnut Creek, CA: Altamira Press.

Carroll, J. L., & Wolpe, P. R. (1996). *Sexuality and gender in society.* New York: HarperCollins.

Cole, T. (1992). *The journey of life: A cultural history of aging in America.* New York: Cambridge University Press.

Covey, H. C. (1989). Perceptions and attitudes toward sexuality of the elderly during the Middle Ages [Abstract]. *Gerontologist, 29,* 93–100.

Cox, H. (2005). *Annual editions: Aging 05/06.* Columbus, OH: McGraw-Hill/Dushkin.

Cummings, E., & Henry, W. (1961). *Growing old: The process of disengagement.* New York: Basic Books.

Demeter, D. (1998). *The human sexuality web: Sex and the elderly.* Retrieved October 10, 2003, from www.umkc.edu/sites/hsw/age/index.html

Dunkle, R., Roberts, B., & Haug, M. (2001). *The oldest of the old in everyday life: Self-perception, coping with change and stress.* New York: Springer.

Ehrenfeld, M., Bronner, G., Tabak, N., Alpert, R., & Bergman, R. (1999). Sexuality among institutionalized elderly patients with dementia. *Nursing Ethics, 6,* 144–149.

Ekerdt, D. J. (1986). The busy ethic: Moral continuity between work and retirement. *Gerontologist, 26*(3), 239–244.

Erikson, E. H. (1984). Reflections on the last stage—and the first. *Harvard Educational Review, 51,* 249–269.

Fischer, D. H. (1977). *Growing old in America.* New York: Oxford University Press.

Fogel, C. I., & Lauver, D. (Eds.) (1990). *Sexual health promotion.* Philadephia: W. B. Saunders.

Francher, J. S., & Henkin, J. (1973). The menopausal queen: Adjustment to aging and the male homosexual. *American Journal of Orthopsychiatry, 43*(4), 670–674.

Freud, S. (1949). *An outline of psychoanalysis* (1st ed.). New York: W. W. Norton.

Friend, R. A. (1990). Older lesbian and gay people: A theory of successful aging. *Journal of Homosexuality, 20*(3/4), 99–118.

Galindo, D., & Kaiser, F. E. (1995). Sexual health after 60. *Patient Care, 29,* 25–38.

Haber, C. (1983). *Beyond sixty-five: The dilemma of old age in America's past.* New York: Cambridge University Press.

Hillman, J. (2000). *Clinical perspectives on elderly sexuality.* New York: Kluwer Academic.

Hordern, A. J. (2003). A patient-centered approach to sexuality in the face of life-threatening illness. *Medical Journal of Australia, 179,* S8–S11.

Human Sexuality. (2005). In *Wikipedia* (Vol. 1). Retrieved March 8, 2005, from www.en.wikipedia.org/wiki/Sexual_behavior

Juska, J. (2003). *A round-heeled woman: My late-life adventures in sex and romance.* New York: Villard Books.

Kart, C. S. (1989). *The realities of aging—An introduction to gerontology.* Boston: Allyn & Bacon.

Katchadourian, H. (1987). *Fifty—Midlife in perspective*. New York: W. H. Freeman.

Katz, S., & Marshall, B. (2003). New sex for old: Lifestyle, consumerism, and the ethics of aging well. *Journal of Aging Studies, 17*, 3–16.

Kelly, J. (1977). The aging male homosexual: Myth and reality. *Gerontologist, 17*, 328–332.

Kimmel, D. C. (1978). Adult development and aging: A gay perspective. *Journal of Social Issues, 34*, 113–130.

Kingsberg, S. A. (2002). The impact of aging on sexual function in women and their partners. *Archives of Sexual Behavior, 31*(5), 431–437.

Kinsey, A. C., Pomeroy, W. B., & Martin, C. E. (1948). *Sexual behavior in the human male*. Philadelphia: Saunders.

Kinsey, A. C., Pomeroy, W. B., Martin, C. E., & Gebhard, P. H. (1953). *Sexual behavior in the human female*. Philadelphia: Saunders.

Laumann, E. O., Paik, A., & Rosen, R. C. (1999). Sexual dysfunction in the United States: Prevalence and predictors. *Journal of the American Medical Association, 281*(6), 537–544.

Lemon, B., Bengtson, V., & Peterson, J. (1972). An exploration of the activity theory of aging. *Journal of Gerontology, 27*, 511–523.

Lenahan, P. (2004). Sexual health and aging. *Clinics in Family Practice, 6*(4), 918–936.

Levy, J. (1994). Sex and sexuality in later life stages. In A. S. Rossi (Ed.), *Sexuality across the life course* (pp. 287–313). Chicago: University of Chicago Press.

Lomranz, L., Bergman, S. E., & Shmotkin, D. (1988). Indoor and outdoor activities of aged women and men as related to depression and wellbeing. *International Journal of Aging and Human Development, 26*, 303–314.

Masters, W. H., & Johnson, V. E. (1966). *Human sexual response*. Boston: Little, Brown.

McDougall, G. J. (1993). Therapeutic issues with gay and lesbian elders. *Clinical Gerontologist, 14*, 45–57.

Miller, K. L., Versi, E., & Resnik, N. M. (1999). Geriatric gynecology and aging. In K. J. Ryan (Ed.), *Kistner's gynecology & women's health* (7th ed., pp. 610–670). St. Louis, MO: Mosby.

Milsten, R., & Slowinski, J. (1999). *The sexual male: Problems and solutions*. New York: W. W. Norton.

National Council on the Aging. (1998, September 28). Half of older Americans report they are sexually active; 4 in 10 want more sex, says new survey. Retrieved November 14, 2003, from www.ncoa.org/content.cfm?sectionID=105&detail=128

Novelli, W. D. (2002). *Helping aging boomers age in place*. Retrieved March 8, 2005, from www.aarp.org/leadership/articles/a2003-01-03-geinplace.html

Palmore, E. (1999). *Ageism: Negative and positive* (2nd ed.). New York: Springer.

Pfeiffer, E., & Davis, G. C. (1972). Determinants of sexual behavior in middle and old age. *Journal of the American Geriatric Society, 20*, 151–158.

Pfeiffer, E., Verwoerdt, A., & Wang, H. S. (1968). Sexual behavior in aged men and women: I. Observation of 254 community volunteers. *Archives of General Psychiatry, 19*, 753–758.

Robinson, B. (1994). *Ageism*. Berkeley: University of California Press.

Rossi, A. S. (Ed.). (1994). *Sexuality across the life course*. Chicago: University of Chicago Press.

Schuster, C. S., & Ashburn, S. S. (1992). *The process of human development: A holistic approach*. Philadelphia: Lippincott.

Sexuality Information and Education Council of the United States (2002). Sexuality and aging revisited. *SIECUS Report, 30(2)*, 1–60.

Sherrill, M. (2003, November/December). Walk on the wild side. *AARP The Magazine*, 52–57.

Stausmire, J. M. (2004). Sexuality at the end of life. *American Journal of Hospice and Palliative Care, 21*, 33–39.

Stiffl, B. (1984). Sexuality and the aging. In B. Stiffl (Ed.), *Handbook of gerontological nursing* (pp. 450–464). New York: Van Nostrand Reinhold.

Stone, J. T., Wyman, J. F., & Salisbury, S. A. (1999). *Clinical gerontological nursing: A guide to advanced practice* (2nd ed.). Philadelphia: Saunders.

Tallis, R., Fillit, H., & Brocklehurst, R. C. (1998). *Brocklehurst's textbook of geriatric medicine and gerontology* (5th ed.). London: Churchill Livingstone.

Trudel, G., Turgeon, L., & Piché, L. (2000). Marital and sexual aspects of old age. *Sexual and Relationship Therapy, 15*(4), 381–406.

United States Census Bureau. (2001). *An aging world: 2001* (Series P95/01–1). Washington, DC: U.S. Government Printing Office.

Verwoerdt, A., Pfeiffer, E., & Wang, H. S. (1969). Sexual behavior in senescence: II. Patterns of sexual activity and interest. *Geriatrics, 24*, 137–154.

Winn, R. L., & Newton, N. (1982). Sexuality in aging: A study of 106 cultures. *Archives of Sexual Behavior, 11*, 283–298.

7

Sexual Orientation and Identity

Michael R. Kauth ◆

For two centuries, Western culture has devoted enormous attention to sexual orientation, particularly, homosexuality (Bullough, 1994). Shifting social beliefs about homosexuality have influenced psychiatric concepts and practices, law and civil rights such as marriage, as well as military service. This chapter describes the concept of sexual orientation, sexual identities in America and in other cultures, current sexuality theories, and recent events involving sexual orientation.

DEFINITIONS AND IDENTITIES

Sexual orientation is the experience of or capacity for erotic or sexual attraction to one or both sexes (Kauth, 2000). *Sexual attraction* is a desire for emotional or physical intimacy and physiological arousal associated with an individual or class of persons. Sexual attraction sometimes leads to sexual behavior with a partner, for example, passionate kissing, oral sex, vaginal intercourse, and so on. In the absence of a partner, sexual desire may lead to sexual fantasies or masturbation. *Sexual (orientation) identity* is the personal identification with a category of sexual attraction: *heterosexual* or *straight* (male-female or other-sex attraction), *homosexual* or *gay/lesbian* (same-sex attraction), and *bisexual* (attraction to both sexes). These labels are thought to reflect particular personality traits and social behaviors but are actually poor indicators of both, as discussed below.

Stigma related to homosexuality, the desire to be perceived as heterosexual and accepted by one's community, as well as the awareness of and comfort with one's own sexual feelings all influence an individual's choice of sexual identity. For many people, sexual identity is about how one wants to be perceived, rather than an indicator of sexual feelings. Prior to identifying as gay or lesbian, many men and women identify as heterosexual, or at least bisexual. African American men and other men of color on the *down low* identify as heterosexual and maintain heterosexual relationships, but engage in clandestine sexual behavior with men (King, 2004). So-called ex-gays, who have undergone treatment to change their same-sex attraction, identify as heterosexual, although their same-sex feelings have not changed (Besen, 2003). For some people, same-sex attraction is not "discovered" until after many years of heterosexual marriage (Rust, 2000a). Are these two latter groups actually bisexual? Further, in the 1970s and 1980s, many feminists identified as lesbians as a political statement, although they did not have sexual relationships with women (Faderman, 1981/1998). Recently, some men and women have reclaimed the epithet *queer* as a provocative challenge to conventional sexual identities (Norton, 1997). A queer sexual identity comes from academic queer theory, which holds that identities are not fixed and do not determine who we are. The label includes gays and lesbians, bisexuals, and *transgendered* persons—people who believe they are actually the other biological sex. However, "queer" has historically referred to people with same-sex attraction, primarily gay men, as illustrated by the popular Bravo television program *Queer Eye for the Straight Guy*. In short, sexual identity labels better reflect social identity than sexual feelings.

PREVALENCE OF SEXUAL IDENTITIES AND CROSS-CULTURAL PERSPECTIVES

The prevalence of sexual orientations depends on how sexual attraction is measured (e.g., erotic desire, romantic feelings, sexual identity, or sexual behavior), what period of time is assessed, and how the culture defines the term "sexual." People in rural India and urban Montreal, Canada, experience different sexualities. However, several Western studies using different methodologies have found that between 2 percent and 6 percent of men and 1–4 percent of women are exclusively same-sex oriented (Fay, Turner, Klassen, & Gagnon, 1989; Kinsey, Pomeroy, & Martin, 1948; Kinsey, Pomeroy, Martin, & Gebhard, 1953; Kontula, 1993; Laumann, Gagnon, Michael, & Michaels, 1994; Wellings, Field, Johnson, & Wadsworth, 1994). About 4 percent of men and women have experienced attraction to both sexes, and between 6 percent and 20 percent of men and 4 percent of women report having one or more same-sex orgasms in their lifetime (Fay et al., 1989; Wellings et al., 1994). In most Western studies, the vast majority of people identify as heterosexual or report exclusive other-sex attraction, although social stigma may inhibit disclosure about same-sex attraction.

In many non-Western and Native American cultures, social roles have greater significance than sexual identities. Among traditional East Asian (Japan, China, and Thailand) and Asian American cultures, as well as Latin and Arab cultures, individuals are referenced by their role in the family social system, not by their sexual feelings, which are private and do not entail a personal identity (Almaguer, 1993; Chan, 1995; Helie-Lucas, 1994). Yet, where Western culture predominates, some individuals adopt labels of sexual identity in conflict with native social values (e.g., Blackwood, 1999; Mogrovejo, 1999; Williams, 1986).

Many non-Western societies have recognized that people experience a variety of sexual feelings. Ford and Beach (1951) found that 64 percent of seventy-six societies around the world viewed same-sex behavior as normal and appropriate for some members of the community at some times. Some societies have even institutionalized same-sex erotic relationships (Greenberg, 1988). Until recently, several Melanesian societies and related cultures in the Pacific supported ritualized same-sex activity for males (Herdt, 1984/1993). Boys were thought to lack the substance to become masculine and fertile, and they engaged in regular oral or anal sexual behavior with older males in order to receive this vital substance. After puberty, these young men in turn provided semen to boys. Most men eventually developed exclusive heterosexual relationships. Women in these cultures were seen as inherently fertile and did not engage in ritualized same-sex relationships.

Among the Basotho of southern Africa, intimate same-sex relationships have played an important role in providing sexual and social information to young women (Gay, 1985). An adolescent girl and an older married woman form a long-term relationship, called *Mummy-Baby*, which includes casual sexual play and sometimes intense genital contact. These intimate relationships bear no stigma as long as the young woman fulfilled her social obligation to marry and produce children. The !Kung (Shostak, 1981) and Mombasa of South Africa (Shepherd, 1987) and aboriginal Australians (Roheim, 1933) also have formed same-sex relationships between younger and older women. Among Mombasans, both boys and girls develop intimate same-sex relationships, and these relationships provide many social and economic advantages (Shepherd, 1987). Mombasan boys, who have little social status, develop relationships with older married men who can provide for them. The boy (*shoga*) takes a passive sexual role with his patron (*basha*). After acquiring personal resources, most, but not all, shoga males end their same-sex relationships and marry. For Mombasan girls, however, the relationship sometimes continues after marriage.

In many cultures, *gender role*—the social performance of masculinity or femininity—determines sexual expression, and gender roles are quite distinct. Among Central and South American, North African, and Mediterranean societies, males are masculine, socially dominant, and active sexual partners (i.e., penetrate their partner), while females are expected to be feminine, submissive, and passive sexual partners (i.e., penetrated by partner) (Carrier, 1980; Espin, 1993). Cross-gender behavior in these cultures violates gender role norms and is stigmatized. Men who are sexually penetrated are considered effeminate, and vice versa, while men who penetrate a male partner bear no stigma and are considered masculine. In some Latin and Mediterranean cultures, anal intercourse with a receptive male may demonstrate *hyper*masculinity and may be witnessed by one's peers (Carrier). In fact, male-dominant societies with rigid gender roles report a high incidence of male-male sexual behavior (Reiss, 1986). For women, however, same-sex encounters in gender-role-rigid societies are often seen as antifamily and are taboo (Espin).

Some cultures have classified individuals who behave or dress as the other sex as a *third gender*, both male and female. Same-sex activity is often associated with third-gendered individuals (Greenberg, 1988). The *waria* of Indonesia (including Java, Sumatra, most of Borneo, West Irian, and other small islands), *hijra* of India, *mahu* of Tahiti, *xanith* of Middle Eastern Oman (Mihalik, 1988), and *washoga* of Muslim Mombasa in Kenya represent third genders (Carrier, 1980). Several Native American Indian societies have reported third and even fourth genders, including the Iroquois, California, Eskimo, Comanche, Cherokee, Illinois, Nadowessi, Chippewas, Koniag, Oglala, Quinault, Crow, Cheyenne, Creek, Yokot, Sioux, Fox, Sac, Zuni, Pima, Mohave, Navajo, Cree, Dakota, Siksika, Arikara, Mandan, Florida, and Yucatan, although the practice has largely ended with increased Westernization (Greenberg; Williams, 1986). Third- or fourth-gendered individuals are sometimes referred to as *berdache* (those with male physiology) or *amazons* (those with female physiology), but the more neutral collective term, *two-spirited* people, is preferred today (Roscoe, 1998). Social roles and statuses for two-spirited people varied across cultures. The Navajo *nádleehi* were farmers, sheepherders, and weavers who often achieved wealth, while Lakota *winkte* were typically powerful spiritual leaders and warriors.

Exclusive same-sex erotic relationships are rare in human history and more typical of contemporary Western culture. While male-female relationships are typical in most societies, same-sex relationships, at least for males, are not uncommon and may have been the norm in some cultures (Bleys, 1995; Cantarella, 1992; Greenberg, 1988). The frequency of same-sex behavior among diverse societies suggests that many people have the capacity for same-sex eroticism or a bisexual orientation (Kauth, 2000).

DESCRIPTIVE MODELS OF SEXUAL ORIENTATION

Despite the attention given to sexual orientation, the concept is poorly defined in the scientific literature and, yet, is a basic construct of sex research (Kauth, 2005). Researchers often omit conceptual or operational definitions of sexual orientation and cite support from studies that employ conflicting models of attraction (Byne & Parsons, 1993; Stein, 1999). Researchers' own implicit assumptions about sexual orientation may serve to maintain conceptual contradictions and dismiss alternative perspectives (Kauth, 2002). Understanding the assumptions behind models of sexual orientation is critical for disentangling a complex literature (Kauth, 2005).

The concept of sexual orientation is related to sex and gender, the structure and nature of sexual orientation, and the role of biology and environment (Kauth, 2005). The foundation of conventional models of sexual orientation is sex and gender. *Sex* refers to biological and physiological characteristics that distinguish males from females (e.g., sex chromosomes, hormone levels, testes, ovaries). *Gender* refers to social characteristics and roles that typify men and women (e.g., masculinity or femininity, husband or wife, clothing, occupations). A writer's choice of terminology suggests specific relationships among sex, gender, and sexual orientation. For example, "same-*sex* orientation" stresses the physiological characteristics of actors and partners, but "same-*gender* orientation" stresses the social characteristics of participants. Some writers (Stein, 1999) employ the hyphenated term *sex-gender* to illustrate the contribution of both constructs and to avoid difficult distinctions, although this practice retains ambiguity.

Structurally, sexual orientation may be *binary, bipolar,* or *multidimensional* (Stein, 1999). A binary sexual orientation involving two mutually exclusive kinds of attraction—same-sex (homosexual) or other-sex (heterosexual)—is a common but false model among both laypeople and researchers. This model views bisexuality as situational (e.g., due to absence of the other sex) or circumstantial (e.g., adolescent experimentation), or as a form of homosexuality (e.g., married men who have sex with men). When a binary sex-gender overlays binary sexual desire, attraction to males becomes a *female* trait, and attraction to females becomes a *male* trait. Same-sex attraction is then a kind of sex-gender inversion, reminiscent of nineteenth-century ideas about homosexuality (Coleman, Gooren, & Ross, 1989). Homosexuality-as-gender-inversion is a popular notion that recurs frequently in the literature.

Bipolar sexual orientation involves a continuum of attractions between exclusive same-sex attraction at one end and exclusive other-sex attraction at the other. This model views attraction to males as inversely related to attraction to females, and some people are expected to experience attraction to both sexes. The Kinsey scale (Kinsey et al., 1948, 1953), a common method for assessing sexual attraction, represents a bipolar model. Surveys of sexual behavior often report a bimodal distribution that is skewed toward the other-sex-attraction pole (Bailey, Dunne, & Martin, 2000; Fay et al., 1989; Laumann et al., 1994). That is, most people report heterosexual behavior, some report same-sex behavior, and few report behavior with both sexes.

Multidimensional models of sexual orientation view same-sex and other-sex attraction as separate dimensions. Shively and DeCecco (1977) have depicted attraction to males and attraction to females as parallel dimensions, each spanning low to strong attraction. Storms (1981) has proposed that these attractions are orthogonal dimensions, forming a grid. This model allows for strong attraction to both sexes, and no attraction to either sex. Klein, Sepekoff, and Wolf (1985) have proposed seven dimensions of sexual orientation, each assessed for three time periods, producing twenty-one scores. Coleman (1987) developed a nine-dimensional model in which current and ideal self-identities are scored, along with physical, gender, sex-role, and sexual orientation. Although these models are conceptually more sophisticated, they are also more complicated and rarely employed in research (Chung & Katayama, 1996).

The models of sexual orientation just discussed tie attraction to sex-gender. However, Ross (1987) has argued that social characteristics—age, physical build, race, personality traits, mentoring, and dominance—and pleasure play a greater role in partner choice than sex or gender. Anthropologists claim that social context and cultural gender roles largely determine partner choice (Blackwood, 1999; Herdt, 1997). Gagnon and Simon (1973) have purported that sexuality exists only in a social context and that *social scripts* determined which relationships are sexual. Diamond (2003) proposed that sexual desire and affectional bonding are functionally independent. Especially for women, affectional bonding may be less oriented toward one or the other sex. Rather, people can be characterized by their capacity to form affectional bonds, regardless of sex of partner.

The nature of sexual orientation refers to whether the concept is viewed as a *natural kind*—universal and invariant—or a *social construction* in which sexual identities and social roles are specific to a sociohistorical period (Stein, 1999). If a natural kind, then sexual attraction is presumed to be experienced today as it was in the past, and similar forms of attraction should be evident across cultures. If so, particular attractions represent kinds of people. Researchers who hold this view use *homosexual* and *heterosexual* as nouns, rather than adjectives, and believe that these sexual kinds of people are represented in non-Western cultures that hold very different ideas about sexuality. However, if sexual orientation is a social construction, then *gay* and *straight* represent specific ideas about personhood, politics, gender, psychology, and sexuality, whose meaning has evolved with changing social beliefs (Foucault, 1978/1990; Katz, 1995). Researchers who hold this view recognize that sexual identities are specific to a particular culture and time and do not describe a universal kind of person. Other writers have claimed that while sexual attractions are universal, their meaning is influenced by individual, social, and cultural factors (Baumeister, 2000; Kauth, 2000).

Finally, the concept of sexual orientation is influenced by presumed biological and environmental effects on attraction (Stein, 1999). Researchers who allege direct environmental effects on sexual orientation tend to view attraction as flexible, while investigators who propose direct biological effects view attraction as relatively stable but perhaps not fixed. The conventional hormonal theory that atypical exposure to fetal androgens results in same-sex attraction is often presented as a direct biological effect (Hershberger, 2001).

Scientists who acknowledge that sexual orientation is a product of indirect, interactive processes involving both biological and environmental factors tend to discuss sexual (orientation) *phenotypes*—the observable and varied features of an organism. Biological and environmental factors such as gender, health, nutrition, age, injury, social class, religion, education, culture, and social experiences all influence the expression of attraction.

Most theories of sexual orientation are simplistic, conceptually flawed, and specific to Western culture, although recent work is notable for greater theoretical sophistication.

THEORIES OF SEXUAL ORIENTATION

Most theories of sexual orientation have attempted to explain homosexuality, which investigators considered aberrant behavior. Heterosexuality was viewed as natural, and received little attention. Below is a brief survey of major theories of sexual orientation. For general surveys, see Katz (1995), Kauth (2000), McKnight (1997), and Rust (2000b).

Evolutionary Psychology

Evolutionary theories attempt to explain *ultimate* causation—*why* a trait developed among ancestral humans to promote reproductive success. Traits that over many generations advantaged reproductive success are called *adaptations* and were dispersed throughout the population (Buss, 1998). Evolutionists have long puzzled over the persistence of same-sex attraction, a trait that presumably leads to few offspring and less reproductive success. Traits can persist without reproductive benefit, as by-products of an adaptation (e.g., poetry) or random effects of a genetic variation, but these are conclusions of last resort.

Wilson (1978) suggested that same-sex-oriented individuals may benefit their siblings' reproductive success if they directed their energies and resources to raising their siblings' children (who share some of their genes). Trivers (1974) has also proposed that altruistic same-sex-oriented individuals advantage their parents by maximizing reproductive success for some offspring and minimizing competition for mates and scarce resources. Both theories rest on shaky assumptions that same-sex-oriented individuals are altruistic and parents can manipulate their children's sexuality. Little evidence supports either assumption (Bobrow & Bailey, 2001; Kirkpatrick, 2000).

Separately, Kauth (2000), Kirkpatrick (2000), and Muscarella (2000) have proposed that same-sex attraction developed as a survival strategy to manage conflict and competition within same-sex groups among ancestral hunters and gatherers. That is, same-sex eroticism facilitated long-term intimate alliances with equal- or higher-status peers and served to manage within-group hostilities and ensure mutual cooperation, loyalty, access to high-quality resources, and social status. An alliance with a high-ranking male may have helped young males achieve social status and ultimately gain access to high-status females, and females may have preferred mates with loyal friends and high social status (Muscarella, 2000). For young females, an alliance with a high-ranking, older female may have been critical for gaining within-group acceptance, quality nutritional and material resources, and assistance during pregnancy and child rearing (Kauth, 2000). In many preagricultural societies, and perhaps in early human societies, very young females leave their natal group to live with their husband's female kin (Campbell, 1985). Sexual behavior may have strengthened same-sex alliances by reducing conflict and providing pleasure. Thus, reproductive success is hypothesized to have been enhanced by erotic relationships with both sexes. Several cultures have favored same-sex alliances (Kirkpatrick, 2000; Muscarella, 2000) and, in the ancient world, sexual relationships with both sexes were not uncommon (Cantarella, 1992; Greenberg, 1988).

Muscarella, Cevallos, Siler-Knogl, and Peterson (2005) found support for perceived advantages of contemporary same-sex erotic alliances. Despite stigma associated with homosexuality, university students viewed same-sex relationships as providing increased social and reproductive opportunities if the individual benefited by greater social status, economic advantages, or career opportunities.

Ultimate causation is contrasted with *proximate* causation or *how* a trait occurs. Proximate causal theories describe immediate events that produce a trait. The following are proximate causal theories.

Psychoanalytic Theory

Freud produced four different theories of male homosexuality and one weak theory of female homosexuality. The theory most repeated by Freud to explain male homosexuality involved a young boy who overvalued his penis and avoided castration anxiety and disgust that mother lacked a penis by choosing sexual partners who resembled himself (Freud, 1905/1953; Lewes, 1988). Later, he speculated that unconscious same-sex erotic identifications represented the most common form of homosexuality (Freud, 1918/1953). In this case, males struggle with their desire to be loved by a father figure (in the way that father loves mother) and yet maintain their (heterosexual) masculinity. Freud suggested that men who admired other men struggled with unconscious homosexual feelings. He explained female homosexuality as a girl's disappointment that her father would not give her a child, leading to her rejection of him and all other men (Freud, 1920/1953).

Although ambivalent about whether homosexuality was a mental illness, Freud saw it as a disruption of normal psychosexual development. Freud is one of the few theorists who proposed theories of heterosexual development. These are described in a later section in this chapter, "Sexual Identity Formation."

Later analytical theorists rejected Freud's view of pansexuality and asserted that heterosexuality was normal and natural (Bergler, 1947). Analysts attempted to explain and cure homosexuality. Based on clinical histories, they purported that men who love men failed to separate from their mothers in early childhood (Socarides, 1968), grew up in dysfunctional families, and had dominant and overprotective mothers and passive and distant fathers (Bieber, 1976). Even so, some analysts warned parents that homosexuality was spread by gay men who seduced children (Lewes, 1988). Women who love women were reported to have had rejecting or indifferent mothers and distant or absent fathers, although less than one-third of lesbians actually described such family dynamics (Wolff, 1971). Other studies have found that gay men and lesbians are no more likely than heterosexuals to come from dysfunctional families (Bell & Weinberg, 1978), and gay men are only slightly more likely than heterosexual men to report a poor father-son relationship (Saghir & Robins, 1973).

Psychoanalytic theories of homosexuality lost favor because analysts failed to substantiate their claims or provide reliable evidence of a cure for homosexuality. Counter findings and pressure from gay rights activists persuaded the American Psychiatric Association to drop homosexuality as a psychiatric disorder in 1973 (Bayer, 1987).

Conversion/Reparative Therapy

Psychoanalytic ideas resurfaced in sexual-orientation conversion therapies, frequently blended with Christian fundamentalism (Besen, 2003). Conversion therapies purport to change homosexual orientation to heterosexual. These therapies explain same-sex attraction as sin, inferiority and social inadequacy, confusion of gender roles, poor masculine identity, weak attachment to the same-sex parent, depression, fetal trauma, and/or poor heterosocial skills. Treatment involves a combination of self-labeling as heterosexual, prayer, Bible study, rejection of gay friends and the gay "lifestyle," suppression of same-sex feelings, sports, heterosexual activity, and, ultimately, marriage. Recipients of conversion therapies are often called "ex-gays." Nicolosi (1991), a leading proponent of conversion, coined the term *reparative therapy* to emphasize that the treatment corrects a problem that prevents full psychological maturity. Nicolosi leads the National Association for Research and Therapy of Homosexuality (NARTH), an organization of conversion therapists whose goals are to make homosexuality a mental illness again and promote a cure for it (Besen). Love in Action, Exodus, Homosexuals Anonymous, Evergreen International, Desert Stream, and Living Waters represent religious-based conversion organizations.

Nicolosi (1991) has claimed to cure one-third of his gay patients and improve heterosexual functioning in another one-third, but has refused to provide verifiable data for examination. However, Beckstead (2001) has described twenty individuals who claimed benefit from conversion therapies.

None had experienced substantial or general heterosexual arousal or decreased attraction to the same-sex, yet all identified as "exclusively heterosexual." Spitzer (2003) has reported a telephone survey of 200 individuals who benefited from conversion therapies, all referred by ex-gay ministries or conversion therapists. Participants were highly religious, and 78 percent had spoken publicly in favor of changing sexual orientation. Most respondents reported change to a predominant or exclusive heterosexual orientation, which Spitzer viewed as credible but probably rare. Critics have strongly challenged Spitzer's methodology, conclusions, and objectivity. The publication of Spitzer's article in the *Archives of Sexual Behavior* was accompanied by twenty-six commentaries from fellow researchers.

Learning and Conditioning Theories

Prominent in the 1960s and the early 1970s, learning theories presumed that people are largely blank slates and that all behavior is learned by being paired with reflexive responses (classical conditioning, e.g., Pavlov's dog salivating to a bell), by being rewarded (operant conditioning, e.g., working for a paycheck), or by punishment (e.g., avoiding a hot burner). Theorists speculated that same-sex attraction resulted from accidental or inadvertent conditioning, such as stimulation of an infant's genitals by the same-sex caregiver, punishment following genital stimulation by the other-sex parent, negative social messages about heterosexual relations, attention from a same-sex person, lack of an other-sex partner when aroused, or inadequate heterosocial skills (Barlow & Agras, 1973; Money, 1988). Indeed, one study found that individuals who learned to masturbate by being manually stimulated by someone of the same sex and who experienced their first orgasm during same-sex contact were more likely to identify as gay as an adult (Van Wyck & Geist, 1984), although sexual attraction may well have preceded behavior. Contrary to prediction, gay men and lesbians often have a great deal of heterosexual experience (Bell, Weinberg, & Hammersmith, 1981), and bisexuals, unaccounted for by learning theorists, presumably have no deficiency in heterosocial skills or lack of arousal to the other sex (Weinberg, Williams, & Pryor, 1994).

To demonstrate that same-sex attraction is learned, researchers have attempted to condition sexual responses to unusual stimuli such as geometric shapes or women's boots, with only limited success (Alford, Plaud, & McNair, 1995). It seems improbable that accidental and infrequent conditioning of same-sex stimuli could produce permanent same-sex attraction in individuals living in a heterosexist society that stigmatizes homosexuality. However, the absence of supportive evidence did not prevent behavior therapists from employing aversive treatments (e.g., electric shock, emetics) to reduce same-sex attraction, but with no greater success. Contemporary conversion therapists continue to employ aversive behavioral therapies (Besen, 2003).

Personality Theories

In a classic study, Green (1987) followed a group of extremely feminine boys who had been referred for treatment and an age-matched group of masculine boys for fifteen years. As young adults, thirty-two (73 percent) formerly feminine boys identified as gay or bisexual, while only one (4 percent) masculine boy was bisexual. Green attributed same-sex attraction among some boys to parenting that permitted feminine behavior and failed to encourage traditional masculine behavior, but cautioned against concluding that childhood femininity leads to male homosexuality. However, in a set of identical twins in the study, the 23-year-old feminine twin was married but acknowledged a strong attraction to males and identified as gay. His masculine twin had a male lover and a pregnant girlfriend and reported a strong attraction to females. Another study of identical male triplets where one brother was gay (HM) and two were heterosexual (HT1 and HT2) further weakens the relationship between male femininity and adult sexual orientation (Hershberger & Segal, 2004). While both HT1 and HM scored similarly on measures of femininity, HT1 endorsed the "desirability" of having male sexual partners, although he had never had sex with men and was currently married.

Nevertheless, Byne and Parsons (1993) have hypothesized that cross-gender traits promote same-sex attraction, citing the prevalence of childhood gender nonconformity among gay men and lesbians. They described male-typical traits as novelty seeking, low harm-avoiding, and reward independent and female-typical traits as low novelty-seeking, harm avoiding, and reward dependent. Presumably, boys who lack one or more male traits feel different from their male peers and are more open to female-typical experiences. Byne and Parsons did not explain how feeling different and spending time with girls leads to male homosexuality.

Bem (1996) has hypothesized that children with cross-gender traits socialize with other-sex children because they fear and feel anxious around same-sex peers. During puberty, this fear and anxiety gets interpreted as sexual arousal, a process Bem called *exotic-to-erotic*. Although the idea of eroticized differences is consistent with heterosexual development, the theory has strange implications for nonheterosexuals. For example, feminine (pregay) boys should be sexualized to masculine (heterosexual) boys, not men and not other gay males. The theory does not account for masculine gay men or feminine heterosexual men. Bem appears to confuse sexual orientation with complementary gender roles and has dismissed bisexuality as irrelevant, when in actuality his model is likely to produce *pan*sexuals (Kauth, 2000). If children eroticized traits or classes of people who differ from their peer group, then sexual attraction may not be limited to one sex, and sex of partner may not be the sole characteristic that influences attraction.

Biomedical Theories

Biomedical theorists generally presume that sexual orientation is a product of genes, exposure to hormones, or some other internal event. Theorists rarely discuss other-sex attraction and often imply a gender inversion model of homosexuality. Typical development is assumed to produce heterosexual, masculine males who play a sexually active role (i.e., the inserter) and heterosexual, feminine females who are sexually receptive. Being natural, heterosexual orientation is given no further explanation. Gay men and lesbians are thought to experience atypical development and possess cross-gender traits. Bisexuals are virtually ignored by biomedical theorists.

Genetic Studies

Linking genes to homosexuality suggests a biological effect. Indeed, Hamer, Hu, Magnuson, Hu, and Pattatucci (1993) found an 82 percent correlation among five consecutive markers on the X chromosome (Xp28) for forty pairs of gay brothers. In addition, the men's maternal uncles were more likely to be gay than were their paternal uncles (7.3 percent versus. 1.7 percent). A follow-up study found a 67 percent correlation among the five markers for thirty-three pairs of gay brothers (Hu et al., 1995). Hamer concluded that at least one form of male-male attraction is transmitted maternally. Lesbian sisters, however, did not share these markers with their gay brothers, suggesting a different mechanism for female homosexuality. Other investigators have reported less convincing data (Rice, Anderson, Risch, & Ebers, 1999), but failed to replicate Hamer's methods.

Traits highly correlated among twins who share identical genetic material also support a biological basis for sexual orientation. Bailey and Pillard (1991) found a 52 percent correlation for homosexuality among fifty-six gay men with an identical twin. Only 22 percent of fifty-four gay men with a nonidentical twin were gay, and 11 percent of adopted brothers were gay. A second study found a 48 percent correlation for homosexuality among seventy-one lesbians with an identical twin compared to 16 percent of thirty-seven lesbians with a nonidentical lesbian twin (Bailey, Pillard, Neale, & Agyei, 1993). Only 14 percent of adopted sisters identified as lesbian. Other researchers have reported a 65 percent correlation for homosexuality among identical male twins and a 30 percent correlation among nonidentical male twins (Whitam, Diamond, & Martin, 1993). This study also included three sets of triplets. In one set, the identical twin brothers were gay, but their nonidentical sister was heterosexual. In the second set, the identical twin sisters were lesbian and their nonidentical sister was not. And, in the third set, all three identical brothers were gay. However, a large sample of Australian twins found only a 20 percent correlation for homosexuality among identical twin males and 24 percent among identical twin females (Bailey et al., 2000). The investigators concluded that subject recruitment procedures inadvertently inflated earlier correlations.

These studies suggest two important points: (a) male homosexuality is more strongly biological (heritable) than female homosexuality, and (b) heritable biological factors alone fail to account for same-sex attraction. Genes only influence neurochemical processes such as hormone production. These processes in turn are influenced by prenatal and postnatal environments. Even identical twins do not share identical prenatal environments.

Hormonal and Neuroanatomic Studies

Most hormonal studies are premised on the notion that same-sex attraction results from atypical prenatal androgen exposure or production. However, extensive literature reviews have found few physiological or postnatal hormonal differences between heterosexuals and gay men and lesbians (Byne & Parsons, 1993; Meyer-Bahlburg, 1984). There is also little evidence that hormonal abnormalities influence same-sex attraction. Women with genetic recessive condition that masculinizes development—congenital virilizing adrenal hyperplasia—have reported increased same-sex attraction (Dittman, Kappes, & Kappes, 1992; Money, Schwartz, & Lewis, 1984), but investigators did not evaluate how knowledge about the condition or its physiological effects (e.g., an enlarged clitoris, shallow vagina, tomboyishness, masculine appearance) may have influenced sexuality. Genetic males with androgen insensitivity are partially or completely unresponsive to androgen, and usually develop a female gender identity and attraction to males and marry men as adults (Collaer & Hines, 1995). However, ultralow prenatal androgen without androgen insensitivity does not appear to increase same-sex attraction (Sandberg et al., 1995). Other genetic conditions that impair androgen synthesis and lower androgen exposure—5-alpha reductase deficiency and 17-beta hydroxysteriod dehydrogenase deficiency—also fail to influence same-sex attraction (Collaer & Hines, 1995), although notable exceptions have been reported (Johnson et al., 1986).

Because direct measurement of prenatal hormones is difficult, most researchers have relied on indicators of fetal hormone exposure to gauge the effects on sexual orientation. These indicators include digit length, fingerprint asymmetries, handedness, birth order, auditory responses, and neuroanatomic structures and functioning. Prenatal androgen exposure in the male fetus typically produces a low second-to-fourth-digit ratio (2D:4D) while low androgen and high estrogen exposure in the female fetus typically produces a high 2D:4D ratio. That is, the second and fourth digits are often similar in length for males but differ in length for females. This effect may be fixed by week fourteen of gestation. Robinson and Manning (2000) have found that gay men had a lower 2D:4D ratio than age-matched heterosexual men, and bisexual men had a lower ratio than gay men. However, Williams et al. (2000) have found a lower ratio only for gay men with older brothers, although Robinson and Manning had reported no birth order effect. Williams et al. (2000) also found a lower 2D:4D ratio among lesbians compared with heterosexual women. Contrary to the conventional androgen theory, these studies suggest that same-sex attraction is associated with high prenatal androgen levels, particularly among males with older brothers. Attraction to both sexes may be associated with very high fetal androgen exposure.

Leftward asymmetry in fingerprint pattern is a female-typical effect that is present as early as seven weeks postconception, and gay men are more likely than heterosexual men to evidence this leftward asymmetry (Hall, 2000). Finger-ridge counts on the left and right hands also differ by sex and sexual orientation. However, among a set of identical male triplets, the predicted pattern held for one heterosexual (HT1) and one gay brother (HM), but the most masculine heterosexual triplet (HT2) had a ridge count similar to his gay brother (Hershberger & Segal, 2004).

Handedness may be determined before birth and shows sex differences. Most adults (89 percent) are right-handed, and men are more likely to be left-handed than women (Gilbert & Wysocki, 1992). Left-handedness is associated with a number of developmental problems that are more typical in males and, thus, linked to androgen exposure. Left-handedness has sometimes been associated with male homosexuality (Lindesay, 1987). A meta-analysis of twenty studies found a higher frequency of non–right-handedness among gay men and lesbians compared to heterosexuals (Lalumière, Blanchard, & Zucker, 2000). However, these studies obscure the point that most gay men and lesbians are right-handed and most left-handers are heterosexual. Among one set of identical male triplets, the heterosexual brothers differed on handedness, and the gay brother was right-handed (Hershberger & Segal, 2004).

A small but consistent birth-order effect has been found among gay men (Blanchard, Zucker, Siegelman, Dickey, & Klassen, 1998). That is, gay men have more older brothers than heterosexual men. Lesbians, however, do not differ from heterosexual women in number of any category of siblings. Blanchard and Klassen (1997) have hypothesized that this birth-order effect among gay men might be explained by a maternal immune response to male-specific fetal hormones, inhibiting heterosexual orientation. The idea that maternal stress blocks male fetal hormones comes from studies of laboratory rats (Dörner, 1979). Male rats exposed to maternal stress hormones more frequently present themselves to males and show little interest in females. Dörner et al. (1980) speculated that pregnant human mothers living during periods of extreme social stress (e.g., the war years in Germany) would have more gay male children and, indeed, they found such an effect although greater social acceptance of homosexuality over time may explain this finding. When mothers of adult gay and heterosexual men were questioned about stressors during pregnancy, they reported similar levels of stress across stages of pregnancy (Bailey, Willerman, & Parks, 1991). Mothers of lesbians reported greater stress during the first and second trimesters, although the theory did not predict female homosexuality. However, other researchers have found that mothers of gay men reported higher levels of stress during the first and second months of pregnancy than mothers of heterosexual men, consistent with the maternal stress theory (Ellis & Cole-Harding, 2001). No differences were found between mothers of lesbian and heterosexual women.

The auditory system differs by sex. Males have an advantage in auditory discrimination tasks, and females hear high frequencies better than males (McFadden & Pasanen, 1998). The inner ear also typically emits sounds— otoacoustic emissions (OAEs)—that differ by sex and are, thus, related to prenatal androgen exposure. Yet, contrary to the conventional androgen theory, McFadden and Pasanen (1998, 1999) found no differences in OAEs among gay, bisexual, and heterosexual men. They hypothesized that variation in timing and concentration of androgen at different brain sites accounts for variation in sexual orientation among men. McFadden and Pasanen (1998, 1999) also found that lesbian and bisexual women demonstrated OAEs that were more male-typical. This is the strongest evidence to date that links female-female attraction to prenatal androgen exposure.

Sex differences in neuroanatomic size and functioning are well documented. Some structural differences in a number of sites have been linked to male homosexuality, but the relevance of these findings is unclear. In most cases, these sites are not known to influence sexual attraction. However, the anterior hypothalamus in humans is thought to be functionally similar to the preoptic area in male rats, which regulates sexual behavior, specifically, mounting behavior. LeVay (1991) found that for presumed gay men and heterosexual women a section of the anterior hypothalamus (third interstitial nuclei) was similar in size but was two to three times larger for heterosexual men. Of course, human sexual behavior is more complex than mounting behavior in rats, and what role the anterior hypothalamus plays in sexual orientation is uncertain.

As for cognitive differences, generally gay men have performed less well on mental rotations (spatial ability) but better on verbal fluency tasks than heterosexual men (Gladue, Beatty, Larson, & Staton, 1990; McCormick & Witelson, 1991). Most functional differences have been attributed to non–right-handed gay men, although right-handed and non–right-handed heterosexual men are more variable than gay men on fluency tasks (McCormick & Witelson, 1991). Gay men and heterosexual women have performed similarly on tests of spatial abilities, which differed significantly from heterosexual men (Rahman & Wilson, 2003; Rahman, Wilson, & Abrahams, 2003). By contrast, lesbians have performed similarly to heterosexual women on many cognitive tasks (Gladue et al., 1990) or better than heterosexual women on visuomotor targeting, and similarly to heterosexual men (Hall & Kimura, 1995). Among a set of identical male triplets discordant for sexual orientation, cognitive functioning was in the predicted direction (Hershberger & Segal, 2004). One important caveat: cognitive studies often describe gay men as making female-typical responses, although gay men's responses are usually intermediate to heterosexual men and women, and not female-typical responses. Such language implies a gender inversion assumption. In sum, the general pattern of cognitive functioning for gay men is consistent with the androgen underexposure theory, but the pattern for lesbians is similar to that for heterosexual women and counter to the androgen theory. The largest differences in functioning between homosexuals and heterosexuals may be due to non–right-handed gay men and butch lesbians.

Synthesis and Conclusions

Overall, the conventional fetal androgen theory poorly explains sexual orientation development. While the theory is consistent with several features of exclusive same-sex attraction in males, it better accounts for non–right-handed, later-born gay men. Bisexual men remain unexplained. The theory also fails to account for female homosexuality, perhaps because female and male sexual orientations have different causes (Baumeister, 2000).

One interactionist theory of sexual orientation presents sexual attraction as an information processing system involving a coordinated network of brain structures (e.g., amygdala, hippocampus, prefrontal cortex, and association cortex) variably sensitized by fetal hormones (Kauth, 2000). Fetal hormone exposure is projected to be a product of timing and duration of exposure to a ratio of sex hormones that results in a complex pattern of effect across brain sites. Thus, masculinization and feminization are expected to vary by brain structure and by degree of effect (Woodson & Gorski, 2000). Byne and Parsons (1993) and Diamond (2003) have hypothesized that genes and fetal hormones influence neural growth and sensitivity, brain structures, cognitive and behavioral traits, and postnatal social experiences in ways that bias toward particular sexual attractions. Kauth (2000) has proposed that site-specific exposure to fetal hormones biases information processing toward attaching emotional significance to particular sex-related stimuli, establishing a range of reactivity to sex stimuli, not a sexual orientation. As children become self-aware, personality traits, social experiences, cultural conditions, and health also influence information processing and the erotic significance of sex-related stimuli—for example, breasts, genitals, body shape, body hair, eye contact, clothes, gestures, and movement. First awareness of sexual attraction may occur around age 10, although this may vary with a number of factors (Herdt & McClintock, 2000). By early adolescence, pubertal hormones may give erotic associations—or lovemaps (Money, 1988)—greater (sexual) significance (Kauth, 2000). Personality, social experiences, cultural beliefs, and sexual behaviors further shape and reinforce sexual attributions. An interactionist model like this one is consistent with human development but difficult to investigate because of its complexity. A major appeal of the linear androgen theory is its simplicity.

Technological advances and methodological sophistication of biomedical research will propel new studies on sexual orientation. Biomedical researchers studying sexuality have traditionally emphasized differences between heterosexuals and gay men and lesbians, although sex differences are far larger. Researchers need to explain how normal variation in fetal hormone exposure among males and females does not affect sexual orientation, since within-sex variation among males is considerable. Indeed, gay men and heterosexual men are more similar than different. In addition, researchers need to explain the development of bisexuality, which has far greater implications for human sexuality than understanding homosexuality.

SEXUAL IDENTITY FORMATION

Heterosexual Identity

Freud (1905/1953) proposed one of the few theories of heterosexual development. He supposed that all children are born capable of erotic attraction to anyone or anything. According to Freud, from an early age, male children know that they have a penis and believe that everyone else does too. Upon learning that females do not have a penis, boys fear that theirs will be taken from them. Gradually, young boys identify with their penis-bearing father and view him as a rival for their mother's affection, a psychic conflict that Freud called the *Oedipal complex*. The fear that father (or other males) will cut off a boy's penis prohibits him from forming erotic attachments to males. Young girls allegedly go through a parallel process. Girls, upon realizing that they do not have a penis but boys do, become jealous. They identify with their mother but blame her for their lack of a penis. The young girl believes that she and her mother are competing for her father's affection, a psychic conflict called the *Electra complex*. In directing their erotic attachments to the other-sex and engaging in heterosexual activity, boys and girls reach Freud's final stage of psychosexual development.

A study of fourteen heterosexual men and twelve women who wrote about their own identity development provides some support for Freud's ideas about male psychosexual development (Eliason, 1995). Most men described arriving at their heterosexual identity by first rejecting a gay identity. However, women often considered a lesbian or bisexual identity before choosing a heterosexual one.

Bisexual Identity

Female bisexuals have reported experiencing other-sex attraction and behavior before same-sex feelings, while male bisexuals have reported experiencing same-sex eroticism before or at the same time as other-sex behavior (Fox, 1995). Despite these differences in timing of attractions, Weinberg et al. (1994) have proposed four stages of collective bisexual identity formation: (a) *initial confusion*— erotic feelings for both sexes are recognized, producing confusion and discomfort; (b) *applying a label*—acknowledgment that sex with both men and women is pleasurable; (c) *settling into an identity*—greater self-acceptance is often associated with meaningful relationships; and (d) *continued uncertainty*—confusion regarding identity stems from exclusive relationships and difficulty managing multiple partners. Although most participants in this study thought that bisexuality was not a phase for them, 40 percent acknowledged that their identity might change in the future (Weinberg et al., 1994). Rust (2000) has noted that bisexuals experience multiple shifts in identity depending on their current partner and argued that a stable identity is not the endpoint for bisexuals. Ault (1996) has noted that some bisexual women adopt "fractured" identities—e.g., lesbian-identified bisexual— in an attempt to maintain identification with lesbian communities and politics. For bisexuals in this culture, sexual identity appears to be a fluid characteristic.

Gay/Lesbian Identity

Cass (1979) proposed an early model of gay/lesbian development, in-volving six stages: (1) *identity confusion*—uncertainty generated by awareness of same-sex feelings; (2) *identity comparison*—awareness of being different pro-duces a great deal of internal conflict; (3) *identity tolerance*—self-acceptance of same-sex desires and sense of belonging to a stigmatized minority; (4) *identity acceptance*—openly disclosing one's same-sex feelings and identity; (5) *identity pride*—newly out gay men and lesbians relish their supportive gay family of friends and reject the heterosexual community as intolerant and hostile; and (6) *identity synthesis*—public and private identities meld into a single self-concept. Collective stage models like this one have been criticized for their simplistic view of development; for ignoring gender, ethnic, class, and geographical differences; and for stressing identification with the gay community (Reynolds & Hanjorgiris, 2000).

Recent models have emphasized that sexual identity development is a diverse and continuous life process. McCarn and Fassinger (1996) have pro-posed separate but parallel processes for individual and group identity for lesbians, with each process having four phases: *awareness, exploration, deepening/ commitment,* and *internalization/synthesis.* Fassinger and Miller (1996) have proposed similar parallel processes for gay men. Both evidence-based models de-emphasize public disclosure and attempt to account for the many influences on identity development.

Gays, lesbians, and bisexuals manage multiple identities, depending on their openness about their sexuality. However, the problem is especially complex for people of color who must balance a sexual minority identity with a racial or ethnic identity that may be more central to their sense of self (Fukuyama & Ferguson, 2000).

CURRENT SOCIAL ISSUES

The U.S. Supreme Court's recent decision to reject sodomy laws and the Massachusetts Supreme Court decision to legalize gay marriage have made homosexuality a frequent topic of public conversation. Gays in the military also remains topical.

Sodomy Laws

In 2003, the U.S. Supreme Court (*Lawrence and Garner v. Texas*, 2003) struck down a Texas state law banning private consensual sex between adults of the same sex. The case stemmed from the 1998 arrest of two Houston men after police entered their home on a false report of a man with gun, filed by a disgruntled former lover. Delivering the majority opinion, Justice Anthony Kennedy stated:

> It suffices for us to acknowledge that adults may choose to enter upon this relationship in the confines of their homes and their own private lives and still retain their dignity as free persons. When sexuality finds overt expression in intimate conduct with another person, the conduct can be but one element in a personal bond that is more enduring. The liberty protected by the Constitution allows homosexual persons the right to make this choice. (p. 6)

The Court also reversed its 1986 *Bowers v. Hardwick* decision that upheld state criminalization of private homosexual conduct. In his dissenting opinion, Justice Antonin Scalia accused the Court of granting a "fundamental right" to homosexual sodomy and buying into the "homosexual agenda" (*Lawrence and Garner v. Texas*, 2003).

In 2003, fourteen states had sodomy laws. Four states—Texas, Kansas, Oklahoma, and Missouri—prohibited oral and anal sex between members of the same sex only; the other ten states—Alabama, Florida, Idaho, Louisiana, Michigan, Mississippi, North Carolina, South Carolina, Utah, and Virginia—and the territory of Puerto Rico banned sodomy for everyone (Summersgill, 2005). Although rarely enforced, sodomy laws created a permanent criminal class of citizens and were routinely cited by courts and legislatures to deny parental rights to gay people. One infamous example is the 1995 Virginia case, *Bottoms v. Bottoms*, in which Sharon Bottoms lost custody of her son to her mother who invoked state sodomy laws to demonstrate Sharon's criminal status and unfitness to raise her child. The child's father had no objections to

Sharon having custody. Sodomy laws have also been used to prohibit gays and lesbians from becoming foster parents or adopting, to deny individuals employment, and to harass student organizations (Summersgill). Justice Kennedy acknowledged the overreaching impact of sodomy laws: "When homosexual conduct is made criminal by the law of the State, that declaration in and of itself is an invitation to subject homosexual persons to discrimination both in the public and private spheres" (*Lawrence and Garner v. Texas*, 2003, p. 18). Justice Scalia, however, lamented the loss of criminal status for gay men and lesbians: "Many Americans do not want persons who openly engage in homosexual conduct as partners in their businesses, as scoutmasters for their children, as teachers in their children's schools, or as boarders in their home" (p. 18).

About eighty-five countries currently criminalize same-sex sodomy (International Gay and Lesbian Human Rights Commission [IGLHRC], 2003). Penalties vary widely, from two to twenty-five years in prison (Mali and Saint Lucia), a life sentence (e.g., India, Singapore, Uganda), or death (e.g., Iran, Pakistan, Saudi Arabia). Same-sex relations still occur in these countries, but are hidden. Sodomy is legal in another 125 countries, including Albania, Argentina, Austria, Cambodia, Canada, Central African Republic, Colombia, Denmark, Eritrea, France, Germany, Israel, Italy, Japan, Jordan, Mexico, New Zealand, Netherlands, Poland, Rwanda, Spain, Sweden, and the United Kingdom (Summersgill, 2005). In addition, a number of countries (e.g., Ecuador, Finland, Israel, South Africa) and ten U.S. states also have policies prohibiting discrimination in the workplace based on sexual orientation (IGLHRC, 1999).

Gay Marriage

The current controversy over gay marriage in the United States began in 1993 when the Hawaii Supreme Court ruled that the state's disallowance of same-sex marriage amounted to gender discrimination ("Trial challenging," 1996). Three gay couples promptly sued for the right to marry. As the court case opened, members of Congress passed the Defense of Marriage Act, allowing states the right to deny recognition of gay marriages licensed in other states, which President Clinton signed into law in 1996 ("Anti gay marriage act," 1996). Critics argued that the law violated the constitutional requirement that states recognize legal contracts in other states. Meanwhile, the Hawaii Legislature amended the state constitution to define marriage as only between a man and a woman.

Three years later, the Vermont Supreme Court ruled that the state constitution allowed gays and lesbians the benefits of marriage ("Vermont's top court," 1999). After contentious debate, the state enacted same-sex civil unions that carried all the benefits of marriage. Then, in 2003, the Massachusetts

Supreme Court ruled that the state had no constitutionally valid reason to deny gays and lesbians the right to marry (Arce, 2004). The Court later clarified that only full marriage rights, not civil unions, would conform to the state constitution.

The Massachusetts Court decision came on the heels of the U.S. Supreme Court ruling on sodomy laws. In his dissent, Justice Scalia had noted, "This reasoning leaves on pretty shaky grounds state laws limiting marriage to opposite-sex couples" (*Lawrence and Garner v. Texas*, p. 17). Events in Canada also fueled the issue. In 2001, a favorable court ruling in Ontario allowed the first gay male couple to marry in a church (Struck, 2004). Soon, six Canadian provinces had begun issuing marriage licenses to gay couples. The Ontario premier Dalton McGuinty proclaimed: "The fact that a gay couple might happen to marry does not threaten me or my marriage or my children's future in any way, shape or form" (Cotter, 2004). In 2003, Canadian prime minister Paul Martin, with approval from the Supreme Court, asked the government to draft a federal law to standardize gay marriage rights.

In the United States, however, President Bush called for a constitutional amendment defining marriage as a union between a man and woman, making gay marriage a presidential campaign issue ("Our government," 2004). Bush accused "activist judges" of making "arbitrary" court decisions and redefining marriage. He openly worried that the Defense of Marriage Act would not "protect" traditional marriage, meaning that states and cities might have to recognize gay marriages.

Despite attempts by the state governor and legislature to halt the process, in May 2004, Massachusetts became the first state to allow same-sex couples to marry ("Same-sex couples," 2004). By November, Congress had failed to pass a federal constitutional amendment, but eleven states approved constitutional amendments to ban same-sex marriage, with eight states also prohibiting same-sex civil unions ("Voters in 11 states," 2004). These eleven states included Arkansas, Georgia, Kentucky, Michigan, Mississippi, Montana, North Dakota, Oklahoma, Ohio, Oregon, and Utah. Missouri and Louisiana had already passed gay-marriage ban amendments. Another fifteen states are prepared to introduce same-sex marriage bans over the next two years. In early 2005, a district court upheld the Defense of Marriage Act, dismissing a lawsuit by two women seeking to have their Massachusetts marriage recognized in Florida (Chachere, 2005). No doubt the U.S. Supreme Court will ultimately decide the legality of gay marriage.

In countries like the Netherlands, where same-sex marriage has been legal for years, the issue is rarely a topic of discussion ("Global view," 2004). Currently, Denmark, the Netherlands, and Belgium grant same-sex couples full civil marriage, while Brazil, Croatia, Finland, France, Germany, Hungary, Iceland, Israel, New Zealand, Norway, Portugal, and Sweden recognize same-sex "domestic partnerships" or civil unions with limited rights ("Global view,"

2004; IGLHRC, 2003b). A number of provinces and cities around the world also recognize civil unions.

Relationships

The 2000 Census has reported 54.5 million married couples and another 4.9 million unmarried heterosexual couples living in the United States (Simmons & O'Connell, 2003). Almost 600,000 unmarried couples were of the same sex. Most same-sex couples (51 percent) were male. One study has estimated that 40–60 percent of gay men and 45–80 percent of lesbians are currently in relationships (Kurdek, 1995). On average, married men were 2.4 years older (49) than their wives, and unmarried men (36.8) were 2.1 years older than their partners (Simmons & O'Connell, 2003). Same-sex couples were in their early forties on average. Male partners differed in age by an average of two years, while female partners differed by only one year.

Nearly nine in ten people marry sometime in their lives, but about half of first marriages end in divorce (U.S. Census Bureau, 2002). The median length of first marriages was eight years. In 2000, 120.2 million Americans were married, and 41 million were widowed, separated, or divorced (Kreider & Simmons, 2003). Just over one-quarter of the population had never married.

Nationally, almost half (46 percent) of married couples and 43 percent of unmarried heterosexual couples had at least one child under age 18 living in the household. One-third of female couples and almost one-quarter of male couples also had children living with them. Perhaps 2–8 million gay men and lesbians are parents of between 4 million and 14 million children (Patterson, 1995). Most same-sex couples bring children from heterosexual relationships. Some couples adopt or foster children where laws permit, and a number of lesbians conceive via artificial insemination.

Gays in the Military

The 1993 "Don't Ask, Don't Tell, Don't Pursue, Don't Harass" policy prohibited openly gay and lesbian personnel from serving in the U.S. military. Gay and lesbian personnel cannot identify as gay or engage in same-sex sexual acts and, since the policy was enacted, about 10,000 service personnel have been discharged for being gay (Servicemembers Legal Defense Network [SLDN], 2004). Even so, an estimated 65,000 gay men and lesbians currently serve in the armed forces, including active duty, National Guard, and reservists (Gates, 2004). While lesbians may comprise about 5 percent of all female military personnel, gay men may account for only 2 percent of personnel. The prohibition of openly gay men and lesbians in the military rests in part on the criminalization of sodomy. Given the Supreme Court's rejection of state sodomy laws, the military's policy on sodomy is likely to be revisited.

The oft-forgotten "Don't Harass" part of the policy was intended to reduce antigay harassment and violence toward gay service members, but has instead institutionalized negative social beliefs about gay men and lesbians (SLDN, 2004). Harassment and witch hunts soared in the first years of the policy. Some personnel have experienced daily antigay remarks from subordinates and superiors. Some were charged for being gay just prior to their retirement, jeopardizing their pension and benefits. The failure of "Don't Ask, Don't Tell" to stop antigay harassment became public in 1999 when Private First Class Barry Winchell was beaten to death with a baseball bat in his sleep by a fellow soldier who believed Winchell was gay. Winchell had endured four months of daily antigay taunts from the two killers prior to his death. Some of Winchell's commanding officers even participated in the harassment.

"Don't Ask, Don't Tell" was enacted over concerns about morale, unit cohesion, recruitment, and heterosexual discomfort serving with gay and lesbian personnel, although support for these claims is anecdotal (Kauth & Landis, 1996). Several countries, including key allies in the current war on terrorism, allow openly gay men and lesbian personnel to serve in the military, including Australia, the Bahamas, Belgium, Canada, Czech Republic, Denmark, Estonia, Finland, France, Germany, Ireland, Israel, Italy, Netherlands, New Zealand, Norway, Portugal, Slovenia, South Africa, Spain, Sweden, Switzerland, and the United Kingdom (International Lesbian and Gay Association [ILGA], 2000). Until recently, the United Kingdom's military policy was similar to that of the United States. The British policy was rescinded in 2000 after the European Court of Human Rights ruled that the ban was unlawful.

SUMMARY

Sexual orientation is largely unexplored territory, and its origins have yet to be discovered. The study of male homosexuality has dominated research on sexual orientation in an attempt to explain less common, socially stigmatized sexual behaviors. However, many cultures have noted considerable diversity in sexual attractions. Understanding attraction to both sexes may be the key to explaining human sexuality.

Conventional theories of sexual orientation have found little support. Interactionist theories are relatively new and have yet to be tested. Some theorists suggest that same-sex attraction developed to facilitate intra-sex relationships and reduce conflict. If so, many people would be capable of attraction to both sexes.

While many other countries have enacted antidiscrimination laws and granted same-sex couples the benefits of marriage, it seems likely that in the current political climate, homosexuality will continue to be a pressing issue in the United States.

REFERENCES

Alford, G. S., Plaud, J. J., & McNair, T. L. (1995). Sexual behavior and orientation: Learning and conditioning principles. In L. Diamant and R. D. McAnulty (Eds.), *The psychology of sexual orientation, behavior, and identity: A handbook* (pp. 121–135). Westport, CT: Greenwood Press.

Almaguer, T. (1993). Chicano men: A cartography of homosexual identity and behavior. In H. Abelove, M. Barale, and D. M. Halperin (Eds.), *The lesbian and gay studies reader* (pp. 255–273). New York: Routledge.

Anti gay marriage act clears Congress. (1996, September 10). *CNN.com*. Retrieved January 17, 2005, from www.cnn.com

Arce, R. (2004, February 6). Massachusetts court upholds same-sex marriage. *CNN.com*. Retrieved January 15, 2005, from www.cnn.com

Ault, A. (1996). Ambiguous identity in an unambiguous sex/gender structure: The case of bisexual women. *Sociological Quarterly, 20*(3), 449–463.

Bailey, J. M., Dunne, M. P., & Martin, N. G. (2000). Genetic and environmental influences on sexual orientation and its correlates in an Australian twin sample. *Journal of Personality and Social Psychology, 78*(3), 524–536.

Bailey, J. M., & Pillard, R. D. (1991). A genetic study of male sexual orientation. *Archives of General Psychiatry, 48*, 1089–1096.

Bailey, J. M., Pillard, R. D., Neale, M. C., & Agyei, Y. (1993). Heritable factors influence sexual orientation in women. *Archives of General Psychiatry, 50*, 217–223.

Bailey, J. M., Willerman, L., & Parks, C. (1991). A test of the maternal stress theory of human male homosexuality. *Archives of Sexual Behavior, 20*(3), 277–293.

Barlow, D. H., & Agras, W. S. (1973). Fading to increase heterosexual responsiveness in homosexuals. *Journal of Applied Behavior Analysis, 6*, 355–366.

Baumeister, R. F. (2000). Gender differences in erotic plasticity: The female sex drive as socially flexible and responsive. *Psychological Bulletin, 126*(3), 347–374.

Bayer, R. (1987). *Homosexuality and American psychiatry: The politics of diagnosis.* Princeton, NJ: Princeton University.

Beckstead, A. L. (2001). Cures versus choices: Agendas in sexual reorientation therapy. *Journal of Gay and Lesbian Psychotherapy, 5*(3/4), 87–115.

Bell, A. P., & Weinberg, M. S. (1978). *Homosexuality: A study of diversity among men and women.* New York: Simon and Schuster.

Bell, A. P., Weinberg, M. S., & Hammersmith, S. K. (1981). *Sexual preference: Its development in men and women.* Bloomington: Indiana University.

Bem, D. (1996). Exotic becomes erotic: A developmental theory of sexual orientation. *Psychological Review, 103*(2), 320–335.

Bergler, E. (1947). Differential diagnosis between spurious homosexuality and perversion homosexuality. *Psychiatric Quarterly, 31*, 399–409.

Besen, W. R. (2003). *Anything but straight: Unmasking the scandals and lies behind the ex-gay myth.* New York: Harrington Park.

Bieber, I. (1976). A discussion of "Homosexuality: The ethical challenge." *Journal of Consulting and Clinical Psychology, 44*, 163–166.

Blackwood, E. (1999). Tombois in West Sumatra: Constructing masculinity and erotic desire. In E. Blackwood and S. E. Wieringa (Eds.), *Female desires: Same-sex relations and transgender practices across cultures* (pp. 181–205). New York: Columbia University.

Blanchard, R., & Klassen, P. (1997). H-Y antigen and homosexuality in men. *Journal of Theoretical Biology, 185*, 373–378.

Blanchard, R., Zucker, K. J., Siegelman, M., Dickey, R., & Klassen, P. (1998). The relation of birth order to sexual orientation in men and women. *Journal of Biosocial Science, 30*, 511–519.

Bleys, R. C. (1995). *The geography of perversion: Male-to-male sexual behaviour outside of the West and the ethnographic imagination, 1750–1918.* Washington Square, NY: New York University.

Bobrow, D., & Bailey, J. M. (2001). Is male homosexuality maintained via kin selection? *Evolution and Human Behavior, 22*, 361–368.

Bullough, V. L. (1994). *Science in the bedroom: A history of sex research.* New York: Basic Books.

Buss, D. M. (1998). Sexual strategies theory: Historical origins and current status. *Journal of Sex Research, 35*, 19–31.

Byne, W., & Parsons, B. (1993). Human sexual orientation: The biologic theories reappraised. *Archives of General Psychiatry, 50*, 228–239.

Campbell, B. (1985). *Human evolution* (3rd ed.). New York: Aldine.

Cantarella, E. (1992). *Bisexuality in the ancient world* (Cormac O'Cuilleanáin, Trans.). New Haven, CT: Yale University.

Carrier, J. M. (1980). Homosexual behavior in cross-cultural perspective. In J. Marmor (Ed.), *Homosexual behavior: A modern reappraisal* (pp. 100–122). New York: Basic Books.

Cass, V. C. (1979). Homosexual identity formation: A theoretical model. *Journal of Homosexuality, 4*(3), 219–235.

Chachere, V. (2005, January 20). Judge in Florida upholds same-sex marriage ban. *Times-Picayune* (New Orleans), p. A13.

Chan, C. S. (1995). Issues of sexual identity in an ethnic minority: The case of Chinese American lesbians, gay men, and bisexual people. In A. R. D'Augelli & C. J. Patterson (Eds.), *Lesbian, gay, and bisexual identities over the lifespan: Psychological perspectives* (pp. 87–101). New York: Oxford University.

Chung, Y. B., & Katayama, M. (1996). Assessment of sexual orientation in lesbian/gay/bisexual studies. *Journal of Homosexuality, 30*, 49–62.

Coleman, E. (1987). Assessment of sexual orientation. In E. Coleman (Ed.), *Psychotherapy with homosexual men and women: Integrated identity approaches for clinical practice* (pp. 9–24). New York: Haworth Press.

Coleman, E., Gooren, L., & Ross, M. (1989). Theories of gender transpositions: A critique and suggestions for further research. *Journal of Sex Research, 26*(4), 525–538.

Collaer, M. L., & Hines, M. (1995). Human behavioral sex differences: A role for gonadal hormones during early development? *Psychological Bulletin, 118*(1), 55–107.

Cotter, J. (2004, December 9). Gay marriage decision sparks diverse reaction. *CNews*. Retrieved January 17, 2005, from www.cnews.canoe.ca

Diamond, L. M. (2003). What does sexual orientation orient? A biobehavioral model distinguishing romantic love and sexual desire. *Psychological Review, 110*(1), 173–192.

Dittman, R. W., Kappes, M. E., & Kappes, M. H. (1992). Sexual behavior in · adolescent and adult females with congenital adrenal hyperplasia. *Psychoneuroendocrinology, 17,* 153–170.

Dörner, G. (1979). Psychoneuroendocrine aspects of brain development and reproduction. In L. Zichella & E. Pancheir (Eds.), *Psychoneuroendocrinology and reproduction.* Amsterdam: Elsevier.

Dörner, G., Geier, T., Ahrens, L., et al. (1980). Prenatal stress as a possible aetiogenetic factor of homosexuality in human males. *Endokrinologie, 75,* 365–368.

Eliason, M. J. (1995). Accounts of sexual identity formation in heterosexual students. *Sex Roles, 32*(11/12), 821–833.

Ellis, L., & Cole-Harding, S. (2001). The effects of prenatal stress and of prenatal alcohol and nicotine exposure on human sexual orientation. *Physiology & Behavior, 74,* 1–14.

Espin, O. M. (1993). Issues of identity in the psychology of Latina lesbians. In L. D. Garnets & D. C. Kimmel (Eds.), *Psychological perspectives on lesbians and gay male experiences* (pp. 348–363). New York: Columbia University.

Faderman, L. (1981/1998). *Surpassing the love of men: Romantic friendship and love between women from the Renaissance to the present.* New York: Quill/William Morrow.

Fassinger, R. E., & Miller, B. A. (1996). Validation of an inclusive model of homosexual identity formation on a sample of gay men. *Journal of Homosexuality, 32*(2), 53–78.

Fay, R. E., Turner, C. F., Klassen, A. D., & Gagnon, J. H. (1989). Prevalence and patterns of same-gender sexual contact among men. *Science, 243,* 338–348.

Ford, C. S., & Beach, F. A. (1951). *Patterns of sexual behavior.* New York: Harper and Brothers.

Foucault, M. (1978/1990). *The history of sexuality: Vol. 1. An introduction* (R. Hurley, Trans.). New York: Vintage Books.

Fox, R. C. (1995). Bisexual identities. In A. R. D'Augelli & C. J. Patterson (Eds.), *Lesbian, gay and bisexual identities over the lifespan: Psychological perspectives* (pp. 48–86). New York: Oxford University.

Freud, S. (1905/1953). Three essays on the theory of sexuality. In J. Strachey (Ed.), *The standard edition of the complete psychological works of Sigmund Freud* (Vol. 7, pp. 123–246). London: Hogarth.

Freud, S. (1918/1953). From the history of an infantile neurosis. In J. Strachey (Ed.), *The standard edition of the complete psychological works of Sigmund Freud* (Vol. 17, pp. 3–22). London: Hogarth.

Freud, S. (1920/1953). The psychogenesis of a case of homosexuality in a woman. In J. Strachey (Ed.), *The standard edition of the complete psychological works of Sigmund Freud* (Vol. 18, pp. 155–172). London: Hogarth.

Fukuyama, M. A., & Ferguson, A. D. (2000). Lesbian, gay, and bisexual people of color: Understanding cultural complexity and managing multiple oppressions. In R. M. Perez, K. A. DeBord, & K. J. Bieschke (Eds.), *Handbook of counseling and psychotherapy with lesbian, gay and bisexual clients* (pp. 81–105). Washington, DC: American Psychological Association.

Gagnon, J., & Simon, W. (1973). *Sexual conduct: The social sources of human sexuality.* Chicago: Aldine.

Gates, G. J. (2004, September 28). *Gay men and lesbians in the U.S. military: Estimates from Census 2000.* Retrieved January 17, 2005, from www.urban. org/url.cfm?ID=411069

Gay, J. (1985). "Mummies and babies" and friends and lovers in Lesotho. *Journal of Homosexuality, 11*(3/4), 55–68.

Gilbert, A. N., & Wysocki, C. J. (1992). Hand preference and age in the United States. *Neuropsychologia, 30*, 601–608.

Gladue, B. A., Beatty, W. W., Larson, J., & Staton, R. D. (1990). Sexual orientation and spatial ability in men and women. *Psychobiology, 18*(1), 101–108.

The global view of gay marriage. (2004, March 4). *CBSNews.com.* Retrieved December 31, 2004, from www.cbsnews.com

Green, R. (1987). *The "sissy boy syndrome" and the development of homosexuality.* New Haven, CT: Yale University.

Greenberg, D. F. (1988). *The construction of homosexuality.* Chicago: University of Chicago Press.

Hall, J. A. Y. (2000). Dermatoglyphic analysis of total finger ridge count in female monozygotic twins discordant for sexual orientation. *Journal of Sex Research, 37*, 315–320.

Hall, J. A. Y., & Kimura, D. (1995). Performance by homosexual males and females on sexually dimorphic motor tasks. *Archives of Sexual Behavior, 24*, 395–407.

Hamer, D. H., Hu, S., Magnuson, V., Hu, N., & Pattatucci, A. M. L. (1993, December 24). Response to male sexual orientation and genetic evidence. *Science, 262*, 2065.

Helie-Lucas, M. (1994). Strategies of women and women's movements in the Muslim world vis-à-vis fundamentalisms: From entryism to internationalism. In O. Mendelsohn & U. Baxi (Eds.), *The rights of subordinated peoples* (pp. 251–275). Delhi: Oxford University Press.

Herdt, G. H. (1984/1993). *Ritualized homosexuality in Melanesia.* Berkeley: University of California.

Herdt, G. H. (1997). *Same sex, different cultures.* New York: Westview Press.

Herdt, G. H., & McClintock, M. (2000). The magical age of 10. *Archives of Sexual Behavior, 29*, 587–606.

Hershberger, S. L. (2001). Biological factors in the development of sexual orientation. In C. J. Patterson & A. R. D'Augelli (Eds.), *Lesbian, gay, and bisexual identities and youth: Psychological perspectives* (pp. 27–51). New York: Oxford University.

Hershberger, S. L., & Segal, N. L. (2004). The cognitive, behavioral, and personality profiles of a male monozygotic triplet set discordant for sexual orientation. *Archives of Sexual Behavior, 33*(5), 497–514.

Hu, S., Pattatucci, A. M. L., Patterson, C., Li, L., Fulker, D. W., Cherny, S. S., et al. (1995). Linkage between sexual orientation and chromosome Xq28 in males but not in females. *Nature Genetics, 11*, 248–256.

International Gay and Lesbian Human Rights Commission. (1999, April). *Antidiscrimination legislation*. Retrieved January 15, 2005, from www.iglhrc.org

International Gay and Lesbian Human Rights Commission. (2003a, July). *Where having sex is a crime: Criminalization and decriminalization of homosexual acts*. Retrieved January 15, 2005, from www.iglhrc.org

International Gay and Lesbian Human Rights Commission. (2003b, November). *Where can you marry: Global summary of registered partnership, domestic partnership, and marriage laws*. Retrieved January 15, 2005, from www.iglhrc.org

International Lesbian and Gay Association. (2000, July). *World legal survey: The armed forces*. Retrieved January 15, 2005, from www.ilga.info/Information/ Legal_survey/ Summary%20information/armed_forces.html

Johnson, L., George, F. W., Neaves, W. B., Rosenthal, I. M., Christensen, R. A., DeCristoforo, A., et al. (1986). Characterization of the testicular abnormality in 5-alpha-reductase deficiency. *Journal of Clinical Endocrinology and Metabolism, 63*, 1091–1099.

Katz, J. N. (1995). *The invention of heterosexuality*. New York: Dutton.

Kauth, M. R. (2000). *True nature: A theory of sexual attraction*. New York: Kluwer Academic/Plenum.

Kauth, M. R. (2002). Much ado about homosexuality: Assumptions underlying current research on sexual orientation. *Journal of Psychology and Human Sexuality, 14*(1), 1–22.

Kauth, M. R. (2005). Revealing assumptions: A guide for describing sexual orientation. *Journal of Bisexuality, 5*(4), xx.

Kauth, M. R., & Landis, D. (1996). Applying lessons learned from minority integration in the military. In G. M. Herek, J. B. Jobe, & R. M. Carney (Eds.), *Out in force: Sexual orientation and the military* (pp. 86–105). Chicago: University of Chicago.

King, J. L. (2004). *On the down low: A journey into the lives of "straight" black men who sleep with men*. New York: Broadway.

Kinsey, A. C., Pomeroy, W. B., & Martin, C. E. (1948). *Sexual behavior in the human male*. Philadelphia: Saunders.

Kinsey, A. C., Pomeroy, W. B., Martin, C. E., & Gebhard, P. H. (1953). *Sexual behavior in the human female*. Philadelphia: Saunders.

Kirkpatrick, R. C. (2000). The evolution of homosexual behavior. *Current Anthropology, 41*, 385–413.

Klein, F., Sepekoff, B., & Wolf, T. J. (1985). Sexual orientation: A multi-variate dynamic process. *Journal of Homosexuality, 11*(1/2), 35–49.

Kontula, O. (1993, November). *Sexual behavior changes in Finland during the last 20 years.* Paper presented at the meeting of the Society for the Scientific Study of Sexuality, Chicago.

Krieder, R. M., & Simmons, T. (2003, October). Marital status: 2000. *Census 2000 Brief.* U.S. Census Bureau. Retrieved January 17, 2005, from www.census.gov/prod/2003pubs/c2kbr-30.pdf

Kurdek, L. A. (1995). Lesbian and gay couples. In A. R. D'Augelli & C. J. Patterson (Eds.), *Lesbian, gay, and bisexual identities over the lifespan: Psychological perspectives* (pp. 243–261). New York: Oxford University.

Lalumière, M. L., Blanchard, R., & Zucker, K. J. (2000). Sexual orientation and handedness in men and women: A meta-analysis. *Psychological Bulletin, 126*(4), 575–592.

Laumann, E., Gagnon, J., Michael, R., & Michaels, S. (1994). *The social organization of sexuality: Sexual practices in the United States.* Chicago: University of Chicago.

Lawrence and Garner v. Texas. (2003) 539 U.S. 558.

LeVay, S. (1991). A difference in hypothalamic structure between heterosexual and homosexual men. *Science, 253*, 1034–1037.

Lewes, K. (1988). *The psychoanalytic theory of male homosexuality.* New York: Meridian.

Lindesay, J. (1987). Laterality shift in homosexual men. *Neuropsychologia, 25*, 965–969.

McCarn, S. R., & Fassinger, R. E. (1996). Revisioning sexual minority identity formation: A new model of lesbian identity and its implications for counseling and research. *Counseling Psychologist, 24*, 508–534.

McCormick, C. M., & Witelson, S. F. (1991). A cognitive profile of homosexual men compared to heterosexual men and women. *Psychoneuroendocrinology, 16*(6), 459–473.

McFadden, D., & Pasanen, E. G. (1998, March). Comparison of the auditory systems of heterosexuals and homosexuals: Click-evoked otoacoustic emissions. *Proceedings of the National Academy of Sciences, 95*, 2709–2713.

McFadden, D., & Pasanen, E. G. (1999, April). Spontaneous otoacoustic emissions in heterosexuals, homosexuals, and bisexuals. *Journal of the Acoustical Society of America, 105*(4), 2403–2413.

McKnight, J. (1997). *Straight science? Homosexuality, evolution and adaptation.* London: Routledge.

Meyer-Bahlburg, H. F. L. (1984). Psychoendocrine research on sexual orientation: Current status and future options. *Progress in Brain Research, 61*, 375–398.

Mihalik, G. J. (1988). More than two: Anthropological perspectives on gender. *Journal of Gay and Lesbian Psychotherapy, 1*(1), 105–118.

Mogrovejo, N. (1999). Sexual preference, the ugly duckling of feminist demands: The lesbian movement in Mexico. In E. Blackwood & S. E. Wieringa (Eds.), *Female desires: Same-sex relations and transgender practices across cultures* (pp. 308–335). New York: Columbia University.

Money, J. (1988). *Gay, straight, and in-between: The sexology of erotic orientation.* New York: Oxford University.

Money, J., Schwarz, M., & Lewis, V. G. (1984). Adult hetorosexual status and fetal hormonal masculinization and demasculinization: 46XX congenital virilizing adrenal hyperplasia and 46XY androgen insensitivity syndrome compared. *Psychoneuroendocrinology, 9*, 405–414.

Muscarella, F. (2000). The evolution of homoerotic behavior in humans. *Journal of Homosexuality, 40*(1), 51–77.

Muscarella, F., Cevallos, A. M., Siler-Knogl, A., & Peterson, L. M. (2005). The alliance theory of homosexual behavior and the perception of social status and reproductive opportunities. *Neuroendocrinology Letters, 26*(6).

Nicolosi, J. (1991). *Reparative therapy of male homosexuality: A new clinical approach.* Northvale, NJ: Jason Aronson.

Norton, R. (1997). *The myth of the modern homosexual: Queer history and the search for cultural unity.* London: Cassell.

Our government should . . . protect the institution. (2004, February 25). *Boston Globe.* Retrieved January 15, 2005, from www.boston.com

Patterson, C. J. (1995). Lesbian mothers, gay fathers, and their children. In A. R. D'Augelli & C. J. Patterson (Eds.), *Lesbian, gay, and bisexual identities over the lifespan: Psychological perspectives* (pp. 262–290). New York: Oxford University.

Rahman, Q., & Wilson, G. D. (2003). Large sexual-orientation-related differences in performance on mental rotation and judgment of line orientation tasks. *Neuropsychology, 17*(1), 25–31.

Rahman, Q., Wilson, G. D., & Abrahams, S. (2003). Sexual orientation related differences in spatial memory. *Journal of the International Neuropsychological Society, 9*, 376–383.

Reiss, I. (1986). *Journey into sexuality: An exploratory voyage.* Englewood Cliffs, NJ: Prentice-Hall.

Reynolds, A. L., & Hanjorgiris, W. F. (2000). Coming out: Lesbian, gay, and bisexual identity development. In R. M. Perez, K. A. DeBord, & K. J. Bieschke (Eds.), *Handbook of counseling and psychotherapy with lesbian, gay and bisexual clients* (pp. 35–55). Washington, DC: American Psychological Association.

Rice, G., Anderson, C., Risch, N., & Ebers, G. (1999, April 23). Male homosexuality: Absence of linkage to microsatellite markers at Xq28. *Science, 284*, 665–667.

Robinson, S. J., & Manning, J. T. (2000). The ratio of 2nd to 4th digit length and male homosexuality. *Evolution and Human Behavior, 21*, 333–345.

Roheim, G. (1933). Women and their life in Central Australia. *Journal of the Royal Anthropological Institute of Great Britain and Ireland, 63*, 207–265.

Roscoe, W. (1998). *Changing ones: Third and fourth genders in Native North America.* New York: St. Martin's Press.

Ross, M. W. (1987). A theory of normal homosexuality. In L. Diamant (Ed.), *Male and female homosexuality: Psychological approaches* (pp. 237–259). New York: Hemisphere.

Rust, P. C. R. (2000a). The biology, psychology, sociology, and sexuality of bisexuality. In P. C. R. Rust (Ed.), *Bisexuality in the United States: A social science reader* (pp. 403–470). New York: Columbia University.

Rust, P. C. R. (2000b). *Bisexuality in the United States: A social science reader.* New York: Columbia University.

Saghir, M. T., & Robins, E. (1973). *Male and female homosexuality.* Baltimore: Williams & Wilkins.

Same-sex couples exchange vows in Massachusetts. (2004, May 17). *CNN.com.* Retrieved January 17, 2005, from www.boston.com

Sandberg, D. E., Meyer-Bahlburg, H. F. L., Yager, T. J., Hensle, T. W., Levitt, S. B., Kogan, S. J., et al. (1995). Gender development in boys born with hypospadias. *Psychoneuroendocrinology, 20*(7), 693–709.

Servicemembers Legal Defense Network. (2004, March 24). *Conduct unbecoming: The tenth annual report on "Don't Ask, Don't Tell, Don't Pursue, Don't Harass."* Retrieved January 17, 2005, from www.sldn.org

Shepherd, G. (1987). Rank, gender, and homosexuality: Mombasa as a key to understanding sexual options. In P. Caplan (Ed.), *The cultural construction of sexuality* (pp. 240–270). London: Tavistock.

Shively, M. G., & DeCecco, J. P. (1977). Components of sexual identity. *Journal of Homosexuality, 3*, 41–48.

Shostak, M. (1981). *Nisa, the life and words of a !Kung woman.* Cambridge, MA: Harvard University.

Simmons, T., & O'Connell, M. (2003, February). Married-couple and unmarried-partner households: 2000. *Census 2000 Special Reports.* U.S. Census Bureau. Retrieved January 17, 2005, from www.census.gov/prod/2003pubs/censr-5.pdf

Socarides, C. (1968). *The overt homosexual.* New York: Grune & Stratton.

Spitzer, R. L. (2003). Can some gay men and lesbians change their sexual orientation? 200 participants reporting a change from homosexual to heterosexual orientation. *Archives of Sexual Behavior, 32*(5), 403–417.

Stein, E. (1999). *The mismeasure of desire: The science, theory, and ethics of sexual orientation.* New York: Oxford University.

Storms, M. D. (1981). A theory of erotic orientation development. *Psychological Review, 88*, 340–353.

Struck, D. (2004, December 10). High court in Canada backs gay marriage. *Washingtonpost.com.* Retrieved January 17, 2005, from www.washingtonpost.com

Summersgill, B. (2005). *Sodomy laws.* Retrieved January 15, 2005, from www.sodomylaws.org

Trial challenging same-sex marriage ban opens in Hawaii. (1996, September 11). *CNN.com.* Retrieved January 17, 2005, from www.cnn.com

Trivers, R. L. (1974). Parent-offspring conflict. *American Zoologist, 14,* 249–264.

U.S. Census Bureau. (2002, February 8). *Nearly 9-in-10 people may marry, but half of first marriages may end in divorce, Census Bureau says.* Retrieved January 17, 2005, from www.census.gov/Press-Release/www/releases/archives/marital_status_living_arrangements/000500.html

Van Wyck, P. H., & Geist, C. S. (1984). Psychosocial development in heterosexual, bisexual, and homosexual behavior. *Archives of Sexual Behavior, 13,* 505–544.

Vermont's top court backs rights for same-sex couples. (1999, December 21). *CNN.com.* Retrieved January 15, 2005, from www.archives.cnn.com

Voters in 11 states overwhelmingly vote against same-sex marriage. (2004, November 3). *The Advocate.* Retrieved December 31, 2004, from www.advocate.com

Weinberg, M. S., Williams, C. J., & Pryor, D. W. (1994). *Dual attractions: Understanding bisexuality.* New York: Oxford University.

Wellings, K., Field, J., Johnson, A. M., & Wadsworth, J. (1994). *Sexual behaviour in Britain: The national survey of sexual attitudes and lifestyles.* Harmondsworth, UK: Penguin Books.

Whitam, F. L., Diamond, M., & Martin, J. (1993). Homosexual orientation in twins: A report on 61 pairs and 3 triplet sets. *Archives of Sexual Behavior, 22,* 187–206.

Williams, T. J., Pepitone, M. E., Christensen, S. E., Cooke, B. M., Huberman, A. D., Breedlove, T. J., et al. (2000, March). Finger-length ratios and sexual orientation. *Nature, 404,* 455–456.

Williams, W. (1986). *The spirit and the flesh: Sexual diversity in American Indian culture.* Boston: Beacon Press.

Wilson, E. O. (1978). *On human nature.* Cambridge, MA: Harvard University.

Wolff, C. (1971). *Love between women.* New York: Harper & Row.

Woodson, J. C., & Gorski, R. A. (2000). Structural sex differences in the mammalian brain: Reconsidering the male/female dichotomy. In A. Matsumoto (Ed.), *Sexual differentiation of the brain* (pp. 229–255). Boca Raton, FL: CRC Press.

8

Gender, Gender Identity, and Sexuality

M. Michele Burnette ◆

Do men have stronger sex drives than women? Are women more emotionally expressive than men? These are common assumptions in today's world that often guide our thoughts and behaviors toward others. The assumption that women and men are characteristically very different is a highly popularized notion and a major topic of discussion in the media (e.g., talk shows, magazines) and popular self-help books. However, scientific research on men and women suggests that they are far more similar than different. Thus, while categorizing and generalizing about what males and females are like may simplify our lives (and provide interesting and lucrative fodder for book writers and the media), these assumptions do not often hold true.

Before moving forward in this discussion, it is important to understand a few general concepts that will be discussed throughout this chapter. *Sex* refers to the biological differences in the sex chromosomes and sex organs of males and females. *Gender* refers to the psychosocial condition of being feminine or masculine, or those traits, interests, and behaviors assumed to be appropriate for a given sex. For example, the sex of a person born with an XY chromosomal makeup, with a penis and testicles, is assumed to be male, but his behavior, personality, and general lifestyle will determine whether or not his gender is masculine or feminine. *Gender roles* are those social behaviors, lifestyles, and personality characteristics that women and men are expected to exhibit. People who adhere closely to these roles are *gender-typed*. A gender-typed female, for example, might dress in feminine clothing, become emotional easily, not show interest in or participate in sports, and dedicate her life to rearing children rather than having a career outside the home. A gender-typed male might work in road construction, watch or participate in sports, and show very little emotion in the face of an upsetting event. But when we assume that all members of a sex possess characteristics and behave in ways that are consistent with gender role expectations, we are *gender stereotyping*—we expect females to be feminine and males to be masculine. Though many men and women do exhibit several characteristics and behaviors in common with other members of their identified sex, this is not universally true. Consider the stay-at-home dad or the woman fighter pilot. When we stereotype, we might fall prey to *gender bias*, that is, we treat men and women differently based on assumptions about members of their sex. Gender bias often leads to unfair treatment. For example, we often rob men of the opportunity to play a primary role in rearing their children because we assume women are by nature more nurturing than men. Or we restrict women from jobs assumed to be suitable only for men. The truth is, many people are *androgynous*, meaning that they exhibit a balance of masculine and feminine characteristics. One final concept is *gender identity* or one's personal view of oneself as male or female, which also may be inconsistent with the individual's biological sex. In general, the dichotomy of maleness and femaleness is an arbitrary notion that can be challenged on both social and biological levels.

PRENATAL SEX DIFFERENTIATION

Prenatal sex differentiation is dependent on two biological factors—chromosomal makeup and hormones. The egg produced by the female always carries an X chromosome; sperm contribute either an X or a Y chromosome. When the sperm and egg unite to form a prenatal organism, if the chromosomal configuration is XX, the fetus is considered female. If the configuration is XY, the fetus is considered male. Ordinarily, the prenatal organism will begin to develop ovaries in the presence of XX, or testes in the presence of XY. However, this process can be interrupted—if the testes do not secrete testosterone between the sixth and twelfth weeks of prenatal development, the organism will automatically develop female sex characteristics—ovaries, uterus, fallopian tubes, and vagina as well as clitoris, labia, and vaginal opening—even with an XY makeup (Money, 1980). As in this example, the expected chromosomal and hormonal processes of sex differentiation occasionally do not occur, and sexual ambiguities result.

The most common chromosomal abnormalities are Klinefelter's syndrome, Turner's syndrome, and intersexuality (also called hermaphroditism). Klinefelter's syndrome occurs when a male has an extra X chromosome (XXY). The result is incomplete masculinization, such as underdeveloped penis and testes, low testosterone levels, and incomplete pubertal maturation, as well as some female physical characteristics, such as partial breast development.

These individuals are infertile and many are mentally handicapped. Turner's syndrome results from a female having only one X chromosome (XO). Individuals with this condition appear female but have no ovaries (or underdeveloped ovaries) and, therefore, do not produce egg cells or sex hormones. In the absence of sex hormones, these women do not develop at puberty without hormone replacement therapy. They also tend to be short and have various physical defects. Unlike these two conditions, the cause of intersexuality is unknown. Hermaphrodites usually have female chromosomes (XX) but genital development is abnormal, resulting in ambiguous genitalia and internal reproductive structures (e.g., one ovary and one testicle, or uterus with male external genitals).

Over- or underexposure to hormones during prenatal development can also cause abnormal sexual development. The embryo may produce abnormal amounts of hormones, or the mother may produce or ingest hormones that affect prenatal development. The most common hormonal abnormalities are congenital adrenal hyperplasia (CAH) and androgen insensitivity syndrome (AIS). In CAH, the adrenal glands of the fetus produce too much testosterone. The result is premature puberty in boys and malelike external genitals in girls. For example, the clitoris may be enlarged and have the appearance of a penis. In AIS, the male fetus has a genetic disorder, which causes the person to be insensitive to testosterone. As a result, the newborn male will not have an internal reproductive system and will have a clitoris and a shallow vagina. At puberty, he is likely to develop breasts. Because they appear female at birth, these chromosomal males are ordinarily reared as females—in fact, by surgically lengthening the vagina and taking estrogen supplements, these individuals usually have satisfactory lives as women (Hines, Ahmed, & Hughes, 2003; Wisniewski et al., 2000). AIS is a condition that highlights the difference between biological sex and gender as well as the difficulty of dichotomizing male and female. According to their chromosomal makeup, these individuals are male; however, their visible physical traits would suggest they are female. In addition, they are generally socialized and identify themselves as female.

GENDER IDENTITY

It is common to assume that one's biological sex will always match one's perception of self as male or female. However, as we just discussed in the case of AIS, this assumption is simply false. Even in the absence of any genetic or hormonal abnormalities, some individuals' gender identity does not correspond to their biological sex. In our society, we find a highly diverse group of individuals who do not conform to traditional notions of a one-to-one correspondence between biological sex and gender in the way they look, behave, or self-identify. We collectively refer to them as *transgendered*. This term is often used to refer to a broad range of individuals, including the intersexed individuals we just discussed, as well as cross-dressers, gay men in drag, "butch" lesbians, and transsexuals (Bullough, 2000). Most relevant to our discussion of gender identity are transsexuals. Cross-dressers, gays, and lesbians are discussed elsewhere in this series. *Transsexuals* are those individuals who think of themselves as the opposite of their biological sex. Many refer to this as feeling "trapped inside the body of the opposite sex." Some transsexuals are content to live as the opposite sex without altering their genitals or physical appearance, but many of them wish to have surgery and take hormones in order to make their bodies appear more like their self-identified sex.

Those who persistently feel "trapped inside the body of the opposite sex" may be diagnosed with gender identity disorder (GID). Signs of GID usually become apparent early in childhood, but it may also develop in puberty. GID is far more common in boys than in girls (4:1). Children with GID are generally very clear about wanting to be the opposite sex and will verbalize this desire openly. However, some may simply take on behavior patterns of the opposite sex and insist on dressing in clothing of the opposite sex. It is important to note that not all children who exhibit these behaviors grow up to live as the opposite sex—many children grow out of it. Those who truly experience GID will become more persistent in their efforts to cross-dress and act like the opposite sex as they grow older (Doorn, Poortinga, & Verschoor, 1994; Money & Lehne, 1999; Zucker, 1995).

How GID exists in the face of a culture that does not accept significant diversions from gender role norms is difficult to understand. Some experts have suggested a biological basis for GID, but the research has not yielded any consistent conclusions (Zucker, 1995). Several environmental factors have also been identified as possible correlates of GID. Boys with GID tend to have more brothers and to be born late in the birth order than non-GID boys (Green, 2000). In addition, children with GID tend to have difficulty identifying with the same-sex parent and have parents who permit and support identification with the opposite-sex parent (Zucker & Bradley, 1995).

Generally, psychotherapy is ineffective in helping an individual feel less distress about her or his cross-gender identity (Zucker, 1995). Some individuals are content to live and dress as the opposite sex, but many seek "sex reassignment," which is having surgery to restructure the genitalia to appear as the opposite sex and taking hormones to change voice quality, muscle mass, hair growth, breast size, and body fat distribution to appear like the opposite sex. Research suggests that in the overall pool of individuals with GID, most suffer from emotional issues throughout life (Hepp, Kraemer, Schnyder, Miller, & Delsignore, 2005). Those individuals who seek and receive sex reassignment are satisfied with the results and generally adjust well psychologically, socially, and sexually (Smith, Van Goozen, Kuiper, & Cohen-Kettenis, 2005). However, they are generally heavily screened in advance to insure that they are psychologically well adjusted before surgery. Postoperative psychotherapy has been recommended in aiding adjustment as well (Rehman,

Lazer, Benet, Schaefer, & Melman, 1999). Transsexualism is indeed an extreme and relatively rare example of how humans transcend common notions of sex and gender. The next section addresses common and more culturally tolerated challenges to traditional notions of gender.

GENDER ROLES AND STEREOTYPES

Recently, a man was discussing his upcoming nuptials and remarked that although his fiancée made more money, she would be quitting her job and moving to the town where he lived. When asked why they would sacrifice the higher income, he remarked that "of course" men should have the higher income and be the primary wage earners. This is a common traditional gender role expectation that persists even in our modern age. Gender role expectations impact our personal relationships in many ways. Traditional gender roles dictate, for example, that women not approach men for dates but that they play the most active role in nurturing a relationship once formed. Men are expected to act "cool" and emotionally distant but be the initiators in sexual interactions. These are all examples of gender-typed behaviors.

Obviously, these roles are not as strictly adhered to today as they were some years ago. Women are more assertive in initiating relationships (and this is often welcomed by men), and men are more comfortable with expressing emotions (also appreciated by women). Despite the fact that so many men and women display flexibility in their gender roles, gender stereotyping is still relatively common. Recall that gender stereotyping occurs when an individual is assumed to engage in certain behaviors or display certain characteristics based on her or his apparent sex, regardless of the extent to which the individual actually exhibits gender-typed behaviors and characteristics. For example, we are stereotyping when we say that all men are primarily motivated to form relationships in order to have sex or that all women are primarily motivated to form relationships to get married and have children. Although some individuals are gender-typed—adhering closely to common notions of male and female—the vast majority of men and women behave similarly most of the time, perhaps more than 98 percent of the time (Canary & Hause, 1993). Thus, stereotypes persist in the face of disconfirming information. Why do they persist? Research suggests that they are sustained because stereotypes bring stability and predictability to a person's life and simplify one's ability to process information about the social environment (Hughes & Seta, 2003). In addition, when men and women do exhibit clear differences, it is in the stereotyped direction, confirming and supporting stereotypic notions (Vogel, Wester, Heesacker, & Madon, 2003).

Life is simplified if we can predict how people will behave based on first appearances rather than having to discover a person's unique qualities. However, problems are likely to arise if one is inflexible about stereotypes and does not accept a person's individuality. Because so many stereotypes are not only inaccurate but also negative, strict adherence to such stereotypes can harm or oppress stereotyped groups. Such gender bias, for example, has often prevented women from pursuing and succeeding in their chosen careers. A contemporary example is the debate over whether or not women should be placed in or near combat (Stone, 2005). Many of the arguments against women in the military, in general, are based on stereotypes and are not supported by research (RAND Research Brief, 1997), and the cost to women is not having equal access to a tremendous number of jobs and advanced positions in the armed services.

ANDROGYNY

So far, this chapter has illuminated the fact that neither sex nor gender is a dichotomous characteristic, and that we cannot easily assume that a person will think, behave, or possess a particular set of characteristics based on our perception of the individual's sex. In fact, people fall on a continuum of masculine and feminine—most men and women are best described as androgynous, having both masculine and feminine characteristics. Only a small number of individuals possess very few either feminine or masculine characteristics—they are referred to as *undifferentiated*. In neither case are these people gender-typed. Where once individuals who were not gender-typed were viewed as deviant, much evidence today suggests that androgyny is the picture of well-being. No longer under pressure to prove one's masculinity or femininity, the androgynous person has a broader repertoire of possible responses to draw from and can choose the most appropriate response for a particular situation. With such a broad repertoire, an individual can function effectively in a variety of situations. To take the case of women in war again, one advantage to having women in the Iraq war is their ability to deal sensitively and effectively with other women and children whom they approach during door-to-door searches (Stone, 2005). Thus, these women are true warriors who also make use of more traditionally "feminine" qualities in a unique and challenging environment.

Researchers have addressed the question of whether or not androgynous individuals enjoy greater psychological well-being than their more gender-typed counterparts owing to their broader repertoires and, therefore, greater ability to act and respond to a variety of demands. Because adolescence is the time when young people begin to take on more adult roles, this question has been studied most extensively in adolescents. Research does suggest that androgynous children and adolescents enjoy greater psychological well-being but so do more masculine children and adolescents (Allgood-Merten & Stockard, 1991; Markstrom-Adams, 1989). This latter finding may be because masculine traits have traditionally been more highly valued by society than feminine traits, giving the more masculine adolescent greater status and acceptance in her or his environment.

THEORIES OF GENDER ROLE DEVELOPMENT

Why are some people gender-typed while others are androgynous? The prominent theories on gender development tend to focus more on the contribution of either nature (heredity) or nurture (learning environment) and less on the relative contributions of both influences. The reader may find that many of these theories complement as well as contradict one another. In addition, most of them focus on how people come to conform to expected gender roles as opposed to why so many people do not.

There are five dominant theories of gender development—three are predominantly based on the notion that gender roles are learned through experience; the other two rely more heavily on the notion that biology determines gender role adherence. The biological theories include behavioral genetics and evolutionary viewpoints, and the environmental theories include Freudian theory, social learning theory, and cognitive developmental theory.

Behavioral Genetics

The behavioral genetics viewpoint posits that gender-typed behaviors are determined through genetic inheritance. In other words, our adoption of these behaviors as well as others is determined by our genetic makeup passed down to us through our biological parents. This position is tested by two primary means. One is by demonstrating that adopted children demonstrate more similar behavior patterns to their biological parents (inheritance) than to their adoptive parents (environment). It is also tested by looking at similarities between monozygotic twins, who are genetically identical, and comparing the extent of those similarities to similarities between dizygotic twins, who are no more genetically similar than any other pair of siblings—they share only about 50 percent of their genes. If a behavioral trait is totally determined by genetics, you would expect identical twins to behave exactly the same 100 percent of the time. This is called a *concordance rate*. You would also expect dizygotic twins to have about a 50 percent concordance on that trait. Few genetic studies have been conducted to assess the relative influence of genetics on gender role development. One study did show some evidence that genetics accounted for the variance in masculine and feminine characteristics in children (20 to 48 percent of the variance). However, they concluded that experiences outside the home, such as peers, have a greater impact than genetics or even parental influence (Mitchell, Baker, & Jacklin, 1989). A recent twin study addressed the contribution of genetics to *atypical* gender development (e.g., boys playing with jewelry and girls playing with swords). This study found that environment contributed more to gender role development than genetic factors, except perhaps in the case of girls who were high in masculinity and low in feminine characteristics. In this case, genetic factors appeared to be the primary determinant (Knafo, Iervolino, & Plomin, 2005).

Evolutionary Theory

The evolutionary position is that gender-typed behaviors that present themselves across all cultures have been selected throughout the centuries in order to insure survival of the species and that these behaviors cannot be explained by environmental factors alone. One would expect to see more variability in these behaviors if they were environmentally determined. Examples of cross-cultural invariability are that in all cultures men are more likely than women to be polygamous (have multiple partners), and women are less likely to commit murder than men. Evolutionary psychologists claim that they can predict similarities between the sexes in those areas where both have been challenged by similar adaptive problems, and differences between the sexes in those areas where they have faced different adaptive problems, throughout time.

For example, David Buss (1995), a prominent evolutionary psychologist, suggested that women are less likely to engage in casual sex than men because the costs of sex are much greater for women. Women are likely to get pregnant and then bear the burden of caring and providing for the child. Men tend to engage in more casual sexual interactions because their evolutionary "goal" is to propagate the species. In addition, they suffer few, if any, lifelong negative consequences. Because of the additional burden women bear, they are more likely to be discriminating and seek out only those sexual partners who appear oriented toward commitment and assuming responsibility for their offspring. While these tendencies may be true in a general sense, in reality there is tremendous variability in the behaviors of men and women. Certainly, we all know men who are very focused on finding the right lifelong mate and women who engage in casual sex without fear of the potential consequences. Perhaps it is best to think of the evolution of behaviors as predispositions that are either exaggerated or diminished by environmental factors (Buss & Schmitt, 1993; Kenrick & Trost, 1993). For example, the invention of effective contraception has given women much greater sexual freedom (Buss, 1994); therefore, women do not have to worry as much about pregnancy and can be less discriminating in their sexual choices.

Overall, it appears that these biological theories of gender role development provide incomplete explanations of how common behaviors are established. It is most likely that environmental factors play as much of, if not a greater, role in gender role development.

Freudian Theory

Sigmund Freud (1856–1939) lived primarily in Vienna, Austria, during what was known as the Victorian era. The Victorian era was marked by extreme sexual oppression. Women, in particular, were denied sexual expression, and, in fact, were considered potential prostitutes if they expressed any sexual feelings at all. This is the context in which Freud's view of gender identification evolved. By today's standards, aspects of this view are sexist. Freud's overall idea of development was that children proceed through a relatively predictable set of stages, including the phallic stage, from about age 3 to 6. He believed that boys and girls learn about what it is to be "male" or "female" by observation and imitation of the same-sex parent's behavior. During the phallic stage, children develop their gender roles through this process. According to him, a boy experiences what Freud called the *Oedipal complex,* during which the boy desires his mother and comes to envy his father, the primary rival for his mother's affection. He then becomes fearful that his father, upon discovering the boy's feelings, will castrate him. Thus, he develops *castration anxiety.* To relieve his anxiety, he suppresses his carnal desires for his mother and identifies with his father by imitating his behaviors, attitudes, and appearance. The girl is also attached to the mother, her primary caregiver. However, during the phallic phase, when genitalia become the object of attention, she discovers that she lacks a penis, and blames her mother and becomes hostile toward her. She then attaches to her father and imagines that she will become pregnant by him and that this will cause her to develop a penis and gain equal status with her father. This is due mostly to the idea that the girl is "envious" of her father's penis and wants to possess it so strongly that she dreams of bearing his children, thus the term *penis envy.* Eventually, recognizing that she cannot possess her father, she identifies and imitates her mother, the woman who does possess him. Freud argued, however, that because the girl is ambivalent about being female (i.e., has penis envy), she adopts an inferiority complex as the "inferior sex." She does not fully adopt her mother's characteristics and her identification is incomplete, causing her to have a poorly developed superego, or conscience. As a result, her values and morals are seen as weaker than men's. Clearly, these are antiquated and sexist notions about the sexes. Freudian theory has little relevance to our current understanding of gender role development except that it opened the door for theorizing about how the social world impacts on the developing child.

Social Learning Theory

The basic tenet of social learning theory is that the roles we assume in life are shaped by events and other people in our lives. In other words, we learn our gender roles through being reinforced or punished and by imitating others. Reinforcement is a stimulus or event that follows a behavior and increases the likelihood that that behavior will occur in the future. Generally, if performance of a behavior results in a pleasant outcome, that behavior will be reinforced. However, the removal of an unpleasant stimulus can also reinforce behavior. Punishment occurs when the onset of an unpleasant stimulus or the termination of a pleasant stimulus following a behavior decreases the likelihood of that behavior occurring in the future. For example, a little boy plays with a doll, but his little male friends make fun of him, so he no longer plays with dolls. In this case, the teasing from his friends punishes playing with dolls. If he picks up a truck and his friends come over to play with him, then playing with trucks is likely to be rewarded by their approval. Reinforcement of gender-typed behavior and punishment of deviations from them establish gender-typed patterns early in life, and these may even take place before birth. Take, for example, parents' preparation for a new baby. If they know the sex, they generally decorate a nursery differently for a boy or a girl—a boy's room might be decorated with sports-related themes, while a girl's might be decorated with cute bunnies. As children grow up, they are influenced by more than their parents' behavior. We are inundated in our society with messages that tell us that boys and girls should behave differently. Take, for example, the highly gender-typed toy commercials that children see while watching cartoons, or the ads on radio and television and in the written media that stress beauty for women and achievement for men.

Beyond the more direct forces of reinforcement and punishment is *role modeling*. Role modeling is the imitation of behaviors of someone admired or liked. Children are most likely to imitate the behavior of someone of the same sex when several members of that sex exhibit that behavior (Bussey & Bandura, 1984; Bussey & Perry, 1982). When, for example, boys see only one or two men (if any) staying home to care for their children while most men are working, they are not likely to aspire to be stay-at-home dads. They are much more likely to model "climbing the corporate ladder" as they see numerous examples of men doing just that.

Social influences on gender role development in our culture cannot be ignored. There is a plethora of research on the influence of parents, peers, teachers, and the media on the development of gender roles, and there is little doubt that all these influence children to develop gender-typed behavior. One of the criticisms of social learning theory is that it focuses almost exclusively on the external environment and ignores the role of other factors, such as thought processes, in gender socialization.

Cognitive-Developmental Theory

There are several cognitive theories of gender development. All are consistent with the social learning perspective in that they assert that children learn gender roles through interactions with their environment. But while social learning theory paints a picture of children as somewhat passive with respect to the influence of their learning environments, most, if not all, cognitive theories emphasize the active role that children play in their own gender socialization. One prominent cognitive theory is cognitive-developmental theory. A major tenet of this theory is that a child's ability to develop gender roles relies on her or his ability to develop *gender constancy*, which occurs when the child accomplishes three things: (1) gender identity—identifies self as male or female: (2) gender stability—recognizes that one's gender does not change over time: and (3) gender consistency—recognizes that one's identity is not altered by changes in gender-typed activities, traits, or appearance. Once the child identifies as male or female, the child will seek out same-sex role models to imitate "appropriate" behaviors. A final tenet of cognitive developmental theory is that a child is motivated internally to bring her or his behavior and thinking in line with one's gender category (Martin, Ruble, & Szkrybalo, 2002).

All of the theories of development that we have reviewed have value. Today's gender role theorists, for the most part, maintain that in order to completely understand gender role development, we need a comprehensive model of development that takes into account biological, social, and cognitive influences (Martin et al., 2002; Martin, Ruble, Szkrybalo, 2004). In fact, some theories, such as social cognitive theory, attempt to integrate cognition into a social learning theory of development and also make note of the contribution of biology and other sociocultural factors (Bussey & Bandura, 1999). Ultimately, all of these factors probably contribute to gender role development, but a truly comprehensive model of these contributions has not yet emerged.

FEMALE AND MALE: INTERACTIONS BETWEEN THE SEXES

In our adult lives, one area where gender-typed behavior and stereotypes impact us most is in interactions between the sexes. With respect to interpersonal interactions, research shows that initial attraction for males and females tends to be toward more gender-typed individuals. However, these relationships tend to become unhappy pairings in the long run (Brehm, 1992; Ickes, 1993; Kenrick & Trost, 1989). In fact, an older but very large survey of men and women revealed that feminine women in relationships with masculine men reported that they were highly dissatisfied with all aspects of their relationships, including their sexual interactions (Ickes). Furthermore, the best interactions between females and males seem to be within couples in which one or both are androgynous. These relationships are more interactive and rewarding than those shared between traditional males and traditional females (Ickes & Barnes, 1978). In addition, other research has shown that both males and females prefer androgynous partners for dates, "one-night stands," and marriage (Green & Kenrick, 1994). In general, it seems that androgynous individuals are more successful at fostering and maintaining healthy heterosocial relationships.

How do gender-typed roles and stereotypes affect sexual interactions? Unfortunately, dissimilarities between the sexes also may create negative outcomes in sexual interactions. Some areas in which gender identification and stereotyping affect sexuality are in expression of sexual intent (i.e., whether or not there is interest in a sexual interaction), initiation of or pressure to engage in sexual interactions, and safer sex practices.

Numerous studies have shown that while women and men are both able to accurately identify flirting behaviors, men have a much greater tendency than women to identify flirting as imparting sexual interest (Henningsen, 2004). Even in casual and brief interactions, men are more likely than women to see members of the opposite sex as being seductive, sexy, and even promiscuous (Harnish, Abbey, & DeBono, 1990; Haworth-Hoeppner, 1998; Johnson, Stockdale, & Saal, 1991). There are several possible reasons why men might overinterpret flirtatious or even neutral interactions as sexual in nature. One may be that men are unduly influenced by the media's tendency to place greater emphasis on women's physical attractiveness and sexual availability as opposed to other attributes such as character and personality. Second, men may be on the lookout for signs of interest from women because men have traditionally been expected to play the role of initiating dates and sexual interactions (Muehlenhard & Rodgers, 1998). Finally, men have traditionally been taught that women play "hard to get" and avoid giving off signs of interest even when they are interested.

The discrepancy in male and female interpretations of sexual interest may, in part, be at the core of the most common form of rape—acquaintance ("date") rape. When males believe that females are interested in a sexual encounter when they are not, and/or that females are more likely to act as if they are not interested, males may continue to pursue sexual interactions even when the female is not interested. In fact, research has shown that males are less likely than females to identify scenarios depicting nonconsensual sex as unacceptable (Freetly & Kane, 1995) perhaps because they do not perceive it as nonconsensual at all, but rather they see it as part of a "mating game."

The traditional view of sexual interactions between men and women has been that men are the initiators, and, as we discussed above, women are the resistors. However, a fairly sizable number of studies now suggest that many women do initiate sexual activity (Clements-Schreiber, Rempel, & Desmarais, 1998). Up to 93 percent of females report that they have initiated sex at some time (Anderson & Aymami, 1993). More surprisingly, research has also documented that women use pressure tactics to get men to engage in sexual interactions with them. Results from a study of coercive sexual strategies used by women suggest that there is at least a modest relationship between a woman's willingness to use coercive strategies and adherence to the gender stereotype that men are always ready and willing to engage in sexual activity (Clements-Schreiber et al., 1998). Thus, stereotypes about men may contribute to inappropriate and potentially harmful behavior in women directed at men. While much attention has been given to how stereotypes about women put them at risk for sexual victimization, little attention has been given to how men might likewise be victimized. The role of harmful gender stereotypes of men in coercive sexuality needs to be explored further.

With the spread of HIV over the last few decades, more attention has been given to how gender stereotypes might have an impact on safer sex practices.

The only way to practice safer sex, besides complete abstinence, is to use a condom each and every time one has oral-genital or genital-genital contact with another person. Until the female condom gains greater popularity, the primary means of protecting against sexually transmitted infections, including HIV/AIDS, is to use a male condom. Obviously, use of a male condom requires significant male cooperation. Women who adhere to traditional notions of male as the aggressor and woman as the passive, less sexual one in heterosexual interactions are not likely to take the initiative to purchase, and, much less, require that their male partners use condoms. In fact, in a study of African American women, those women who never used condoms and were hence characterized as sexually nonassertive expressed that they did not use condoms out of concern for how their male partners would react to their requests to wear a condom (Wingood & DiClemente, 1998). Furthermore, a more traditional woman is more likely to prefer sex in the context of an ongoing relationship as opposed to casual sex. When a woman waits until she gets to know a man well before having intercourse, she is more likely to assume that he is "safe" (i.e., does not carry any sexually transmittable infections). In fact, one study supported this idea that women preferring "relational" sex were less likely to use a condom than women who did not place an emphasis on relational sex (Hynie, Lydon, Cote, & Weiner, 1998).

ARE MEN AND WOMEN SEXUALLY DIFFERENT?

The previous discussion might raise the question of whether or not true sexual differences between men and women actually exist. For example, are men always primed for sex, and women less interested or less sexually arousable than men? In general, objective data using direct physiological measures of genital responses and self-report data regarding arousability to sexual stimuli suggest that both men and women are aroused most by explicit sexual material (as opposed to romantic content) and that women are just as physiologically arousable as men (Heiman, 1977; Schmidt & Sigusch, 1970; Schmidt, Sigusch, & Schafer, 1973; Sigusch, Schmidt, Reinfeld, & Wiedemann-Sutor, 1970). Research further shows that men and women are also most highly aroused to *female-initiated* sexual interactions. How are men and women different in sexual arousal? When shown several different types of sexual interactions (male to male, female to male, female to female, group versus individual), heterosexual women and men are similar in that they show greatest arousal to group sex and least arousal to male homosexual sex. However, men found lesbian sex (between two women) most arousing, followed by heterosexual sex. Women showed the opposite pattern (Steinman, Wincze, Sakheim, Barlow, & Mavissakalian, 1981); heterosexual sex was more arousing than lesbian sex.

What can be learned from this brief review of gender and sexuality? In general, neither gender nor sexuality is clearly a dichotomous category. Not only is there a great deal of variability in expression of masculinity and femininity in men and women, but there is also not always a clear distinction between male and female sex. Some individuals have genetic or hormonal conditions that make their biological sex ambiguous as well. If people do not fit into clear categories of male and female, masculine and feminine, what about similarities and differences between men and women? Overall, men and women have more similarities than differences in how they behave, especially with respect to interpersonal and sexual relationships.

REFERENCES

Allgood-Merten, B., & Stockard, J. (1991). Sex role identity and self-esteem: A comparison of children and adolescents. *Sex Roles, 25*, 129–139.

Anderson, P. B., & Aymami, R. (1993). Reports of female initiation of sexual contact: Male and female differences. *Archives of Sexual Behavior, 22*(4), 335–343.

Brehm, S. S. (1992). *Intimate relationships.* New York: McGraw-Hill.

Bullough, V. L. (2000). Transgenderism and the concept of gender. *International Journal of Transgenderism, 4*(3). Retrieved July 22, 2002, from www .symposion.com/ijt/gilbert/bullough.htm

Buss, D. M. (1994). *The evolution of desire: Strategies of human mating.* New York: Basic Books.

Buss, D. M. (1995). Psychological sex differences: Origins through sexual selection. *American Psychologist, 50*, 164–168.

Buss, D. M., & Schmitt, D. P. (1993). Sexual strategies theory: An evolutionary perspective on human nature. *Psychological Review, 2*, 204–232.

Bussey, K., & Bandura, A. (1984). Influence of gender constancy and social power on sex-linked modeling. *Journal of Personality and Social Psychology, 42*, 1292–1302.

Bussey, K., & Bandura, A. (1999). Social cognitive theory of gender development and differentiation. *Psychological Review, 106*, 676–713.

Bussey, K., & Perry, D. G. (1982). Same-sex imitation? *Sex Roles, 8*, 773–784.

Canary, D. J., & Hause, K. S. (1993). Is there any reason to research sex differences in communication? *Communication Quarterly, 41*, 129–144.

Clements-Schreiber, M. E., Rempel, J. K., & Desmarais, S. (1998). Women's sexual pressure tactics and adherence to related attitudes: A step toward prediction. *Journal of Sex Research, 35*(2), 197–205.

Doorn, C. D., Poortinga, J., & Verschoor, A. M. (1994). Cross-gender identity in transvestites and male transsexuals. *Archives of Sexual Behavior, 23*, 185–201.

Freetly, A. J. H., & Kane, E. W. (1995). Men's and women's perceptions of non-consensual sexual intercourse. *Sex Roles, 33*, 785–803.

Green, B. L., & Kenrick, D. T. (1994). The attractiveness of gender-typed traits of different relationship levels: Androgynous characteristics may be desirable after all. *Personality and Social Psychology Bulletin, 20*, 244–253.

Green, R. (2000). Birth order and ratio of brothers to sisters in transsexuals. *Psychological Medicine, 30*(4), 789–795.

Harnish, R. J., Abbey, A., & DeBono, K. G. (1990). Toward an understanding of "The Sex Game": The effects of gender and self-monitoring on perceptions of sexuality and likeability in initial interactions. *Journal of Applied Social Psychology, 20*(16), 1333–1334.

Haworth-Hoeppner, S. (1998). What's gender got to do with it: Perceptions of sexual coercion in a university community. *Sex Roles: A Journal of Research, 38*(9/10), 757–779.

Heiman, J. R. (1977). A psychophysiological exploration of sexual arousal patterns in females and males. *Psychophysiology, 14*(3), 266–274.

Henningsen, D. D. (2004). Flirting with meaning: An examination of miscommunication in flirting interactions. *Sex Roles: A Journal of Research, 50*(7/8), 481–489.

Hepp, U., Kraemer, B., Schnyder, U., Miller, N., & Delsignore, A. (2005). Psychiatric comorbidity in gender identity disorder. *Journal of Psychosomatic Research, 58*(3), 259–261.

Hines, M., Ahmed, S. F., & Hughes, I. A. (2003). Psychological outcomes and gender-related development in complete androgen insensitivity syndrome. *Archives of Sexual Behavior, 32*(2), 93–101.

Hughes, F. M., & Seta, C. E. (2003). Gender stereotypes: Children's perceptions of future compensatory behavior following violations of gender roles. *Sex Roles: A Journal of Research, 49*(11/12), 685–691.

Hynie, M., Lydon, J. E., Cote, S., & Weiner, S. (1998). Relational sexual scripts and women's condom use: The importance of internalized norms. *Journal of Sex Research, 35*(4), 370–380.

Ickes, W. (1993). Traditional gender roles: Do they make, and then break, our relationships? *Journal of Social Issues, 49*, 71–85.

Ickes, W., & Barnes, R. D. (1978). Boys and girls together—and alienated: On enacting stereotyped sex roles in the mind-sex dyads. *Journal of Personality and Social Psychology, 36*, 669–683.

Johnson, C., Stockdale, M., & Saal, E. (1991). Persistence of men's misperceptions of friendly cues across a variety of interpersonal encounters. *Psychology of Women Quarterly, 15*, 463–475.

Kenrick, D. T., & Trost, M. R. (1989). A reproductive exchange model of heterosexual relationships: Putting proximate economics in ultimate perspective. In C. Hendrick (Ed.), *Review of personality and social psychology* (Vol. 10, pp. 148–172). New York: Guilford Press.

Kenrick, D. T., & Trost, M. R. (1993). The evolutionary perspective. In A. E. Beall & R. J. Sternberg (Eds.), *The psychology of gender* (pp. 148–172). New York: Guilford Press.

Knafo, A., Iervolino, A. C., & Plomin, R. (2005). Masculine girls and feminine boys: Genetic and environmental contributions to atypical gender development in early childhood. *Journal of Personality and Social Psychology, 88*(2), 400–412.

Markstrom-Adams, C. (1989). Androgyny and its relationship to adolescent psychosocial well-being: A review of the literature. *Sex Roles: A Journal of Research, 21*, 325–340.

Martin, C. L., Ruble, D. N., & Szkrybalo, J. (2002). Cognitive theories of early gender development. *Psychological Bulletin, 128*(6), 903–933.

Martin, C. L., Ruble, D. N., & Szkrybalo, J. (2004). Recognizing the centrality of gender identity and stereotype knowledge in gender development and moving toward theoretical integration: Reply to Bandura and Bussey. *Psychological Bulletin, 130*(5), 702–710.

Mitchell, J. E., Baker, L. A., & Jacklin, C. N. (1989). Masculinity and femininity in twin children: Genetic and environmental factors. *Child Development, 60*, 1475–1485.

Money, J. (1980). *Love and sickness: The science of sex, gender difference, and pair-bonding.* Baltimore: Johns Hopkins University Press.

Money, J., & Lehne, G. K. (1999). Gender identity disorders. In R. T. Ammerman & M. Hersen (Eds.), *Handbook of prescriptive treatments for children and adolescents* (2nd ed., pp. 214–228). Boston: Allyn & Bacon.

Muehlenhard, C. L., & Rodgers, C. S. (1998). Token resistance to sex: New perspectives on an old stereotype. *Psychology of Women Quarterly, 15*, 447–461.

RAND Research Brief. (1997). *Military readiness: Women are not the problem.* Retrieved June 20, 2005, from www.rand.org/publications/RB/RB7515/

Rehman, J., Lazer, S., Benet, A. E., Schaefer, L. C., & Melman, A. (1999). The reported sex and surgery satisfactions of 28 postoperative male-to-female transsexual patients. *Archives of Sexual Behavior, 28*(1), 71–89.

Schmidt, G., & Sigusch, V. (1970). Sex differences in responses to psychosexual stimulation by films and slides. *Journal of Sex Research, 6*, 268–283.

Schmidt, G., Sigusch, V., & Schafer, S. (1973). Responses to reading erotic stories: Male-female differences. *Archives of Sexual Behavior, 2*, 181–199.

Sigusch, V., Schmidt, G., Reinfeld, A., & Wiedemann-Sutor, I. (1970). Psychosexual stimulation: Sex differences. *Journal of Sex Research, 6*, 10–24.

Smith, Y. L., Van Goozen, S. H., Kuiper, A. J., & Cohen-Kettenis, P. T. (2005). Sex reassignment: Outcomes and predictors of treatment for adolescent and adult transsexuals. *Psychological Medicine, 35*(1), 89–99.

Steinman, D. L., Wincze, J. P., Sakheim, D. K., Barlow, D. H., & Mavissakalian, M. (1981). A comparison of male and female patterns of sexual arousal. *Archives of Sexual Behavior, 10*(6), 529–547.

Stone, A. (2005, May 20). Panel's decision reheats women-in-combat debate: Pentagon to review issue that some say renews cultural battle. *U.S.A. Today.* Retrieved June 7, 2005, from www.usatoday.com/printedition/news/20050520/a_womencombat20.art.htm

Vogel, D. L., Wester, S. R., Heesacker, M., & Madon, S. (2003). Confirming gender stereotypes: A social role perspective. *Sex Roles: A Journal of Research, 48*(11/12), 519–528.

Wingood, G. M., & DiClemente, R. J. (1998). Pattern influences and gender-related factors associated with noncondom use among young adult African American women. *American Journal of Community Psychology, 26*, 29–51.

Wisniewski, A. B., Migeon, C. J., Meyer-Bahlburg, H. F., Gearhart, J. P., Berkovitz, G. D., Brown, T. R., et al. (2000). Complete androgen insensitivity syndrome: Long-term medical, surgical, and psychosexual outcome. *Journal of Endocrinological Metabolism, 85*(8), 2664–2669.

Zucker, K. J. (1995). Gender identity disorders: A developmental prespective. In L. Diamant & R. D. McAnulty (Eds.), *The psychology of sexual orientation, behavior, and identity: A handbook* (pp. 327–354). Westport, CT: Greenwood Press.

Zucker, K. J., & Bradley, S. J. (1995). *Gender identity disorder and psychosexual problems in children and adolescents.* New York: Guilford Press.

9

The Social Construction of Sexuality: Religion, Medicine, Media, Schools, and Families

Laina Y. Bay-Cheng ◆

- It is important to remember that helping your child stay healthy is an ongoing job. Parents need to know that sexually active adolescents face greater physical and emotional health risks than any other segment of the population. . . . With so much at stake, it is more important than ever for parents to encourage their adolescents to delay sexual involvement, preferably until marriage. Abstinence is, without question, the healthiest choice for adolescents, both physically and emotionally.

- In most dating relationships there is a natural progression of physical intimacy. If no barriers are put into place, this progression generally leads to sexual inter-course. Most experts agree that once couples move beyond hugging and light kissing, hormones encourage further physical contact.

  Progression of physical intimacy:

  - Holding hands
  - Holding each other around the waist or shoulder (hugs)
  - Kissing on the lips
  - "French" (open mouth) kissing
  - Touching breasts
  - Touching sexual organs
  - Sexual intercourse.[1]

These excerpts from www.4parents.gov, a Web site launched in early 2005 by the U.S. Department of Health and Human Services, are readily recognizable as tips to help parents understand and communicate with their adolescent children about sexuality. However, a closer reading reveals a deeper level of information and education. Specifically, adolescent sexuality is implicitly defined as an inherently, universally risky venture that is virtually unstoppable once activated. What is more, by referring to "marriage" (a social institution that only heterosexual couples have access to, except in Massachusetts), "breasts," and "sexual intercourse" in its discussion of sexuality, this site favors heterosexuality over other forms of sexual identities, relationships, and behaviors. This position is made clear elsewhere on the Web page where reference is made to nonheterosexual "lifestyles," a word typically used by conservatives to imply that lesbian, gay, bisexual, or transgendered identities, relationships, and behaviors are a matter of choice and therefore can—and should—be changed. This deeper level of analysis and process of reading between lines is referred to as *deconstruction*: a dissection of the obvious message in order to reveal its parts and underlying assumptions, which may be hidden by the whole. By studying the message within the message, the passages above become significant not just as a helpful guide to parents seeking information and tips on how to talk about sex with their teenagers, but also as a conveyer of a particular set of social norms and values.

The term "deconstruction" is drawn from the theoretical framework of *social constructionism*. The basic tenet of social constructionism was most popularly and succinctly defined by Berger and Luckmann (1966) as the position that "reality is socially constructed." In other words, there is no single, objectively true world or reality that we just live in; we are not passive residents of a prefabricated setting, just soaking up and responding to the view. Instead, our realities, which consist of our relationships and identities, are constantly being produced or constructed through our actions, reactions, and interactions. We do not just inhabit the social world; we are simultaneously building it, too.

From this perspective, nothing is stable or universal; race, gender, "right" and "wrong"—none are fixed or foregone conclusions. In this way, social constructionism is not just a strategy for answering the same old questions; it allows us to ask entirely new questions. For instance, suppose you are concerned about gender issues such as the disproportionate number of men working in the sciences or male violence against women, but you also buy into the idea that gender is innate (e.g., women are naturally less adept at logic and spatial relations; men are inherently more aggressive), then there is only so much you can do to rectify the inequality. After all, the difference is natural and, at some point, we revert back to a "boys will be boys" conclusion. However, if approached from a social constructionist perspective, a new level of analysis and intervention is opened up; anatomy no longer must be destiny. Rather than a reflection of inalterable biological difference, gender itself is seen as a social construct, a deeply ingrained but nonetheless changeable one. By questioning and deconstructing the very "reality" of gender, new solutions to sexism and misogyny are revealed.

Using the analytical tool of deconstruction, this chapter will examine questions about sexuality that only social constructionism allows us to ask: How is sexuality constructed in contemporary American culture? What social institutions authorize this construction as correct and real? How are the social norms associated with our construct of sexuality delivered and disseminated among us? Optimally, each of these questions warrants a chapter (or a book, or even several books) unto itself. Clearly, one chapter to cover all of these questions cannot possibly do them justice. However, I hope to be able to provide at least a thumbnail sketch of the meanings and mechanisms of the social construction of sexuality.

INTRODUCING SOCIAL CONSTRUCTIONISM

Social constructionism emerged out of a critique of the principles and priorities that have dominated American and European schools of thought since the Enlightenment. The post-Enlightenment period, commonly referred to as modernity, is typified by a reliance on the scientific pillars of objectivity and logic. Facilitated by the advances in technology, modernist science focused on the primacy of nature and the pursuit of singular, finite, and knowable facts. Postmodernism, which is used to describe a wide-ranging critique of modernist principles and values, rejects the suggestion that there is a single, true reality, or that humans, for instance, possess a single, uniform "nature" or way of being. To the contrary, postmodernism endorses the existence and validity of multiple realities, multiple truths, and multiple ways of being—one no more "true," "real," or "better" than another.

The challenge raised by postmodernist scholarship has commonly been conceived as a debate between social constructionism and *essentialism*. "Essentialism" is used by social constructionists to refer, typically negatively, to the modernist belief that an entity or phenomenon contains a central, natural essence—a core truth that is immutable, universal, and innate (DeLamater & Hyde, 1998). For instance, in his theory of the life and death instincts (Eros and Thanatos, respectively), Sigmund Freud (1940) proposed an essentialist view of human nature as always—across both time and culture—being motivated by the selfish needs for pleasure and domination. However, rather than accept the notion that *all* humans are aggressive and that this is an unchangeable, inborn trait, social constructionism looks for exceptions and alternatives: Can human behavior across time and around the world really be simply reduced to the need for either pleasure or aggression? Do pleasure and aggression themselves look the same and mean the same across time and around the world? Finally, if we *do* see evidence of humans being motivated by pleasure and aggression across time and around the world, is this because these drives really, truly exist or because this is what our own skills of perception have been trained to see? An essentialist answers this final question with the former: we are observing actual reality, which exists regardless of whether we are there to observe it or not. A social constructionist, on the other hand, endorses the latter: what we see is a reality that we are simultaneously constructing to be "true"; motives for pleasure and aggression exist precisely because we look for—and decide that we find—them.

SOCIALLY CONSTRUCTING SEXUALITY

Although individuals have particular sexual interests, styles, and peccadilloes, most people believe in the general common denominator of an instinctual, deeply seated, and utterly natural human sex drive. Americans tend to endorse a *drive reduction model* (Gagnon & Simon, 1973) of sexuality; that is, our innate, constantly surging sex drive must be actively restrained or it will threaten to overrun all good and common sense. This position is exemplified by one of the statements that opened this chapter: "If no barriers are put into place, this progression generally leads to sexual intercourse. Most experts agree that once couples move beyond hugging and light kissing, hormones encourage further physical contact." What is more, it is believed that this drive is predominantly focused on coitus—penile-vaginal intercourse—and is satisfied by orgasm (at the very least for the man; possibly, but not necessarily, for the woman). Indeed, the urge to have sex (i.e., coitus) is linked to evolution and the survival of the species—what could be more natural than that?

However, closer inspection of our cultural discourse (everything said, printed, performed, or expressed—verbally or otherwise) about sexuality reveals that it is not that simple. Our expectations and norms of sexuality extend beyond this seeming lowest common denominator of a generic, unformed sex drive. To the contrary, we expect that it (1) be aimed at members of the "opposite" sex who are within a certain age range;[2] (2) involve a certain kind of sexual behavior (penile-vaginal intercourse culminating in male orgasm) in a particular relational context (ideally a monogamous, legally sanctioned marriage); and (3) be robust enough to compel people to have (or at least want) sex at a particular rate of frequency. If we over- or undershoot any of these targets, or aim for entirely different targets, we are labeled as being impotent, oversexed, frigid, a tease, a pervert, a slut, a fag, and so on. There are a seemingly limitless number of ways in which we criticize ourselves and each other for our deviations—in size, stamina, style, etc.—from the perceived sexual norm. In addition, many of our notions of sexual deviance are thoroughly enmeshed with racism and other forms of prejudice: animalistic, predatory black men; loose working-class women; emasculated, geeky Asian men; hot, insatiable Latina women (Reid & Bing, 2000). Indeed, far from being a simple, naturally occurring drive within us, sexuality is a carefully scripted social construct with very narrow boundaries.

The social constructionist take on sexuality does not deny that most humans have an innate capacity for the physiological states of arousal (e.g., vaginal lubrication, penile erection) and orgasm. Everything beyond that most basic physiological potential (e.g., what cues provoke arousal, how an individual responds after arousal, etc.), however, is socially constructed (Tiefer, 2004; White, Bondurant, & Travis, 2000). What is more, social constructionists also argue that it is precisely these other, socially dependent aspects of sexuality that are meaningful, not the base potential for arousal. For instance, Paul Abramson and Steven Pinkerton (2002) explain that until it is processed by the brain according to cultural scripts, a kiss or a caress has no sexual significance: "The sensory signals arriving at the brain following stimulation of an erogenous zone are not inherently pleasurable, or even inherently sexual. Instead, interpretation of these signals by the brain is required for the impinging sensations to be recognized as sexually pleasurable. It is this interpretive stage that admits the profound influences of culture and context in the experience of sexual pleasure" (pp. 8–9).

In this sense, sexuality is thoroughly social and context dependent. The act of coitus, for instance, might be construed as an expression of intimacy ("making love"), a casual act of physical gratification ("hooking up"), a violation of bodily and personal integrity (rape), a form of labor performed in exchange for resources (prostitution), or even a military strategy (as in the case of systematic wartime rape). These varied interpretations of coitus depend not just on the time, place, and situation but also on which participant you ask. These examples show how an identical physical act, penile-vaginal intercourse, may have radically divergent meanings and consequences. On a similar note, Hope Landrine (1998) argues for the need for contextualized understandings of behavior by comparing the distinct meanings of anal intercourse among young Latina women and gay men:

> When contextually defined, when understood as an act-in-context, the behavior here is not unprotected anal intercourse except in the most superficial way of thinking about complex human beings. For these particular Latinas, the behavior was "trying to maintain virginity for, but still have intercourse with, men who are demanding both," and that surely is not the behavior gay men engage in when they exhibit similar, superficial, mechanical movements. Comparisons across groups on superficially similar movements cannot be made because the acts-in-context are different behaviors and have different meanings. (p. 86)

As suggested by the number and variety of sex-related slurs and taunts, there are many ways in which one might stray (advertently or not) from *normal* sexuality. As Tiefer (2004) explains, there are several definitions for the term "normal": it can refer to a *statistical* average (as in "most people do it"); it can refer to a seemingly objective *clinical* standard of healthfulness (as in "physically and mentally fit people do it"); and it can also refer to an *ideal* (as in "all people should at least strive to do it"). Although social construction is a dynamic process that varies significantly according to time and place, it is possible to point to five critical pillars of the dominant construction of normal sexuality in the contemporary United States:

1. Our instinctual sex drive is constantly surging and must be actively restrained by laws, morals, and individual willpower (i.e., the drive reduction model).
2. "Real" sex is coitus (i.e., penile-vaginal intercourse)—everything else is foreplay (e.g., hand-genital contact, oral sex) or perverted (e.g., anal sex; bondage).
3. Heterosexuality is normal (statistically, clinically, and ideally).
4. In sexual relationships and encounters, men and women occupy distinct gender roles.
5. Sexuality is for adults only.

What is most important to note about each of these components is that they all claim to be innate, constant, and universal. In other words, this is a thoroughly essentialist view of sexuality. By disguising the construct of sexuality as natural, essentialist positions make it indisputable, a given that we seldom even notice, never mind question (that is just the way it is). For example, Gagnon and Simon (1973) argue that sexuality is no more biologically driven than any other behavior, but because the drive reduction model so thoroughly saturates how we think, feel, and experience sexuality, its influence on and direction of our sexual and relational behaviors are virtually invisible. The deconstruction of sexuality, however, makes it—and its alternatives—visible.

Similarly, this presumably universal, innate, and constant sex drive does not have a generically sexual goal; it is specifically aimed toward coitus. This is not surprising given that the "naturalness" of our sex drive is based on the presumed evolutionary imperative of procreation: we are driven not just to seek sexual gratification in any old way, but we are specifically driven to coitus in order to reproduce. While some sexuality theorists clearly delineate the difference between the pleasure and procreative functions of sexuality (White et al., 2000), popular opinion does not typically make this distinction. Indeed, there is little doubt that "real sex" is equated to coitus. This was famously articulated by President Clinton with regard to his relationship with Monica Lewinsky and his denial that fellatio qualified as "sexual relations." The status of oral sex and whether it should "count" as real sex or not has also been called into question after numerous reports in the popular media regarding the prevalence and incidence of fellatio among adolescents (Jarrell, 2000). Professionals and parents have expressed concern that teens are engaging in casual oral sex, seeing it as more of a dalliance than an intimate relational behavior.

Given that, by definition, coitus involves male and female genitalia, it logically follows that our drive-reduction, coitus-centered construction of sexuality is also thoroughly *heteronormative*, meaning that only heterosexuality is explicitly and implicitly deemed normal; homosexual behaviors and relationships are marginalized. Of course, the extent and consequences of this marginalization can vary: some people view homosexuality as a hateful sin or an unfortunate pathology; seemingly more tolerant people may see it as comprising a minority, but as no less worthy than heterosexuality. Although this final position may not seem particularly prejudicial or untrue (after all, homosexual relationships and activities are in the statistical minority), this liberal position among some individuals does not change the fact that virtually every American social institution privileges heterosexuality and penalizes homosexuality. Straight couples can get married; they can share health insurance; they can express affection for one another in public without fear of negative attention (or outright hostility or danger); and their relationships and sexual behaviors are represented—favorably—in research, the media, and politics. All of these serve to normalize heterosexuality and marginalize homosexuality, whether as a sin, a pathology, or, at best, a statistical aberration.

The heteronormativity of our construction of sexuality does not give all heterosexually behaving people an automatic pass on sexual stigmatization, though. Indeed, as will be demonstrated throughout this chapter, it is not enough to just be "straight" and have intercourse; carefully scripted roles must be adhered to. Although social dimensions such as class, race, and religion influence the specific sexual script one must follow, gender is arguably the central determinant of sexual behavior (Fausto-Sterling, 2000). Even the very first building block of our construction of sexuality, the drive reduction model, is gendered: men are believed to have an almost irrepressible sex drive, whereas women are less sexually compelled (and have historically been cast as wholly asexual) (Holland, Ramazanoglu, Sharpe, & Thomson, 1999). This treatment of sexual gender difference as fundamental truths is evident not only in popular rhetoric (e.g., the book, game, and TV show *Men Are from Mars, Women Are from Venus*), but also in academic scholarship in the field of evolutionary psychology (Buss, 1995). It is also used to further justify the more elaborate sexual scripts that have been developed around sexual relationships and behaviors (Morokoff, 2000): Girls and women are passive recipients, whereas boys and men are active initiators; girls and women must be responsible sexual "gatekeepers" (i.e., they must learn how to say "no") since boys and men are physically unable to control their sexual impulses; girls and women have sex out of love, whereas boys and men agree to love in order to have sex; boys and men are studs if they have frequent sex or numerous partners, whereas girls and women are sluts if they do. Despite thoughtful and impassioned critiques of these problematic assumptions regarding gender difference, they are alive and well in the sexuality discourse produced through the media, in schools, and in families, as we will explore later in this chapter.

Finally, as will be discussed at length in relation to school sexuality education and sexual socialization within families, sexuality is also largely considered to be an adults-only terrain in the United States. This belief grows out of both our essentialist, drive reduction notions of sexuality, and our social construction of adolescence. Indeed, just as gender, sexuality, and race are socially constructed, so too are developmental stages (Holland, 2001; Lapsley, Enright, & Serlin, 1985). In her critique of popular views of adolescence, Nancy Lesko (1996) argues that adolescence as a developmental stage is constructed such that youth are trapped in a sort of developmental no-man's-land: they no longer possess the presumed virtues and appealing vulnerability of childhood; but they are also denied access to the credibility and legitimacy granted to adults. The notion of "coming of age," for instance, asserts the superiority of adults and reduces youth to a secondary position as not-quite-adults.

Essentialist concerns regarding humans' innate, surging sex drives are therefore compounded by our dominant construction of adolescence as a time of recklessness, rebellion, and "raging hormones." Indeed, one of the least challenged presumptions about adolescence is that it is a tumultuous period in which teens' moods and motives are overrun by hormones (Steinberg & Scott, 2003). From this perspective, the "natural" sex drive that compels all of us is not only particularly robust in adolescents, but it is also less likely to be reined in by one's sense of responsibility and good judgment, which many believe—reflecting yet another component of our construction of adolescence—youth are cognitively incapable of possessing. All of this leaves adults with a challenging mandate: since teens are too young to have sex, we must do everything in our power to obstruct them from doing so. However, teens are more sex-crazed and less responsible than adults, leaving us with an uphill battle, to say the least.

In addition, discussions of teen sex or adolescent sexuality tend to imply that teens are simply having sex with each other and that we, as responsible adults, must stop them and save them from themselves (i.e., their hormones and their recklessness). It becomes evident that "teen sex" is a misnomer, however, when one looks at the statistics of who is having sex with whom. One national study found that 37 percent of adolescent women between 15 and 19 years of age have male partners who are at least three years their senior (i.e., adult men) (Darroch, Landry, & Oslak, 1999). What is more, several studies indicate that the primary problem associated with teen sex—teen pregnancy—is more likely to occur when adolescent women have sex with adult men (Males, 1998). These statistics certainly put a different spin on what, or who, is the problem with teen sex.

AUTHORIZING SEXUALITY: RELIGION AND MEDICINE

Religion

Prior to the Enlightenment and the premium placed on science in the modern world, the Christian church (which I use to refer to Catholic and Protestant denominations) served as the ultimate authority governing sexuality. Relying on and generating doctrines that associated certain (most) sexual relationships and behaviors with varying levels of sin, the church established and disseminated norms, including strict prohibitions regarding masturbation and premarital or extramarital sexual relations (especially for women). The concept of "sin," which characterized all violations of the religious boundaries placed on sexuality, played a central role in pre-Enlightenment constructions of sexuality. With the rise of modernism, however, the scientific concepts of disease and disorder replaced sin as the marker of deviations from sexual norms. Kim Phillips and Barry Reay (2002) articulate this by quoting Donzelot: "The priest pre-ceded the doctor as the manager of sexuality" (p. 10).

Although religion is no longer the sole authority regarding sexuality, it would be misguided to minimize its continued role in the construction of sexuality. This is especially true in the United States, which is widely regarded as the most religious among industrialized nations (Whitehead, Wilcox, Ros-tosky, Randall, & Wright, 2001). For instance, despite the racial and ethnic diversity of the country, the majority of Americans claim theistic beliefs and specifically identify with Christian denominations. According to the results of a recent Gallup poll reported in the *New York Times*, 46 percent of all Americans identify as evangelical or born-again Christians (Kristof, 2003). Indeed, through its significant influence on American politics and therefore federal funding, the Christian church exerts substantial control over sexuality-related research, policies, and programs such as sexuality education (Irvine, 2002).

In addition to this indirect influence, religion also plays a direct role in the construction of sexuality at local and personal levels. Research regarding the association between religion and sexuality has been primarily focused on whether religion serves as a protective factor against the perceived risks of sexuality by reducing nonmarital sexual activity itself. If we take a moment to deconstruct this basic research question, it becomes clear that it operates on the drive reductionist assumption that *something* is needed to help people withstand the urge to have sex; that without religious, legal, or social deterrents of some sort, people will engage in sex willy-nilly and put themselves, and others, at all kinds of risk. Nevertheless, the preponderance of evidence does indicate that religiosity, both in terms of personal beliefs and public practices such as at-tending services, is associated with less frequent sexual activity among adults (Poulson, Eppler, Satterwhite, Wuensch, & Bass, 1998; Wyatt, 1997) and ad-olescents (Holder et al., 2000).

Although this appears to suggest that religiosity is "good" for one's sexual health (presuming one strives for lower rates of sexual activity), another set of research findings complicates this picture: religion is also associated with lower levels of *safe* sexual activity (i.e., condom and contraceptive use) (Holder et al., 2000; Wilcox, Rostosky, Randall, & Wright, 2001). Another study by Marlena Studer and Arland Thornton (1987) indicated that religious teen women were less likely to use "medical" contraceptives (e.g., methods such as the pill, which require a medical examination and prescription) than other methods, including condoms, spermicides, withdrawal, and the rhythm method. They explain this finding by suggesting that it is difficult for highly religious individuals to plan in advance for safer sex (e.g., get a prescription for the pill), since premarital sex and sometimes contraception are at odds with the values of most Christian denominations. In a similar vein, teens who take virginity pledges, an exercise commonly promoted by popular faith-based sexuality education programs, have been found to initiate intercourse approximately eighteen months later than their peers who have not taken such pledges. However, when they did have sex, teens who had taken virginity pledges were one-third less likely to use contraception at first sex than their nonpledging peers (Bearman & Brückner, 2000). Thus, it appears that the construction of sexuality by religious institutions as sinful and shameful is a bit of a double-edged sword: although there is evidence that it enables adolescents and unmarried adults to delay or reduce rates of sexual activity, it also appears to *dis*able them from taking necessary health precautions when they do engage in sexual behaviors.

As cited earlier, religion no longer is the leading authority on sexual health and well-being; indeed, this is a position it has ceded, in large part, to medicine. Reflecting this shifting social position, religious institutions now frequently draw on scientific knowledge, which they help direct and fund, of course, to bolster their doctrinal principles opposing premarital sex (e.g., by promoting information regarding the risks of sexually transmitted infections [STIs]) as well as the rationale for changing their approaches to other sexual issues (e.g., citing the declassification of homosexuality as a mental illness as grounds for accepting same-sex relationships that are based on principles of monogamous love and commitment). Indeed, medicine, to which we now turn, has assumed the top, most visible, role in dictating the boundaries of normal sexuality.

Medicine

One of the hallmark features of modernism is its conviction in the supremacy of objectivity and logic. Medicine, as the scientific study and treatment of the human body, is revered as the ultimate authority on the conditions and potential of human life. Through its predominant focus on physiological, as opposed to social, grounds and remedies for sexual "dysfunctions" and abnormalities, the interdisciplinary study of sexuality reveals its reliance on *medicalized* notions of human experiences and relationships. Tiefer (2004) defines medicalization as "a major social and intellectual trend whereby the concepts and practices of medicine come to exercise authority over particular areas of life" (p. 181). She continues to describe American culture as in a state of "biomania," in which our attention is exclusively trained on the body (hormones, brain chemistry, brain structure, DNA, and so on), and we are fixated on medical explanations and techniques to reveal the reasons and cures for all conditions and complaints. Although advances in medical knowledge and technology have certainly enriched many aspects of life, Tiefer warns that the total dominance of the medical model in sexuality, both as a field of research and as an aspect of life and relationships, has eliminated alternative understandings and knowledge about sexual experiences, development, and relationships.

The appeal of a medical model for assessing human behavior is that it identifies, using presumably objective criteria, what is "normal." However, this is not a simple or innocuous act. As Tiefer (2004) explains, "The normative basis of the health model is absolutely inescapable—the only way we can talk about 'signs and symptoms' or 'treatments and cures' or 'diagnosis and classification' is with regard to norms and deviations from norms" (p. 189). This might not be objectionable if science and medicine were somehow truly unbiased endeavors. However, as cited by numerous postmodernist and feminist critical theorists, there is no value-free objective science (Riger, 1992). From the selection of research questions to pursue, to the funding of particular projects and how widely their results may be disseminated, scientific study is implicitly and explicitly driven by subjective biases and values. White et al. (2000) make the point that as a result of religious and social norms that continue to regard procreation as the best (i.e., most acceptable) reason for sexual behavior, sexuality research is largely focused on procreation. However, this focus on procreation initiates a sort of domino effect: (1) if procreation is at the center, then the majority of research is about coitus (therefore excluding a wide range of noncoital sexual behaviors that individuals might engage in); (2) given that, by definition, coitus involves male and female genitalia, research about coitus is largely hetero-normative; and (3) this study of heterosexuality, especially with its narrow focus on a single sexual act, tends to "naturalize" gender, treating gender roles and differences as biologically based and therefore inevitable and immutable.

For these reasons, critics charge that medicalized approaches are about much more than the unbiased scientific study of sexuality. In contrast, they construct healthy, normal sexuality as coitus-centered, heterosexual, and attached to traditional gender roles. In their dissections of the history and effect of Viagra, both Tiefer (2004) and Loe (2004) explore how the gendered and heteronormative idea of male virility is a central component of our construction of sexuality. In addition, the hype around erectile dysfunction, including the production of several Viagra-type drugs, their accompanying aggressive advertising campaigns, and the emergence of an analogous focus on female sexual performance reflect science's preference for studying measurable, physiological phenomenon (e.g., signs of arousal, occurrence of orgasm) as opposed to the far more complicated and intangible aspects of sexuality, such as pleasure and intimacy.

As discussed earlier in this chapter, before the "personnel of science and medicine replaced the churches' ministers and priests as the custodians, confessors, and controllers of sex" (Phillips & Reay, 2002, p. 15), faith-based constructions of sexuality also identified normal sexuality and stigmatized other sexualities (behaviors, relationships, feelings). In this sense, the consequences of a medicalized social construction of sexuality are no different than those of a faith-based one; the mark of "sin" is simply replaced by the diagnosis of "sick." However, as Tiefer (2004) points out, the health model does not quite work with sexuality:

> Who's to say, for example, that absence of interest in sex is abnormal according to the clinical definition? What sickness befalls the person who avoids sex? What disability? Clearly, such a person misses a life experience that some people value very highly and most value at least somewhat, but is avoiding sex "unhealthy" in the same way that avoiding protein is? Avoiding sex seems more akin to avoiding travel or avoiding swimming or avoiding investments in anything riskier than saving accounts—it's not trendy, but it's not sick, is it? (p. 10)

Tiefer's position, not a unique one, is that what is damaging to an individual is *thinking* that one is somehow damaged, inferior, or inadequate—if one is not having enough sex, not having good enough sex, not having the right kind of sex with the right kind of partner, or perhaps not wanting to have sex enough. In this sense, the medicalized construction of sexuality, with its judgments of health and promise of more frequent, more satisfying, more normal sex, may ironically be bad for our sexual health.

DISSEMINATING SEXUALITY: THE MEDIA, SCHOOLS, AND FAMILIES

Social constructionism does not view power or authority as a fixed entity or object that an individual or institution possesses or not. Instead, power and authority, just as meaning and significance, are produced through social interactions; they do not independently exist. According to these tenets, for instance, religious doctrine is meaningless without believers, and a church is insignificant as a structure if no one attends its services. Similarly, science and medicine must be regarded as expert in order to hold sway in individuals' lives. Without the status and prestige of expertise, science and medicine would be (and have been) dismissed as heresy or quackery. The following section reviews the ways in which the media legitimates the authority and expertise of medicine. What is more, the norms authorized by medical experts must be conveyed to the masses; although doctor-patient consultation represents one means of disseminating information and norms, it is hardly the most efficient. Through the media, school-based sexuality education, and the institution of the family, however, individuals are continually exposed to and directed to internalize the five components of our construction of sexuality.

The Media

Magazines, television, movies, and the Internet all serve as the mouthpiece of medicine and play a critical role in the medicalized construction of sexuality. A glance at the headlines of current women's and men's magazines will offer clear evidence of the media's role in the construction of sexuality as well as the dissemination of sexual "expert" advice: "Secrets of your sex drive: Why you want it when you want it . . . and how to want it more" (*Cosmopolitan*, 2005, June); and "Sex by sundown: Cheap tricks that pay off big" (*Maxim*, 2005, May). In addition, the news media play an important role in relaying scientific and medical discoveries and knowledge to the general public. Most recently, a Swedish study regarding differences between the reactions of homosexual and heterosexual men to particular scents made the headlines of major print, television, and online media. The study's design does not allow for conclusions about which came first: the difference in scent receptivity or the identity as gay. That is, it is possible that men who frequently or exclusively have sex with men develop a different smell response as a result of their sexual behaviors, rather than having homosexual relationships as a result of an inborn biological difference. However, as Anne Fausto-Sterling (2000) warns, popular media reports of scientific studies frequently distort research findings by overlooking or misrepresenting more nuanced aspects of the work or by only choosing to report studies that confirm particular positions or viewpoints (thereby increasing their audience and subsequent profit). Indeed, with regard to the study about scent reception, some media outlets, such as the *New York Times* (Wade, 2005), mentioned (albeit at the end of the article) that causality cannot be deduced from this study, while others blatantly distorted the findings with headlines such as "Hormone sniff test indicates biological base for sexual orientation, researchers report" (Schmid, 2005). Rather than present a more complex, ambiguous, and accurate story of the research findings, the media packaged a simpler, more popular version, one that bolsters an essentialist construction of sexual orientation.

In addition to its role in perpetuating a medicalized construction of sexuality, the popular media also socialize viewers and readers into other aspects of "normal" sexuality. Specifically, through their explicit and implicit messages, media such as magazines and television contribute to the coitus-centered, heteronormative, and traditionally gendered norms of sexuality. Studies by Laura Carpenter (1998) and Meenakshi Durham (1998) deconstructed the gendered messages contained in girls' magazines such as *Seventeen*, noting the ways in which they teach girls to adhere to gendered sexual norms of feminine appearance and the role of girls and women to please others (especially boys and men). At the same time, such magazines send messages of the importance of sexual virtue, warning girls not to give in to sexual temptation. In this way, they direct girls to be sexual looking but not sexual acting. Men's magazines such as *Maxim* and *Stuff* contain similarly gendered content, though it is aimed at encouraging a male target audience to objectify women and view themselves as entitled to sexual fulfillment (Krassas, Blauwkamp, & Wesselink, 2003; Ward, 2003). In her extensive review of the media's role in sexual socialization, Ward (1995) found that although television programming tends to be less sexually graphic than magazines, and primarily relies on innuendos and discussions about sexuality rather than depictions of it, shows and commercials participate in the sexual objectification of women while also treating dating and sexuality as a sort of competition or game.

In her analysis of the content of magazines, Melissa Tyler (2004) observed that their messages were not just reflective of medicalization or sexist norms of sexuality. She argued that headlines such as "10 seconds to a 10 minute orgasm" and "7 easy steps to orgasm heaven" were signs of how corporate culture was becoming part of our construction of sexuality. She likened articles about how to increase the efficiency and effectiveness of one's sexual performance and how to get maximum pleasure with minimum effort to the priorities of the business world of maximizing profit while minimizing cost. In her estimation, this sort of content is not helpful to readers; rather, it provides more yardsticks for readers to measure themselves and others against.

Although the research in this field is more limited than one would expect, most of it pertaining to television and magazines, there is evidence that exposure to sexual content in the media influences sexual attitudes and behavior. Over the course of Ward's (1995) review, and in her own subsequent research (Ward, Hansbrough, & Walker, 2005), she found evidence that increased exposure to sexual content in the media, particularly through soap operas and music videos, was related to more liberal sexual attitudes (e.g., acceptance of nonmarital sex) as well as more sexist gender attitudes (e.g., acceptance of sexual harassment). In her review, she also found that youth who either consumed a lot of media or were at least very involved in the media they did consume (i.e., they did not watch a lot of TV but were very invested when they did) overestimated how much sex others were having. However, she warns against oversimplifying these findings. Many of the studies in this field are correlational, meaning that it is impossible to determine if individuals with liberal sexual attitudes seek out shows and magazines with a lot of sexual content, or if the content itself fosters liberal sexual attitudes (in other words, which came first: the attitudes or the media content?).

In addition, a fairly consistent finding among the studies she reviewed was that girls and women appeared to be more affected by media content than boys and men. This relates to a critical factor when thinking about how the media's sexual content is related to its audiences' sexual behavior: every viewer and every reader approaches each television show or magazine from a unique position and therefore takes away different messages. This consideration of one's social location (e.g., race, class, gender) and personal history when assessing the impact of the media is at the core of the Media Practice Model (Steele, 2002). As an example, the effect of race was demonstrated in a study of adolescent women's perceptions of magazines aimed at teen girls (Kaplan & Cole, 2003). In contrast to focus groups of young white women whose conversations revolved around the gender and sexuality content in *Seventeen*, a group of young black women were more concerned with the representation of race, specifically their impressions that there were not enough images of black girls and women and that those that were included made them seem less attractive and feminine than their white counterparts. Indeed, viewers and readers are not passive or blank slates that mindlessly consume whatever media is in front of them; instead, not only do we choose what we watch or what we read, we also interpret them differently based on our particular histories and backgrounds.

When comparing the sexual content of the news media (e.g., newspapers) with that of the entertainment media (e.g., television sitcoms), a somewhat divided picture emerges. While both these media construct sexuality according to the drive reduction, coitus-centered, heteronormative, gendered, and adults-only principles, they also diverge from one another. On the one hand, entertainment media such as movies, music videos, and fictional television programs tend to glamorize and simplify sex and sexuality: the people are beautiful and successful and the sex tends to be exciting and consequence-free (Cope-Farrar & Kunkel, 2002). The news media, on the other hand, tend to report on the darker sides of sexuality: rates of STIs in the United States and around the world, sexual predators seeking victims over the Internet, and the incidence of date rape, especially among youth. As we will see in the next section, school-based sexuality education delivers a far less mixed message, focusing almost exclusively on the dangers of sex.

Schools

Without a doubt, sexuality education is an ongoing process that involves familial, peer, romantic, and sexual relationships; it certainly is not confined to classroom lessons in middle and high school. Indeed, much of the point of this chapter is that we are constantly learning about sexuality and soaking up norms of sexuality from all different social institutions and relationships. However, formal school-based sexuality education (SBSE) warrants distinct attention as it serves as a public, official face of our culture's sexual norms and ideals. Recently, SBSE has been at the center of a cultural debate between a conservative, largely Christian sexual agenda—in favor of abstinence until marriage and in opposition to abortion and equal rights for lesbian, gay, bisexual, and transgendered-identified individuals—and a liberal agenda that advocates for safer sex (including, but not limited to, abstinence) and respect for a range of reproductive and sexual choices. Beginning with federal legislation in 1996 as part of welfare reform (Personal Responsibility and Work Opportunity Reconciliation [PRWOR] Act), states have received significant federal funding for abstinence-only SBSE. This funding has been regularly increased since 1996, including an 18.5 percent funding increase for abstinence-only programs in President Bush's proposed budget for 2006 (SIECUS, 2005). In order for a program to qualify for this support, it should satisfy a list of criteria—the program "teaches that sexual activity outside of the context of marriage is likely to have harmful psychological and physical effects" and "teaches that bearing children out-of-wedlock is likely to have harmful consequences for the child, the child's parents, and society" (Hauser, 2004). Comprehensive sexuality education, on the other hand, which characterized most school-based curricula from the 1960s until the mid-1990s (Moran, 2000), includes information on a range of sexual health options (e.g., abstinence, condoms, and contraception) and adopts a "values clarification" stance whereby youth are encouraged to reflect on and develop an individual set of moral values to guide their sexual decision-making (Morris, 1994).

Many researchers and practitioners in the field of sexuality education are sharply critical of the reliance of SBSE, particularly of abstinence-only programs, on scare tactics as a means of discouraging adolescent sexual behaviors. SBSE curricula are frequently dominated by images of diseased genitals, misleading statistics regarding the failure rates of condoms, and narratives of guilt and regret from sexually active youth (see Kantor, 1992/1993). In 1973, Gagnon and Simon remarked that "learning about sex in our society is learning about guilt; conversely, learning how to manage sexuality constitutes learning how to manage guilt" (p. 42). Some argue that through this exclusively sex-negative depiction, sexuality educators are not only failing to equip youth with the information they require to make careful decisions regarding their sexual relationships and behaviors, but are also failing to instill in them a positive, healthy sense of their sexualities (Welsh, Rostosky, & Kawaguchi, 2000). In thinking about the particular position of adolescent women, Raymond (1994) warned: "Ironically, in our indiscriminate portrayals of teenage girls as sexual victims, we may be failing to teach them about genuine sexual autonomy and consequently ensuring that they *will be* victims" (p. 132).

It is in the context of SBSE that the drive reduction model and the adults-only perspective feed into tremendous anxiety at the prospect of adolescents being sexual. What makes this especially tricky is that we not only fear what will become of adolescents if they are sexual with one another (though, as mentioned earlier, teens are not only being sexual with other teens), but we also simultaneously believe that adolescents are essentially hypersexual (Steinberg & Scott, 2003). It is precisely this intersection of our social constructs of sexuality and of adolescence that is used to justify the scare tactics and absolutist (i.e., just say no) approach so common among SBSE curricula. Michel Foucault (1976/1990), one of the most prominent figures in social constructionism, described the "pedagogization of children's sex" as a strategy designed to produce or construct knowledge and power vis-à-vis sexuality. This process construes youth sexuality as both natural (in the sense that there is an innate sex drive in all functional humans) and unnatural (children are and should be asexual), and hinged on a drive reduction model of sexuality, thus providing the rationale for the formal regulation of children and youth sexuality (e.g., through SBSE).

From the vantage point of social constructionism and through the process of deconstruction, it becomes apparent that SBSE is not just delivering a single lesson regarding sexuality. In addition to information and statistics about STIs and reproductive anatomy, sexuality education also transmits a particular set of norms and standards regarding sexuality: not only is it a biological drive, but it is—ideally—also focused on heterosexual penile-vaginal intercourse (i.e., real sex) within a monogamous adult relationship that generally conforms to conventional gender roles (Haywood, 1996; Raymond, 1994; Redman, 1994). In this sense, SBSE is not simply instructing students about the birds and the bees, nor is it only telling them to "just say no." It is participating in a more complicated process of construction by treating some sexual behaviors and relationships as "normal" and others, by default, as less healthy, less desirable, and less moral. This represents the hidden curriculum of SBSE: the socialization of youth into a particular set of sexual and relational behaviors.

That SBSE is motivated by more than a desire to protect youth from negative sexual outcomes (e.g., unwanted pregnancy and STIs) is evidenced by the fact that abstinence-only programs receive political and economic support from the federal government even though research does not show that they are the most effective means of promoting sexual health among youth (Kirby, 2001), and the majority of American parents want their teens to learn about safer sex options other than abstinence (Henry J. Kaiser Family Foundation, 2000). Indeed, support for abstinence-only SBSE does not come from empirical research or popular opinion; rather, it is driven by religious and political ideology that uses threats of sickness and immorality to enforce a heteronormative and gendered construction of sexuality.

Interestingly, much of the debate regarding SBSE involves families, specifically parents. When first proposed at the beginning of the twentieth century, it was argued that SBSE was necessary because the lower classes—for example, immigrants, North-migrating black laborers, non-Protestants, and nonwhites—were not capable of providing their children with sufficient moral instruction (as per white, Protestant, middle-class norms) (Morris, 1994). In this (racist and classist) sense, SBSE was seen as a way to redress what was lacking in familial environments. This stands in sharp contrast to current discourse regarding SBSE, in which conservative white, Protestant leaders argue that sexuality education exclusively belongs in the home.

Families

The social construction of sexuality in the context of familial relationships has received surprisingly little and fairly superficial attention. I refer to this as "superficial" given that research in the field has been limited to a focus on adult-adolescent communication, even though sexual socialization is a process that occurs over the entire course of a parent-child relationship, and because it is typically only concerned with explicit, verbal communication rather than the multitude of nonverbal forms of teaching and learning that parents and their children engage in. What is more, this section of the chapter should probably be called "Parents" as opposed to "Families" since there has been very little research on the role of siblings in sexual socialization. The research that has been conducted has yielded mixed findings: some studies suggest that younger siblings become sexually active at a younger age than their older siblings (Rodgers, Rowe, & Harris, 1992) or are more likely to become pregnant if an older sister is a teenaged mother (East & Shi, 1997), whereas others find that younger siblings are more conservative in their sexual attitudes and behaviors, perhaps out of disapproval of their older siblings' sexual activity (Kornreich, Hearn, Rodriguez, & O'Sullivan, 2003).

Much of the research on parent-child communication regarding sexuality has been focused on whether parents are having "sex talks" with their children and what specific topics they include (DiLorio, Pluhar, & Belcher, 2003). Surveys have shown that both youth and their parents want parents to be a main source of sexuality education (Wyatt & Riederle, 1994). However, despite this mutual interest, research about *what* is being communicated, along with other studies of exactly *who* is communicating with whom and *how*, reveals a pretty substantial disconnect between parents and their children.

First of all, the confluence of three factors—the drive reduction model of sexuality, the position that only adults should be sexual, and the belief that teens are hypersexual—leaves parents fearful that talking about sex will somehow encourage youth to have sex (Fine, 1988). This worry lingers despite the fact that there is no evidence that talking to youth about sex compels them to have more of it (Kirby & Coyle, 1997). In her interviews with American and Dutch parents regarding the rules and limits they set for their teenaged children's sexuality, Amy Schalet (2000) found that the American parents frequently described their teens as not only too young to have sex, but also too young to know that they were too young to have sex (again, reflecting the essentialist presumptions regarding the developmental capabilities and limitations of adolescents described earlier in this chapter). Therefore, the American parents felt that setting limits on potentially sexual interactions (e.g, coed parties) was part of being a good, responsible caregiver. The Dutch parents, tapping into a different construction of both sexuality and adolescence, felt that their role was to adjust to and accommodate their adolescents' emerging sexual interests, relationships, and behaviors. Schalet describes Dutch parents' efforts to negotiate with their adolescent children and employ an ethic of mutual consideration that involves compromise and communication among all family members, children and, adults alike. She uses the following quote from a Dutch father to illustrate such negotiation and reconciliation:

> You [live] here with each other, [so] you have to take each other into account. That means that it can be necessary to consult with one another about what television program to watch, or what time to eat dinner. From time to time, someone will have to compromise. We [the parents] too. [This applies also] to whether boyfriends can sleep here, or whether they cannot because we have other guests. (p. 92)

Aside from this fear that talk about sex will incite the act itself, parents frequently report feeling like they do not know how or what to say to their adolescents. In fact, this is regarded to be such a common obstacle that there are public service announcements on television encouraging parents to talk with their teenagers, and community programs designed to educate parents about sexuality so that they will be able to educate their children at home. Indeed, in their review of related research, DiLorio et al. (2003) cite studies indicating that the more knowledgeable and confident in their knowledge parents are, the more likely they are to discuss sexuality with their children.

However, while increasing a parent's knowledge about sexuality may increase the likelihood that they will talk with their children about sexuality, this does not remedy another major problem: many parents report that they and their children have conversations about sex, but unfortunately, their children do not agree. Across studies that asked parents and their children if they had talked with one another about sex, 72–98 percent of the parents reported that they had; however, only 13–83 percent of the children recalled such conversations taking place (DiLioro et al., 2003). In another study, Jaccard, Dittus, and Gordon (1998) found that 73 percent of the mothers in their sample claimed to have discussed sex with their teenagers, but only 46 percent of the teenagers corroborated this.

Researchers who are curious about the reasons for this apparent disconnect between what parents say and what youth hear have suggested that parents may be talking as they claim, but that they are communicating in ineffective ways. Studies have shown that when discussing sexual matters, mothers become more authoritative and didactic in their style and are more inclined to lecture than to engage in a conversation of mutual turn-taking (Kahlbaugh, Lefkowitz, Valdez, & Sigman, 1997; Lefkowitz, Kahlbaugh, & Sigman, 1996). This may be due to a few factors: a lack of modeling about how to talk about these issues (because parents' own parents did not have such conversations with them), the concern mentioned earlier that talking about sex will somehow encourage sex, and the discomfort and embarrassment that parents frequently report when talking to their children about sexuality (which, of course, may be due to the first two factors) (Wyatt & Riederle, 1994).

Research in this area also demonstrates that parents are communicating in selective ways. That is, who says what to whom varies significantly and largely according to gender. In their review, DiLorio et al. (2003) cite evidence that when it comes to sex talks, mothers are doing more of the talking than fathers. What is more, mothers are more likely to talk with daughters than with sons; and when fathers do talk about sexuality, they are more likely to do so with sons than with daughters. Of greatest importance to the subject of this chapter, however, is the difference in what parents (typically mothers) tell their daughters compared to their sons. In keeping with the gender norms that dominate mainstream sexual scripts, daughters are more frequently instructed in ways to be successful sexual gatekeepers (Downie & Coates, 1999; O'Sullivan,

Meyer-Bahlburg, & Watkins, 2000). This finding reveals important underlying gender assumptions: (1) boys and men have a naturally stronger (insatiable and irrepressible) sex drive and therefore are unreliable as gatekeepers, and (2) girls are asexual or at least sexually passive, making them suitable gatekeepers. These combine to justify the well-known sexual double standard: if a boy is sexual he is a stud, but if a girl is sexual she is a slut. The tendency to talk to girls but not boys about sexual responsibility implies that the burden of gatekeeping—and the blame for failure to do so—is exclusively that of girls.

CONCLUSION

The focus of this chapter has been on the social institutions that authorize and disseminate norms of sexuality in the contemporary United States, norms that essentialize sexuality as driven by a deep-seated, instinctual urge to have penile-vaginal intercourse, within traditionally gendered adult relationships. In the past, religion served as the primary authority regarding sexuality. Although it retains significant influence, this role has largely been usurped by science, which presents a seemingly objective, medicalized view of sexuality. Heteronormative, coitus-centered, and gendered norms are further transmitted through the social institutions of the media, schools, and families, reproducing a narrow, essentialist construction of sexuality.

However, as discussed at the beginning of this chapter, social constructionism allows us to revisit and reevaluate what seem to be foregone conclusions about what is natural—what must be, or has always been. In doing so, social constructionism shows us how to read between lines and recognize the implicit meanings and norms that shape our behavior, which in turn further shapes our reality. Thus, social constructionism creates new ways of viewing social issues.

What is more, it also allows us to see ourselves and the potential for change in new and exciting ways. In contrast to the inevitability and stability proposed by essentialist perspectives, social constructs are dynamic and must be constantly produced and reproduced in order to exist. If, for example, we all stopped using race in our identification and categorization of ourselves and others, if no one called anyone "white," "black," or "Asian" anymore, then these labels would cease to have meaning or even exist. Race is not an independent entity; it is fueled by our thoughts and interactions. Of course, one point here is absolutely critical: this example is not meant to suggest that the repercussions of race, specifically, the damage done by oppression and the benefits afforded by privilege, are somehow imagined; or that these do not affect the lived experiences of individuals, families, communities, and nations; or that the legacy and injustices of racism can be easily undone. The point and perspective offered by social constructionism is not that race and racism do not exist in our world; it is that *they do not have to*. Race exists as it does only because we think and say so (see Chapter 10 by Lewis in this volume).

Indeed, social constructs are not stable, and social construction is not a one-way, top-down process. Individuals are not passive recipients of institutions' teachings; they also exert influence and play an active role in the existence not only of social constructs but also of institutions themselves. Without sufficient membership, for instance, churches must close their doors. In a recent study, Ellingson, Tebbe, van Haitsma, and Laumann (2001) described the challenge faced by churches that must negotiate between denominational doctrine (the source of their institutional authority and legitimacy) and the needs and norms of their local communities (the source of their institutional viability). They cite several examples of congregations diverging from larger denominational conventions (e.g., bans on performing same-sex unions) in response to the more accepting and open norms of the local culture. In doing so, these individual churches influence the "normative frameworks" for sexuality in the local community, but also may have an impact on the larger denomination's policies and stances toward particular sexual issues. This is an example of how social construction is an ongoing, dynamic process that occurs through the relations and transactions between social systems of all sizes: individuals, local churches, and the upper levels of denominational leadership and doctrine.

Similarly, dominant sexual norms and constructs are also altered and influenced through alternative channels and communities. The Internet has emerged as an alternative site of sexuality expression, interaction, and education. To use sexuality education as an example, in sharp contrast to school settings (where the curricular content is closely regulated by federal, state, and local funders and administrators), anyone can say anything on the Web—a double-edged sword, to be sure. However, despite the numerous risks (e.g., spreading misinformation), the opportunities for sexuality education offered by the Internet are exciting. While conservative positions regarding sexuality are well represented online (see Irvine, 2005), they are counterbalanced by alternative, sex-positive Web-based sources of information and interaction (Bay-Cheng, 2005). Furthermore, the Internet offers unique opportunities for building communities among sexually stigmatized and marginalized individuals (Stern & Handel, 2001) and for challenging the narrow construction of sexuality that is being produced and reproduced through religion, medicine, the media, schools, and families.

Much of the content here has criticized biomania and the medicalization of sexuality for disguising variable, alterable cultural biases as universal, fixed biological truths and for stigmatizing our deviations from those constructed norms as signs of inherent inadequacy or dysfunction. If we did not have science to draw boundaries of normal and abnormal; healthy and sick; big, good, or frequent enough, what would sexuality look like? Would we see it as a relationship that we engage in rather than an individual capacity? Tiefer (2004) draws a humorous analogy to friendship:

People use the phrase "my sexuality" as though they are only sexual in one way. They say that really comfortably, but I'm not so comfortable with that, because the sexuality that I have with one person is very different than I have with another person. My experience—I think everybody's experience as they get older—is one of enormous fluctuation in my sexual life. Sexuality is more situational, like friendship. You have the potential for friendship, but it's not like you walk around saying, "Gee, my friendship is really going strong today." (p. 93)

This is one suggestion for how our conceptions of sexuality might be changed through the deconstruction of dominant norms. However, social constructionism does not offer or recommend specific endpoints or goals; indeed, this would be wholly antithetical to the social constructionist, postmodern framework, which endorses the existence and validity of multiple truths and realities. What it can do for us in our study of sexualities (ours and others') is free us from artificial starting points (e.g., an innate drive toward coitus), externally imposed standards of performance, and the limited and limiting pursuit of so-called real, normal sex.

NOTES

1. *Abstinence* (n.d.). Retrieved May 15, 2005, from www.4parents.gov/topics/abstinence.htm.
2. This conception of gender as a polarized categorical variable is itself a social construct that has been rigorously critiqued and deconstructed. For example, see Fausto-Sterling (2000).

REFERENCES

Abramson, P. R., & Pinkerton, S. D. (2002). *With pleasure: Thoughts on the nature of human sexuality* (Rev. ed.). Oxford: Oxford University Press.
Bay-Cheng, L. Y. (2005). Left to their own devices: Disciplining youth discourse on sexuality education electronic bulletin boards. *Sexuality Research and Social Policy, 2,* 37–50.
Bearman, P. S., & Brückner, H. (2000). *Promising the future: Virginity pledges as they affect transition to first intercourse.* New York: Columbia University Press.
Berger, P., & Luckmann, T. (1966). *The social construction of reality: A treatise in the sociology of knowledge.* Garden City, NY: Basic Books.
Buss, D. M. (1995). Psychological sex differences: Origins through sexual selection. *American Psychologist, 50,* 164–168.
Carpenter, L. M. (1998). From girls into women: Scripts for sexuality and romance in *Seventeen* magazine, 1974–1994. *Journal of Sex Research, 35,* 158–168.
Cope-Farrar, K. M., & Kunkel, D. (2002). Sexual messages in teens' favorite prime-time television programs. In J. D. Brown, J. R. Steele, & K. Walsh-Childers

(Eds.), *Sexual teens, sexual media: Investigating media's influence on adolescent sexuality* (pp. 59–78). Mahwah, NJ: Lawrence Erlbaum.

Darroch, J. E., Landry, D. J., & Oslak, S. (1999). Age differences between sexual partners in the United States. *Family Planning Perspectives, 31,* 160–167.

DeLamater, J. D., & Hyde, J. S. (1998). Essentialism vs. social constructionism in the study of human sexuality. *Journal of Sex Research, 35,* 10–18.

DiLorio, C., Pluhar, E., & Belcher, L. (2003). Parent-child communication about sexuality: A review of the literature from 1980–2002. *Journal of HIV/AIDS Prevention and Education for Adolescents and Children, 5,* 7–32.

Downie, J., & Coates, R. (1999). The impact of gender on parent-child sexuality communication: Has anything changed? *Sexual and Marital Therapy, 14,* 109–121.

Durham, M. G. (1998). Dilemmas of desire: Representations of adolescent sexuality in two teen magazines. *Youth and Society, 29,* 369–389.

East, P. L., & Shi, C. R. (1997). Pregnant and parenting adolescents and their younger sisters: The influence of relationship qualities for younger sister outcomes. *Developmental and Behavioral Pediatrics, 18,* 84–90.

Ellingson, S., Tebbe, N., van Haitsma, M., & Laumann, E. O. (2001). Religion and the politics of sexuality. *Journal of Contemporary Ethnography, 30,* 3–55.

Fausto-Sterling, A. (2000). *Sexing the body: Gender politics and the construction of sexuality.* New York: Basic Books.

Fine, M. (1988). Sexuality, schooling, and adolescent females: The missing discourse of desire. *Harvard Educational Review, 58,* 29–53.

Foucault, M. (1976/1990). *The history of sexuality: Vol. 1. An introduction.* New York: Vintage Books.

Freud, S. (1940). *An outline of psychoanalysis.* New York: W. W. Norton.

Gagnon, J. H., & Simon, W. (1973). *Sexual conduct: The social sources of human sexuality.* Chicago: Aldine.

Hauser D. (2004). *Five years of abstinence-only-until-marriage education: Assessing the impact.* Washington, DC: Advocates for Youth.

Haywood, C. (1996). Sex education policy and the regulation of young people's sexual practice. *Educational Review, 48,* 121–129.

Henry J. Kaiser Family Foundation. (2000). *Sex education in America.* Menlo Park, CA: Author.

Holder, D. W., Durant, R. H., Harris, T. L., Daniel, J. H., Obeidallah, D., & Goodman, E. (2000). The association between adolescent spirituality and voluntary sexual activity. *Journal of Adolescent Health, 26,* 295–302.

Holland, J., Ramazanoglu, C., Sharpe, S., & Thomson, R. (1999). Feminist methodology and young people's sexuality. In R. Parker & P. Aggleton (Eds.), *Culture, society and sexuality: A reader* (pp. 457–472). London: University College London Press.

Holland, S. (2001). Representing children in child protection assessments. *Childhood, 8,* 322–339.

Irvine, J. M. (2002). *Talk about sex: The battles over sex education in the United States.* Berkeley: University of California Press.

Irvine, J. M. (2005). Anti-gay politics online: A study of sexuality and stigma on national websites. *Sexuality Research and Social Policy, 2,* 3–21.

Jaccard, J., Dittus, P., & Gordon, V. V. (1998). Parent-adolescent congruency in reports of adolescent sexual behavior and in communications about sexual behavior. *Child Development,* 69, 247–261.

Jarrell, A. (2000, April 3). The face of teenage sex grows younger. *New York Times,* pp. 1, 8.

Kahlbaugh, P., Lefkowitz, E. S., Valdez, P., & Sigman, M. (1997). The affective nature of mother-adolescent communication concerning sexuality and conflict. *Journal of Research on Adolescence, 7,* 221–239.

Kantor, L. M. (1992/1993). Scared chaste? Fear-based education curricula. *SIECUS Report, 21,* 1–15.

Kaplan, E. B., & Cole, L. (2003). "I want to read stuff on boys": White, Latina, and black girls reading *Seventeen* magazine and encountering adolescence. *Adolescence, 38,* 149–159.

Kirby, D. (2001). *Emerging answers: Research findings on programs to reduce teen pregnancy.* Washington, DC: National Campaign to Prevent Teen Pregnancy.

Kirby, D., & Coyle, K. (1997). School-based programs to reduce sexual risk-taking behavior. *Children and Youth Services Review, 19,* 415–436.

Kornreich, J. L., Hearn, K. D., Rodriguez, G., & O'Sullivan, L. F. (2003). Sibling influence, gender roles, and the sexual socialization of urban early adolescent girls. *Journal of Sex Research, 40,* 101–110.

Krassas, N. R., Blauwkamp, J. M., & Wesselink, P. (2003). "Master your Johnson": Sexual rhetoric in *Maxim* and *Stuff* magazines. *Sexuality and Culture, 7,* 98–119.

Kristof, N. D. (2003, March 4). God, Satan, and the media. *New York Times on the Web.* Retrieved March 6, 2003, from www.nytimes.com

Landrine, H. (1998). Cultural diversity, contextualism, and feminist psychology. In B. M. Clinchy & J. K. Norem (Eds.), *Gender and psychology reader* (pp. 78–103). New York: New York University Press.

Lapsley, D. K., Enright, R. D., & Serlin, R. C. (1985). Toward a theoretical perspective on the legislation of adolescence. *Journal of Early Adolescence, 5,* 441–466.

Lefkowitz, E. S., Kahlbaugh, P. E., & Sigman, M. D. (1996). Turn-taking in mother-adolescent conversations about sexuality and conflict. *Journal of Youth and Adolescence, 25,* 307–321.

Lesko, N. (1996). Denaturalizing adolescence: The politics of contemporary representations. *Youth and Society, 28,* 139–161.

Loe, M. (2004). *The rise of Viagra: How the little blue pill changed sex in America.* New York: New York University Press.

Males, M. (1998). Adult partners and adult contexts of "teenage sex." *Education and Urban Society, 30,* 189–206.

Moran, J. P. (2000). *Teaching sex: The shaping of adolescence in the 20th century.* Cambridge, MA: Harvard University Press.

Morokoff, P. J. (2000). A cultural context for sexual assertiveness in women. In C. B. Travis & J. W. White (Eds.), *Sexuality, society, and feminism* (pp. 299–319). Washington, DC: American Psychological Association.

Morris, R. W. (1994). *Values in sexuality education: A philosophical study*. Lanham, MD: University Press of America.

O'Sullivan, L. F., Meyer-Bahlburg, H. F. L., & Watkins, B. X. (2000). Mother-daughter communication about sex among urban African American and Latino families. *Journal of Adolescent Research, 16*, 269–291.

Phillips, K. M., & Reay, B. (2002). *Sexualities in history*. New York: Routledge.

Poulson, R. L., Eppler, M. A., Satterwhite, T. N., Wuensch, K. L., & Bass, L. A. (1998). Alcohol consumption, strength of religious beliefs and risky sexual behavior in college students. *Journal of American College Health, 46*, 227–232.

Raymond, D. (1994). Homophobia, identity, and the meanings of desire: Reflections on the cultural construction of gay and lesbian adolescent sexuality. In J. M. Irvine (Ed.), *Sexual cultures and the construction of adolescent identities* (pp. 115–150). Philadelphia: Temple University Press.

Redman, P. (1994). Shifting ground: Rethinking sexuality education. In D. Epstein (Ed.), *Challenging lesbian and gay inequalities in education* (pp. 131–151). Philadelphia: Open University Press.

Reid, P. T., & Bing, V. M. (2000). Sexual roles of girls and women: An ethnocultural lifespan perspective. In C. B. Travis & J. W. White (Eds.), *Sexuality, society, and feminism* (pp. 141–166). Washington, DC: American Psychological Association.

Riger, S. (1992). Epistemological debates, feminist voices: Science, social values, and the study of women. *American Psychologist, 47*, 730–740.

Rodgers, J. L., Rowe, D. C., & Harris, D. F. (1992). Sibling differences in adolescent sexual behavior: Inferring process models from family composition patterns. *Journal of Marriage and the Family, 54*, 142–152.

Schalet, A. T. (2000). Raging hormones, regulated love: Adolescent sexuality and the constitution of the modern individual in the United States and the Netherlands. *Body and Society, 6*, 75–105.

Schmid, R. E. (2005, May 10). Hormone sniff test indicates biological base for sexual orientation, researchers report. *St. Louis Post-Dispatch*, p. A3.

Sexuality Information and Education Council of the United States. (2005, February 9). *18.5% boost in funding for unproven abstinence-only-until-marriage programs in President Bush's proposed FY 2006 budget*. Retrieved May 15, 2005, from www.siecus.org/media/press/press0089.html

Steele, J. R. (2002). Teens and movies: Something to do, plenty to learn. In J. D. Brown, J. R. Steele, & K. Walsh-Childers (Eds.), *Sexual teens, sexual media: Investigating media's influence on adolescent sexuality* (pp. 227–252). Mahwah, NJ: Lawrence Erlbaum.

Steinberg, L., & Scott, E. S. (2003). Less guilty by reason of adolescence: Developmental immaturity, diminished responsibility, and the juvenile death penalty. *American Psychologist, 58*, 1009–1018.

Stern, S. E., & Handel, A. D. (2001). Sexuality and mass media: The historical context of psychology's reaction to sexuality on the Internet. *Journal of Sex Research, 38*, 283–291.

Studer, M., & Thornton, A. (1987). Adolescent religiosity and contraceptive usage. *Journal of Marriage and the Family, 49*, 117–128.

Tiefer, L. (2004). *Sex is not a natural act and other essays* (2nd ed.). Boulder, CO: Westview Press.

Tyler, M. (2004). Managing between the sheets: Lifestyle magazines and the management of sexuality in everyday life. *Sexualities, 7*, 81–106.

Wade, A. (2005, May 10). For gay men, different scent of attraction. *New York Times*, p. A1.

Ward, L. M. (1995). Talking about sex: Common themes about sexuality in the prime-time television programs children and adolescents view most. *Journal of Youth and Adolescence, 24*, 595–615.

Ward, L. M. (2003). Understanding the role of entertainment media in the sexual socialization of American youth: A review of empirical research. *Developmental Review, 23*, 347–388.

Ward, L. M., Hansbrough, E., & Walker, E. (2005). Contributions of music video exposure to black adolescents' gender and sexual schemas. *Journal of Adolescent Research, 20*, 143–166.

Welsh, D. P., Rostosky, S. S., & Kawaguchi, M. C. (2000). A normative perspective of adolescent girls' developing sexuality. In C. B. Travis & J. W. White (Eds.), *Sexuality, society, and feminism* (pp. 111–140). Washington, DC: American Psychological Association.

White, J. W., Bondurant, B., & Travis, C. B. (2000). Social constructions of sexuality: Unpacking hidden meanings. In C. B. Travis & J. W. White (Eds.), *Sexuality, society, and feminism* (pp. 11–33). Washington, DC: American Psychological Association.

Whitehead, B. D., Wilcox, B. L., Rostosky, S. S., Randall, B. A., & Wright, M. L. C. (2001). *Keeping the faith: The role of religion and faith communities in preventing teen pregnancy*. Washington, DC: National Campaign to Prevent Teen Pregnancy.

Wilcox, B. L., Rostosky, S. S., Randall, B. A., & Wright, M. L. C. (2001). Reasons for hope: A review of research on adolescent religiosity and sexual behavior. In B. D. Whitehead, B. L. Wilcox, S. S. Rostosky, B. A. Randall, & M. L. C. Wright (Eds.), *Keeping the faith: The role of religion and faith communities in preventing teen pregnancy*. Washington, DC: National Campaign to Prevent Teen Pregnancy.

Wyatt, G. E. (1997). *Stolen women: Reclaiming our sexuality, taking back our lives*. New York: Wiley.

Wyatt, G. E., & Riederle, M. H. (1994). Reconceptualizing issues that affect women's sexual decision-making and sexual functioning. *Psychology of Women Quarterly, 18*, 611–625.

10

Sexuality, Race, and Ethnicity

Linwood J. Lewis ◆

How can we understand the relationship between race/ethnicity and sexuality? Do persons of different ethnic groups have different ways of being sexual? There are many correlates of sexual behavior, orientation, and identities—social class, education, neighborhood organization, and gender, as well as race and ethnicity. We cannot reduce the diversity of human sexual experiences to differences between persons based on ethnic or racial characteristics. The sexual experiences of persons in the world clearly occur at the intersection of multiple social identities. Yet, race and sexuality (as well as gender) seem to be important, basic aspects of the Western sense of "self." Michel Foucault (1978) suggests that sexuality captures a sense of "truth" about ourselves; Jeffrey Weeks (1986) suggests that there is an assumption in Western culture that our sexuality is "the most spontaneously natural thing about us" and that it gives us our identities and a sense of self as man or woman, "normal" or "abnormal" or "natural" or "unnatural" (p. 13). I would suggest that race also gives us a basic sense of identity and our place within society, which is more apparent for ethnic and racial minorities, but in fact exists for all of us.

For many audiences, both academic and nonacademic, ethnicity and race may seem to be natural categories, which emerge from a biological or physiological base and do not change over historical time (Morning, 2004). Sexuality also shares this sense of the natural, meaning that it is *presocial*, or falling outside of human societies to alter or control; highlights essential or intrinsic and fixed defining aspects of a person, particularly in reference to their gender;

and is *universal*, thus extending across national boundaries (Tiefer, 2004). However, as I will make clear later in this chapter, race and sexuality are profoundly social constructs, which change quite often over time and place. The central thesis of this chapter is that sexual behavior and beliefs are used in a racially organized social context to define what it means to be a member of an ethnic or racial group. Sexuality is also used to police the boundaries between ethnic and racial groups and serves to highlight racial and ethnic hierarchies (Nagel, 2003). In order to support this thesis, I will (1) highlight the differences between race and ethnicity, (2) briefly describe the history of the concept of race, (3) describe and contrast the history, sexual practices, and attitudes of U.S. white, Latino, and black populations, and (4) describe some theories from the sexual scientific literature that can inform the relationship between race and sexuality. I have chosen to examine white, Latino, and black populations because these are the largest racial/ethnic groups in the United States, together accounting for 93 percent of all Americans in the 2000 U.S. Census.

WHAT IS RACE?

Race is most often defined as the placement of individuals and groups into categories based on physical characteristics such as skin color, hair texture, and facial structure (Braun, 2002; Goldberg, 1993). It is commonly assumed that members of a race also share a host of nonphysical characteristics including behaviors, customs, and belief systems. Race differs from ethnicity, which we will define here as a category of persons who share language, culture, history, religion, and/or geographic origin (Haney-Lopez, 1997). All members of an ethnic group need not share all of the characteristics of the group, but there is a sense of shared origins and familial roots (e.g., blood). Race may be seen today as primarily physical (with a subtext of culture added), while ethnicity is more cultural (with a subtext of biology added) (Haney-Lopez; Omi & Winant, 1994). There is enormous confusion about the differences between race and ethnicity: each is often defined in terms of the other, and this confusion has existed since the beginning of the use of the term "race" in its modern sense in the seventeenth century. The differentiation of these concepts is important in understanding the relationship among race, ethnicity, and sexuality.

One example of this is the confusion between the racial term "black" and the ethnic term "African American." In this chapter, I use the former to refer to the broadest grouping of persons whose ancestors were of African descent, and the latter to refer to those specific Americans whose ancestors were brought to the United States as African slaves. Thus, the racial term black contains various ethnicities, including African American, a number of Afro-Caribbean ethnic groups (e.g., Jamaican, Haitian, Trinidadian), as well as recent immigrants from various countries in Africa (e.g., Nigerian Americans, South African Americans). The distinction between race and ethnicity is important because very different ethnic groups are often collapsed into the same racial demographic category; yet, they may have very different histories, cultures, and conflicting relations with other members of their racial category. This is especially important when looking at issues of sexuality. For example, some Afro-Caribbeans hold themselves in contradistinction to African Americans, whom they may perceive as morally suspect, lazy, and sexually undisciplined (Kasinitz, Battle, & Miyares, 2001; Waters, 1999). The use of broad racial/ethnic categories in the sexuality literature masks ethnic, generational, and cultural diversities.

Given the indeterminacy of race as a category, it may not seem that it is a useful construct in understanding sexuality. In fact, there are calls from various disciplines to remove race as a scientific construct, because it does not appear to have biological meaning. There is no biological evidence that humans can be reliably organized into racial categories that mirror common categories of race (Lewontin, 1972; Montagu, 1942/1997). It has been demonstrated that 85.4 percent of genetic variation occurs within racial groups and 8.3 percent between population groups within a race; only 6.3 percent of genetic variance occurs between racial groups (Braun, 2002; Lewontin). However, to do away with the concept of race would be a mistake because although race may not appear to have biological currency, it does have enormous social significance.

At the microsocial level of individual interactions, we notice the physical characteristics of a person that are associated with different races, and this informs our expectations of that person. Omi and Winant (1994), in their classic work *Racial Formation in the United States*, note the discomfort that arises when we meet someone who is racially ambiguous, and our comments when someone violates our perception of what that person's race should be— "Funny, you don't look [b]lack" (p. 59). Racial expectations and stereotypes (e.g., whites' inability to jump higher than blacks, the exaggerated sexuality and criminality of blacks and Latinos) are testimony to a racially organized social structure. These beliefs are used to justify broader, macrolevel social "policies" such as housing and job discrimination as well as to explain why differences in the life circumstances of different racial groups, such as poverty and high rates of incarceration, exist in the first place. Beliefs and expectations about sexuality are organized racially, and so, ignoring race would deprive us of a tool in understanding human sexual experience, particularly in twenty-first-century America.

A Brief History of Race

It is important to understand the history of the use of race in order to understand how race and sexuality are connected at present, and why they are so inextricably linked. The focus of much of this section is on Africans; I am suggesting that the earliest conceptions of race by Europeans were in response to their experiences and treatment of Africans among other indigenous peoples.

The organization of persons into races is a relatively new phenomenon. The modern conception of race was first articulated in the seventeenth century during the Enlightenment. The first published use of race in the modern sense was by François Bernier (1684/2000), a French traveler who described his journeys in a text entitled "A New Division of the Earth." Bernier described four races (curiously, he described the regions that members of these races lived in but did not give the names of three of the races). The first group comprised persons from northern Europe, southern Europe, North Africa, and parts of southeastern and western Asia (e.g., Siam [Thailand], Borneo, Persia [Iran]); the second, persons from all of sub-Saharan Africa; the third, persons from China, Japan, Tartary, and the Philippines; and the fourth, persons from northern Finland, who were called the Lapps. Bernier noted physical characteristics that were associated with each group. The skin color, hair texture, and sparseness of hair of the African group was compared to that of the European group, as was the different body structure of the East Asian group. The Lapps were described as "little stunted creatures with thick legs, large shoulders, short neck and a face elongated immensely; very ugly and partaking much of the bear" (Bernier, p. 6).

In describing the skin of the European group, Bernier noted the wide variation in skin colors and asserted that the darkness of the skin of some members was due to exposure to sun, as opposed to the Africans, whose skin remained the same if transported to a cold country. Of course, other European travelers had noted physical differences between themselves and the indigenous peoples they met, but Bernier was the first to group humans based on these characteristics. Interestingly, aspects of sexuality were discussed by Bernier in this first publication of racial ideas. He spent considerable space describing the beauty of women found in each of the locations (except for the Lapps) and the physical characteristics that signified beauty in Bernier's eyes. There were some subtle ideas of racial hierarchy in Bernier's text, as he spoke of seeing "handsome [women] among the blacks of Africa, who had not those thick lips and squat nose" (Bernier, 1684/2000, p. 3). Travelogues that included discussion of the sexual nature of other peoples were a common part of European cultures in general; sailors were a particularly avid audience, reading both for knowledge and for sexual titillation (Bergreen, 2004). Bernier's text highlights some of the features of later discussions of race in its conflation of ethnic, racial, and national origins. However, there is little of the increasing stigmatization of non-European ethnic/racial groups that followed racial thinking in later years.

Enlightenment philosophers such as Immanuel Kant, John Locke, and David Hume extensively explored the idea of race. Their organization of humans into races increasingly betrayed a European ethnocentrism, which placed Europeans at the top of a racial hierarchy. This hierarchy later helped to justify the colonization, enslavement, and exploitation of the indigenous peoples of Africa and the New World. For example, Kant (1775/1997) writes

of four races—whites, Negros, the Hunnic (Mongolian), and the Hindustanic—
the original rootstock of human races being the white race. Kant believed
that differences in climate were responsible for the physical and behavioral differences between whites and the other races: "Besides all this, damp heat promotes strong growth in animals in general; in short, the Negro is produced,
well-suited to his environment; that is strong, fleshy, supple, but in the midst of
the bountiful provision of his motherland lazy, soft and dawdling" (Kant, 1764/
1997, p. 46).

These differences were seen as hereditary and permanent. Kant also established European national differences in the ability to perceive beauty and
the sublime, which signified a refined intellectual and moral cultivation. He
stated that Germans are the Europeans best able to perceive both qualities,
whereas the Africans have, "by nature, no feeling that rises above the trifling"
(Kant, 1764/1997, p. 54). He briefly explored gender and sexual relations
among non-Europeans and Europeans. Europeans, according to Kant, were the
first (and only) race to raise sex to the sublime by interlacing it with morality
and, by doing so, raise the status of women. In contrast, non-European men
placed women in virtual slavery because of the insecurity of their dominance as
men. Kant cited a report of a "Negro" carpenter, who mocked whites as fools
for making concessions to their wives and then complaining when they drove
men mad. Kant commented that the carpenter may have had a point, but, "in
short, this fellow was quite black from head to toe, a clear proof that what he
said was stupid" (Kant, 1764/1997, p. 57). It is clear from this passage that it
is skin color that drives Kant's hierarchy of races, a common theme of Enlightenment racial thought. Furthermore, these groupings are seen as absolute,
such that all members of a racial category share the characteristics cited for the
group.

Stigmatization of Racial Differences and Justification for Slavery

Examination of Enlightenment ideas about race, and particularly about
Africans, shows generally increasing stigma about certain races as one moves
into the eighteenth century. The increased exploitation of indigenous peoples
by Europeans after 1492 was primarily responsible for the transformation of
European ideas about race. As exploitation of natural resources and colonization by Europeans increased, there was a societal need to account for this
exploitation (West & Zimmerman, 1987). Initially, this justification was on
religious grounds. For example, religious fervor was an important determinant
of Spanish policy in the New World, and it was argued that it was necessary to
have a religious presence in the New World. A continuing controversy about
the nature of the indigenous peoples of the Americas and their subsequent
treatment hinged on the nature of their souls and their capacity to be converted to Christianity. In 1550, Ginés de Sepúlveda argued that the native

peoples of the Americas were incapable of being converted because they were so inferior in terms of wisdom, virtue, and basic humanity. Bartolemé de Las Casas idealized the lives of the native peoples and argued that they were in fact capable of understanding Christianity and should be converted. In the end, Las Casas may have been indirectly responsible for the continued miseries of the native peoples as forced conversions to Christianity destroyed native cultures (Goldberg, 1993).

From the sixteenth to the eighteenth century, there were changes in the way slavery was practiced, which required changes in justification for Europeans and Americans. Initially, slavery was an extended form of indentured servitude, with the prospect of freedom for African slaves. Many of the American colonies had substantial populations of freed Africans who were Christianized and partly integrated into colonial society as artisans and other laborers (Adams & Sanders, 2003; D'Emilio & Freedman, 1997). As economic reliance on the forced labor of slaves to clear and work the land increased in the American South, it added impetus for change to a permanent enslavement for both slaves and their descendents. The practice of slavery made fortunes in the New World and in Europe, as the infamous Triangle Trade moved slaves from Africa to the New World in return for rum, molasses, and other goods, which bought manufactured goods for sale in Africa. As slavery became increasingly integrated into the economic and social fabric of the colonies, Americans attempted to account for this practice to each other and to the world by asserting the inferiority of Africans.

As Enlightenment ideas came to the fore in the eighteenth century, discussion shifted to concepts of basic human rights. Humans have rights to life and liberty, and we have a moral obligation to guarantee those rights; we also have the right to rebel in the face of abrogation of those rights by an unjust government. Enlightenment values suggest that what separates humans from other animals is the ability to reason. Linnaeus used the binomial *Homo sapiens* ("thinking man") to differentiate humans, while John Locke (1689/1931) suggested that only rational beings should be afforded natural equality and, thus, full moral treatment. There was a logical disconnect between the brutality and permanence of slavery and the increased calls for basic human rights to life and liberty by American colonists. Abolitionists on both sides of the Atlantic remarked on this hypocrisy at the time (Adams & Sanders, 2003). There needed to be a resolution of the dichotomy between the ideal of the human right to life and liberty and the loss of these rights for African slaves and, to a lesser extent, Native Americans. The solution was found in redefining the important characteristics that determined whether one was human, and pointing to the lack of these characteristics in Africans.

John Locke's writings are widely cited as strong influences on American ideas on liberty and political Liberalism. But it has also been suggested that some of his work served as direct justification for African slavery and confiscation of Native American lands (Goldberg, 1993; London, Pieterse, & Parekh, 1995).

Locke's concept of *nominally essential qualities*, qualities that are created from a society's shared ideas about an object, was used to justify racial hierarchy (Goldberg). The logic is as follows: societies identify qualities that define objects. So, we note that balls are round and roundness is an essential quality of an object called ball. If Englishmen decide that the color black is an indication of irrationality, then irrationality becomes part of the essence of blackness. All objects (including persons) that share that essence also partake of the quality of irrationality. Africans are black of skin; therefore, they are irrational and irrationality is a nominally essential quality of African-ness. Tying the nature of Africans to irrationality is an important step in the moral justification of slavery because rationality is seen as the hallmark of humanity (Goldberg). By defining Africans as irrational beings, they were denied moral treatment as well as the right to engage in rebellion and escape. For those who trafficked in African slaves, it provided a fig leaf to defend their social and moral right to engage in the practice. At the end of the eighteenth century, it allowed a compromise between Southern slave owners and Northerners who were uncomfortable with the practice so as to ratify the Articles of Confederation and, later, the U.S. Constitution (Adams & Sanders, 2003).

This act of intellectual legerdemain was not universally agreed upon at the time of the Enlightenment. Johann Gottfried von Herder (1800) criticized Kant's anthropological views on race and on the supposed inferiority of blacks. In *Outlines of a Philosophy of the History of Man*, Herder pointed out that dark skin color is not uniform in Africans; that the cuticles, bodily fluids, and other tissues are not black in color; and that the climate darkens pale European skin to resemble Africans; thus implying that these differences are not permanent. He also pointed out that the lack of empirical knowledge of African civilizations precluded comparisons between African and European cultural achievements. Finally, he pointed out that the known diversity of physical forms in Africa makes it difficult to form judgments of Africans as a whole. James Beattie (1770/1997) argued against Hume's ideas of the innate inferiority of Africans by pointing out that if a slave can neither read, write, nor speak a European language and is not permitted to do anything without the permission of his master, then Europeans should not expect the slave to distinguish himself.

In summary, these ideas of the inferiority of Africans, which were floated as reasons for justifying slavery, became reified as "truths" of what it means to be African. Reification occurs when a society creates an interpretation of an event, and then, without additional evidence, believes that the interpretation reflects concrete reality. It was forgotten that the viability of organizing people into races was argued and contested from race's inception. It was also forgotten that the stigmatization of the black race was originally posited as a justification for African enslavement. Ideas of irrationality and inferiority came to be seen as a natural entailment, or the essence, of blackness. These ideas about race were then generalized, so that race was thought to represent natural categories for all humans, categories that exist independent of social forces. This forgotten set of controversies explains why there has been an obsession about racial differences in intelligence in the United States until the present day (e.g., Herrnstein & Murray, 1994). Ideas about the irrationality of Africans, which allowed their poor treatment, became reified ideas about native intelligence of persons of African descent in general. These reified ideas also become justification for present social inequalities and inequalities in distribution of resources.

RACE AND SEXUALITY

The link between race and inferiority also explains why sexuality became so important to European and American imaginings about race. Sexuality became an important part of the construction and reinforcement of Africans as irrational beings. If the sexual behavior of Africans is animallike, then it becomes more evidence for their irrationality. Sexuality was also seen as an arena to assert control over African bodies. Sexual exploitation of African slaves began as soon as they were captured. Women and children were permitted to walk freely on the decks of many slave ships to allow ready sexual access by sailors. Both slave owners and overseers engaged in sexual relations with male and female slaves (Collins, 2004; D'Emilio & Freedman, 1997). The rape of female slaves was widespread, but the state of sexual relations between whites and slaves was more complex, and spanned from sexual assault to romantic attachments. It is difficult to parse the differences between voluntary and involuntary sexual relations between slaves and owners,[1] but examination of slave narratives strongly suggests that the choices for women were sharply circumscribed (Jacobs, 1861/2000).

The regulation of sexuality was an important part of Western Christianity in general. St. Augustine, the fourth-century Christian theorist, was a member of the Manichaeans, a religious sect that believed that all matter including flesh was evil and corrupting and that spirit was good. He left the sect, but Manichaean ideas about the corrupting influence of the physical realm on the soul permeated his writings and became part of Christian dogma (Mendelson, 2000; Parrinder, 1987). Humans can and must control their sexuality in ways that other animals cannot, in order to reach the Divine. During the Enlightenment, the use of "reason" allowed for the control of sexuality. African sexuality was posited as uncontrollable, and so it became additional evidence for the irrational nature of Africans. So, even as slavers sexually assaulted their captives, and slave owners engaged in voluntary and involuntary sexual liaisons with slaves, a continuing narrative of African sexual lasciviousness and Christian sexual temperance became a part of our ideas about race.

By the end of the eighteenth century, sexual and racial ideologies became mutually supporting. Assumed differences between African sexuality and European sexuality were cited as additional evidence for the "naturalness" of sexuality. White Christian men and women were expected to act in certain ways; in order to maintain a white racial identity, sexuality must be approached in a Christian fashion. The juxtaposition of white sexuality against black sexual incontinence strengthened the idea of what it meant to be white.

The historian Barbara Welter (1978) described the nineteenth-century concept of the Cult of True Womanhood, or the cult of domesticity, which asserted that (white) womanly virtue resided in piety, sexual purity, submissiveness, and domesticity. This ideal, explicitly promoted by eastern U.S. ministers and woman-oriented literature from about 1820 to 1860, was implicitly racial as well—African American women worked outside of the home both before and after Emancipation, and their purported lack of sexual purity was evidenced by supposed illegitimacy during this time (Walker, 1998). Of course, slaves were not legally allowed to marry, since they were property and thus could not enter into contracts. Nonlegal marriages were performed in slave communities by African Americans. These ties were binding, and families struggled to keep in contact even if their members were spread out in other communities (Gutman, 1976). Despite this, high rates of conception outside of legal unions were seen as evidence of African American lack of sexual control and indifference to ties of kinship (D'Emilio & Freedman, 1997).

Sexual Policing of the Boundaries of Race

The first Africans documented to have set foot in America did so in Virginia in 1619. The racial and ethnic boundaries between blacks and whites have been the focus of much of the negotiation of race. In part, American culture grew out of the interaction between Africans and whites; eventually, both slave and slave owner wore the same clothes, ate the same food, and worshipped the same god, albeit in different churches. This long physical intimacy led to sexual intimacy, so that both often shared the same parent as well. In this context, it became difficult to see the boundaries between slaves and free persons as each began to resemble the other, and so state laws were enacted to adjudicate white lineage. The law of hypodescent, or the one-drop rule, was used: if a person had one ancestor who was of African descent, then that person was considered to be black. This simplified the policing of racial boundaries.

Racial boundaries were policed even more strictly after Emancipation in 1865, because blacks were no longer separated from whites by the fact of slavery. The practice of lynching, or extralegal execution (usually by hanging), was said to occur mainly in order to stop sexual assaults by ethnic minority men. However, lynching often took place in areas where blacks were exercising political power, and most historians suggest that it was a thinly veiled tactic of intimidation or redistribution of assets (D'Emilio & Freedman, 1997; Messerschmidt, 1998; Painter, 1991). It was also suggested that sexual assault was actually the purported cause of lynching in only one-third of the cases (Painter). Blacks were often seen as political rivals, particularly in the American

South, where, in many counties, they actually outnumbered whites. During Reconstruction, lynching, among other tactics, was used to control access to the ballot for African American voters. After Reconstruction, lynching was used to uphold Jim Crow laws, as well as to discourage upward economic mobility by African Americans (Messerschmidt; Painter).

During the late nineteenth and early twentieth century, *scientific racism*—race-based biological explanations for the subaltern status of African Americans—dominated the discourse concerning race in America. Charles Darwin's work on the origin of species was invoked to explain differences between races, as well as the consequences of racial competition for those races that were not able to compete well. All persons of African descent were considered to be inferior because of heritable physical traits that distinguished them from all other groups. Explanations of the evolution of the black race and social policy based on these explanations fell into two broad streams during this period: *accommodationist racists*, who believed that blacks were at a lower stage of evolutionary development and, with proper caretaking, could progress and eventually join (white) society; and *competitive racists*, who believed that change was not possible for blacks and segregation was necessary to preserve the achievements of the white race (Fredrickson, 1987). The sexuality of blacks was thought to present a moral danger to white American society, as a corrupting influence on upstanding citizens. Black sexual needs were purported as unrefined by civilization and thus needed to be controlled by the state for their own good as well as society's good. Their presence was seen as a danger to racial purity and evolutionary fitness; their status in society was thought to be determined by heredity and unchecked reproduction was believed to threaten the ability of the nation to compete with other nations. Antimiscegenation laws, or state laws prohibiting sexual intercourse or marriage (and thus reproduction) of persons from two different races, date from this time.

> Section 4189 of the same Code declares that "if any white person and any negro, or the descendant of any negro to the third generation, inclusive, though one ancestor of each generation was a white person, intermarry or live in adultery or fornication with each other, each of them must, on conviction, be imprisoned in the penitentiary or sentenced to hard labor for the county for not less than two nor more than seven years." (Code of Alabama, cited in *Pace v. State [of Alabama]*, 1883)

Although these laws were largely found in the South and were enforced largely among black-white unions, they were more often enforced when black men attempted to marry white women. White men still maintained sexual access to black women, whether that access was voluntary or not. Often, white men were not prosecuted for the rape of black women; when blacks acted in extralegal ways by attacking white male rapists to protect themselves from sexual assault, they were themselves the target of lynching (D'Emilio & Freedman, 1997, p. 217).

In the mid-to-late twentieth century, there was a gradual increase in the number of interracial unions in the United States. Interethnic marriages were fairly common among European ethnic groups, and antimiscegenation laws were not uniform across the country (Pagnini & Morgan, 1990). As the liberation movements of the 1960s and 1970s (Civil Rights and Black Power movements, Gay Liberation and Women's Liberation movements) liberalized sexual interactions in general, pressure was applied to overturn these laws at the national level. The U.S. Supreme Court declared antimiscegenation laws unconstitutional in *Loving v. State of Virginia* in 1967. The number of interracial unions increased from 310,000 in 1970 to 1,160,000 in 1992. This was an increase from 0.7 percent of all marriages in 1970 to 2.2 percent in 1992 (Qian, 1999). At present, the ways in which ethnic and racial boundaries relating to sex are enforced are informal and implicit (such as through social pressure and stigma) rather than through the formal actions of the government. If we examine the research literature on sexual networks, we see that sexual interactions among racial groups are still largely endogamous (within racial groups) (Laumann, Gagnon, Michael, & Michaels, 1994); when exogamy (between racial groups) occurs, it tends to recapitulate class and gender boundaries (Qian).

In summary, the history of the concept of race and its implementation in American society has led to a sociocultural context in which sexuality, race, and ethnicity form a mutually reinforcing framework. As individuals negotiate this framework, they may or may not be aware of the ways in which the sociocultural context affects the sexual choices that one makes as an individual. However, individuals are also integrated into this framework—each one of us has a sexual, ethnic, and racial identity that influences our sexual interactions as members of the groups we see ourselves a part of.

EXAMINATION OF SEXUAL ATTITUDES AND BEHAVIORS IN SELECTED RACIAL GROUPS IN THE UNITED STATES

How has the history of race and sexual interactions between races influenced sexual behavior in different racial groups? In the following sections, I examine white, black, and Latino/a sexual attitudes and behaviors. It is a significant challenge to locate sexual scientific data in ethnic groups because of the indeterminacy of most investigations with regard to racial and ethnic group membership. For example, two of the largest and most comprehensive national surveys of adult sexuality, the Kinsey studies (e.g., Kinsey, Pomeroy, & Martin, 1948) and the National Health and Social Life Survey (NHSLS) (Laumann et al., 1994) break their data down into racial groups (white, black), but for the white and black data, there is no systematic analysis of the ethnic composition of these groups. These data will therefore focus on broader racial categories in examining sexual behavior and beliefs. Each of the following sections will (1) describe the group under study, (2) focus on elements of the history and present social conditions relevant to sexual behavior and beliefs within the racial group, and (3) describe data on sexual behaviors and beliefs collected within the past twenty years.

White Americans

White Americans form the largest racial group in the United States, topping 194 million or 69.1 percent in the 2000 U.S. Census. This does not include the 3.4 million who self-identified as white and another race and are not of Latino origin, or those Latinos who also self-identified as white (16.9 million). In terms of ancestry, the 2000 Census asked respondents to write in their ancestry or ethnic origin. The three highest ethnic ancestries reported in the census data by those who self-identified as white-only were German (29.8 million), Irish (18.9 million), and English (16.4 million).

History

The importance of white racial identity and culture for sexual behavior may not be apparent to most Americans. White identity often goes unremarked and unnoticed by the individual and the society because of the way in which ideas about whiteness and American identity are created and experienced in the United States.

Because there was no long-standing American ethnic identity in terms of a shared history, ties of kinship and blood, or geographic origin held by all Americans, such an identity had to be created and recreated throughout the nation's history. Through most of American history, one of the basic elements of American citizenship was a white identity. This was policed through custom and law; nonwhites were denied citizenship by law (e.g., Naturalization Act of 1790). Racial ideas were applied not only to those groups whose skin color, hair texture, and facial structure marked them as different, but also to European ethnic groups as well. For example, in the United States during the eighteenth and early nineteenth centuries, the Irish were not considered to be members of the white race. Differences in language, religion, and cultural practices, particularly around sexual and courtship practices, led to widespread discrimination for the Irish.[2] Similar experiences awaited other European immigrants (e.g., Italians, Russians, Greeks) into the United States during the nineteenth and twentieth centuries. Discriminatory practices led to extreme pressure for those groups who might become white to assimilate or subsume their ethnic identities and cultural practices into an undifferentiated American identity. The rhetoric around the concept of the "melting pot" suggests that immigrants shed their differences and become American. Immigrant groups who do not choose to "fit in" by retaining their language of origin or cultural practices face pressure from society to conform.

The loss of a specific ethnic identity and cultural experience may lead white Americans to perceive themselves as lacking a race or ethnicity because these two factors may not appear to be salient in their daily life. In many parts of the United States, whites may not have any meaningful interaction with ethnic minority persons, either because of de facto segregation or because of low numbers of ethnic minority persons in general. Researchers who are not immune to social and cultural influences on theorizing may also perceive race and ethnicity as factors that affect nonwhites primarily, and thus ignore the possible effects of white racial cultures on sexuality. While there is substantial empirical evidence for white sexual behaviors and attitudes, as well as differences between racial groups, there is not as much empirical or theoretical work on the effect of white racial identity on sexual behavior or attitudes.

Sexual Behavior and Beliefs

Much of the data in this section is from the NHSLS. This is a large-scale probability sample of 3,432 U.S. men and women between 18 and 59 years of age, of which 2,707 respondents self-identified as white. When we examine age at first vaginal intercourse, white men and women tended to engage in intercourse later than other groups. For the cohort of NHSLS respondents born between 1963 and 1967, the mean age at first intercourse for black men was 15½; white men, 17½; white women, $17\frac{3}{4}$; and black women, 17 (Laumann et al., 1994, p. 325). This difference may be related to differences in the onset of puberty. The mean ages at the onset of pubic hair, breast development, and menarche, respectively, were 9.5, 9.5, and 12.1 years for black girls; 10.3, 9.8, and 12.2 for Mexican American girls; and 10.5, 10.3, and 12.7 for white girls (Wu, Mendola, & Buck, 2002).

The developmental progression of engagement in sexual activity in adolescence is fairly consistent for white men and women. Smith and Udry (1985) examined longitudinally the order in which black and white adolescents engaged in precoital behaviors in their progression to intercourse. For white adolescents, there was a predictable progression from the unclothed caressing of breasts to feeling male and female sex organs and then vaginal intercourse.

In the NHSLS data, white respondents tended to be liberal and fairly secular in their attitudes about sexuality: 44 percent of white men and 57 percent of white women reported that religion shaped their sexual behavior, while 22 percent of white men and 30 percent of white women agreed that premarital sex was wrong (Mahay, Laumann, & Michaels, 2001). In terms of sexual behavior, whites were also less conservative than other groups: 75 percent of whites engaged in oral sex in their lifetime, although the percentage of men engaging in active anal intercourse was roughly similar across racial groups (approximately 3–4 percent). The median number of partners since age

18 for whites was three, which was higher than for all other groups except blacks (four partners) (Laumann et al., 1994, p. 181).

Homosexuality. In the sexuality literature, there are distinctions made among sexual identity, sexual behavior, and sexual orientation or desire. The percentage of homosexual- and bisexual-identified persons varies from less than 1 percent for black women to 3.7 percent for Hispanic men in the NHSLS. For white men, this is 3 percent and for white women, 1.7 percent. For women, this was the highest reported percentage, and for men it was the second highest (Laumann et al., 1994, p. 305).

Stereotypes in American society suggest that homosexuality or rather gay and lesbian identities seem to be associated with whites, particularly among ethnic minority groups (Boykin, 2005). Media depictions of gay men and lesbians are more likely to be white, which is consistent with the numbers of whites in the population as a whole. The Gay Liberation movement in the 1970s was a largely white male movement, and much of the activism around HIV/AIDS in the 1980s and 1990s was conducted by middle- and upper-middle-class white gay men (Epstein, 1996). Whites also tend to be less likely to hold negative attitudes toward homosexuality in general, although religious conservatives (Burdette, Ellison, & Hill, 2005) and white men tend to have higher levels of sexual prejudice (Bonilla & Porter, 1990; Herek & Capitanio, 1996).

Sexual dysfunction. Sexual dysfunction has not been discussed in racial terms in the research literature until recently (Lewis, 2004; Working Group on a New View of Women's Sexual Problems, 2001). But examination of the literature suggests that quite a bit is known about sexual dysfunction in white populations. Very often, the data on sexual dysfunction does not contain the ethnic background of the research participants; when it does, the vast majority of the studies examine largely white samples and cannot make informed analyses of the causes or prevalence of sexual dysfunction in ethnic minority populations (e.g., Benet & Melman, 1995; Feldman, Goldstein, Hatzichristou, Krane, & McKinlay, 1994). Eleven to 29 percent of white women reported sexual problems in the NHSLS; these ranged from a lack of interest in sex (29 percent), to inability to experience orgasm (24 percent), to anxiety about sexual performance (11 percent). Seven to 29 percent of white men reported sexual problems such as climaxing too early (29 percent) and an inability to experience orgasm (7 percent) (Laumann, Paik, & Rosen, 2001). While these rates seem high, they are lower in comparison to other racial/ethnic groups.

Latinos

Latinos form the second largest racial group in the United States.[3] In the 2000 U.S. Census, 35.3 million people (12.5 percent of the U.S. population) self-identified as Hispanic or Latino. The largest ethnic ancestries reported were Mexican (20.6 million), Puerto Rican (3.4 million), and Cuban

(1.2 million). There is enormous diversity found within Latino ethnic groups. Major challenges lie in defining this population, deciding exactly who fits into this category, accounting for differences in self-definition, and understanding the relationship between culture of origin and host culture and its effects on sexuality.

For example, do we define being a Latino as being a citizen of a Spanish or Portuguese language country? How then do we account for Chinese Cubans, who came to Cuba in the nineteenth century as laborers? Are they Asian or Latino? In the U.S. Census, Hispanic/Latino status is described as an ethnicity and Latinos can also self-identify as members of other races. Thus, a Latino respondent can identify as black and Hispanic, or white and Hispanic, or Native American and Hispanic. On the face of it, this makes sense; because of the diversity of skin colors and ethnic group intermarriage and immigration, Latinos can be of African, Chinese, Amerindian, or Asian Indian descent among other groups, sometimes within the same person. The individual histories of Latin countries may also determine the racial characteristics of their inhabitants. Argentina was founded by the Spanish and for many years has carried out an explicit policy of promotion of white European immigration. Because of this, the ethnic breakdown in Argentina is 97 percent white (mostly Spanish and Italian) and 3 percent nonwhite, mestizo (mixed white and Amerindian ancestry), Amerindian, or other groups (Central Intelligence Agency, 2005a). The Dominican Republic, on the other hand, because of a larger African slave population and high rates of intermarriage, has an ethnic breakdown of 16 percent white, 11 percent black, and 73 percent mixed (CIA, 2005b).

Another challenge lies in the expectation that a person from Argentina and a person from the Dominican Republic have had similar experiences before immigration to the United States. A white Argentinean may be of high social class in Argentina, and if they appear white to American eyes (including English fluency), they may also enjoy that class and racial status in the United States without ever experiencing racial discrimination. Yet, they are members of the same racial/ethnic category as a dark-skinned Dominican, who may experience quite a bit of racial discrimination. Social class is an important aspect of identity and varies across national origin and immigration status in the United States. Given this, it may be difficult to characterize Latino sexual behavior as a whole, although there is some research suggesting that there are enough similarities between Latino ethnic groups to make such a discussion meaningful (Carballo-Dieguez, Dolezal, Nieves-Rosa, & Diaz, 2000). There are multiple levels of complexity in the analysis of Latino sexualities. The best course available in assessing the work in this area is to be as painstaking as possible in the ethnic identification of Latino respondents—what is the country of origin of the sample; what is the level of acculturation, age of arrival, generation, and length of residence in the United States for immigrant samples.

History

From reading this chapter, as well as much of the scholarship on race, it may seem that racial interactions were primarily between whites and blacks in the United States. However, there are long and continuing histories of Latino-white interactions that vary across particular Latino ethnic groups. In general, the treatment of Latinos often paralleled the treatment of Native Americans in the United States. For example, the appropriation of land and other material resources belonging to Mexicans and Mexican Americans occurred in the Southwest and California before and after the Treaty of Guadalupe Hidalgo in 1848 (Carrasco, 1998). The interactions between whites and Mexicans in the Southwest were complex. Mexicans were seen as inferior, particularly as tensions rose between Mexico and the United States. But it is important to remember that in the early nineteenth century, white Americans were initially immigrants into much of the Southwest, and so there was integration of whites into Mexican culture. After the Treaty of Guadalupe Hidalgo and the discovery of gold in California, the relationship between the numbers of whites and Mexican Americans changed, and we see the implementation of public policy to limit the economic power of Mexican Americans (Takaki, 1993).

Sexual relations between Mexicans and whites were different than that between blacks and whites. They typically occurred in one of three fashions (D'Emilio & Freedman, 1997). At first, white men intermarried Mexican women and assimilated into Mexican society. This occurred earlier in the nineteenth century, when small numbers of white male trappers, miners, and traders interacted with Mexican society. Later, as more whites entered the Southwest, Mexican women assimilated into white society through inter-marriage. They often had to endure increased stigmatization as dirty and immoral, particularly as relations between Mexico and the United States soured in the wake of the Mexican-American War (1846–1848). Their husbands attempted to reinvent stigmatized Mexican women as Spanish "ladies" in order to ease their integration into white society. The third type of sexual relation was more exploitative, as white men used their social privilege in similar ways as with blacks to subjugate and control Mexican mestizo sexuality (D'Emilio & Freedman, 1997). This exploitative relationship was mirrored in the law as well, as Mexican labor was alternatively called for and cracked down upon by the United States throughout the nineteenth and twentieth centuries (Carrasco, 1998). Tensions in the southwestern part of the country and California among whites, blacks, and Latinos exist to the present day, and continue to affect the perception of Mexicans and Mexican Americans in the United States.

Acculturation is a significant issue for Latino immigrants (Zea, Reisen, & Díaz, 2003). The terms of immigration—whether there was a significant population of the migrating group in the United States, the social class and resources of the group, and the relationship between the home country and the United States—all help in determining how immigrating members of the group negotiate American society. This also has effects on the context in which sexuality occurs. For example, traditional Mexican ideas about marriage and the sexual relationship between men and women changed for Mexicans migrating to the United States. Ideals of companionate marriage present in the country were internalized by acculturating Mexican Americans and their children. These ideas also were introduced into Mexico through the media, returning migrants, and direct communication between Mexicans living in the United States and in Mexico (Hirsch, 2003). The lack of distance between these two countries, the political situation in Mexico, and the pattern of temporary and permanent migration to the United States were strong influences on ideas of marriage for Mexicans. It is also important to remember that not all Latinos are immigrants. Mexican Americans have been in California for 300 years, well before it was a part of the United States. In 1848, when the Treaty of Guadalupe Hidalgo ceded control of California and the rest of the Southwest, the Mexican inhabitants were granted immediate American citizenship according to the terms of the treaty.

Sexual Behavior and Beliefs

The major challenge in outlining sexual beliefs and behaviors of Latinos from empirical data lies in sampling biases. As many researchers in this area have noted, sexual experiences vary in persons within the same ethnic group, as the (social and physical) distance from the country of origin changes, as well as across generations (e.g., Hirsch, 2003). Given this, data that are collected for Latinos should contain information about national origin and generational status for immigrant samples if at all possible. For example, the NHSLS does contain information about the national origin of Latinos, but these data are not always made a part of analyses in the literature.

With regard to age at first intercourse, Upchurch, Levy-Storms, Sucoff, and Aneshensel (1998) reported a median age of 16.5 years for Latino males and 17.3 years for Latino females in a largely Mexican American sample. Another interesting finding was that Latinas were nearly half as likely to engage in sexual activity as white females. This difference was not likely due to differences in the onset of puberty, but rather differences in family structure. When differences in family structure were controlled for, the difference in sexual activity was not a significant one. The NHSLS data suggests that Latinos are more likely to engage in their first sexual experience with a partner they were in love with (Mahay et al., 2001).

In the NHSLS data, Mexican American respondents tended to be more traditional in their attitudes about sexuality than were whites. This difference did not manifest in the percentages, but in the statistical analysis, which controlled for age, religion, and educational status. Fifty-one percent of Mexican men and 60 percent of women reported that religion shaped their sexual behavior, while 27 percent of Mexican men and 42 percent of women agreed that premarital sex was wrong (Mahay et al., 2001). The statistical analyses showed that Mexican Americans were nearly three times as likely to state that premarital sex was wrong, and nearly twice as likely to state that religion shaped their sexual behavior. In terms of sexual behavior also, Mexican Americans were more conservative than whites; 65 percent of Mexican men and 61 percent of women engaged in oral sex in their lifetime. When controlling for other variables, Mahay et al. suggest that Mexican Americans were half as likely to have engaged in oral sex. The median number of partners since age 18 for Latinos was two, which was lower than for all other groups except Asians (one partner) (Laumann et al., 1994, p. 181).

Overall, examination of the NHSLS data suggests that Latinos find fewer sexual practices appealing when compared to whites. Although Latinos were more likely to espouse conservative sexual values, the percentage of premarital sex was not different for them compared to whites. This and other data suggest that there is evidence for a romantic script that adolescent and young adult Latinos followed in their initial explorations of sex. The data also suggest that Latino sexuality may be tied in a more explicit fashion to gender, as Latinas were much more likely than other groups to state that their first sexual experience was with someone they loved.

The gender scripts *machismo* and *marianismo* suggest that sexuality is a positive expression of gender, but only under certain circumstances. Marianismo is a cultural script employed by Latino ethnic groups to organize the behavior of women. This scenario constrains the heterosexual behavior of women as passive partners within relationships with men and, within sexual relationships, places expectations of sexual abstention before marriage and a restraint of sexual expression after marriage (Seal, Wagner-Raphael, & Ehrhardt, 2000). Machismo suggests that men must prove their masculinity through acts of bravery, fearlessness, and strength, and that these acts must have a public aspect, as machismo is a performance whose appreciation must come from other people (Cheng, 1999). According to these scripts, young women with a desire for sex have to couch their desire in romantic terms, stating that they had sex because they were in love and their male partner wanted to have sex. Young men have to attempt to prove their masculinity by boasting of sexual prowess and demonstrating that prowess as much as possible (Díaz, 1998). Of course, there are many cultures in the United States that also have similar gender norms, but the strength of these scripts in Latino communities and their interaction with other norms have powerful effects on the sexual behavior of Latinos. There is strong evidence of this when homosexuality is explored in Latino samples.

Homosexuality. In examining homosexuality in Latino communities, the cultural distinctions across ethnic groups about what constitutes homosexuality become apparent. In the NHSLS data, 3.7 percent of Latino men self-identified as either homosexual or bisexual, the highest of all the racial groups (Laumann et al., 1994, p. 305). But this percentage may be compromised by the meaning of this self-identify for Latinos. For many heterosexually identified Latino men, being the insertive partner in same-sex anal intercourse (*el bugarron*) does not make a man a homosexual; it is the act of being penetrated that makes one homosexual. Homosexuality is thought of as a problem of gender such that men who have same-sex desires and act on them by being penetrated are not real men (*no hombre hombre*) (Carrier, 1976; Díaz, 1998).

For many homosexually oriented men, their identities as a man and as a Latino are at odds with their sexual desires, and thus they may organize their behavior to conform to ideas of masculinity. Some men may internalize engendered sexual prejudice, be more concerned with the loss of an erection and avoid becoming comfortable using condoms, and ignore HIV prevention messages aimed at gay men because those men are *loca* (crazy females) and thus different from themselves (Díaz, 1998). Others may choose to drink alcohol or use drugs in order to help dissociation from sexual feelings or feelings of shame (Hughes & Eliason, 2002). Familism, a cultural ideal that emphasizes the importance of family and family emotional bonds, also makes it difficult for men to negotiate homosexuality. Since homosexuality is so stigmatized, it increases the difficulty of coming out to one's family and increases the shame and emotional pain if a man is rejected by his family. There may also be conflict between cultural values of *respeto* (respect for others) and familism such that Latinos may not come out to their families because to do so would breach the respect shown to elders (Rosario, Schrimshaw, & Hunter, 2004). Some Latino men choose to avoid this possibility by living a double life, which can lead to more stress (Meyer, 2003).

Latina lesbians experience significant stigma as well, as they must negotiate compulsory heterosexuality and the expectation that as women they must have a family and children of their own (Espin, 1987). There are cultural possibilities for strong and enduring emotional ties between women (*amigas intimas*) (Espin, 1993), but a lesbian identity is strongly stigmatized in Latino communities. There is the perception here, as in black communities, that homosexuality is a behavior that was forced on Latinos by (white) Americans. The stigma attached to the word may be so strong that some Latinas use the words *amigas* or *companeras* in their self-identification. Again, there is an expectation that homosexuality is a gender problem, so that homosexually oriented women may feel pressure to conform to a butch or masculinized role (Espin, 1993). These cultural meanings may also compromise the percentage (1.1 percent) of Latina women who self-identified as either homosexual or bisexual (Laumann et al., 1994, p. 305).

Attitudes toward homosexuality are largely negative among Latinos. In the NHSLS data, Mexican American men and women constitute the highest percentage of respondents who stated that homosexuality was wrong (84 percent and 85 percent, respectively) (Mahay et al., 2001, p. 215). Controlling for other variables, Mexican American men are twice as likely and women three times as likely as whites to endorse this negative attitude. Many Latinos face racial and ethnic discrimination and prejudice within white gay and lesbian communities as well (Díaz, Ayala, Bein, Henne, & Marin, 2001; Siegal & Epstein, 1996).

Sexual dysfunction. Interestingly, when examining the NHSLS data on sexual dysfunction, Latinos tend to endorse the lowest levels of these sexual problems. However, most of the differences between Latinos and whites in the statistical analyses conducted by Laumann et al. (2001) are not significant. Twelve to 30 percent of Latina women reported sexual problems in the NHSLS. These ranged from a lack of interest in sex (30 percent), to inability to experience orgasm (22 percent), to anxiety about sexual performance (12 percent). Five to 27 percent of Latino men reported sexual problems such as climaxing too early (27 percent) and anxiety about their performance (5 percent) (Laumann et al., 2001).

When we examine women's experience of sexuality in marriage, there is evidence of generational and perhaps migrational differences in their perceptions of their sexual lives. Hirsch (2003) reported that in more traditional marriages based on mutual respect and social decorum (*respeto*), Mexican women expected no sexual pleasure in their sexual interactions with their husbands. If it did occur, then it was seen as a bonus; if it did not, then it was a private matter for the woman to deal with (Hirsch, 2003, p. 213). In the more companionate marriages experienced by the urban, more educated, and/or immigrant women, trust and mutual disclosure (*confianza*) led to greater expectation of intimacy and sexual pleasure for women and for men. Although this division between immigration, education, location, and type of marriage expectations is not a hard and fast rule (respeto and confianza are found through Mexican society in Mexico and abroad), these factors are important in understanding how sexual problems are defined and discussed (Fontes, 2001).

Blacks or African Americans

The U.S. Census uses the terms "black" and "African American" synonymously, as does the vast majority of the research literature on sexuality, so it may not be possible to make clear distinctions between racial and ethnic data in this section. Black Americans are the third largest racial group in the United States, with 34.7 million or 12.3 percent who self-identified as black or African American alone in the 2000 Census. One million self-identified as black alone or in combination with other races (e.g., black and white) and of Latino origin, and nearly 1.8 million as black and one or more other races. Of those who answered black as their only racial affiliation, the largest ethnic ancestries are as follows: 21.7 million self-identified as African American, 1.1 million as African, 604,000 as Jamaican, and 452,000 as Haitian. An additional 2.1 million answered black or Afro-American. The remaining of the total 34.7 million gave answers as diverse as Fijian (199 respondents) to Herzegovinian (2 respondents).

Without knowing the salience of these ethnic identities for the individual, it is impossible to determine their effects on the sexual experiences of individuals, but there are broad statements that can be made about cultural scenarios about African Americans in general.

Twenty-first-Century Perceptions/Stereotypes of African American Sexuality

In many ways, the present perceptions of African American male and female sexualities are an extension of the ideas we have explored earlier. For the past thirty years, the sexuality of native African Americans has continued to be presented largely as a problem. In the psychological and public health literatures, much focus has been placed on increases in adolescent pregnancy and illegitimacy as problems found in black communities, although the birthrate in all communities had increased during the mid-twentieth century, and actually peaked in the 1950s (Luker, 1996). The number of babies born to women out of wedlock across all age-groups has remained stable or declined, depending on which group of women one chooses to focus on, and the rates of black adolescent pregnancies out of wedlock dropped 40 percent in the 1990s (Martin et al., 2002). Yet, in popular culture and the media, myths of black women as "baby factories," and high rates of illegitimacy in black communities as indicative of black sexual immorality continued to be produced throughout the twentieth century (Walker, 1998).

Multiple sexual stereotypes about blacks are continually in flux, transformed by new representations in popular culture both within and outside of black communities. Present scenarios about black women include the "black bitch," a loud, rude, and sexually aggressive woman, and the "ho" or "hoochie mama," a materialistic, sexually available woman who uses her sexuality for material gain (Collins, 2004). These stereotypes, which are stigmatized because they violate patriarchal expectations about women's sexuality and its control, coexist in hip hop culture alongside black female performers who speak out against misogyny and objectification.

Much has been made of hip hop as the major creator of sexual stereotypes about black men and women, as well as its production by African Americans. Because it was created by poor and working-class African Americans and Latinos (hip hop was invented in dance clubs and parties in the Bronx, in the late 1970s), hip hop has heightened credibility as an authentic portrayal of African American (sexual and gender) values. But the largest consumers of hip hop are white: according to music industry sales statistics, 70–75 percent of hard-core rap albums are purchased by white consumers (Speigler, 1996). Although the musicians and producers are largely persons of color, consumers ultimately control what is produced by their purchasing patterns; many of the major labels that were originally owned by African Americans (e.g., Def Jam Records, Russell Simmons) have been bought by mainstream recording companies. This suggests that although hip hop may have reflected, and for many still reflects, working-class and poor African American cultural values of masculinity and femininity, there may also be a commodification and packaging of hip hop to reflect expectations about African American male and female sexuality by non–African American consumers. This suggestion would be anathema for hip hop artists, for whom "keeping it real" or maintaining black working-class ties and values, and not selling out, is a core value.

African American male sexuality has continued to be represented as dangerous and violent, and also close to the primitive, and thus more potent than other groups who have been exposed to the emasculating effects of civilization. Past cultural scenarios of the primitive, rapacious black "Buck" and the Reconstruction-era rapist, who is a danger to white womanhood, have been updated to presentations of the hypermasculine black (working-class) man. Images of black hypermasculinity present an urban aesthetic of physical prowess and strength, respect through the imminent threat or use of violence, misogyny, leeriness of emotional ties to lovers, and a particular kind of sexual aggressiveness (Henry, 2002). This aggressiveness is demonstrated through the persona of the "playa," who collects sexual conquests, often through implicit or explicit deception of their female partners (Anderson, 1997; Collins, 2000; hooks, 2004). "Pimp culture" is also an element found within hip hop; the pimp is glorified as a man who makes money and controls women despite social sanctions against him. The pimp is transgressive—he goes against mainstream social values and so holds street credibility for black and white consumers alike.

Yet, hip hop culture is multifaceted. It is not only "booty flyin' across the screen," but is also a major venue for poetry, political commentary, and activism by young African Americans and Latinos (Kitwana, 2003; Rivera, 2002). Some of the same artists who extend hypermasculinity and misogyny in their work are also advocates for political change, often within the same album (Kitwana, 2003; Powell, 1998). Older African Americans, as well as feminist-oriented critics, contest the values displayed in hip hop culture as misogynistic and counter to the values of civil society (Powell).

Hip hop, however, has a visibility and perceived authenticity in the United States that makes it a major player in the production and distribution of ideas about African Americans (Kitwana, 2003). Its worldwide distribution through music, videos, and motion pictures inspired by hip hop sensibilities makes it central among the first experiences of non-American audiences to African Americans.

In the context of the protean nature of hip hop and black cultures in general, it is interesting to examine the sexual behavior of blacks in the United States. High rates of HIV infection in black communities may also have had an effect on individual sexual behaviors, even though it may not have had an effect on the discussion of HIV in American popular culture at large. A Kaiser Family Foundation report focusing on media coverage of HIV/AIDS from 1981 to

2002 noted that less than 2 percent of all recent HIV/AIDS reporting centered on ethnic minorities, although HIV/AIDS is the leading cause of death for African Americans between 25 and 44 years of age (Kaiser Family Foundation, 2004).

Sexual Behavior and Beliefs

The overall picture of the sexual experiences of blacks is in stark contrast to the cultural stereotypes of black sexuality, which in general suggests that African Americans are sexually voracious, enjoy more sex, and enjoy sex more than other ethnic or racial groups. With regard to specific sexual practices, African Americans tend to be more conservative sexually as compared to other racial groups. According to NHSLS data, black men and women are less likely (20–30 percent less) to engage in fellatio and cunnilingus than other ethnic/racial groups, both the last time they engaged in sexual activity and ever in their lifetime (Mahay et al., 2001). Both genders are also less likely to have found fellatio and cunnilingus as appealing sexual activities. Black women are less likely to have engaged in anal sex in their lifetime (9.6 percent). Anal sex, while not a part of the sexual repertoire of most Americans, had been experienced by 26 percent of American men and 20 percent of American women in the NHSLS (Laumann et al., 1994, p. 99). Black men and women are more likely to have not masturbated at all in the past year. However, the amount of pleasure experienced by black men and women does not seem to be different when compared to other groups.

When we examine age at first vaginal intercourse, black men tend to be younger than white men, white women, and black women. For the cohort of NHSLS respondents born between 1963 and 1967, the mean age at first intercourse for black men was 15½; white men, 17½; white women, 17¾; and black women, 17 (Laumann et al., 1994, p. 325). As suggested earlier, this difference may be related to differences in the onset of puberty, and girls who mature earlier begin to date and engage in sexual behavior earlier than later-maturing girls (Brooks-Gunn, 1987).

Data from other studies suggest that the order in which adolescents progress to vaginal intercourse is different for black adolescents than for whites. In Smith and Udry's study (1985), there was not a consistent progression over time for most black adolescents; some experienced a similar progression from petting to intercourse while others did not. This is also supported by other qualitative research that suggests there is a historical cohort effect such that African American men who came of age sexually in the 1950s and 1960s experienced a progression similar to that reported in Smith and Udry's study (Bowser, 1994). Younger men who came of age in the 1980s were more likely to have engaged in vaginal intercourse as one of their first sexual encounters rather than moving from petting to intercourse.

Homosexuality. Attitudes about homosexuality/sexual identity are contradictory in black samples. Research has been sparse in this area, but suggests that blacks are more likely to hold negative attitudes toward homosexuality than whites (Ernst, Francis, Nevels, & Lemeh, 1991). It has been suggested that religiosity may be one reason for high levels of sexual prejudice (homophobia) in African American samples, as well as strong endorsement of masculine ideology (Battle & Lemelle, 2002). Cultural descriptions of black hypermasculinity are heterosexually oriented, and cultural stereotypes about black sexuality in general are implicitly heterosexual. Some early-twentieth-century commentators suggested that homosexuality would be unknown in blacks because homosexuality is unnatural; thus blacks, who were closer to nature, would not exhibit this unnatural behavior (Collins, 2004). These attitudes are also found within black communities; many homosexually oriented black men and women have reported that they have been told that homosexuality is a white phenomenon (Edwards, 1996; Peterson, 1992). Other homosexually oriented black men and women refuse to identify as gay or lesbian because these labels are seen as being white labels, or because they have experienced racial prejudice in white gay communities (Boykin, 2005; Greene, 2000). Other terms in use in African American communities include "same-gender loving" and "two-spirited" (Malebranche, Peterson, Fullilove, & Stackhouse, 2004). There is also evidence that black men who have sex with men (MSM) are less likely to identify as homosexual and are more likely to consider themselves heterosexual (Edwards, 1996). This has clear implications for public health interventions targeted toward gay men: black MSM may be less likely to listen and act upon public health interventions that they do not perceive as relevant to their own lives.

Sexual dysfunction. The research literature suggests that black men and women experience high rates of sexual dysfunction (Laumann et al., 2001; Lewis, 2004; Wyatt, 1997). Thirteen to 44 percent of black women reported sexual problems in the NHSLS; these ranged from a lack of interest in sex (44 percent), to inability to experience orgasm (32 percent), to experiencing pain during sex (13 percent). Thirty-two percent reported that sex was not pleasurable as well. Nine to 34 percent of black men reported sexual problems such as climaxing too early (34 percent) and being unable to experience orgasm (9 percent) (Laumann et al., 2001). Additional analyses showed that black women are nearly twice as likely as white women to report lack of interest in sex, while black men are more than twice as likely as white men to report that sex is not pleasurable (Laumann et al., 2001). Gail Wyatt (1997) writes of the challenge of many African American women to enjoy sex in the face of negative stereotypes about black female sexuality. Tricia Rose (2003), in presenting a set of narratives from black women about sexuality and intimacy, comments on the frequency of physical and sexual abuse in childhood that her respondents mentioned. Although there is little data on erectile dysfunction (ED) across racial/ethnic groups other than whites, I have suggested elsewhere that African American men suffer disproportionately from medical conditions such as diabetes and hypertension that are associated with ED, such that between 900,000 and 1.1 million African Americans may experience ED (Lewis, 2004). It is important to realize that despite the challenges faced by black men and women in negotiating sexuality, there is little difference in the amount of unhappiness in sexuality reported in the NHSLS.

EXPLAINING RACE, ETHNICITY, AND SEXUALITY

How do researchers explain these differences among black, white, and Latino sexualities? I have to acknowledge the difficulty in writing this part of the chapter, because there is little explicit theory about race and sexuality in the psychological and sexual scientific literature. In many ways, all of the anthropological literature on sexuality in differing cultural contexts is about the relationship among culture, sexual behaviors, and meanings of sexuality. But in the sense that we connect race, ethnicity, and sexuality in the United States, there is little theory about the normative connection among these aspects of identity (Lewis & Kertzner, 2003).

In many ways, the scientific research on human sexuality in the United States is largely the study of white American sexualities. For example, Kinsey's groundbreaking work *Sexual Behavior in the Human Male* is based on a total sample of 5,300 white American and Canadian men. Kinsey did collect data from black American and Canadian men, but in this work, he suggests that he has not collected the numbers needed to make inferences from comparisons across races. Note that Kinsey, as many other researchers, states his analysis (or lack of analysis) primarily in terms of racial comparisons rather than by examining sexual behavior within ethnic groups. Lastly, although Kinsey and his colleagues interviewed only white males, they titled their book *Sexual Behavior in the* Human *Male*. The equation of "human" and "white" has not been unusual in the social sciences in the past, and is a problem that still exists to a lesser extent today (Graham, 1992).

Whiteness has not been commonly examined or remarked on in the sexuality research literature, except in relation to ethnic "minority" groups. When this occurs, it seems as if there is a belief that the study of white Americans removes the influence of race/ethnicity, as if whiteness was a lack of ethnic or racial identity. An alternate view is that white racial identity is normative, and something extra needs to be added to the analysis when ethnicity and race are examined, namely, the presence of nonwhite participants (Azibo, 1988). When comparative work is done, often there is an inequity in the groups examined, with white and middle-class samples compared to samples of ethnic minority persons living in poverty. Even when variables such as income are controlled for, so that persons from different racial/ethnic groups but of similar income level are compared, other factors may impact how income is experienced in two different groups. These differences are attributed to cultural differences, although social class and factors outside of the individual (e.g., stigma) may influence sexual practices and beliefs.

There are many studies that document racial and ethnic group differences in sexual behavior and attitudes. These studies answer, to a greater or lesser extent, questions of *who* does *what* and *when* in sexuality research. These descriptive studies, when the quality is high, can provide a wealth of information about varieties of human experiences of sexuality. However, questions of how and why the connections between sexuality and ethnic/racial group membership occur have not been addressed in the sexuality literature. This is consistent with the larger challenge of lack of theorization in the field in general (Stevenson, 2002). One broad distinction between theories about sexuality lies between essentialism and social constructionism (DeLamater & Hyde, 1998).

Modern essentialism in sexuality research is described as the belief that (1) sexuality is determined (often biologically) such that individuals have no choice in their sexual behavior, orientation, or identity; (2) there are underlying "true" essences or categories that organize human sexuality (e.g., "homosexuals," "heterosexuals," "men," "women"); (3) these essences are universal, so they are shared by all members of the group and cut across historical, national, and cultural boundaries (DeLamater & Hyde, 1998). *Social constructionism* suggests that our definitions of sexuality, race, and ethnicity are socially agreed upon and are reproduced when we act on these conventions of sexuality, race, and ethnicity. Because they are socially agreed upon, it is argued that they have no independent existence apart from the culture/society they are produced in (Bohan, 1993).

Essentialism is often confused with biological determinism, which states that biological factors are responsible for the behavior under study. The important idea in essentialism is that essences are internal to the person, persistent across the lifetime, and the behaviors associated with the essence will inevitably occur (Bohan, 1993). Biological determinism can be a type of essentialism, but there can be other explanations for the origin of essences. For example, cultural essentialism suggests that culture determines how a member of a cultural group will behave. Biological reasoning and the use of the natural are often invoked to explain why these essences occur, but there are also examples of cultural essentialism as well.

Racial essentialism clearly describes how race was conceived of from the sixteenth to the early twentieth century. During this period, the focus on biology as a way of explaining racial group differences naturalized differences between groups. In the twentieth century, sociologists and anthropologists fought against these ideas of racial biological essentialism by highlighting the cultural and social aspects of American life and their effects on ethnic minority sexual behavior. For example, W. E. B. Du Bois (1903/1990) examined the historical and economic antecedents to the breakdown of African American monogamy, which in turn led to family dissolution, lack of moral values, and, ultimately, criminal behavior, alcoholism, and other forms of damage to African American communities. The balance of work on ethnic/racial minority sexuality in the twentieth century can be seen as a tension between biological models of essentialism and sociocultural explanations for differences between white and ethnic minority, largely, African American samples.

As sociocultural explanations of racial/ethnic differences became more social constructionist in their approach, they moved from suggesting that all members of a race receive the same socialization to questioning the basis of shared ideas about sexuality. There also came to be a focus on the meaning of sexual behavior to the individual and the society of which they were a part. At the present time, essentialist ideas about race and sexuality have fallen out of vogue in academic circles, particularly if they focus on biological ideas about race. The biological meaningfulness of race has been challenged by biologists, anthropologists, and now geneticists, who suggest that genetic data does not support the typology of race as conceived in the nineteenth and early twentieth centuries (e.g., Graves, 2001; Lewontin, 1972; Montagu, 1942/1997).

Sexual Scripting Theory

Present theorizing about sexuality and race acknowledges that culture is responsible for the ways in which members of ethnic/racial groups come to organize their sexual lives, but there are not many theories that explicitly address the process. One theory that does begin to address the cultural acquisition of sexual knowledge is Sexual Scripting Theory (SST). John Gagnon and William Simon presented this theory in their book *Sexual Conduct* (1973), arguing that sexuality was not a single, unitary natural phenomenon. They suggest that sexuality is "far from being natural" and is "located well within the realm of the social and the symbolic" (Plummer, as cited in Simon, 1996, p. x). In SST, social groups create *sexual scripts*, which are sets of behaviors, beliefs, and the meanings attached to them that are constructed by an individual and social group, and are agreed as sexual. Because sexual scripts are not limited to sexual behavior but include meaning, a sexual scripting approach begins to address the challenge of understanding the meanings of sexual behavior to those who are being sexual. These scripts change over historical time and across national boundaries.

Sexual scripts are held at three differing levels: (1) the cultural or social level, where abstract ideas about sexuality are created and shared among members of the culture; scripts found at this level are described as *cultural scenarios*; (2) the interpersonal level, where individuals act on their chosen set of sexual ideas in conjunction with other persons; scripts at this level are called *interpersonal scripts*; and (3) the intrapersonal level, where individuals' internalized ideas about their own sexuality are located; scripts at this level are called *intrapsychic scripts*. Each of these levels is analytically distinct yet inextricably linked to the other.

Cultural scenarios are the scripts built by cultural or social groups for explaining the (sexual) experiences of people. Cultural scenarios provide the raw material for the construction of more personal scripts by members of that culture by limiting choices of behavior and beliefs and by setting rules of appropriate behavior and responses to others' behavior. The majority of ideas about black sexuality discussed earlier in this chapter are cultural scenarios. These scenarios include beliefs concerning black (and white) masculinity held by African Americans, European Americans, and other racial/ethnic groups; expectations of male-female relations; and moral prescriptions for appropriate and inappropriate sexual practices, among others. Scenarios can be about persons outside of the group as well as within the group. These scenarios impact on relations between groups; sexual scenarios can have a deadly effect when combined with social power because of the emotional and societal valence contained within them. Historical analyses, such as the analysis of race in this chapter, can highlight the construction of cultural scenarios over time, making clear why some scenarios have more currency at present than others.

Cultural scenarios, which refer to the beliefs about the behavior of groups, are abstract in SST—the theory does not directly address the actual behaviors and beliefs in individuals acting in a concrete world. An excellent example of a cultural scenario is the concept of marianismo. The actual behavior engaged in by Latinas, and the extent to which marianismo is adhered to or resisted by individuals can be very different from the scenario, and is affected by the social environment in which the actual behavior occurs. The actual "rules" that an individual woman holds for how she interacts with her partners are interpersonal scripts. Some women may enact the marianismo scenario with their husbands in their own life without thinking about or changing their behavior at all. Other women may interact with their partner and find that neither is satisfied with enacting marianismo between themselves. Individuals take these external cultural scenarios, internalize them as a part of the creation and continuation of the self, and in conjunction with other persons, and use transformed cultural scenarios as interpersonal scripts to organize actual behavior in real-world contexts.

Interpersonal scripts govern the actual interactions between the actor and other persons, but also allow room for improvisation. Cultural scenarios are not simply downloaded verbatim into individuals. Individuals select the cultural scenarios that are most consistent with their own ideas and experiences of sexuality and incorporate them into their own menu of sexual acts. Interpersonal scripts help in the production of behavior—overt, observable events that occur in the interaction of social actors in the real world. Because interpersonal scripts are behavioral scripts, this is the level that is usually examined in much of the sexuality research. There tends to be little reference to cultural scenarios or intrapsychic scripts.

Intrapsychic scripting is the compilation of events, persons, and possibilities that cause sexual excitement for the individual, whether or not it is socially sanctioned. These scripts provide the individual motivation to act in a sexual manner, at the same time demarcating what is rejected sexually (Simon & Gagnon, 1987). Intrapsychic scripts form a part of sexual identity (e.g., "I like women, therefore I'm straight") and are part of the cognitive and affective frameworks that form our sexual selves.

In my own work, I characterize statements like "My mother told me that men should use condoms all the time" as cultural scenarios about safer sex; the actual words and techniques a person uses to get their partner to use a condom as interpersonal scripts; and the person's own ideas about condoms, "Condoms don't feel comfortable and I don't like them," as intrapsychic scripts.

The usefulness of this theory is that it may answer questions about the relationship between the collective and the individual. Sexual scripting can explain why individuals have similar ideas about sexuality within a particular racial/ethnic group, as well as why there is enormous variety in the sexual activities in which people actually engage. It also explains rather well the dynamic nature of sexuality, as individuals can, over time, create and implement new forms of sexuality. If these new forms are enjoyed by a number of people, then they can become new cultural scenarios employed by others. Unfortunately, although SST organizes ideas of sexuality well, and appears to have been reasonably applied to investigations of sexuality by racial/ethnic group in the research literature (Gilmore, DeLamater, & Wagstaff, 1996; Mahay et al., 2001), there is not yet a set of mechanisms for determining how individuals internalize scenarios or make choices of what scenarios to internalize (Weis, 1998).

CONCLUSION

Examining race or ethnicity is just one way of organizing and understanding sexuality. Sexuality is defined and experienced within a web of biological, psychological, and sociocultural factors. This web is dynamic, meaning that it changes in historical time, in ontogenetic (individual developmental) time, and as individuals become more experienced sexually within the context of their society and the sexual communities in which they live. Other important loci of identity (e.g., gender, social class, religion) also clearly impact on the construction of sexuality and in turn are also constructed by sexuality. This brief overview does not do justice to the rich literatures necessary to develop a complete snapshot of this moving target. But it is clear that reductionistic approaches that narrow and homogenize do not lead to a clear and veridical understanding of race, ethnicity, and sexuality. Interdisciplinary approaches with multiple methods of analysis should allow the field to move from a mere description of sexuality to a deeper appreciation of sexuality in context.

ACKNOWLEDGMENTS

This research was supported by center grant P50 MH43520 from the National Institute of Mental Health to the HIV Center for Clinical and Behavioral Studies (Anke A. Ehrhardt, Ph.D., Principal Investigator).

NOTES

1. Of course, the issue of agency calls into question whether any sexual relationship between slaves and their owners can be considered consensual in the face of this clearest of power differentials. How does one describe the choices faced by slaves such as Harriet Jacobs (1813–1897), who was forced to choose between her owner, a man who wished to make her his concubine, and another white man, whose sexual interest and fathering of her children would protect her from her owner's advances? This tactic did not work in the end. After the birth of her two children, Jacobs was forced to live in a crawlspace in her grandmother's home for seven years to hide from the advances of her owner. Jacobs's experiences were narrated in her autobiography, *Incidents in the Life of a Slave Girl* (1861/2000).

2. During the mid–nineteenth century, political deals made between Irish American ward leaders and white, Anglo Saxon elites for Irish votes led to increasing civil rights for Irish Americans and assimilation into white racial culture (Ignatiev, 1996).

3. I use the term "race" here because although the U.S. Census designated Hispanic/Latino as an ethnic category, the social treatment of Latinos in the United States suggests that Latinos are treated as if they are a different race (Haney-Lopez, 1997). Since race has little biological validity, the only currency that race holds is in its social effects (Graves, 2001). Concerns about intermarriage, passing, structural inequalities such as access to health care and housing, as well as the grouping of multiple national groups into a single category suggest that "Latino/a" acts as a race in all but name.

REFERENCES

Adams, F. S., & Sanders, B. (2003). *Alienable rights: The exclusion of African Americans in a white man's land, 1619–2000.* New York: HarperCollins.

Anderson, E. (1997). *Code of the street.* Chicago: University of Chicago Press.

Azibo, D. (1988). Understanding the proper and improper usage of the comparative research framework. *Journal of Black Psychology, 15,* 81–91.

Battle, J., & Lemelle, A. J. (2002). Gender differences in African American attitudes toward gay males. *Western Journal of Black Studies, 26,* 134–139.

Beattie, J. (1770/1997). A response to Hume. In E. C. Eze (Ed.), *Race and the Enlightenment: A reader* (pp. 34–37). Malden, MA: Blackwell.

Benet, A. E., & Melman, A. (1995). The epidemiology of erectile dysfunction. *Urologic Clinics of North America, 22,* 699–709.

Bergreen, L. (2004). *Over the edge of the world: Magellan's terrifying circumnavigation of the globe.* New York: HarperCollins.

Bernier, F. (1684/2000). A new division of the earth. In R. Bernasconi & T. L. Lott (Eds.), *The idea of race* (pp. 1–4). Indianapolis, IN: Hackett.

Bohan, J. S. (1993). Regarding gender: Essentialism, constructionism, and feminist psychology. *Psychology of Women Quarterly, 17,* 5–21.

Bonilla, L., & Porter, J. (1990). A comparison of Latino, black and non-Hispanic white attitudes toward homosexuality. *Hispanic Journal of Behavioral Sciences, 12,* 437–452.

Bowser, B. P. (1994). African-American male sexuality. In A. S. Rossi (Ed.), *Sexuality across the life course* (pp. 127–150). Chicago: University of Chicago Press.

Boykin, K. (2005). *Beyond the down low: Sex, lies and denial in black America.* New York: Carroll & Graf.

Braun, L. (2002). Race, ethnicity, and health: Can genetics explain disparities? *Perspectives in Biology and Medicine, 45,* 159–174.

Brooks-Gunn, J. (1987). The impact of puberty and sexual activity upon the health and education of adolescent girls and boys. *Peabody Journal of Education, 64,* 88–112.

Burdette, A. M., Ellison, C. G., & Hill, T. D. (2005). Conservative Protestantism and tolerance toward homosexuals: An examination of potential mechanisms. *Sociological Inquiry, 75,* 177–196.

Carballo-Dieguez, A., Dolezal, C., Nieves-Rosa, L., & Diaz, F. (2000). Similarities in the sexual behavior and HIV risk factors of Colombian, Dominican, Mexican, and Puerto Rican MSM residing in New York City. *Journal of Psychology and Human Sexuality, 12,* 49–67.

Carrasco, G. P. (1998). Latinos in the United States: Invitation and exile. In R. Delgado & J. Stepancic (Eds.), *The Latino/a condition: A critical reader* (pp. 77–85). New York: New York University Press.

Carrier, J. M. (1976). Cultural factors affecting urban Mexican male homosexual behavior. *Archives of Sexual Behavior, 5,* 103–124.

Central Intelligence Agency. (2005a). *World factbook—Argentina.* Retrieved March 20, 2005, from www.cia.gov/cia/publications/factbook/geos/ar.html# People

Central Intelligence Agency. (2005b). *World factbook—Dominican Republic.* Retrieved March 20, 2005, from www.cia.gov/cia/publications/factbook/ geos/dr.html

Cheng, C. (1999). Marginalized masculinities and hegemonic masculinity: An introduction. *Journal of Men's Studies, 7,* 295–315.

Collins, P. H. (2000). *Black feminist thought: Knowledge, consciousness and the politics of empowerment* (2nd ed.). New York: Routledge.

Collins, P. H. (2004). *Black sexual politics: African Americans, gender and the new racism.* New York: Routledge.

DeLamater, J., & Hyde, J. S. (1998). Essentialism vs. social constructionism in the study of human sexuality. *Journal of Sex Research, 35,* 10–18.

D'Emilio, J., & Freedman, E. B. (1997). *Intimate matters: A history of sexuality in America* (2nd ed.). Chicago: University of Chicago Press.

Díaz, R. M. (1998). *Latino gay men and HIV: Culture, sexuality and risk behavior.* New York: Routledge.

Díaz, R. M., Ayala, G., Bein, E., Henne, J., & Marin, B. V. (2001). The impact of homophobia, poverty, and racism on the mental health of gay and bisexual Latino men: Findings from 3 US cities. *American Journal of Public Health, 91,* 927–932.

Edwards, W. J. (1996). A sociological analysis of an in/visible minority group: Male adolescent homosexuals. *Youth and Society, 27,* 334–355.

Epstein, S. (1996). *Impure science: AIDS, activism, and the politics of knowledge.* Berkeley: University of California Press.

Ernst, F. A., Francis, R. A., Nevels, H., & Lemeh, C. A. (1991). Condemnation of homosexuality in the black community: A gender-specific phenomenon? *Archives of Sexual Behavior, 20,* 579–585.

Espin, O. M. (1987). Psychological impact of migration on Latinas. *Psychology of Women Quarterly, 11,* 489–503.

Espin, O. M. (1993). Issues of identity in the psychology of Latina lesbians. In L. D. Garnets & D. C. Kimmel (Eds.), *Psychological perspectives on lesbian and gay male experiences* (pp. 348–363). New York: Columbia University Press.

Feldman, H. A., Goldstein, L., Hatzichristou, D. G., Krane, R. J., & McKinlay, J. B. (1994). Impotence and its medical and psychosocial correlates: Results of the Massachusetts male aging study. *Journal of Urology, 151,* 54–61.

Fontes, L. A. (2001). The new view and Latina sexualities: Pero no soy una maquina. In E. Kashak & L. Tiefer (Eds.), *A new view of women's sexual problems* (pp. 33–38). New York: Haworth Press.

Foucault, M. (1978). *The history of sexuality: Part 1. An introduction.* New York: Pantheon Books.

Fredrickson, G. M. (1987). *The black image in the white mind: The debate on Afro-American character and destiny, 1817–1914.* Hanover, NH: Wesleyan University Press.

Gagnon, J. H., & Simon, W. (1973). *Sexual conduct: The social sources of human sexuality.* Chicago: Aldine.

Gilmore, S., DeLamater, J., & Wagstaff, D. (1996). Sexual decision making by inner city black adolescent males: A focus group study. *Journal of Sex Research, 33,* 363–371.

Goldberg, D. (1993). *Racist culture.* Cambridge, MA: Blackwell.

Graham, S. (1992). "Most of the subjects were white and middle class": Trends in published research on African Americans in selected APA journals, 1970–1989. *American Psychologist, 47,* 629–639.

Graves, J. L. (2001). *The emperor's new clothes: Biological theories of race at the millennium.* New Brunswick, NJ: Rutgers University Press.

Greene, B. (2000). African American lesbian and bisexual women. *Journal of Social Issues, 56,* 239–249.

Gutman, H. G. (1976). *The black family in slavery and freedom, 1750–1925*. New York: Pantheon Books.

Haney-Lopez, I. (1997). *Retaining race: LatCrit theory and Mexican American identity in* Hernandez v. Texas. Retrieved April 2, 2005, from personal.law.miami.edu/~fvaldes/latcrit/archives/harvard/haney.htm#N_1_

Henry, M. (2002). He is a "bad mother *$%§!#": Shaft and contemporary black masculinity. *Journal of Popular Film and Television, 30*, 114–119.

Herder, J. G. von (1800). *Outlines of a philosophy of the history of man*. London: Printed for J. Johnson by Luke Hansard.

Herek, G. M., & Capitanio, J. P. (1996). "Some of my best friends": Intergroup contact, concealable stigma, and heterosexuals' attitudes toward gay men and lesbians. *Personality and Social Psychology Bulletin, 22*, 412–424.

Herrnstein, R. J., & Murray, C. (1994). *The bell curve*. New York: Free Press.

Hirsch, J. S. (2003). *A courtship after marriage: Sexuality and love in Mexican transnational families*. Berkeley: University of California Press.

hooks, b. (2004). *We real cool: Black men and masculinity*. New York: Routledge.

Hughes, T. L., & Eliason, M. (2002). Substance use and abuse in lesbian, gay, bisexual and transgender populations. *Journal of Primary Prevention, 22*, 263–298.

Ignatiev, N. (1996). *How the Irish became white*. New York: Routledge.

Jacobs, H. A. (1861/2000). *Incidents in the life of a slave girl*. New York: Signet Books.

Kaiser Family Foundation. (2004). AIDS at 21: Media coverage of the HIV epidemic 1981–2002 (Publication # 7023). Menlo Park, CA: Author. Retrieved January 6, 2006 from www.kff.org/kaiserpolls/7023.cfm

Kant, I. (1764/1997). On national characteristics. In E. C. Eze (Ed.), *Race and the Enlightenment: A reader* (pp. 48–57). Malden, MA: Blackwell.

Kant, I. (1775/1997). On the different races of man. In E. C. Eze (Ed.), *Race and the Enlightenment: A reader* (pp. 38–48). Malden, MA: Blackwell.

Kasinitz, P., Battle, J., & Miyares, I. (2001). Fade to black? The children of West Indian immigrants in southern Florida. In R. G. Rumbaut & A. Portes (Eds.), *Ethnicities: Children of immigrants in America* (pp. 267–300). Berkeley: University of California Press.

Kinsey, A. C., Pomeroy, W. B., & Martin, C. E. (1948). *Sexual behavior in the human male*. Philadelphia: Saunders.

Kitwana, B. (2003). *The hip hop generation: Young blacks and the crisis in African American culture*. New York: Perseus Books Group.

Laumann, E. O., Gagnon, J. H., Michael, R. T., & Michaels, S. (1994). *The social organization of sexuality: Sexual practices in the United States*. Chicago: University of Chicago Press.

Laumann, E. O., Paik, A., & Rosen, R. C. (2001). Sexual dysfunction in the United States: Prevalence and predictors. In E. O. Laumann & R. T. Michael (Eds.), *Sex, love and health in America: Private choices and public policies* (pp. 352–376). Chicago: University of Chicago Press.

Lewis, L. J. (2004). Examining sexual health discourses in a racial/ethnic context. *Archives of Sexual Behavior, 33*, 223–234.

Lewis, L. J., & Kertzner, R. M. (2003). Toward improved interpretation and theory building of African American male sexualities. *Journal of Sex Research, 40,* 383–395.

Lewontin, R. C. (1972). The apportionment of human diversity. *Evolutionary Biology, 6,* 381–398.

Locke, J. (1689/1931). *Essay concerning human understanding.* Cambridge, MA: Harvard University Press.

London, J. P., Pieterse, N., & Parekh, B. (Eds.). (1995). *The decolonization of imagination: Culture, knowledge, and power.* Atlantic Highlands, NJ: Zed Books.

Luker, K. (1996). *Dubious conceptions: The politics of teenage pregnancy.* Cambridge, MA: Harvard University Press.

Mahay, J., Laumann, E. O., & Michaels, S. (2001). Race, gender and class in sexual scripts. In E. O. Laumann & R. T. Michael (Eds.), *Sex, love and health in America: Private choices and public policies* (pp. 197–238). Chicago: University of Chicago Press.

Malebranche, D. J., Peterson, J. L., Fullilove, R. E., & Stackhouse, R. W. (2004). Race and sexual identity: Perceptions about medical culture and healthcare among black men who have sex with men. *Journal of the National Medical Association, 96,* 97–107.

Martin, J. A., Hamilton, B. E., Ventura, S. J., Menacker, F., Park, M. M., & Sutton, P. D. (2002). Births: Final data for 2001. *National Vital Statistics Reports, 51*(2). Retrieved May 13, 2005, from www.cdc.gov/nchs/data/nvsr/nvsr52/nvsr52_10.pdf

Mendelson, M. (2000). Saint Augustine. In *The Stanford Encyclopedia of Philosophy* (Winter 2000 Edition). Retrieved March 22, 2005, from www.plato.stanford.edu/archives/win2000/entries/Augustine

Messerschmidt, J. W. (1998). Men victimizing men: The case of lynching, 1865–1900. In L. H. Bowker (Ed.), *Masculinities and violence* (pp. 125–151). Thousand Oaks, CA: Sage.

Meyer, I. H. (2003). Prejudice, social stress, and mental health in lesbian, gay, and bisexual populations: Conceptual issues and research evidence. *Psychological Bulletin, 129,* 674–697.

Montagu, A. (1942/1997). *Man's most dangerous myth: The fallacy of race* (6th ed.). Walnut Creek, CA: AltaMira Press.

Morning, A. J. (2004). *The nature of race: Teaching and learning about human difference.* Unpublished doctoral dissertation, Princeton University, NJ.

Nagel, J. (2003). *Race, ethnicity, and sexuality: Intimate intersection, forbidden frontiers.* New York: Oxford University Press.

Omi, M., & Winant, H. (1994). *Racial formation in the United States: From the 1960s to the 1990s.* New York: Routledge.

Pace v. State (of Alabama). 106 U.S. 583 (1883). Retrieved January 6, 2006 from http://laws.findlaw.com/us/106/583.html

Pagnini, D. L., & Morgan, S. P. (1990). Intermarriage and social distance among U.S. immigrants at the turn of the century. *American Journal of Sociology, 96,* 405–432.

Painter, N. I. (1991, November 11). Who was lynched? *Nation, 253*(16), 577.

Parrinder, G. (1987). A theological approach. In J. H. Geer & W. T. O'Donohue (Eds.), *Theories of human sexuality* (pp. 21–48). New York: Plenum Press.

Peterson, J. L. (1992). Black men and their same-sex desires and behaviors. In G. H. Herdt (Ed.), *Gay culture in America: Essays from the field* (pp. 147–164). Boston: Beacon Press.

Powell, K. (1998). *Keepin' it real: Post-MTV reflections on race, sex, and politics.* New York: Random House.

Qian, Z. (1999). Who intermarries? Education, nativity, region, and interracial marriage, 1980 and 1990. *Journal of Comparative Family Studies, 30*, 579–597.

Rivera, R. (2002). Hip hop and New York Puerto Ricans. In M. Habell-Palan & M. Romero (Eds.), *Latino/a popular culture* (pp. 127–143). New York: New York University Press.

Rosario, M., Schrimshaw, E. W., & Hunter, J. (2004). Ethnic/racial differences in the coming-out process of lesbian, gay, and bisexual youths: A comparison of sexual identity development over time. *Cultural Diversity & Ethnic Minority Psychology, 10*, 215–228.

Rose, T. (2003). Longing to tell: Black women talk about sexuality and intimacy. New York: Picador.

Seal, D. W., Wagner-Raphael, L. I., & Ehrhardt, A. A. (2000). Sex, intimacy, and HIV: An ethnographic study of a Puerto Rican social group in New York City. *Journal of Psychology and Human Sexuality, 11*, 51–92.

Siegel, K., & Epstein, J. A. (1996). Ethnic-racial differences in psychological stress related to gay lifestyle among HIV-positive men. *Psychological Reports, 79*, 303–312.

Simon, W. (1996). *Postmodern sexualities.* New York: Routledge.

Simon, W., & Gagnon, J. H. (1987). A sexual scripts approach. In J. H. Geer & W. T. O'Donohue (Eds.), *Theories of human sexuality* (pp. 363–383). New York: Plenum Press.

Smith, E. A., & Udry, J. R. (1985). Coital and non-coital sexual behaviors of white and black adolescents. *American Journal of Public Health, 75*, 1200–1203.

Speigler, M. (1996). Marketing street culture: Bringing hip-hop style to the mainstream. *American Demographics, 18*(11), 29–34.

Stevenson, M. R. (2002). Conceptualizing diversity in sexuality research. In M. W. Wiederman & B. E. Whitley, Jr. (Eds.), *Handbook for conducting research on human sexuality* (pp. 455–478). Mahwah, NJ: Lawrence Erlbaum.

Takaki, R. (1993). *A different mirror: A history of multicultural America.* Boston: Little, Brown.

Tiefer, L. (2004). *Sex is not a natural act and other essays* (2nd ed.). Boulder, CO: Westview Press.

Upchurch, D. M., Levy-Storms, L., Sucoff, C. A., & Aneshensel, C. S. (1998). Gender and ethnic differences in the timing of first sexual intercourse. *Family Planning Perspectives, 30*, 121–127.

Walker, A. (1998). Legislating virtue: How segregationists disguised racial discrimination as moral reform following *Brown v. Board of Education* [Electronic version]. *Duke Law Journal, 47*, 399–424.

Waters, M. C. (1999). *Black identities: West Indian immigrant dreams and American realities.* Cambridge, MA: Harvard University Press.

Weeks, J. (1986). *Sexuality.* New York: Routledge.

Weis, D. L. (1998). Conclusion: The state of sexual theory. *Journal of Sex Research, 35*, 100–114.

Welter, B. (1978). The cult of true womanhood: 1820–1860. In M. Gordon (Ed.), *The American family in socio-historical perspective* (pp. 372–392). New York: St. Martin's Press.

West, C., & Zimmerman, D. (1987). Doing gender. *Gender & Society, 1*, 125–151.

Working Group on a New View of Women's Sexual Problems. (2001). A new view of women's sexual problems. In E. Kashak & L. Tiefer (Eds.), *A new view of women's sexual problems* (pp. 1–8). New York: Haworth Press.

Wu, T., Mendola, P., & Buck, G. M. (2002). Ethnic differences in the presence of secondary sexual characteristics and menarche among US girls. *Pediatrics, 110*, 752–757.

Wyatt, G. E. (1997). *Stolen women: Reclaiming our sexuality, taking back our lives.* New York: Wiley.

Zea, M. C., Reisen, C. A., & Díaz, R. M. (2003). Methodological issues in research on sexual behavior with Latino gay and bisexual men. *American Journal of Community Psychology, 31*, 281–291.

11

Commercial Sex: Pornography

Dan Brown ◆

Human sexuality has perhaps stimulated more attention than any other aspect of human behavior (Kinsey, Pomeroy, & Martin, 1948). From ancient times, artistic representations of human sexuality have portrayed such images as exaggerated sexual organs (Webb, 1982) and explicit participation in sexual intercourse (Brewer, 1982). Perhaps the height of commercialized use of sexual images in the ancient world occurred by 800 B.C.E. with the works of the Greeks and the Romans (Lane, 2001). Pornography, derived from *pornographos*, the Greek term for writing about prostitutes (Hyde, 1964), is at least as old as prostitution itself (Zillmann & Bryant, 1989). Walter Kendrick (1987) traces the term *pornography* through successive generations of dictionaries, finding that it did not appear in Samuel Johnson's work of 1755 and concluding that the term was born sometime between 1755 and 1857, when the word appeared in a medical dictionary. However, scientific and legal consensus about a definition of pornography remains elusive. A 1986 federal government commission charged with studying pornography defined the term as "material predominantly sexually specific and intended for the purpose of sexual arousal" (U.S. Department of Justice, 1986, pp. 228–229). A more complete discussion than that contained here of definitional factors related to pornography is available elsewhere (Brown, 2003).

James V. P. Check and Ted H. Guloien (1989) describe the distinctions between erotica, degrading pornography, and violent pornography. Dolf Zillmann (1984b), distinguishing pornography from erotica by the absence of coercion and violence, explains the typical themes of pornography as including fellatio, cunnilingus, and sexual intercourse in a multitude of positions, especially anal intercourse, in most instances involving more than two people and frequently portraying females as being overly attentive to serving male sexual appetites. Some authors (e.g., Brownmiller, 1975) suggest that all erotica are degrading, especially to women.

William A. Fisher and Azy Barak (1989) group pornography into three types. *Degrading pornography* is sexually explicit content that debases or dehumanizes people, perhaps reducing inhibitions against treating them with cruelty. *Violent pornography* refers to "material that prescribes the normativeness and utility of sexual violence, usually directed against women" (p. 290). *Erotica*, in their scheme, refers to sexual content that is nondegrading and nonviolent. They explain that systematically categorizing sexually explicit content into these three categories remains beyond the reach of current research (Fisher & Barak, 2001).

Court action against displays of pornography generally requires demonstration that the work in question is *obscene*, as defined by the U.S. Supreme Court in *Miller v. California* (1973). The *Miller* decision holds that a finding of obscenity requires that an average person, applying contemporary community standards to evaluate the whole work, would find it appealing to the prurient interest by portraying in a patently offensive way some sexual behavior that is proscribed by a state law. The work must contain no serious literary, artistic, or scientific value. Only child pornography is automatically obscene in the United States, and prosecutions against persons for activity regarding other forms of pornography require that a court rule the material to be obscene.

SCOPE OF PORNOGRAPHY USE

Pornography in the United States grew from a relatively hidden underground business in the 1950s to a publicly available commercial juggernaut in the twenty-first century. Revenues earned by the pornography industry exceed gate receipts of all American sporting and musical events combined (Lane, 2001). Reflecting growing public concern about the availability of pornography, two federal commissions reported on pornography (U.S. Commission on Obscenity and Pornography, 1970; U.S. Department of Justice, 1986).

Eric Schlosser (1997) summarizes the pornography industry, noting its start after World War II and transformation from a minor operation to an important phenomenon. He cites sociologist Charles Winick as observing that sexuality in America changed more in the last twenty years than in the previous 200 years, partly because the ease of in-home access to pornography changed the under-the-counter pornography culture.

The first commission on pornography (U.S. Commission on Obscenity and Pornography, 1970) found parts of the pornography industry to be somewhat "chaotic" (p. 7), rather than well organized and centralized. Richard Morais (1999) recalls that *Forbes* magazine reported in the 1970s about pornography as a business of organized crime that operated as a largely underground cash enterprise. He observes that the Supreme Court's *Miller* decision, applying the First Amendment protection of free speech for pornography, allowed pornography to be sold openly as a legal product.

Schlosser found that about 100 hard-core pornographic films were produced in 1978. Subsequently, Morais reports, legal pornography revenues reached $56 billion worldwide by 1998, and he lists several large multinational companies offering pornographic products and enjoying listing on major stock exchanges. Businesses, such as Castle Superstores, openly sell pornographic and sex-related products that once were hidden from public view.

Scope of Print Pornography

Only 21 percent of the mass-market book industry was deemed by the 1970 Commission on Pornography as falling within its mission. That figure included paperback books and book club books. The commission found the market strengthening for adults-only paperback books, for which "it is probably not possible to exceed the candor, graphic descriptions of sexual activity, and use of vulgar language" (p. 15).

Among best-selling paperback books that sold between January 1969 and July 1970, the commission identified eighteen sexually oriented titles that remained on the list for at least one month. During 1969, 40 percent of the top twenty hardcover fiction books qualified as sexually oriented, and three of the top four nonfiction titles related to sex. The $179 million category of adult trade books made up only 6.8 percent of the $2.6 billion book industry at the time of the commission's report.

Frederick Lane (2001), writing about the entrepreneurs of pornography, lists several magazines that emerged as entertainment for the troops in the World War II era. By the time of the 1970 commission report, a variety of magazines could be described as sexually oriented, but the commission struggled with criteria to define whether particular publications should be so identified. The commission's final report discussed such categories as "romance" and "barbershop" magazines as possibly pornographic, but it identified a category of magazines, "men's sophisticates" (p. 14), as having the greatest degree of sexual orientation among the mass-market magazines. These publications specialized in nude females in modeling poses. About 41 million such magazines sold in 1969, earning about $31 million or about 1.2 percent of the mass-market periodical industry sales.

Perhaps the best-known illustration of pornography as commercial success story is Hugh Hefner's empire built around *Playboy* magazine, a publication treated as outside the other groups of sexually oriented magazines by the 1970 commission. *Playboy* began on a shoestring in 1953, printing 175,000 copies in its first year and 400,000 in its second, and selling 5.5 million copies per month in 1969 (Lane, 2001).

Scope of Film and Video Pornography

Describing the pornographic films of the era, the 1970 Commission on Pornography included a category of "skin flicks" (U.S. Commission on Obscenity and Pornography, 1970, p. 9) with low production costs and emphasis on sexually arousing content. Such films, called *exploitation films*, received little advertising, were little known among the public, and tended to play in a limited number of theaters. However, the commission noted that the distinctions between these films and major releases were beginning to blur by the late 1960s, with sexual themes and nudity becoming more common in mainstream films.

Schlosser (1997) described a major assault on the industry after the report of the Attorney General's Commission on Pornography in 1986. Ironically, that effort occurred when the pornography industry was enjoying unprecedented growth. William A. Linsley (1989) cites 165,000 people involved in the commercial activity surrounding delivering pornography to the public— monthly sales of 20 million pornographic magazines, weekly ticket sales of 2 million to X-rated movies, annual box office receipts of $500 million for the films, and 10–15 percent of the videotape market.

In 1990, 1,275 new hard-core films entered the American market (Morais, 1999). Between 1991 and 1996, the production of new hard-core pornographic videos grew by 500 percent to almost 8,000 new productions in 1996 (Schlosser, 1997). In 1998, 8,948 new hard-core video productions appeared for public consumption (Morais).

Pamela Paul (2004) reports annual production of 11,000 pornographic films in 2003, dwarfing the approximately 400 motion pictures produced by all the major Hollywood motion picture studios combined. Schlosser (1997) cites data from *Adult Video News* as showing that pornographic video rentals in the United States grew from 75 million in 1985 to 490 million in 1992, an increase of 656 percent. Reflecting the success of the pornography industry, that monthly pornography trade publication reaches nearly 300 pages and is filled with advertising (Morais, 1999).

By 1996, 665 million pornographic video rentals occurred, representing another 35.7 percent increase. Paul (2004) found that by 2003, more than 800 million rental pornographic videos and DVDs were seen by Americans annually, and 20 percent of all video rentals were pornographic. In-home orders in 1996 for pornographic pay-per-view films topped $150 million, and guest orders in hotels for pornographic films reached about $175 million in the United States.

Schlosser (1997) reports that 1996 American spending on sexually explicit entertainment exceeded $8 billion, similar to the $8.3 billion they spent on purchasing all sorts of books and maps during that year. Pornography spending in 1996 exceeded the $6.3 billion spent by Americans in 1996 at motion-picture box offices and the $6.4 billion that they spent attending all spectator sporting events (U.S. Bureau of the Census, 1998). Seidman (2003) cited reports by Egan (2000), Laslow (1999), and Rich (2001) that yearly sales of pornographic materials surpassed $10 billion, more than half of which went for videos and films.

The focus of pornography on home consumption also brought new business entities into the industry that previously had nothing to do with selling sex (Schlosser, 1997). Major corporations in industries such as tele-phone, cable television, hotel, and motel chains provide pornography for fees. Because pornography consumers no longer need adult theaters, many of them folded. Los Angeles adult theaters dwindled to about six by 1997, after once exceeding thirty. Similarly, adult bookstores declined and began showing videos on-site.

Nonchain video stores often turn to pornography to compete with chains. Schlosser (1997) cites Paul Fishbein of *Adult Video News* as reporting that 25,000 American video stores, almost twenty times the number of adult bookstores, offered hard-core pornography in the mid-1990s.

Scope of Computer Pornography

Computers offer options in the delivery of pornography. Subscription services provide channels for generally available content, such as bulletin boards and conferencing arrangements, and confidential content delivered to individual accounts. Additional revenues flow from sales of sexual devices, other forms of pornography, and advertising by sexually oriented businesses.

In the early 1990s, access to computer bulletin boards via telephone modems often involved charges for the time connected, as well as fee for receiving images. Despite slow modems and expensive services, one porno-graphic bulletin board service earned $3.2 million in 1993 (Lane, 2001).

With peer-to-peer computer file exchange software, users can trade files with people anywhere in the world. However, this vehicle accounted for less than 1 percent of the child pornography on the Internet after 1998 (Sub-committee on Commerce, Trade, and Consumer Protection, 2004).

Marty Rimm (1995) conducted the first systematic research on pornog-raphy over the Internet in 1994, finding a wealth of pornographic imagery and text easily available to consumers. Researchers identified Internet pornography users in all fifty states, most of Canada, forty different countries, and other territories worldwide. Among sampled Usenet newsgroups, 83.5 percent of all materials posted within one week to the sample group contained pornography. Among all the more than 100,000 items posted to the top forty Usenet groups within one month, 20.4 percent were pornographic. About 9 million people visited the five most popular sexually explicit Web sites in April 1998, representing about 15 percent of the total number of Web users in that year (Cooper, Scherer, Boies, & Gordon, 1999).

Small hobbyists were not the only people exchanging pornography on the Internet. Print pornography peddlers like *Playboy*, *Penthouse*, and *Hustler* host some of the most popular online sites. The *Playboy* Web site opened in 1994, offering free previews of monthly magazines. The site received 4.3 million visits in October 1997 and generated revenues of $2.5 million in one quarter during 1999 (Lane, 2001).

Morais (1999) cited Forrester Research reports of Internet pornography revenues reaching about $1 billion annually, including such enterprises as the Internet Video Network, a channel reaping $7 million each year from such content as strip shows. Lane (2001) cites estimates by industry analysts of Internet pornography revenues of nearly $2 billion annually by the fall of 1999. According to Paul (2004), by July 2003, the Internet contained 260 million pages of pornography, up by 1800 percent from 1998. She reports that pornography accounted for 7 percent of Web pages indexed by Google, an Internet search engine. That proportion represents 231 million pages of Web pornography.

The federal government's General Accounting Office (GAO) reported that 400,000 commercial pornographic Web sites operated in 2003, and the number grew to 1.6 million by the issuance of a report by a congressional subcommittee in May 2004 (Subcommittee on Commerce, Trade, and Consumer Protection, 2004). The report notes that 34 million people visit pornographic Web sites each month, about 25 percent of the monthly Web traffic.

Rosen (2004) cites data from the Internet Filter Review showing that pornography on the Internet makes up $2.5 billion of the worldwide $57 billion business of pornography. This Internet contribution includes, according to the review, 4.2 million pornographic Web sites that are visited annually by 72 million people, including 40 million Americans. About 25 percent of all searches conducted daily on the Internet seek pornographic materials (Rosen), and sex is the most frequently sought topic on the Internet (Cooper et al., 1999).

Internet pornography has become so widespread that people confront it without meaning to. A national survey (Finkelhor, Mitchell, & Wolak, 2000) of 1,501 children of ages 10–17 who regularly use the Internet found that 25 percent of the respondents had found on the Internet, within the previous year, unwanted images of naked people or of people having sex. Among these incidents, 94 percent involved naked people, 38 percent referred to people engaged in sex, and 8 percent portrayed violence in addition to the nudity or sex.

A congressional report (Subcommittee on Commerce, Trade, and Consumer Protection, 2004) found that Internet pornography peddlers frequently use false domain names and fake advertising to entice people to their Web sites when they are not seeking sexual content. Searches conducted by the GAO found pornography in 56 percent of searches using terms that are popular in finding children's materials online. Pornographers intentionally lure children to their Web sites by using nonsexual terms, such as *Cinderella*, enticing visitors to retrieve files on peer-to-peer exchanges that allow Internet users to trade files of various types, including music.

Scope of Telephone Pornography

In the 1980s, the pornography industry found new ways of reaching audiences, such as Dial-A-Porn telephone (Brown & Bryant, 1989). Telephone companies in the 1920s offered dial-up services with such content as weather reports. The Federal Communications Commission ruled in the early 1980s that the telephone companies were responsible only for transmission and billing, while information providers using telephone services were responsible for content. Dial-A-Porn began in 1983 after winning a 1982 New York lottery that determined what dial-up services could operate in that state, expanding the business by leasing telephone lines from other lottery winners. The services offered credit-card billing for calls to paid performers and monthly billing of calls to designated prefixes, such as 976.

Typical content of Dial-A-Porn calls included verbal descriptions of sexual activities, sometimes as imaginary participation, and one service logged 180 million calls during the year ending February 28, 1984. During that year, such calls accounted for 44 percent of the calls to 976 exchanges operated by Pacific Bell (U.S. Department of Justice, 1986). By 1996, Americans spent more than $750 million annually in making such calls (Schlosser, 1997).

Lane (2001) provides details of how the phone sex business operates, calling it an extremely simple business to enter and operate to earn impressive revenues. A range of people, from small business entrepreneurs to individuals in foreign countries, operate profitable phone sex enterprises, and large American corporations such as AT&T earn hundreds of millions of dollars each year from the combination of phone sex and Internet access.

Examples of Video Game Pornography

Atari introduced the home video game *Pong* to the public in 1975 and enjoyed popularity in American homes by the early 1980s (Lane, 2001). In 1982, AMI introduced adult games for the Atari player, selling 750,000 cartridges by the end of that year. Those games connected with a television set, and the graphics were poor. An alternative emerged for the early versions of personal computers as text-based games.

Adult games, such as *Softporn* in 1984, engaged players in seeking to win by engaging in sex acts with characters in the games. Similar games that included sexually oriented text, but not sexually explicit visuals, sold $20–25 million during 1991 alone. Omitting explicit visuals permitted selling the games through well-known retail outlets.

In 1996, *Tomb Raider* was released for game consoles, becoming popular and spawning spin-offs in various media, including motion pictures. The game sold 2.3 million copies in 1998. Although *Tomb Raider* was not sexually explicit, amateur Web sites began offering chances to see the buxom lead character, Lara Croft, in the nude and play games with Croft appearing naked. None of the explicit imitators sold as well as *Tomb Raider* because of their inability to market through mainstream retail outlets (Lane, 2001). Clearly, video game pornography justifies increased research attention because of popularity and the child audience.

PUBLIC OPINION POLLS ABOUT PORNOGRAPHY

Public opinion surveys in the United States from the 1930s through the 1980s show that pornography use was common (Bryant & Brown, 1989). The 1985 Attorney General's Commission on Pornography contended that such surveys show that the public was becoming more tolerant of pornography (U.S. Department of Justice, 1986), although some disagreed (e.g., Smith, 1987).

The survey of perhaps the largest number of people was conducted by the Institute for Sex Research, including more than 10,000 people between 1938 and 1963 (Gebhard & Johnson, 1979). Because of the abundance of young, white-collar respondents, the survey results do not necessarily represent the entire population. Asked whether they had ever seen a film containing sexual intercourse or homosexuality, 16.1 percent of white males who had attended college said they had. So did 29 percent of white males who never attended college, and 17.3 percent of black males. Such films had been seen by 2 percent of females who had attended college, 7.2 percent of females who never attended college, and 4.5 percent of black females.

The 1970 Commission on Pornography found that 33 percent of females and 54 percent of males had seen pornography by age 17, up from 10 percent and 20 percent respectively at age 12 (Abelson, Cohen, Heaton, & Suder, 1971). Another such study reported that 19 percent of males and 9 percent of females reported having seen explicit sexual material by age 12, 54 percent and 33 percent respectively at age 17, and 74 percent and 51 percent respectively by age 20 (Wilson & Abelson, 1973).

A 1978 Gallup poll covering 1972–1977 reported that 52 percent of respondents believed that sexually explicit books, magazines, and films contain useful sexual information. Respondents who found explicit content to have harmful consequences seemed to outnumber those who saw pornography as positive. For example, 67 percent agreed with a statement that pornography leads to a decline in public morals, 76 percent agreed with a statement that it causes a loss of respect for women, and 73 percent agreed with a statement that it instigates rape or sexual violence in some people. Only 34 percent agreed that pornography safely assists people with sexual dysfunction, and 47 percent agreed with a statement that it improves the sex lives of some couples.

A Gallup poll of more than 1,000 adults conducted in 1985 for *Newsweek* magazine reported that 37 percent of the respondents reported having purchased a magazine like *Playboy* (Press et al., 1985). *Hustler* magazine purchases were reported by 13 percent of the respondents, 7 percent reported attending an X-rated movie within the previous year, and 9 percent reported having purchased or rented such a videotape or film within the previous year.

Bryant and Brown cited a summary by T. W. Smith (1987) of polling data showing reported the proportion of respondents who had seen sexually explicit films within the previous year, covering 1973–1986. Fluctuating as low as 15 percent in 1978, the data reflected a steady upward trend from 1978 through 1986 to 24.8 percent.

Testifying before the Attorney General's Commission on Pornography, Jennings Bryant (1985b) reported data from telephone surveys showing a much higher rate of using pornography. From three groups of respondents, each including 100 males and 100 females, he found that 94.3 percent of the total 600 respondents had seen sexually explicit R-rated films, with the mean at 14.4 films per person. The groups included students aged 13–15 and 16–18 and adults aged 19–39. Nearly everyone in the latter two groups reported having looked at or read *Playboy* or *Playgirl* or similar magazines, with adult males reporting experience with an average of 26.5 issues. The average age of first experience with such materials among all three groups was 11 years for males and 12 years for females.

When the survey addressed consumption of hard-core pornography depicting people engaged in sexual activity, the average age among all respondents was 13.5 years, and 69 percent of both males and females reported having seen X-rated films. Among the members of the group aged 13–15, 92 percent reported having seen such a film, whereas the adults reported first exposure at an average age of about 18 years. Among the16- to 18-year-olds, 84 percent reported having seen an X-rated film. Among all respondents, 70 percent of females and 55 percent of males reported having been introduced by someone else to hard-core films.

Bryant compared these figures with those obtained from students enrolled in college classes, which provided nearly 100 percent participation in the surveys, finding about half of the usage reported in telephone surveys. He acknowledged that people willing to participate in a telephone survey about their experience with pornography might be more liberal in their sexual attitudes than those who would not consent, calling for more research to clarify the differences in findings from the different surveys.

Alan Sears (1989) cited a July 1986 *Time* magazine poll showing that 72 percent of the surveyed members of the public wanted a government crackdown on pornography, and 92 percent favored such action against child pornography. He also cited a 1986 Gallup poll reporting that 73 percent of the respondents would ban certain types of extremely explicit pornography.

Paul (2004) contends that pornography on the Internet fostered a huge increase in pornography consumption and promoted greater interest in hardcore pornography over milder forms. Despite the warnings such as those described in this chapter from social scientists, the majority of respondents to surveys about online sexuality find little harm in online pornography. Paul cites a survey of 7,037 adults by the San Jose Marital and Sexuality Center as reporting that two-thirds of the users of online sexually explicit Web sites find no impact on their sex with partners. However, 75 percent of the respondents indicated that they masturbated while looking at these sites.

Ethan Seidman (2003) cited Goodson, McCormick, and Evans (2000) in reporting that 43.5 percent of a sample of Texas college students had seen sexually explicit Internet content at least once. Seidman surveyed 102 male and 208 female college students, finding greater usage of pornography than previously published reports. He found that both men (80 percent) and women (59.2 percent) actively sought pornography within a year of the survey. More than a third of the men reported using pornography at least once each week, but only 1.5 percent of the women reported such frequent use. Among women, 43.1 percent reported never having seen pornography within the previous year, but only 20.8 percent of the men had not. Men typically use pornography alone, often masturbating at the same time. Women more often use pornography with a partner and without masturbating. Seidman reported that this pornography use was *not* predicted by lack of availability of sexual partners, elevated anxiety, feelings of ineptitude in romance, feelings of depression, or interpersonal difficulties.

A national survey (Rideout, 2004) of 1,001 parents of children aged 2–17 conducted by the Kaiser Foundation in July and August 2004 addressed parental concerns about the media. "Inappropriate" content seen by children viewing entertainment media was described by 63 percent of parents as making them "very concerned" (p. 5). Television was of greatest concern to 34 percent of the respondents, but 20 percent named all media equally, 16 percent named the Internet, 10 percent named movies, 5 percent named video games. Among the types of media content prompting parental concern, excessive sexual content received the most emphasis, being named by 60 percent of the responding parents. Relating to the beliefs that sexual and violent content on TV affects behavior of children, 53 percent of the parents agreed that behavior is affected "a lot" (p. 7).

Clear conclusions about pornography use in America seem inappropriate in light of the wide variance in definitions, wording of survey questions, composition of survey samples, and response biases of respondents (Bryant & Brown, 1989). However, most Americans have apparently seen pornography by the time they reach high school. Few people report no exposure, and most report being introduced to pornography by peers. Stereotypical categorization of pornography users as loners with poor social skills seems inaccurate, with users typically coming from all walks of life. Although most research reports that differences in use of pornography exist between males and females, some authors (e.g., Burt, 1976; Thomas, 1986) contend that such differences stem from the type of pornographic content offered in the marketplace.

CONTENT OF PORNOGRAPHY

Print Media

Through the 1950s, open display of pornography was rare in the United States, with such printed materials being relegated to back rooms of places that appeared from the street to be ordinary newsstands (Brown & Bryant, 1989). With increasing public display of printed pornography by the 1960s, the materials used for pornographic magazines improved through the use of four-color printing on glossy paper. The predominant sexually explicit magazine content portrayed simulated sex acts with no exposed genitals because such display would have likely opened the publishers to prosecution for distributing obscenity (U.S. Department of Justice, 1986).

By the mid-1960s, nudist magazines dared to display genitalia, and soon after, other magazines began to feature attractive models engaged, not only in nudist camp activities, but also in sexual behavior. By the late 1960s, magazines featured photographs of both male and female genitalia, usually portraying a single individual but sometimes more than one person. Although sadomasochism emerged in publications during the period, portraying less explicit sexual photographs, such content was not a major factor in the commercial marketing of pornography.

Textual descriptions of sexual matters became generally considered to be immune from prosecution for obscenity law violations after U.S. Supreme Court decisions liberalized views about published obscenity by the late 1960s. The U.S. Commission on Obscenity and Pornography reported that many textual works published by the early 1970s presented extremely graphic descriptions of sexual matters. Most of these books were "designed to appeal to heterosexual males, but about 10% portrayed material attractive to male homosexuals, about 5% focused on fare catering to fetish enthusiasts, and almost none were intended to appeal to females" (Brown & Bryant, 1989, p. 6).

Romance magazines also seemed to promise in photographs more sexual emphasis than the text delivered in the 1960s. An analysis of eight different romance magazines of the era revealed frequent kissing and coitus, but rarely found homosexual activity or oral-genital contact. The practice of promiscuity in the stories resulted in severe consequences (Sonenschein, 1970).

The 1970 Commission on Pornography and Obscenity identified adult paperback novels as containing a considerable amount of pornography (Massey, 1970). One of the largest examinations of these books reported increasing frequency of paperback sexual content from 1967 through 1970, followed by a leveling off from 1970 through 1974. This degree of emphasis represented three to fifteen times the proportion of space devoted to sexual content in such mass-market sex novels as *Fear of Flying*. This paperback sexuality tended toward fulfillment of male sexual fantasy, with a recurring theme of female beauty rescued from sexual resistance by a virulent male (Smith, 1976).

Crime magazines in the 1980s frequently relied on sexually oriented cover images and sexual violence to attract readers. About twenty publications in this category attracted a circulation of nearly 1 million in 1980, despite the tendency of the magazine stories to fall short of the amount of emphasis on explicit sex (Dietz, Harry, & Hazelwood, 1986).

By 1986, the Attorney General's Commission on Pornography reported more than 2,300 magazine titles available for sale in sixteen pornography outlets found in six eastern American cities (U.S. Department of Justice, 1986). Few of these magazines received the attention of systematic research. However, an analysis of pictures and cartoons in all *Playboy* and *Penthouse* issues from 1973 to 1977 found increasing amounts in both numbers and proportion of sexual violence in both publications, with 13 percent of the cartoons published in *Penthouse* being sexually violent (Malamuth & Spinner, 1980). Another study of *Playboy* issues from 1954 to 1983 found that only 8.7 cartoons per thousand and 3.8 pictorials per thousand contained sexual violence (Scott & Cuvelier, 1987).

An examination of all 430 magazines offered for sale during 1979–1980 at an adult bookstore in Times Square in New York City revealed that almost all of the content was offered for a target audience of males (Winick, 1985). More than 80 percent of the models appeared to be of ages 20–30, and wide variation of attractiveness occurred. Activities suggested mostly middle-class occupations, and more than half of the models appeared to be married. Satisfaction with sexual activity predominated, with few examples of forced sex. Examination of the bondage content, however, revealed an imbalance of power among the sexual partnerships, with 71 percent of such relationships portraying male dominance.

Sari Thomas (1986) studied the 1980s portrayals of gender and social class in pictorial pornography. She divided nine magazines that focused on sexually explicit photographs as designed to appeal to different sociological groups: upwardly mobile heterosexual males, working-class heterosexual males, homosexual males, and heterosexual females. *Playboy*, *Penthouse*, and *Oui* represented the content that targeted upwardly mobile heterosexual males. These magazines emphasized air-brushed photographs of young, mostly white, and extremely beautiful females in poses that seemed to naturally suggest sexual activity. *Blueboy* and *Mandate* magazines portrayed male models emulating the style of *Playboy*, *Penthouse*, and *Oui*. *Cheri*, *Gallery*, and *Hustler* magazines represented working-class pornographic publications, offering a wider variety of female models differing in age, race, and beauty. These photographs depicted more graphic displays of sexual organs in poses that appeared to be designed to sexually arouse male viewers.

Thomas (1986) found that the female models portrayed in photographs in publications targeted to males were generally younger than the males who appeared in *Playgirl* magazine. She estimated the ages of the female models at 18–35, compared with 25–40 for the male models. Body types among the male models lacked the somewhat exaggerated proportions that were apparent among the female models, as well as the degree of physical attractiveness. Males were also presented in poses more akin to merely posing for a picture, rather than those of sexual allure.

Films and Electronic Media

Naked females appeared in films by 1899, and filmed sexual intercourse appeared soon thereafter (Slade, 1984). By the 1920s, nude males appeared in a small number of films targeting homosexuals. From the early practice of showing pornographic films in all-male clubs, they became known as *stag films*, and they tended to run for only 10–12 minutes. Stag films tended to be of poor quality, black and white, and silent. They were sold in plain, numbered containers lacking titles and featuring females revealing their breasts, although underground outlets offered explicit versions showing sexual intercourse. In the 1960s, after several U.S. Supreme Court decisions made convictions for selling obscenity more difficult to prosecute, the technical quality of stag films began improving, and the explicitness of content grew bolder. By the end of the 1960s, films with focus on female genitalia, sexual intercourse, and oral sex were common, and the numbers on containers had been replaced with both titles and suggestive scenes.

Early stag films and those available through the 1950s tended to avoid any semblance of plot. However, by the 1960s, the genre adopted the storytelling characteristics of the more mainstream media. The 1970 U.S. Commission on Obscenity and Pornography reported that the topics for sexually explicit films included "perversion, abortion, drug addiction, wayward girls, orgies, wife swapping, vice dens, prostitution, promiscuity, homosexuality, transvestism, frigidity, nymphomania, lesbianism, etc." (p. 74).

In the 1970s, pornographic films emerged as an economic force. More than 2,000 such films were produced in 1973, with the pace slowing down a bit to 700–800 annually after 1975 (Slade, 1984). A study of pornographic films from their outset to the 1970s found little violence in the genre, violence being at variance with the usual theme of insatiable female sexual appetites. The increase in the presence of violence in such films during the 1970s appeared to be substantial, but remained present in a relatively small proportion, probably not exceeding 10 percent. Although pornographic films tended to portray less frequent violence than more mainstream films of other types, the degree of violence portrayed in pornography is more extreme, tends to show females as victimized by males, and tends to omit portrayal of negative consequences of sexual abuse (Brown & Bryant, 1989).

With the introduction of the video cassette recorder in the latter part of the decade, the most popular-selling prerecorded video cassettes contained pornography, and the industry grew bolder in a variety of ways. More graphic content, including homosexuality and sadomasochism, became common, and adult theaters openly promoted their wares (U.S. Department of Justice, 1986). During this period, public protests tended to focus on hard-core materials that were often promoted as triple-X to highlight their explicit brand of pornography, as opposed to adult or X-rated films and videos. The latter classification appeared in full view of the buying public in legitimate multi-interest outlets (Palys, 1986).

Palys studied 150 sexually explicit videos, finding that they contained an average of eleven sex scenes each. Among his sample videos, 77 percent of the analyzed scenes contained sex acts, and he separated the videos into two categories: *adult* and *triple-X* videos. The fifty-eight adult videos included more aggression, and the triple-X videos contained more oral sex.

Bradley S. Greenberg (1994) cites findings from an examination (Cowan, Lee, Levy, & Snyder, 1988) of forty-five pornographic videos as showing that more than half of the scenes portrayed "domination or exploitation" (p. 168), usually men abusing women. These videos resembled Palys's (1986) triple-X category. More than half of the videos (60 percent) included sex acts, with the average video including ten such acts. Heterosexual activity occurred 78 percent of the time, 11 percent included lesbian sexual behavior, 2 percent portrayed bisexual activity, and 9 percent displayed masturbation. No male homosexuality occurred in the sample.

EFFECTS OF PORNOGRAPHY

Much of the literature about the effects of pornography deals with negative impact, but Kinsey suggested using sexually explicit films for sex education in the late 1940s (Yaffe, 1982). For example, preadolescent and adolescent school children, normal adults, medical students, health professionals, people with mental disabilities, and people with sexual dysfunction have been involved with such therapeutic use of pornography (Bryant & Brown, 1989).

Observing that many Americans believe pornography is vulgar but without effects on its viewers, Victor Cline (1994) suggests that such a view denies the idea of education in suggesting that people are not affected "by what they see" (p. 230). He notes that pornography has useful results, specifically for couples who want to modify their sexual behavior or attitudes. He observes that such patients would have specific prescriptions of materials to view delivered by a licensed therapist, similar to the way a patient with a different problem would receive a prescription for chemical medication. The patients would not merely turn to whatever pornographic images happened to become available because so much of pornography that is commercially available serves as *miseducation*, conveying false, misleading impressions about human sexuality. Cline describes pornography as offering up models of unhealthy and antisocial sexual behavior, such as "sadomasochism, abuse, humiliation of the female, involvement of minors, incest, group sex, voyeurism, exhibitionism, bestiality, and so on" (p. 231). Rimm's (1995) analysis of pornography available online also confirms a marked disparity between the sexual behaviors that Americans profess to practice and the sexual behaviors portrayed in pornography.

Although pornography use in therapeutically supervised situations can have a positive effect in generating sexual arousal, enhancing sexual satisfaction, Cline (1994) treated approximately 300 people with sexual illnesses over a period of many years in his clinical psychology practice, concluding that "pornography has been a major or minor contributor or facilitator in the acquisition of their deviation or sexual addiction" (p. 233). He reports finding a cause-effect relationship between pornography use and harm from the use among his patients.

Feminist writers accuse pornography of degrading women and subordinating them to men, and leading to hostile male attitudes toward women (Brownmiller, 1975). Catherine MacKinnon and Andrea Dworkin (1997) cowrote an antipornography ordinance that was enacted in December 1983 by the city of Minneapolis. The law promulgated the concept of pornography as a violation of human rights and was later considered by Indianapolis, Los Angeles County, the Commonwealth of Massachusetts, Germany, Sweden, and the Philippines (MacKinnon & Dworkin). MacKinnon (1997) provides a long list of harms of pornography as revealed in the testimony of women at the December 1983 Minneapolis hearings about the ordinance.

The 1986 Attorney General's Commission on Pornography also reported a litany of harms from women's testimony saying that they were victimized by pornography producers and users. The report listed categories of harm resulting from consumption of pornography, including physical harm, psychological harm, and social harm (Sears, 1989).

Zillmann includes such harms of pornography as compulsive use and self-serving attitudes about the sexual desires of others (Zillmann, 1994a). Most of the public's attention in the discussion about the possible harm generated by pornography seems to center around sexual violence. Bryant and Zillmann (2001) list a number of harms of the use of pornography and contend that harm involving sexual violence, although of legitimate concern, represents only the most blatant of concerns. They recommend more attention to subtle harms of pornography links with sexual callousness among young people and interference by pornography in the intimate lives of partners. This interference occurs because pornography reduces the arousal produced by sexual cues that normally occur in relationships, and leads to unrealistic beliefs about sexual behaviors that are acceptable to partners. Pornography users may develop improbable ideas about reasonable sexual abilities, leading to sexual dissatisfaction with the sex life with a current partner. Bryant and Zillmann observe that research evidence documents the occurrence of these harms.

RESEARCH ON PORNOGRAPHY

The 1970 Commission on Pornography financed a great deal of new research about pornography, and the Attorney General's Commission attempted to call forth the results of scientific research in policy formation, but the results were more or less surprising, depending on whether the researchers maintained objectivity. Zillmann and Bryant (1989) pointed out that not everyone in the scientific community agreed that social science research was the best available method to inform such policy making. They observe that some social scientists used the opportunity to advocate positions consistent with personal consumption preferences and attitudes, leading to questioning of the validity of research on pornography. To address that problem, they produced a book designed to offer diverse views from which readers could draw more informed conclusions.

In that book, Kathryn Kelley, Lori Dawson, and Donna M. Musialowski (1989) describe the three faces of sexual explicitness as including empirical investigations, the interface of internal fantasy and external stimuli, and the potential of sexually explicit materials in dealing with sexual deviance and dysfunction. These authors defined sexual explicitness as clearly obvious representation of sexual activity and found that many of the variations observed in responses are associated with a theme of personality traits. They list sexual attitudes and experience as other important mediators of responses to sexually explicit content. They acknowledge that the same content may produce opposite reactions in different people and that sexually explicit content may produce responses deemed both negative and positive.

Physiological changes such as blood pressure readings and other measurements of the sympathetic nervous system are readily observable in people viewing pornography. Enjoyment of pornography, in fact, depends on increased levels of sympathetic activity (Zillmann, 1984b). Long-term consumption of pornography tends to reduce initial resistance to such material (Zillmann, 1989), and enjoyment of pornography has been demonstrated to remain even or decrease after prolonged exposure. Zillmann and Bryant (1982, 1984) showed that these effects persisted after two weeks following the end of such viewing. In plain language, consuming pornography quickly tends to reduce the enjoyment of consuming it. The activity no longer produces the level of excitement that occurred at first look, and more extreme imagery is needed to produce the same degree of early excitement.

A systematic study of the research literature published in peer-reviewed scholarly journals between 1971 and 1991 produced 152 empirical studies of the effects of pornography (Lyons, Anderson, & Larson, 1994). Analysis of this body of research resulted in the conclusion that using pornography produces measurable causal effects, particularly for aggressive pornography and for written pornography. Apparently, written pornography produced more powerful effects, perhaps because of its stimulation of the imagination in users and because of the relatively higher likelihood that visual pornography will soon become boring. Consistent with this finding, audio pornography ranked after written pornography and before visual pornography in consistently producing statistically significant effects.

Some people are more at risk than others to suffer lasting effects from using pornography. Among males who are predisposed to sexually aggressive behavior, pornography users display degrees of sexual aggression that exceed four times that of sexually aggressive males who do not use pornography (Malamuth, Addison, & Koss, 2000). Aggressive males may differ in their responses to pornography from nonaggressive males (Allen, D'Alessio, & Emmers-Sommer, 2000; Malamuth & Check, 1983; Malamuth, Check, & Briere, 1986).

Viewing Behavior

The primary research technique for measuring prolonged consumption of pornography also emerged from the work of the 1970 Commission (Howard, Reifler, & Liptzin, 1971). The protocol involved exposure to pornography followed by an interval of no exposure before taking measurements of possible effects. The pioneering study showed pornographic films to college students over a three-week period. Eight weeks after the end of the screening, measurements were taken during the showing of a pornographic film and also afterward. The physiological measures confirmed that the primary response after steady exposure to pornography was boredom from seeing similar material. Although pornography's initial impact on physiological arousal is powerful, content that once was exciting soon loses its capacity to elicit a thrill (Zillmann, 1984b).

Zillmann and Bryant (1986) found that participants who engaged in prolonged pornography consumption and were subsequently allowed to choose their own viewing materials preferred more unusual forms of sexually explicit content, such as bestiality and sadomasochism. This effect occurred with both male and female participants and reflected the results of interviews about repeat customers at adult book and video stores. Zillmann (1994a) predicts that experienced consumers of pornography will turn to sexually explicit materials containing violence because of the loss of excitement generated by more common forms. He suggests that if explicit sexuality appears openly in nonsexual environments, such as on billboards, on public transportation, on materials at checkout counters, on television, and other generally available public displays, people seeking sexually gratifying stimulation will soon turn to more radical forms of sexual imagery to meet their requirements (Zillmann, 1984a). This same habituation to pornography, he explains, corresponds with frequent references in clinical literature that habituation occurs frequently in monogamous relationships. Primate males tend to lose their tendencies toward sexual excitement to the same sexual stimuli over time, although the phenomenon remains to be proved with research on humans.

Investigations of whether couples who view pornography together change their sexual behavior produced conflicting results. Couples with ten years or more of marriage changed sexual repertoires little and showed no expansion after four weekly sessions of viewing pornography (Mann, Sidman, & Starr, 1971). However, more recent reports (Bryant, 1985a; Wishnoff, 1978) showed that sexually experienced couples adjusted behavior after steady exposure to pornography.

Pornography and Aggression

Aggression tends to decline with exposure to pornography for both males (Zillmann, Bryant, Comisky, & Medoff, 1981) and females (Baron, 1979). Zillmann (1984b) explains this reduction by observing that common pornography contains generally pleasant nonviolent, noncoercive material. The conclusion is consistent with findings that aggression among viewers resulted from aggressive content, rather than from sexually explicit images in the content (Zillmann, Bryant, & Carveth, 1981). Both males and females enjoy watching pornography, which stimulates sexual desire, and research disproves the notion that sexual frustration from ending the viewing of such material increases aggression (Sapolsky & Zillmann, 1981).

These conclusions have both agreement (Malamuth & Ceniti, 1986) and disagreement from other researchers who measured the results of prolonged repeated exposure to aggressive pornography. In laboratory settings, Edward Donnerstein (1980a, 1980b) and his colleagues (Donnerstein & Berkowitz, 1981) found that viewers were aggressive toward women after viewing pornography. Other studies (e.g., Linz, Donnerstein, & Adams, 1989) linked aggression and viewing aggressive pornography when the content displays sexual aggression rather than mere sexual content.

Also, not everyone agrees that nonviolent pornography generates no aggressive behavior, although researchers concede that the level of aggression generated by such fare is less than that arising after viewing aggressive pornography (Lyons et al., 1994; U.S. Department of Justice, 1986). Does such promoted aggression rise to the level of criminal behavior?

Pornography and Criminal Behavior

The final report of the Attorney General's Commission (U.S. Department of Justice, 1986) links viewing pornography and imitating violent behavior seen in it, and some authors (e.g., Russell, 1988) charge that viewing pornography causes rape. Although rapists and child molesters have admitted using pornography as a stimulant before and during their crimes (Marshall,

1988), scientific proof of a causal connection is not available, and research has not demonstrated that youths' consumption of pornography leads to their becoming sex offenders (Davis & McCormick, 1997).

Ethical and legal restrictions on research protocols make it difficult, if not impossible, to prove that using pornography causes violent behavior. Consequently, the frequency with which pornography viewers imitate what they see lacks scientific analysis (Harris, 1994).

College men who saw pornography were more likely than viewers who did not, to say that they might rape someone if they could be sure of avoiding prosecution (Check & Guloien, 1989). Describing such admissions by research participants as evidence of sexual callousness, Bryant and Zillmann (2001) found that sexual callousness strengthens from viewing of both violent and nonviolent pornography. Research findings have not yet demonstrated that violent pornography is more powerful than nonviolent pornography in producing impact on imitative behavior (Zillmann, 2000). Even when the pornographic content includes scenes of suffering by rape victims, participants viewing the content show no greater tendency to admit a willingness to commit rape than those who saw noncoercive pornography.

It is also difficult to prove a link between actual illegal behavior and viewing pornography. Researchers acting ethically and legally cannot conduct studies that would show such causation. Doing so would subject the research participants to the possibility of great harm. Therefore, whatever researchers know about such connections comes from interviewing criminals and studying their crimes. Bryant and Zillmann (1996) found such evidence conflicting and inconclusive.

When pornography was more easily available, rates of sex crimes in Japan and Denmark declined, but the same was not true in Australia and the United States. Mere availability does not explain these results, and researchers need more knowledge of the effects of cultural differences when evaluating the effects of pornography on criminal sexual behavior.

James Weaver (1994), summarizing research connecting pornography with sexual callousness, concedes that research fails to prove the connection. Young people today are more likely to have received initial sexual orientation from pornography than are people of earlier generations. Weaver further notes that consuming pornography produces a loss of respect for "female sexual autonomy" (p. 224) and lessening of male restraint of aggression against women. These two factors commonly appear in the beliefs and attitudes of male sexual offenders. M. Douglas Reed, analyzing the clinical evidence about pornography, states: "Pornography to addicted sex offenders is as dangerous as matches and gasoline to an arsonist" (1994, p. 265).

Child pornography involves criminal behavior. Federal law (U.S. Code, 2004) prohibits producing, advertising, or distributing sexually explicit images of models under the age of 18. Kenneth Lanning and Ann Burgess (1989) describe child pornography as a record of child abuse because it cannot be produced except by victimizing a child. Possessing child pornography is illegal under both state and federal laws and is not openly sold anywhere in the United States. However, Lanning and Burgess observe that child pornography is exchanged in almost every American community.

They divide child pornography into commercial and homemade, depending on the purpose for which the content is created. They explain that pedophiles are primarily responsible for importing child pornography into the United States because their motivation includes collection, as well as commercial sale. Commercial dealers find the risks of prosecution too great to justify their own production, but the quality of homemade productions sometimes is good enough that it becomes commercially distributed.

Prolonged Pornography Consumption and Family Values

Zillmann and Bryant (1988a) studied the effects of prolonged exposure to pornography on family values. They found that the short-run, immediate gratification values of pornographic content undermine those of the family, which center on caring, responsibility, and commitment. Consumers of such fare reported diminished desire for marriage and having children, especially female children.

Zillmann cites several detailed analyses (Brosius, 1992; Brosius, Staab, & Weaver, 1991; Palys, 1984; Prince, 1990) of the content of pornography showing that images predominantly portray people engaging in sexual activity soon after first meeting, expecting no long-term relationships with each other, and maintaining contact only for as long as completing sex requires. Furthermore, pornography often features sex with many partners, all of whom appear to feel ecstasy from the experience. Schlosser (1997) writes that pornography deals with a wide variety of content preferences, including heterosexual, homosexual, interracial, bondage, fetishes, and more. These images, suggests Zillmann, undermine notions that sex should be part of personal commitment, even promoting the idea that such commitment is confining and likely to prevent achievement of sexual fulfillment.

Zillmann and Bryant (1988b) found that prolonged consumption of pornography affected the perceptions of pornography users, who may be presumed to seek greater sexual satisfaction through such consumption. However, the research findings suggest that the portrayal of idealized sexual performance and sexual partners generates the opposite impact. Verifying that such idealizing may be no different from that occurring in nonpornographic content, such as advertising, they used the Indiana Inventory of Personal Happiness. The instrument revealed that satisfaction with nonsexual issues remained unaffected, although all items related to sexuality reflected this rising dissatisfaction.

A related study (Weaver, Masland, & Zillmann, 1984) found that users of prolonged pornography reported less satisfaction with sexual partners, even when their partners were part of a long-term relationship. The partners seemed less attractive and less satisfying as sexual performers. Questions about the partners' willingness to remain faithful emerged, as did greater willingness for pornography viewers and their partners to sanction sexual relationships outside of marriage. Recreational sex attained higher-rated importance for prolonged pornography viewers, and they expressed greater willingness to use sex as a tool for gaining favor.

Prolonged consumption of pornography itself significantly changed perceptions about family values and fostered greater acceptance of sexual promiscuity (Zillmann, 1994a). These findings were attributable specifically to the pornography use, as distinguished from being the result of generally changing attitudes in society. Such prolonged pornography use was accompanied by a decline in expectations that intimate sexual partners will remain faithful to each other, a finding that consistently occurred among males, females, students, and nonstudents. Prolonged use of pornography produced greater acceptance of sexual behavior with people other than marriage partners as well as with people other than the regular partner outside of marriage. Additionally, the prolonged pornography users showed greater tolerance for their partners straying from faithfulness. In other words, this consumption weakened notions that sexual intimacy should be reserved for a person's exclusive sexual partner, whether in or out of marriage.

This fostering of acceptance for multiple sex partners also demonstrates consequences for ideas about sexual activity and health. Prolonged use of pornography fostered beliefs that sex without restraints is "wholesome and healthy; and moreover, that any sexual restraint poses health risks" (Zillmann, 1994a, p. 206).

Prolonged pornography use led to lowered acceptance of the importance of marriage to society and greater likelihood of believing that marriage will become obsolete. Again, these findings emerged in males, females, students, and nonstudents. Pornography consumption also reduced expressed desire to have children, apparently making family commitments seem unnecessarily burdensome.

In addition to affecting ideas about marriage, prolonged consumption of pornography affected perceptions of grounds for divorce. Sexual infidelity became less accepted as suitable grounds for divorce among pornography users, and unacceptable sexual interest and initiative became more acceptable grounds. For reasons unrelated to sex, pornography consumption produced no differences in perceptions about grounds for divorce.

Sexual Callousness toward Women and Rape

Several feminist authors have accused pornographers of teaching women to perceive themselves as lacking power and behaving more submissively (Baldwin, 1984). The general notion of perceiving females as submissive and fearful has been called the *cultural climate hypothesis* (Krafka, Linz, Donnerstein, &

Penrod, 1997). Research support for this phenomenon is available from studies showing aggressive pornography to males (Donnerstein, Linz, & Penrod, 1987). Aggressive pornography was defined as sexually explicit images of the use of force or coercion, usually involving rape or assault. A lesser degree of support emerged from display of such content to females (Krafka et al., 1997).

The rape myth suggests that women invite rape, and research shows that the influence of mild pornography leads men to hold women responsible for being raped. People who saw such images also gave less credibility to claims by women that they were raped (Wyer, Bodenhausen, & Gorman, 1985). The stimulus materials contained images of women in sexually alluring poses. Women who saw the materials were less inclined to react the same way, however, giving the alleged rape victim more credibility and less responsibility for the alleged rape than women in a control group.

Another study assessed recommended rape sentences after conviction based upon whether the respondents had experienced prolonged exposure to pornography (Zillmann & Bryant, 1982). Although women issued longer prison sentences to the convicted rapists than did men, both women and men gave more lenient sentences after three weeks of exposure to pornography during a six-week study.

Prolonged exposure to both nonviolent and violent pornography has been demonstrated to increase the likelihood that males report willingness to commit rape (Check, 1985). Even eliminating from experiments men with predispositions to violence and men who might have been angry before seeing violent pornography produced this same attitude toward women (Donnerstein, 1984). After viewing pornography in which women were victimized by violence in scenes rated as sexually arousing, men rated the female victims as having suffered less injury than did men who did not see that content (Linz, 1985).

Edward Donnerstein and Daniel Linz (1986) found that young adults displayed increased tendencies of sexual callousness toward women after seeing violent pornography over a prolonged period. Unlike Zillmann and Bryant, however, these authors concluded that the violence, instead of the sexually explicit content, produced the effect. The same authors were involved in other published research that found desensitization of male viewers of violent pornography in which females were victimized (Linz et al., 1989). Studies do, however, reveal that realistic portrayals of the consequences of sexual violence produced less male sexual arousal than violent pornography portraying female victims who become sexually aroused during the assault against them (Linz & Donnerstein, 1989).

Seeing films portraying sexually aggressive females led males to project similar perceptions onto women judged by others as not being sexually permissive (Zillmann & Weaver, 1989). In other words, women perceived in pretests as nice girls were seen by male viewers of sexually explicit content as being promiscuous. Women who saw such films were less willing to see innocence in female victims in cases involving clearly guilty male perpetrators of violence against women, including rape. The same effect appeared in male viewers when they saw sexually explicit films portraying rape and erotic violence, but the effect failed to appear when males saw content portraying consensual sex and female-instigated sex. The authors concluded that viewing pornography trivialized rape among both men and women, contradicting earlier studies by Linz and Donnerstein (1990) and Donnerstein et al. (1987) that the violence, not the sex, produced sexual callousness.

After analyzing the available research on television violence, Haejung Paik and George Comstock (1994) supported Zillmann and his colleagues, concluding that the sexual content, not the violence, was primarily responsible for generating sexual callousness. Other authors (Jansma, Linz, Mulac, & Imrich, 1997) suggest that measuring interactions between men and women after they view sexually violent pornography would improve the research about sexual callousness, citing Elizabeth Perse's (1994) finding that acceptance of rape myths influences decisions to use pornography. Bryant and Zillmann (2001) observed that meta-analyses (e.g., Allen, D'Alessio, & Brezgel, 1995; Allen, Emmers, & Giery, 1995), or comprehensive studies of wide collections of research investigations, have concluded that nonviolent pornography is almost as powerful as violent pornography in promoting sexual callousness against women.

Effects of Internet Pornography

Access to sexually explicit content on the Internet is usually either characterized as sexual exploration, or pathological, related to addictive behavior and compulsive attitudes. Both mental health professionals and the public seem to believe that too much Internet sexuality is harmful, just as both groups believe that too much sex is harmful (Cooper et al., 1999). In one of the earliest studies (Durkin & Bryant, 1995) of using the Internet for sexual purposes, online sexual communication was seen as helping people maintain sexual fantasies that might have disappeared sooner without the interactive and immediate feedback. Cooper et al. (1999) cited previous works (Cooper & Sportolari, 1997) in noting that sexual communication via the Internet reduced the emphasis on physical appearance relative to shared interests, values, and emotions.

Their survey of 9,177 visitors to the MSNBC Web site found that 92 percent spent eleven or fewer hours per week engaging in online activities related to sexuality, and 61 percent admitted falsifying their age in online sexual pursuits. All of the participants in this survey were people who use the Internet for sexual content. Five percent admitted pretending to be a person of a different sex during these activities. Although 87 percent of the respondents professed to feel no shame or guilt, 70 percent kept their online sexual activity secret. The researchers found no differences in survey respondents' use of the Internet for sexual purposes and their general use of sexual materials off-line, mostly for entertainment rather than sexual arousal. Twenty percent of the respondents reported feeling sexually aroused while using the Internet for sexual purposes, while 88 percent found the experience exciting. No interference with any part of living was reported by 68.2 percent of the respondents, and only 12 percent believed that they were downloading sexual materials from the Internet too frequently.

People spending eleven or more hours weekly in online sexual pursuits were defined as heavy users, and they were more likely to use Internet chat rooms and newsgroups than other users. The authors of the survey found that heavy Internet use for sexual purposes was associated with factors related to psychological difficulty. These factors include distress, sexual compulsiveness, and sensation seeking. An important proportion, about 8 percent, of users of online sexual materials scored high on these measures, seemed distressed, and admitted that their behavior causes some problems in their lives. This proportion resembles the proportion of the general population that suffers from sexual compulsivity, reported by these authors at about 5 percent. More research is needed to determine the direction of this association between time spent seeking sex online and psychological distress. To date, research has not been able to say whether distressed people seek sex online or whether seeking sex online leads to distress.

SHOULD PORNOGRAPHY BE CENSORED?

In Favor of Censoring Pornography

Although the 1970 Commission on Pornography found pornography mostly inoffensive and recommended the repeal of laws restricting its availability to adults (U.S. Commission on Obscenity and Pornography, 1970), the 1986 Commission differed. The latter commission ruled that the production and distribution of pornography violates civil rights of the public and is an abuse that can be legally and constitutionally stopped (U.S. Department of Justice, 1986).

Regardless of how strongly some people may be offended by pornography, it enjoys protection under the First Amendment to the U.S. Constitution (Zillmann, 1994b). The First Amendment protects the right to publish and distribute and to consume content. This freedom is staunchly defended, not only by the pornography industry, but also by such groups as the American Civil Liberties Union. Sears (1989) contends that an absolute application of the First Amendment ignores damage to performers who may be coerced in the production of pornography, damage to people confronted with the content, and potential damage through the relationships between consumption and antisocial behavior. He suggests several citizen alternatives to censorship, such as organizing pickets, supporting boycotts of businesses, and campaigning to inform the public about the negative effects of pornography.

Sears points out that government has the power to restrict the publication and sale of obscenity and child pornography, which enjoys no First Amendment protection and the mere possession of which can be constitutionally prohibited. Sears disagrees with common claims that laws restricting obscenity are too confusing to enforce. He contends that such laws are clearer than many other laws that receive regular enforcement, such as fraud, antitrust, and self-defense. After reviewing the history of U.S. Supreme Court decisions regarding obscenity and pornography, Sears finds an array of constitutional legal tools to fight such content. He includes both civil actions to control display, such as zoning, as well as criminal prosecution for illegal production and distribution. Sears contends that the Court has upheld the principle of restricting obscenity and pornography in ways that are adaptable to the emerging new technologies.

Another defense of pornography involves claims of privacy, which Sears dismisses. He argues that visual pornography forfeits any legitimate claim to privacy after production teams record and publish what might otherwise be considered private behavior.

Against Censoring Pornography

Linsley (1989) contends that the sheer numbers of people producing and consuming pornography show public acceptance of it. He suggests three premises that must be met to justify censorship of pornography: clearly defined pornography, identifiable harm, and proof that censorship preserves essential freedom.

Linsley contends that pornography and obscenity have become inseparable in the minds of many, and both are practically impossible to define. He quotes decisions of the U.S. Supreme Court to establish the inability to consistently define pornography, to distinguish between content judged as obscene and protected speech, citing such examples from *Miller v. California* (1973) as *prurient interest, patent offensiveness*, and *serious literary value*. The term *pornography*, he contends, is subjective and lacks legal foundation. Such nebulous terms cannot fairly be used to proscribe conduct because citizens cannot know in advance which acts violate the law.

Congressional Action and First Amendment Conflicts

Congress attempted to regulate the sending of obscene or indecent content via the Internet to minors, those under age 18, with the Communications Decency Act of 1996 (CDA). This law was struck down by the U.S. Supreme Court (*Reno v. American Civil Liberties Union*, 1997) as overbroad.

The Court directed that less intrusive measures be used before the First Amendment rights of adults could be threatened by attempts to restrict the availability of content to children. The Court also criticized the law for using vague definitions of such terms as *indecent* and *patently offensive* in describing content that could be restricted, noting that valuable educational and artistic materials could be included using such terms as the basis for regulation (Rosen, 2004).

Congress passed the Child Pornography Prevention Act of 1996, including computer-generated sexually explicit images of children under content banned as child pornography. Again, the U.S. Supreme Court found the law unconstitutionally vague (*Ashcroft v. Free Speech Coalition*, 2002).

Congress again focused on Internet pornography and children with the Child Online Protection Act (COPA) in 1998, particularly on content designed for commercial purposes. Congress used language from *Miller v. California* (1973) to specify what would be restricted. The U.S. Supreme Court ruled in the *Miller* case that community standards would govern what is obscene, but the Court ruled (*Ashcroft v. Free Speech Coalition*, 2002) that local standards could not effectively be applied to the Internet and called instead for a national standard in such a venue (Rosen, 2004). These cases illustrate the conflict between protecting the rights of those considered to be particularly vulnerable to the influence of Internet and computer-generated pornography and the First Amendment.

CONCLUSIONS

Reaching the bottom line on the impact of pornography depends on perspective. The economic impact is unquestionable. Researchers differ about the effects on attitudes and behavior. For example, some analyses of the research on pornography effects (e.g., Fisher & Grenier, 1994) question the findings and methods of research on aggressive pornography. These objections have been criticized (Malamuth et al., 2000) as being inaccurate, unrepresentative, and lacking validity.

Existing research tends to focus mostly on sexually violent pornography and its impact on rape to the exclusion of emphasis on more subtle and common forms of pornography (Zillmann, 1989). Strategies used in this research often follow disparate methodologies that produce findings that fail to fit into a consistent body of knowledge, resulting in a lack of clear understanding of research results and fodder for those who would attack research about pornography. Such critics use different studies with inconsistent findings as ammunition for their attacks. Despite clear social science research findings about the harms of using pornography and despite clear testimony about suffering from victims of pornography, some researchers and members of the legal community do not accept that pornography causes harm.

However, other systematic meta-analyses (e.g., Allen, D'Alessio, et al., 1995; Allen et al., 2000; Allen, Emmers, et al., 1995) have been praised

(Malamuth et al., 2000) for their rigorous methodology. These studies report consistent and strong effects from the use of pornography.

Despite these differences, Zillmann (1994b) argues that research provides a strong foundation for public policy dealing with pornography. Inconsistencies in the body of research are explainable to the satisfaction of informed researchers, and the bulk of the findings are consistent in demonstrating harm from pornography. Conceding that censorship is neither desirable nor constitutional, he recommends that policy makers focus on education designed to enlighten the public about such ills as sexual callousness, support for rape and rapists, and other improper sexual attitudes. While falling short of demonstrating that pornography ruins families and personal relationships, the scientific evidence supports the contention that prolonged consumption of pornography influences the attitudes and dispositions of the users toward intimate sexual partners, sexual health, marriage, and family values.

REFERENCES

Abelson, H., Cohen, R., Heaton, E., & Suder, C. (1971). National survey of public attitudes toward and experience with erotic materials. *Technical report of the Commission on Obscenity and Pornography* (Vol. 6). Washington, DC: U.S. Government Printing Office.

Allen, M., D'Alessio, D., & Brezgel, K. (1995). A meta-analysis summarizing the effects of pornography. Part II: Aggression after exposure. *Human Communication Research, 22*, 258–283.

Allen, M., D'Alessio, D., & Emmers-Sommer, T. M. (2000). Reactions of criminal sexual offenders to pornography: A meta-analytic summary. In M. Rolloff (Ed.), *Communication Yearbook 22* (pp. 139–169). Thousand Oaks, CA: Sage.

Allen, M., Emmers, T., & Giery, M. A. (1995). Exposure to pornography and acceptance of the rape myths. *Journal of Communication, 45*, 5–26.

Ashcroft v. Free Speech Coalition. (2002). 122 S. Ct. 1389, 1406.

Baldwin, M. (1984). The sexuality of inequality: The Minneapolis pornography ordinance. *Law and inequality, 2*, 629–653.

Baron, R. A. (1979). Heightened sexual arousal and physical aggression: An extension to females. *Journal of Research in Personality, 13*, 91–102.

Brewer, J. S. (1982). A history of erotic art as illustrated in the collections of the Institute for Sex Research (The "Kinsey Institute"). In A. Hoch & H. I. Lief (Eds.), *Sexology: Sexual biology, behavior and therapy* (pp. 318–321). Amsterdam, the Netherlands: Exerpta Medica.

Brosius, H. (1992). Sex und pornographie in den Massenmedien: Eine Analyse ihrer Inhalte, ihrer Nutzung und ihrer Wirkung [Sex and pornography in the mass media: An analysis of content, use, and effects]. In R. Frohlich (Ed.), *Der andere Blick: Aktuelles zur Massenkommunikation aus weiblicher Sicht* [The different view: Current research in mass communication from a female viewpoint] (pp. 139–158). Bochum: Brockmeyer.

Brosius, H., Staab, J., & Weaver, J. B. (1991, May). *Exploring the social "reality" of contemporary pornography*. Paper presented at the International Communication Association Meeting, Chicago.

Brown, D. (2003). Pornography and erotica. In J. Bryant, D. Roskos-Ewoldsen, & J. Cantor (Eds.), *Communication and emotion: Essays in honor of Dolf Zillmann* (pp. 221–253). Mahwah, NJ: Lawrence Erlbaum.

Brown, D., & Bryant, J. (1989). The manifest content of pornography. In D. Zillmann & J. Bryant (Eds.), *Pornography: Research advances and policy considerations* (pp. 3–24). Hillsdale, NJ: Lawrence Erlbaum.

Brownmiller, S. (1975). *Against our will: Men, women, and rape*. New York: Simon and Schuster.

Bryant, J. (1985a). Effects of pornography: Research findings. *Testimony to the U.S. Attorney General's Commission on Pornography*. Houston, TX.

Bryant, J. (1985b, March). *Frequency of exposure, age of initial exposure, and reactions to initial exposure to pornography*. Report presented to the Attorney General's Commission on Pornography, Houston, TX.

Bryant, J., & Brown, D. (1989). Uses of pornography. In D. Zillmann & J. Bryant (Eds.), *Pornography: Research advances and policy considerations* (pp. 25–55). Hillsdale, NJ: Lawrence Erlbaum.

Bryant, J., & Zillmann, D. (1996). Violence and sex in the media. In D. W. Stacks & M. B. Salwen (Eds.), *An integrated approach to communication theory and research* (pp. 195–209). Mahwah, NJ: Lawrence Erlbaum.

Bryant, J., & Zillmann, D. (2001). Pornography: Models of effects on sexual deviancy. In C. D. Bryant (Ed.), *Encyclopedia of criminology and deviant behavior* (pp. 241–244). Philadelphia: Brunner-Routledge.

Burt, M. E. H. (1976). Use of pornography by women: A critical review of the literature. *Case Western Reserve Journal of Sociology, 8*, 1–6.

Check, J. V. P. (1985). *The effects of violent and nonviolent pornography*. Ottawa: Department of Justice.

Check, J. V. P., & Guloien, T. H. (1989). Reported proclivity for coercive sex following repeated exposure to sexually violent pornography, non-violent dehumanizing pornography, and erotica. In D. Zillmann & J. Bryant (Eds.), *Pornography: Research advances and policy considerations* (pp. 159–184). Hillsdale, NJ: Lawrence Erlbaum.

Cline, V. B. (1994). Pornography effects: Empirical and clinical evidence. In D. Zillmann, J. Bryant, & A. C. Huston (Eds.), *Media, children, and the family: Social scientific, psychodynamic, and clinical perspectives* (pp. 229–247). Hillsdale, NJ: Lawrence Erlbaum.

Cooper, A., Scherer, C. R., Boies, S. C., & Gordon, B. L. (1999). Sexuality on the Internet: From sexual exploration to pathological expression. *Professional Psychology: Research and Practice, 30*(2), 154–164.

Cooper, A., & Sportolari, L. (1997). Romance in cyberspace: Understanding online attraction. *Journal of Sex Education and Therapy, 22*, 7–14.

Cowan, G., Lee, C., Levy, D., & Snyder, D. (1988). Dominance and inequality in X-rated videocassettes. *Psychology of Women Quarterly, 12*, 299–311.

Davis, C. M., & McCormick, N. B. (1997). *What sexual scientists know about . . . pornography* [Brochure]. Society for the Scientific Study of Sexuality. Allentown, PA. Retrieved May 15, 2001, from www.ssc.wisc.edu/ssss/wssk_prn.htm

Dietz, P. E., Harry, B., & Hazelwood, R. R. (1986). Detective magazines: Pornography for the sexual sadist. *Journal of Forensic Sciences, 31*(1), 197–211.

Donnerstein, E. (1980a). Aggressive-erotica and violence against women. *Journal of Personality and Social Psychology, 39*, 269–277.

Donnerstein, E. (1980b). Pornography and violence against women. *Annals of the New York Academy of Sciences, 347*, 277–288.

Donnerstein, E. (1984). Effects of pornography. In D. Scott (Ed.), *Symposium on media violence and pornography: Proceedings and resource book* (pp. 78–94). Toronto, Ontario: Media Action Group.

Donnerstein, E., & Berkowitz, L. (1981). Victim reactions in aggressive erotic films as a factor in violence against women. *Journal of Personality and Social Psychology, 41*, 710–724.

Donnerstein, E., & Linz, D. (1986). Mass media sexual violence and male viewers: Current theory and research. *American Behavioral Scientist, 29*, 601–618.

Donnerstein, E., Linz, D., & Penrod, S. (1987). *The question of pornography: Research findings and policy implications.* New York: Free Press.

Durkin, K. F., & Bryant, C. D. (1995). Log onto sex: Some notes on the carnal computer and erotic cyberspace as an emerging research frontier. *Deviant Behavior: An Interdisciplinary Journal, 16*, 179–200.

Egan, T. (2000, October 23). Technology sent Wall Street into market for pornography. *New York Times*, p. AI.

Finkelhor, D., Mitchell, K., & Wolak, J. (2000). *Online victimization: A report on the nation's youth.* Washington, DC: National Center for Missing and Exploited Children.

Fisher, W. A., & Barak, A. (1989). Sex education as a corrective. In D. Zillmann & J. Bryant (Eds.), *Pornography: Research advances and policy considerations* (pp. 289–320). Hillsdale, NJ: Lawrence Erlbaum.

Fisher, W. A., & Barak, A. (2001). Internet pornography: A social psychological perspective on Internet sexuality. *Journal of Sex Research, 38*(4), 312–324.

Fisher, W. A., & Grenier, G. (1994). Violent pornography, antiwoman thoughts, and antiwoman acts: In search of reliable effects. *Journal of Sex Research, 31*(1), 23–38.

Gallup, G. R. (1978). *Public opinion 1972–1977* (Vol. 2). Wilmington, DE: Scholarly Resources.

Gebhard, P. H., & Johnson, B. (1979). *The Kinsey data: Marginal tabulations of the 1938–1963 interviews conducted by the Institute for Sex Research.* Philadelphia: Saunders.

Goodson, P., McCormick, D., & Evans, A. (2000). Sex and the Internet: A survey instrument to assess college students' behavior and attitudes. *CyberPsychology & Behavior, 3*, 129–149.

Greenberg, B. S. (1994). Content trends in media sex. In D. Zillmann, J. Bryant, & A. C. Huston (Eds.), *Media, children, and the family: Social scientific, psychodynamic, and clinical perspectives* (pp. 215–227). Hillsdale, NJ: Lawrence Erlbaum.

Harris, R. J. (1994). The impact of sexually explicit media. In J. Bryant & D. Zillmann (Eds.), *Media effects: Advances in theory and research* (pp. 163–211). Hillsdale, NJ: Lawrence Erlbaum.

Howard, J. L., Reifler, C. B., & Liptzin, M. B. (1971). Effects of exposure to pornography. *Technical report of the Commission on Obscenity and Pornography* (Vol. 8, pp. 97–169). Washington, DC: U.S. Government Printing Office.

Hyde, H. M. (1964). *A history of pornography.* New York: Farrar, Straus and Giroux.

Jansma, L. L., Linz, D. G., Mulac, A., & Imrich, D. J. (1997). Men's interactions with women after viewing sexually explicit films: Does degradation make a difference? *Communication Monographs, 64*, 1–24.

Kelley, K., Dawson, L., & Musialowski, D. M. (1989). Three faces of sexual explicitness: The good, the bad, and the useful. In D. Zillmann & J. Bryant (Eds.), *Pornography: Research advances and policy considerations* (pp. 57–91). Hillsdale, NJ: Lawrence Erlbaum.

Kendrick, W. (1987). The secret museum: Pornography in modern culture. New York: Viking Press.

Kinsey, A. C., Pomeroy, W. B., & Martin, C. E. (1948). *Sexual behavior in the human male.* Philadelphia: Saunders.

Krafka, C., Linz, D., Donnerstein, E., & Penrod, S. (1997). Women's reactions to sexually aggressive mass media depictions. *Violence Against Women, 3*(2), 149–181.

Lane, F. S. (2001). *Obscene profits: The entrepreneurs of pornography in the cyber age.* New York: Routledge.

Lanning, K. V., & Burgess, A. W. (1989). Child pornography and sex rings. In D. Zillmann & J. Bryant (Eds.), *Pornography: Research advances and policy considerations* (pp. 235–255). Hillsdale, NJ: Lawrence Erlbaum.

Laslow, J. (1999, April 26). Internet helps boost adult video sales to record highs. *Adult Video News.* Retrieved May 8, 2005, from www.avn.com/htm Uavn/news/nws/news297.html

Linsley, W. A. (1989). The case against censorship of pornography. In D. Zillmann & J. Bryant (Eds.), *Pornography: Research advances and policy considerations* (pp. 343–359). Hillsdale, NJ: Lawrence Erlbaum.

Linz, D. (1985). *Sexual violence in the media: Effects on male viewers and implications for society.* Unpublished doctoral dissertation, University of Wisconsin, Madison.

Linz, D., & Donnerstein, E. (1989). Effects of counterinformation on rape myths. In D. Zillmann & J. Bryant (Eds.), *Pornography: Research advances and policy considerations* (pp. 259–288). Hillsdale, NJ: Lawrence Erlbaum.

Linz, D., & Donnerstein, E. (1990, April/May). Sexual violence in the media. *World Health, 43*, 26–28.

Linz, D., Donnerstein, E., & Adams, S. M. (1989). Physiological desensitization and judgments about female victims of violence. *Human Communication Research, 15*, 509–522.

Lyons, J. S., Anderson, R. L., & Larson, D. B. (1994). A systematic review of the effects of aggressive and nonaggressive pornography. In D. Zillmann, J. Bryant, & A. C. Huston (Eds.), *Media, children, and the family: Social scientific, psychodynamic, and clinical perspectives* (pp. 271–310). Hillsdale, NJ: Lawrence Erlbaum.

MacKinnon, C. A. (1997). The roar on the other side of silence. In C. A. MacKinnon & A. Dworkin (Eds.), *In harm's way* (pp. 3–36). Cambridge, MA: Harvard University Press.

MacKinnon, C. A., & Dworkin, A. (Eds.) (1997). *In harm's way.* Cambridge, MA: Harvard University Press.

Malamuth, N. M., Addison, T., & Koss, M. (2000). Pornography and sexual aggression: Are there reliable effects and can we understand them? In J. R. Heiman (Ed.), *Annual Review of Sex Research* (Vol. 11, pp. 26–91). Mason City, IA: Society for the Scientific Study of Sexuality.

Malamuth, N. M., & Ceniti, J. (1986). Repeated exposure to violent and non-violent pornography: Likelihood of raping ratings and laboratory aggression against women. *Aggressive Behavior, 12,* 129–137.

Malamuth, N. M., & Check, J. V. P. (1981). The effects of mass media exposure on acceptance of violence against women: A field experiment. *Journal of Research in Personality, 15,* 436–446.

Malamuth, N. M., & Check, J. V. P. (1983). Sexual arousal to rape depictions: Individual differences. *Journal of Abnormal Psychology, 92*(1), 55–67.

Malamuth, N. M., Check, J. V. P., & Briere, J. (1986). Sexual arousal in response to aggression. Ideological, aggressive and sexual correlates. *Journal of Personality and Social Psychology, 50,* 330–340.

Malamuth, N. M., & Spinner, B. (1980). Longitudinal content analysis of sexual violence in the best selling erotica magazines. *Journal of Sex Research, 16,* 226–237.

Mann, J., Sidman, J., & Starr, S. (1971). Effects of erotic films on sexual behavior of married couples. *Technical report of the Commission on Obscenity and Pornography* (Vol. 8, pp. 170–254). Washington, DC: U.S. Government Printing Office.

Marshall, W. L. (1988). The use of explicit sexual stimuli by rapists, child molesters, and nonoffender males. *Journal of Sex Research, 25,* 267–288.

Massey, M. (1970). A marketing analysis of sex-oriented materials. *Technical report of the Commission on Obscenity and Pornography* (Vol. 4, pp. 3–98). Washington, DC: U.S. Government Printing Office.

Miller v. California. (1973). 413 U.S. 15.

Morais, R. C. (1999, June 14). Porn goes public. *Forbes, 163*(12), 214–221.

Paik, H., & Comstock, G. (1994). The effects of television violence on antisocial behavior: A meta-analysis. *Communication Research, 21*(4), 516–546.

Palys, T. S. (1984, June). *A content analysis of sexually explicit videos in British Columbia.* Working papers on pornography and prostitution (Research Report No. 15). Ottawa: Department of Justice.

Palys, T. S. (1986). Testing the common wisdom: The social content of video pornography. *Canadian Psychology, 27*(1), 22–35.

Paul, P. (2004, January 19). The porn factor: In the Internet age, pornography is almost everywhere you look. *Time, 163*(3), 99.

Perse, E. M. (1994). Uses of erotica and acceptance of rape myths. *Communication Research, 21*(4), 488–518.

Press, A., Namuth, T., Agrest, S., Gander, M., Lubenow, G. C., Reese, M., et al. (1985, March 18). The war against pornography. *Newsweek*, 58–66.

Prince, S. (1990). Power and pain: Content analysis and the ideology of pornography. *Journal of Film and Video, 42*(2), 31–41.

Reed, M. D. (1994). Pornography addiction and compulsive sexual behavior. In D. Zillmann, J. Bryant, & A. C. Huston (Eds.), *Media, children, and the family: Social scientific, psychodynamic, and clinical perspectives* (pp. 249–269). Hillsdale, NJ: Lawrence Erlbaum.

Reno v. American Civil Liberties Union. (1997). 521 U.S. 844.

Rich, F. (2001, May 20). Naked capitalists. *New York Times Magazine*, 50.

Rideout, V. (2004). *Parents, media, and public policy: A Kaiser Family Foundation Survey*. Retrieved February 11, 2005, from www.kff.org/entmedia/entme dia092304pkg.cfm

Rimm, M. (1995). Marketing pornography on the information superhighway: A survey of 917,410 images, descriptions, short stories, and animations downloaded 8.5 million times by consumers in over 2000 cities in forty countries, provinces, and territories. *Georgetown Law Journal, 83*(5), 1849–1934.

Rosen, J. (2004). The end of obscenity. *New Atlantis*, 75–82.

Russell, D. E. H. (1988). Pornography and rape: A causal model. *Political Psychology, 9*(1), 41–73.

Sapolsky, B. S., & Zillmann, D. (1981). The effect of soft-core and hard-core erotica on provoked and unprovoked hostile behavior. *Journal of Sex Research, 17*, 319–343.

Schlosser, E. (1997, February 10). The business of pornography. *U.S. News & World Report, 122*(5), 42–51.

Scott, J. E., & Cuvelier, S. J. (1987). Sexual violence in *Playboy* magazine: A longitudinal content analysis. *Journal of Sex Research, 23*(4), 534–539.

Sears, A. (1989). The legal case for restricting pornography. In D. Zillmann & J. Bryant (Eds.), *Pornography: Research advances and policy considerations* (pp. 323–342). Hillsdale, NJ: Lawrence Erlbaum.

Seidman, E. L. (2003). The pornographic retreat: Contemporary patterns of pornography use and the psychodynamic meaning of frequent pornography use for heterosexual men. *Dissertation Abstracts International, 64*(8), 4063. (UMI No. 3102959).

Slade, J. W. (1984). Violence in the hard-core pornographic film. *Journal of Communication, 26*(1), 148–163.

Smith, D. D. (1976). The social content of pornography. *Journal of Communication, 26*(1), 16–24.

Smith, T. W. (1987). The polls—a review: The use of public opinion data by the Attorney General's Commission on Pornography. *Public Opinion Quarterly, 51*, 249–257.

Sonenschein, D. (1970). Love and sex in the romance magazines. *Journal of Popular Culture, 4*(2), 398–409.

Subcommittee on Commerce, Trade, and Consumer Protection. (2004). *Online pornography: Closing the door on pervasive smut.* Washington, DC: U.S. Government Printing Office.

Thomas, S. (1986). Gender and social–class coding in popular photographic erotica. *Communication Quarterly, 34*(2), 103–114.

U.S. Bureau of the Census. (1998). *Statistical abstract of the United States: 1999* (119th ed.). Washington, DC: U.S. Government Printing Office.

U.S. Code. (2004). 18 § 2251.

U.S. Commission on Obscenity and Pornography. (1970). *Report of the Commission on Obscenity and Pornography.* New York: Random House.

U.S. Department of Justice. (1986, July). *Attorney General's Commission on Pornography: Final Report.* Washington, DC: U.S. Government Printing Office.

Weaver, J. B. (1994). Pornography and sexual callousness: The perceptual and behavioral consequences of exposure to pornography. In D. Zillmann, J. Bryant, & A. C. Huston (Eds.), *Media, children, and the family: Social scientific, psychodynamic, and clinical perspectives* (pp. 215–227). Hillsdale, NJ: Lawrence Erlbaum.

Weaver, J. B., Masland, J. L., & Zillmann, D. (1984). Effect of erotica on young men's aesthetic perception of their female sexual partners. *Perceptual and Motor Skills, 58,* 929–930.

Webb, P. (1982). Erotic art and pornography. In M. Yaffe & E. C. Nelson (Eds.), *The influence of pornography on behavior* (pp. 80–90). London: Academic Press.

Wilson, W. C., & Abelson, H. I. (1973). Experience with and attitudes toward explicit sexual materials. *Journal of Social Issues, 29*(3), 19–39.

Winick, C. (1985). A content analysis of sexually explicit magazines sold in an adult bookstore. *Journal of Sex Research, 21*(2), 206–210.

Wishnoff, R. (1978). Modeling effects of explicit and nonexplicit sexual stimuli on the sexual anxiety and behavior of women. *Archives of Sexual Behavior, 7,* 455–461.

Wyer, R., Bodenhausen, G. V., & Gorman, T. F. (1985). Cognitive mediators of reactions to rape. *Journal of Personality and Social Psychology, 48,* 324–338.

Yaffe, M. (1982). Therapeutic uses of sexually explicit material. In M. Yaffe & E. C. Nelson (Eds.), *The influence of pornography on behavior* (pp. 119–150). London: Academic Press.

Zillmann, D. (1984a). *Connections between sex and aggression.* Hillsdale, NJ: Lawrence Erlbaum.

Zillmann, D. (1984b). Effects of nonviolent pornography. In D. Scott (Ed.), *Symposium on media violence and pornography: Proceedings and resource book* (pp. 95–115). Toronto, Ontario: Media Action Group.

Zillmann, D. (1989). Effects of prolonged consumption of pornography. In D. Zillmann & J. Bryant (Eds.), *Pornography: Research advances and policy considerations* (pp. 127–157). Hillsdale, NJ: Lawrence Erlbaum.

Zillmann, D. (1994a). Erotica and family values. In D. Zillmann, J. Bryant, & A. C. Huston (Eds.), *Media, children, and the family: Social scientific, psychodynamic, and clinical perspectives* (pp. 199–213). Hillsdale, NJ: Lawrence Erlbaum.

Zillmann, D. (1994b). The regulatory dilemma concerning pornography. In J. E. Wood, Jr., & D. Davis (Eds.), *Problems and conflicts between law and morality in a free society* (pp. 117–148). Waco, TX: Baylor University.

Zillmann, D. (2000). Influence of unrestrained access to erotica on adolescents' and young adults' dispositions toward sexuality. *Journal of Adolescent Health, 27*(2, Suppl. 1), 41–44.

Zillmann, D., & Bryant, J. (1982). Pornography, sexual callousness, and the trivialization of rape. *Journal of Communication, 32*(4), 10–21.

Zillmann, D., & Bryant, J. (1984). Effects of massive exposure to pornography. In N. M. Malamuth & E. Donnerstein (Eds.), *Pornography and sexual aggression* (pp. 115–138). Orlando, FL: Academic Press.

Zillmann, D., & Bryant, J. (1986). Shifting preferences in pornography consumption. *Communications Research, 13,* 560–578.

Zillmann, D., & Bryant, J. (1988a). Effect of prolonged consumption of pornography on family values. *Journal of Family Issues, 9*(4), 518–544.

Zillmann, D., & Bryant, J. (1988b). Pornography's impact on sexual satisfaction. *Journal of Applied Social Psychology, 18,* 438–453.

Zillmann, D., & Bryant, J. (1989). *Pornography: Research advances and policy considerations.* Hillsdale, NJ: Lawrence Erlbaum.

Zillmann, D., Bryant, J., & Carveth, R. A. (1981). The effect of erotica featuring sadomasochism and bestiality on motivated intermale aggression. *Personality and Social Psychology Bulletin, 7,* 153–159.

Zillmann, D., Bryant, J., Comisky, P. W., & Medoff, N. J. (1981). Excitation and hedonic valence in the effect of erotica on motivated intermale aggression. *European Journal of Social Psychology, 11*(3), 233–252.

Zillmann, D., & Weaver, J. B. (1989). Pornography and men's sexual callousness toward women. In D. Zillmann & J. Bryant (Eds.), *Pornography: Research advances and policy considerations* (pp. 95–125). Hillsdale, NJ: Lawrence Erlbaum.

12

The Sex Trade:
Exotic Dancing and Prostitution

Vern L. Bullough and Richard D. McAnulty ◆

I was a prostitute for eight years, from the time I was fifteen up until I was 23, and I don't know how you can possibly say, as busy as you are as a lady of the evening, that you like every sexual act, that you work out your fantasies. Come on, get serious! How can you work out your fantasies with a trick that you are putting on an act for?

—L. Bell, 1987, pp. 49–50

Every night, between the peak hours or 9 p.m. and 1 a.m., perhaps a quarter of a million Americans pick up the phone and dial a number for commercial phone sex. The average call lasts 6 to 8 minutes, and the charges range from 89 cents to $4 a minute. . . . Three quarters of the callers are lonely hearts seeking conversation with a woman. The sexual content of the call is often of secondary importance. . . . most calls are answered by "actresses"—bank tellers, accountants, secretaries, and housewives earning a little extra money at the end of the day.

—Schlosser, 1997, pp. 48–49

We are not bad people. We are regular people. You know, I live in a regular neighborhood. I'm a regular person. . . . Just I'm a dancer. I think it's important for people to know that we are just regular people and that we do have lives. We do have families, we do have kids, you know, and we're not . . . out to wreck homes. . . . We're just out there to make a dollar, just like anybody else.

—H. Bell, Sloan, & Stickland, 1998, p. 358

In its various forms, the sex trade is one of the most lucrative industries in the world. The global pornography industry alone generates over $55 billion in revenues each year, making it the third most profitable industry after the trade of weapons and of illicit drugs (Morais, 1999). The global sex industry thrives in some parts of the world, southeast Asia in particular. In Thailand, prostitution fuels the sex industry, which employs tour operators and travel agencies that offer special package deals. Sex tourism contributes upward of $4 billion per year to the Thai economy (Bishop & Robinson, 1998). The sex trade caters to men. The vast majority of the sex tourists to the capital of Thailand, nearly 90 percent, are men. In fact, the customers of prostitutes, whether male or female, are men. Although less visible in other parts of the world, including the United States, the sex trade thrives in most cultures.

Of all the forms of sex trade, one in particular has a long and controversial history—prostitution. The lengthy existence of the various forms of commerce reveals that there are sufficient numbers of consumers to sustain these trades. Topless or exotic dancing also has a long history; as a form of entertainment for hire, however, it is probably a more recent phenomenon.

This chapter offers an overview of the above two common forms of sex trade. Research on prevalence and the different forms of these practices is reviewed. Additionally, research findings on sex trade workers and their customers are summarized. Finally, we also consider the sociocultural and individual factors that support the sex trade, along with divergent perspectives on the benefits and problems associated with the trade.

EXOTIC DANCING

We use the term "exotic dancing" to refer to any form of sexually suggestive dancing for hire. The dancers are designated by a variety of terms, including topless dancers, strippers, exotic dancers, and adult entertainers. The latter term is apparently preferred by dancers because it carries less of a negative connotation than the other labels. Entertainment featuring nude or topless dancing has gained popularity in recent years. In one national sex survey, 16 percent of men and 4 percent of women reported having been to a club featuring nude or seminude dancers (Laumann, Gagnon, Michael, & Michaels, 1994). According to the *Exotic Dancer Directory*, an industry publication, there are over 2,000 clubs offering adult entertainment in the United States. It is estimated that most major metropolitan areas have several dozen clubs that offer adult entertainment, and these numbers seem to be steadily growing. These clubs provide acts consisting of performances by dancers in various stages of undress. Depending on local ordinances, the entertainers may be topless or completely nude. Although illegal in the United States, some countries such as Thailand permit live sex acts featuring sexual intercourse and lesbian acts on stage (Manderson, 1992). In the United States, the only physical contact between dancers and customers that is sometimes permitted involves "lap dancing." Lap dancing consists of individual, and usually private, performances during which the dancer may rub her thong-clad genitals against a customer's clothed lap. The entire performance takes place in the customer's lap or between his legs. As one performer described it, a lap dance basically involves "the dancer grinding her genitals against his, and the man knows he can expect to get off" (Lewis, 1998). Although some instances of lap dancing allegedly escalate to actual sexual activity, including mutual masturbation and oral sex, most dancers object to the association of exotic dancing with prostitution. Most dancers insist on the enforcement of the "no touching" provision that is required by club management and local jurisdictions as a way of reinforcing the distinction between the "art" of exotic dancing and the practice of prostitution (Lewis, 1998).

Exotic dancing is not a new trade. There are several historical accounts of scantily clad female dancers providing entertainment for royalty. The biblical Dance of the Seven Veils allegedly involved an exotic dance by King Herod Antipas's own daughter to entertain the audience. Burlesque theater was a precursor to modern striptease or exotic dancing. One of the first descriptions of topless dancers was offered by Skipper and McCaghy (1970) who conducted a field study of thirty-five performers. Using a semistructured interview, the authors gathered information on the physical, social, and psychological attributes of "strippers." They characterized the participants as usually being the firstborn in a family from which the father figure was absent, as reaching puberty precociously, having sexual experiences at an early age, and possessing the physical endowment (large breasts) desired in the trade. The dancers tended to demonstrate early independence, often leaving home at an early age. Presumably, this early departure from home represented an urge to escape an aversive environment. Their need for affection was met by their occupational choice, the public display of the body as a means of securing approval and recognition. In addition, the opportunity to dance topless for pay came about at a time of great financial need in these women's lives. The authors concluded that performers "became strippers more by chance than design, more by drift than aspiration" (p. 400). Thus, this description of dancers provides the picture of a troubled childhood, with early sexualization, and an opportunistic motivation for entering the profession.

A similar depiction of topless dancers as relatively unstable and desperate women was offered by Salutin (1971). Salutin added that dancers, by necessity, were uninhibited about their bodies, inclined to engage in prostitution occasionally, and sexually promiscuous. In Salutin's estimation, although most dancers were married or were in a long-term heterosexual relationship, most were open to sexual experimentation in various forms, which she attributed directly to the occupation. Again, the portrayal of topless dancers is mostly negative, accentuating the image of a "deviant profession."

Enck and Preston (1988) analyzed the nature of interactions between dancers and customers. Their conclusions were based on the observations of a student who secured a waitress job in a topless club (she elected not to be listed as a coauthor because of the stigma associated with her profession). Enck and Preston emphasized the "counterfeit intimacy" that characterized the interactions between dancers and patrons. In their analysis, performances are orchestrated to provide an illusion of sexual intimacy, thus constituting a form of role-playing in which the actors have distinctive parts and goals. For dancers, the ultimate goal is to generate an income, and the method is by acting in a sexually provocative fashion. Several ploys used by dancers were identified, including making each customer feel special, sexually desirable, and appearing emotionally and/or sexually needy. For the customer, the primary goal is to obtain a "sexual experience." Customers' ploys include claiming an emotional attachment to a dancer, complaining of being lonely or deprived, and boasting of physical or financial resources. Despite their portrayal of the interactions as shallow and "counterfeit," Enck and Preston postulated that the profession provides a source of fulfillment, for customers and dancers alike, that conventional or "legitimate" institutions had failed to provide for these individuals. Therefore, adult entertainment is sometimes viewed as a useful and legal outlet for unmet needs.

In contrast to the negative portrayals of adult entertainers provided by earlier studies, findings of a more recent study revealed a more positive picture. The personality profiles and background characteristics of thirty-eight topless dancers were compared to those of a control group of restaurant waitresses (McAnulty, Satterwhite, & Gullick, 1995). Overall, the dancers were not found to be more psychologically maladjusted. Both groups were above average in extraversion and openness to new experiences, and the dancers had higher incomes, earning four times the salary of waitresses. The dancers viewed themselves as more physically attractive, but also reported more preoccupation with body image than did the waitresses. No differences were found in criminal history. The vast majority of all participants reported a heterosexual orientation, and virtually all were in dating or committed relationships. Anecdotal information suggested that none of the dancers engaged in prostitution, which was strictly prohibited by club regulations and is illegal.

One finding consistently reported in studies of topless and nude dancers is that the primary motivation for entering the profession is financial (McAnulty et al., 1995; Skipper & McCaghy, 1970). The same finding has been noted for male strippers (Dressel & Petersen, 1982). Although many people consider adult entertainment to be a deviant occupation, topless dancers are not inherently deviant individuals. Some researchers have suggested that deviance is mostly in the eyes of the beholder. In other words, a career or lifestyle is deviant *only* if society labels it so. Undoubtedly, individuals attracted to a profession like exotic dancing will tend to be more disinhibited and more comfortable with their bodies than most. Some of these same issues will be revisited as we cover another profession, prostitution. However, unlike topless and nude dancing, prostitution is almost always considered a deviant occupation.

PROSTITUTION

Prostitution refers to the profession involving the indiscriminate exchange of sexual favors for economic gain, or the commercialized sale of sexual services in which sex is a commodity (de Zalduondo, 1991). For the prostitute, the practice represents a means of deriving or supplementing an income. Therefore, prostitutes are referred to as sex trade workers. In some cases, the prostitute may exchange sexual acts for illicit drugs; for example, the so-called crack whores trade sex for crack cocaine (Fullilove, Lown, & Fullilove, 1992). A person who trades sexual favors for a job promotion would not be labeled a prostitute, although this includes some of the same elements as prostitution. What separates prostitution from this example is the repeated and indiscriminate nature of selling sexual services.

Historical Perspective

Prostitution has been called the "oldest profession." In reality, it is probably not any older than such social roles as medicine man and priest. However, prostitution has always been and continues to be one of the most controversial occupations. Much ambivalence toward the practice of selling sexual favors as an occupation is reflected throughout history. On one hand, prostitution is often viewed as a deplorable practice, but its lengthy existence reveals that there has always been a demand for sex at a price. This ambivalence is illustrated by the writings of early religious figures. Biblical texts refer to Mary Magdalene as a "woman of the city, a sinner," and many references to harlots are found throughout the Bible. In the fourth century, the Christian bishop Augustine viewed prostitutes as shameful while also noting that they served as useful outlets for lustful desires. Similarly, Thomas Aquinas, Italian priest and philosopher of the Middle Ages, believed that prostitutes helped prevent the spread of lustful sins (Bullough & Bullough, 1977). Napoleon Bonaparte is quoted as saying that "prostitutes are a necessity. Without them, men would attack respectable women on the street." In Victorian-era England, prostitutes were viewed as unfortunate but essential sexual outlets for men's needs; the trade prevented "worse offenses" such as having sexual encounters with other men's wives or with virgins (Taylor, 1970).

The ambivalence toward prostitution is evident in the various governmental policies and interventions. President Juan Perón of Argentina ordered the legalization of prostitution in 1954. The Argentine government and public health department reasoned that legalizing the commerce of sex would help control the spread of sexually transmitted diseases and prevent men from engaging in sexually deviant behavior (Guy, 1991). In the same country, Dr. Nicolás V. Greco wrote that banning prostitution led men to seek "artificial methods" (such as masturbation) or "sexual perversions" (homosexuality in this case) for sexual release. Greco and others believed that prostitution encouraged heterosexuality and, therefore, reinforced the institutions of marriage and family. Lacking any scientific evidence to support these views, Greco quoted St. Thomas Aquinas and St. Augustine. Prostitution has remained a legal institution in Argentina since 1955. Historical records suggest that prostitution has generally been viewed as a necessary "evil," one that might be tolerated to prevent worse evils.

Prostitution across Cultures

In most cultures, prostitution is viewed as a deviant profession. This is clearly illustrated by the choice of terms used to describe prostitutes in our culture—such as "hooker," "whore," and other terms that are perhaps less pejorative, such as "working girls," "ladies of the night," and *femmes fatales* (from the French for "deadly women"). There is much variability in the prevalence of prostitution across cultures and in cultural attitudes toward the sale of sex. Many societies have quietly tolerated the practice, while others are more accepting of prostitution within specified boundaries. In ancient Greece and Mesopotamia, temple prostitutes, both male and female, were common and the practice was associated with religious rituals. Having sex with the prostitutes was considered a form of worship. Temple prostitution was also practiced in India. The Hindu temple of Samanâtha reportedly had over 500 "dancing girls" who provided music for the god and sensual pleasure for male worshippers (Bullough & Bullough, 1978). Prostitution also flourished in medieval Europe.

Some societies have banned the practice outright, whereas it is regulated in some parts of the world. In countries where prostitution is legalized, such as France and the Netherlands, prostitutes must be registered and submit to periodic medical evaluations for sexually transmitted diseases. Prostitution is more prevalent in male-dominated, or patriarchal, societies, where women have a comparatively low status. In such societies, women typically are considered inferior, have fewer opportunities for success and independence, and are expected to cater to men's needs and desires (Cusick, 2002). Prostitution is most prevalent in patriarchal, economically depressed countries that do not have severe sanctions for nonmarital sex, such as Mexico, Brazil, Ivory Coast, and Thailand. Thailand alone, for example, has an estimated 2 million female sex workers (Buckingham, Meister, & Webb, 2004). Prostitution also flourishes in societies that prize female virginity. Under conditions of a limited supply of eligible female partners, there is often a demand for a sex trade. In situations where men greatly outnumber available women, there is competition for female partners, and some men will be willing to pay for sexual encounters. Declining numbers of eligible women could be due to higher mortality rates (which was common in the past due to severe anemia and complications during childbirth), a cultural requirement of female virginity, or a double standard that tolerates male sexual experimentation but demands female sexual restrictiveness. In general, prostitution is most common in restrictive societies and least common in sexually open societies. Presumably, in an open and tolerant society, where the genders have equal rights and opportunity, there would be no need for a clandestine sex trade (Goode, 1990). However, it should be noted that even liberal countries such as Denmark report a thriving sex trade. And in a study of Norwegian men, 13 percent admitted having paid for sex with a prostitute (Høigård & Finstad, 1986/1992).

Prostitution in the United States

Even in societies where prostitution is illegal, such as the United States (outside of a few counties in Nevada), it exists and even thrives in some urban areas. In the state of Nevada, prostitution is legal but regulated. Each county in the state has the right to allow prostitution in designated areas. Nevada's best-known brothel, the Mustang Ranch, closed in 1999 amid allegations of fraud. Potterat, Woodhouse, Muth, and Muth (1990) estimated that 80,000 women worked as prostitutes in the United States in the 1980s. However, these are probably underestimates due to the clandestine nature of the profession and the tendency of some prostitutes to drift in and out of the trade. Potterat and colleagues estimated that prostitution tends to be a short-term career, four to five years for most. However, Freund, Leonard, and Lee (1989) found that the streetwalkers they studied had been in the trade for an average of eight years. In the Janus and Janus (1993) survey, 4 percent of the women admitted having traded sex for money. In one study in New York City, 22 percent of the gay and bisexual male adolescents admitted to exchanging sex for money or drugs (Rotheram-Borus et al., 1994). Interestingly, we find no comparable survey of heterosexual male adolescents.

Although it is impossible to accurately estimate the number of prostitutes in the United States, survey results suggest that fewer men have experience with prostitutes today than in the 1940s. Kinsey, Pomeroy, and Martin (1948) noted that two out of three white males that they surveyed admitted having had sex with a prostitute at least once, and up to 20 percent described themselves as regular customers. Later surveys suggested a significant decline in men's experiences with prostitutes. In the Janus survey (Janus & Janus, 1993), 20 percent of men admitted having paid for sex. A similar pattern is noted in the number of men who report that their first sexual encounter occurred with a prostitute: approximately 54 percent of high school graduates and 20 percent of college graduates who participated in Kinsey's survey were sexually initiated by prostitutes, compared to 10 percent in a survey conducted more than twenty years later (Hunt, 1974). This pattern was also documented by Laumann et al. (1994) who found that 7 percent of 55- to 59-year-old men had their first sexual encounter with a prostitute, compared to 1.5 percent of 18- to 24-year-olds. The preferred explanation for this trend is the decreased double standard during the second half of the twentieth century, which made more women open to premarital sexual experimentation. Consequently, this increase in available sexual partners reduced men's inclination to pay a stranger for sexual activity (Edgley, 1989).

The Prostitute

The term "prostitute" is derived from the Latin word *prostitutus*, meaning "to set forth" or to be exposed for sale. This refers to the advertising of sexual services by the prostitute, whether in manner of dress, verbal propositions, or location. The corresponding legal term, "solicitation," is a reference to the offer of sexual activity for a fee.

The consistent pattern in contemporary society and throughout history is for the customers of prostitutes to be men. The most common form of prostitution involves women who sell sexual favors to heterosexual men. The second most common group consists of homosexual male prostitutes who cater to gay men. Male prostitutes who make themselves available to women are called "gigolos," and they are reportedly very uncommon. Lesbian prostitutes are considered extremely rare. Despite what customers may believe, the prostitute does not engage in the practice for personal sexual satisfaction, but rather as a financial enterprise. Prostitutes do not generally derive pleasure from their repeated encounters with customers and, in fact, generally resent them. For the practitioner, prostitution entails the provision of a service for a fee. Female prostitutes earn over thirteen times the salary of nonprostitutes (Earls & David, 1989). By definition, the transactions are void of emotional involvement. The briefer the encounter is, the sooner the prostitute can return to work and generate more income. One prostitute commented, "[W]hen I have intercourse I move around just a little. Then the customers get more turned on, so it goes faster. Otherwise, it's so gross; besides, I get sore if it takes too long" (Høigård & Finstad, 1986/1992, p. 68). Street prostitutes may have a dozen or more anonymous sexual encounters during the course of an evening (Cordelier, 1976/1978; Heyl, 1979). In one study of prostitutes, the average number of customers per day was four, with some prostitutes reporting up to ten encounters in a day (Freund et al., 1989).

Female Prostitutes

There are different classes of female prostitutes. From society's perspective, the most deviant form involves *streetwalkers*, the most common and visible prostitutes. Streetwalkers are virtually indiscriminate in accepting customers, have a relatively low fee for services, and generally have numerous patrons in one night. Compared to the other types of prostitutes, streetwalkers are more vulnerable to arrest and abuse by customers. Most streetwalkers work for a pimp, usually a man who provides protection in return for a large percentage of monies earned by the prostitute.

Over 60 percent of the streetwalkers studied by Freund et al. (1989) engaged in fellatio and 23 percent had vaginal intercourse with customers. Consistent with reports from female prostitutes, kissing is uncommon (Freund, Lee, & Leonard, 1991). As one prostitute stated, "Like most girls, I personally refuse to let a client kiss me on the mouth. . . . I make a distinction between my vagina and my mouth. I think it's only normal, we've got our dignity too" (Jaget, 1980, p. 167).

Streetwalkers advertise their services in several ways. They tend to wear provocative and revealing clothing and will generally frequent areas known for prostitution. Finally, upon gaining the attention of potential customers, they often make subtle ("Want to party?") or direct ("I can show you a good time") propositions. The cost of services is negotiated early in an encounter, with fee varying depending on the type of sexual act requested; fellatio is often cheaper than intercourse (Winick & Kinsie, 1971).

Prostitutes who work in *brothels* (whorehouses), and special massage parlors or clubs have higher status. Being in an establishment that employs prostitutes has some advantages: it is safer, and business is often more regular. However, there is also a risk of arrest because police squads periodically raid such facilities. Outside of a few counties in Nevada, there are no legally recognized brothels in the United States although some clandestine facilities definitely exist. In countries where prostitution is legal and regulated, brothel prostitution is prevalent. Typically, brothels are managed by a "madam" who collects a percentage of all earnings in the establishments (Heyl, 1979). Massage parlors are sometimes fronts for brothels. The masseuse will generally provide a massage, with other services (often fellatio or masturbation) available to clients for an additional charge. Such extra services are of course illegal in the United States. This association between prostitution and massage parlors has led many legitimate masseurs and masseuses to emphasize that they do not provide sexual services. One way to stress the legitimacy of massage services is by specifying that they consist of "therapeutic massages."

At the highest level of prostitution are the *call girls*, who often operate through an escort service. Escort services advertise that they provide male or female escorts for social occasions. Their advertisements stress that their services are confidential and discreet. One large city in the southeastern United States advertised no less than 106 such escort agencies. The nature of their advertisements suggests that these agencies are thinly veiled covers for prostitution (e.g., "Fantasy Girls," "Wild College Girls," "Affairs of the Heart").

Call girls demand a higher price, are more selective, and typically have a small regular clientele (Greenwald, 1970). They often operate independently and live a luxurious life in comparison to other types of prostitutes (Winick & Kinsie, 1971).

Contrary to streetwalkers and brothel prostitutes, call girls do not usually have multiple encounters in one evening. The case of Heidi Fleiss, "the Hollywood Madam," made the headlines in 1993 for operating an exclusive call-girl service that catered to wealthy men in California (Fleiss was quoted as saying, "I took the oldest profession on Earth, and I did it better than anyone on Earth"). This case was sensational to the media and public not because it involved prostitution but due to the allegations that Fleiss's customers included politicians and popular actors (Birnbaum, 1993).

Equivalent roles to those of contemporary prostitutes could be found in ancient Greece, where *pornoi* (a term meaning "the writing about [or by] prostitutes") referred to the lowest class of prostitutes and *hetairae* (meaning "companion") represented the higher-class courtesans (Bullough & Bullough, 1978, 1995). The latter held high unofficial status, were educated and socially sophisticated, and commanded a higher price for their services. Ancient Greek culture epitomized gender inequality. Therefore, wives were responsible for childrearing and domestic duties, while the hetairae served as social and sexual companions. In both cases, woman was considered man's property, either for his sexual enjoyment or for domestic comfort.

Male Prostitutes

Although both are old practices and probably involve similar prevalence rates, male prostitution has received less attention than female prostitution. Prior to 1963, even less was known of male prostitution than is known today. That year, John Rechy published *City of Night*, a novel about the travels of a boy from Texas who becomes a prostitute and plies his trade throughout the United States. The novel served as a window into the seamier side of male prostitution and increased public awareness about the "profession."

Male prostitutes tend to practice their trade intermittently in comparison to female prostitutes (Winick & Kinsie, 1971). The vast majority of male prostitutes offer their services to gay men. Interestingly, the majority of male prostitutes do not describe themselves as being gay. In their study of 224 male street prostitutes, Boles and Elifson (1994) found that only 18 percent described themselves as homosexual, while nearly 36 percent considered themselves to be bisexual, and 46 percent were heterosexual in their self-reported sexual orientation. The average age was 28 years and most had been in the trade for close to ten years. The services offered by male prostitutes vary as a function of their reported sexual orientation: heterosexual prostitutes were unlikely to participate in anal intercourse whereas nearly 65 percent of homosexual male prostitutes engaged in receptive anal intercourse. Twenty-three percent of bisexual male prostitutes participated in receptive anal intercourse (Boles & Elifson). In a study of male prostitutes in London, West and de Villiers (1993) reported that the ages ranged from 16 to 21 years. Fellatio and masturbation of customers are the most commonly reported sexual activities by male prostitutes. Anal intercourse occurs somewhat less frequently and commands a higher fee.

As for female prostitutes, the primary motive for male prostitution is making money (Boles & Elifson, 1994). Some male prostitutes report initially being attracted to the excitement of life of the streets and the prospect of multiple sexual encounters. However, the novelty rapidly wears off and the main reason for continuing is financial. As one male prostitute put it, "I'm hustling money—not sex" (Boles & Elifson, p. 44). Male sex trade workers apparently earn less money than their female counterparts (Shaver, 2005).

Several types of male prostitutes have been identified. *Hustlers* are viewed as the male counterpart of streetwalkers. Like streetwalkers, they tend to have multiple indiscriminate encounters during the course of an evening. These encounters may take place in public places, such as parks, rest rooms, or in customer automobiles. However, in contrast to streetwalkers, hustlers generally do not have pimps. *Drag queen* sometimes refers to gay prostitutes who cross-dress while working.[1] The majority of gay cross-dressers, however, are not prostitutes. Some of the customers of drag queen prostitutes may mistake them for women, especially if the prostitute restricts his sexual activity to performing fellatio on the customers. *Call boys* are equivalent to call girls in that they have a regular clientele and live a more comfortable life. *Kept boys* are financially supported by an older male, or "sugar daddy," in exchange for sexual favors. Finally, *gigolo* refers to heterosexual males who are paid for sex by female customers, although gigolos are fairly rare. Compared to female prostitutes, very little research has been conducted on the types of male prostitutes, with the exception of hustlers. This classification of male prostitutes is somewhat arbitrary because some will function in several of these roles over time (Earls & David, 1989).

Child Prostitutes

One of the most disturbing aspects of the sex trade is the exploitation of children. Worldwide, it is estimated that several million children and adolescents are involved in prostitution (Willis & Levy, 2002). In the United States alone, over 244,000 children are at risk of sexual exploitation, which includes prostitution and child pornography (Estes & Weiner, 2001). Child prostitution has been reported throughout the world, from Boise, Idaho, to Bangkok, Thailand, and London, England. Both boys and girls are involved and their ages range from 10 to 17. Many adult prostitutes actually started their careers in adolescence when they ran away to escape physical, mental, or sexual abuse at home. According to Williard (1991), low self-esteem and a lack of marketable skills may lead some runaways into prostitution as a means of survival on the streets. Most commonly, an adult, either a pimp or even a parent, is involved in their initiation in the trade. Campagna and Poffenberger (1988) described a pimp who recruited 12- to 14-year-old girls from a shelter for runaways while another met desperate youths at bus stations. The initiation into prostitution often included instilling a false sense of security and the lure of easy money. The use of drugs is another common means of facilitating the exploitation of children and adolescents.

Child prostitution has long-term adverse effects on the victims. Of particular concern is the global trafficking of women and children as sex trade workers involving as many as 700,000 victims per year (U.S. Department of State, 2002), 30 percent of whom are children (Kelly, 2002). With increased recognition of the problem of sexual exploitation of children, efforts are being made to prosecute the exploiters and prevent the tragic effects on the victims. In August 1996, nearly 2,000 representatives from 122 countries assembled in Stockholm, Sweden, for the first World Congress against Sexual Exploitation of Children. This meeting called for international attention on the plight of sexually exploited children, concluding that it is the responsibility of each nation to protect children and to prosecute perpetrators of such crimes, which are apparently increasingly prevalent.

Customers of Prostitutes

Far more interest has been shown in prostitutes than in their customers by both researchers and the legal system. We know that prostitutes are more likely to be arrested than their customers, and the criminal charges are more serious (Boyle & Noonan, 1987). According to Margo St. James (1987), a former female prostitute and an advocate for the rights of sex trade workers, few men are arrested for prostitution. Those few men are usually male prostitutes rather than customers. This trend in prosecuting prostitutes more severely than their customers is not new. In the eighteenth century, convicted male customers were fined but the female prostitute was publicly flogged. Her crime has consistently been viewed as worse than his. Prostitution remains the only sexual offense for which more women than men are convicted.

In the trade, customers are referred to as "johns" or "tricks." Their demographic characteristics cross all socioeconomic and racial strata. In one study of the customers of an escort service, based on an address listing obtained during a raid, the majority of clients were Caucasian, married, and affluent (Adams, 1987). Monto (2005) reported that a significant proportion of customers are married, although they are less likely to be married than noncustomers, and they are more likely to be dissatisfied with their marriages. Customers tend to visit prostitutes from their own ethnic and racial background (Monto, 2004). From their interviews with 101 customers of New Jersey streetwalkers, Freund et al. (1991) reported that 42 percent were married and most resided in the surrounding areas. Average age in the sample was 40. Most men were regular customers (93 percent made monthly visits and 63 percent reported weekly encounters) and had been visiting the prostitutes for more than one year. Furthermore, 55 percent of the customers were "regulars" who had sex with the same prostitute during their outings. Sex usually occurred outdoors, such as in back alleys, or in the client's car. The preferred sexual activity was fellatio, and vaginal intercourse was a close second (see also Monto, 2001).

Several motives for using prostitutes have been delineated, including variety, loneliness, sexual deviance, curiosity, and deprivation (Edgley, 1989; Monto, 2004, 2005; Pitts, Smith, Grierson, O'Brien, & Misson, 2004). Some customers seek the anonymous and indiscriminate nature of sex with a prostitute. The encounters do not require emotional commitment or preliminary courting, just sex. The prostitute holds no expectation of the client other than financial remuneration. The customer may believe that he is unable to obtain sexual favors without paying for them. Several situations would apply, including men whose wives object to certain sexual practices (such as fellatio), men who have serious physical deformities or social anxiety, and those who have deviant or kinky sexual proclivities. For example, some customers solicit from prostitutes unusual sexual activities that their regular partners find objectionable, such as bondage, spanking, or the use of unusual costumes or sex toys. The illicit and risky nature of an encounter with a prostitute is attractive to some men. Finally, some customers employ the services of prostitutes when their regular partners are unavailable, due to travel or illness.

Although there is an implicit agreement between the customer and the prostitute that the exchange will be superficial and temporary, customers usually want the illusion that the prostitute is interested in them personally and sexually. In fact, customers may become frustrated or angry if the prostitute seems detached, unresponsive, or hurried (Monto, 2004). As with exotic dancing (Enck & Preston, 1988), the customers of prostitutes are paying for a semblance of intimacy; some even describe the transactions as love relationships and insist that they have a special place in the prostitute's life. The challenge for the prostitute is to negotiate a fee for a brief encounter while maintaining the illusion of sexual desire and interest in the customer (Berstein, 2001).

There are a host of reasons for visiting a prostitute, but sexual initiation is no longer a common motive. Whereas prostitutes functioned essentially as sex educators by initiating many young men in the 1930s and 1940s, in contemporary society, few men seek their sexual initiation from sex trade workers.

The Life of Prostitution

In contrast to the fairly positive depictions of the lives of prostitutes in such films as *American Gigolo* and *Pretty Woman*, the actual existence of most prostitutes is anything but glamorous. Most studies and autobiographies portray prostitutes as frequently coming from dysfunctional backgrounds, as suffering from psychological and medical problems, and as living on the fringe of society (Earls & David, 1989). Such findings lead one to question why an individual would choose this profession. Do prostitutes select this stigmatized and often risky occupation in full appreciation of these factors, or is it a desperate choice when no other viable options avail?

Motives for Entering Prostitution

The social and personal dynamics of entering into prostitution have been the subject of study. Poverty and limited alternatives are commonly reported factors that may lead a person to select prostitution as an occupation. Most streetwalkers, for example, have limited educational backgrounds; less than one-third of a sample of 309 streetwalkers had completed high school (Kramer & Berg, 2003). In some Third World nations, impoverished parents actually sell their daughters to be placed in brothels. McCaghy and Hou (1994) reported that one-third of Taiwanese prostitutes entered the trade to provide financial assistance to their parents. Another third became prostitutes because of personal debts. The remainder entered the sex trade out of desperation or exploitation. As one prostitute reported, "I was sold to an illegal wine house by my foster father. That is the way I began my life as a prostitute. I was often beaten by him since I was three. When I was sold I did not have much choice" (p. 261).

In the United States and Canada, a significant number of those entering the trade are adolescent runaways. A history of childhood sexual abuse is commonly reported by prostitutes (Potterat, Rothenberg, & Muth, 1998; Simons & Whitbeck, 1991). In one study of 200 adolescent and adult female prostitutes, 67 percent reported being sexually abused by a father or father figure (Silbert & Pines, 1981a, 1981b). Typically, they have escaped a troubled home and find themselves isolated with virtually no financial resources. Williard (1991) estimated that 75 percent of juvenile prostitutes are runaways or "castaways," youths who are actively encouraged to leave home by parents. In their study of adolescent runaways, Rotheram-Borus et al. (1992) found that 13 percent of males and 7 percent of females had provided sexual favors in return for money or drugs. Nadon and colleagues (1998), however, did not find higher rates of childhood abuse in a sample of forty-five adolescent prostitutes when compared to a matched sample of thirty-seven nonprostitute adolescents. Childhood abuse alone does not explain why some adolescents enter the sex trade, although it represents one of several vulnerabilities (Cusick, 2002). It is clear though that prostitution is an alluring option for survival on the streets for a number of destitute males and females (Earls & David, 1989). For these reasons, street prostitution is sometimes referred to as a "survival crime" (Kramer & Berg, 2003).

Rather than an abrupt entry into the trade, becoming a prostitute is usually a gradual, insidious process. Most often, a person is introduced to prostitution by a friend or acquaintance (Cusick, 2002). In some cases, the prospective prostitute is gradually introduced to the sex trade by a man who poses as a boyfriend or caretaker. After earning the trust of the vulnerable teenager, the "boyfriend" fosters a dependency while restricting contacts with outsiders. The grooming process extends to making the teenager feel helpless and submissive. After pressuring the adolescent to engage in sex with one of the "boyfriend's" male friends, the prospective prostitute is gradually pressured or coerced into having paid encounters with strangers (Swann, 1998). At some point, the novice prostitute realizes that his or her "boyfriend" is actually a pimp.

Risks of the Business

The lifestyle of prostitutes entails many risks, including violence from customers and pimps, criminal arrest, and sexually transmitted diseases. According to Høigård and Finstad (1986/1992), the prostitutes' risk of assault by customers increases proportionately with the number of customers. Nineteen of twenty-six prostitutes they interviewed had experienced violence from customers, ranging from "slaps to rape, from confinement to threats of murder" (p. 58). Nearly two-thirds of the 211 male prostitutes studied by Simon, Morse, Osofsky, Balson, and Gaumer (1992) feared violence by customers.

Substance abuse is another problem commonly reported by prostitutes. Forty-four percent of the young male prostitutes studied by Pleak and Meyer-Bahlburg (1990) admitted having a drug or alcohol problem. All of the male prostitutes studied by Simon et al. (1992) were substance users, primarily alcohol, cocaine, and marijuana, and 80 percent were polysubstance abusers. Boles and Elifson (1994) found that over half of the male prostitutes in their study were injectable drug users: 54 to 71 percent used crack cocaine and 16 to 20 percent had abused heroin. Cocaine was reportedly the drug of choice with nearly 80 percent reporting a history of abuse.

Similar trends are reported among female prostitutes. The vast majority, 86 percent, in one sample of 237 female streetwalkers reported drug usage. One-half of the women had used injectable drugs (Potterat et al., 1998). In most cases, substance abuse preceded women's entry into prostitution, suggesting that they entered the trade as a means of supporting their drug habits. Some female crack-cocaine users report exchanging sex for the drug. In one sample of 150 users, 43 percent admitted having traded oral sex or vaginal intercourse for cocaine (Sterk, Elifson, & German, 2000). Problematic substance abuse may therefore represent another motive for becoming a prostitute.

Although contagion from prostitution accounts for a relatively small percentage of total cases of HIV disease worldwide, in some countries prostitution represents the major vector in the spread of HIV disease. In a study of 1,000 prostitutes in Kenya, 85 percent tested positive for HIV (Lambert, 1988). In some brothels in Thailand, up to 70 percent of prostitutes were infected (Gray et al., 1997; Manderson, 1992). In the United States, estimates of HIV infection among prostitutes range from none to 60 percent, depending on location and the prostitute's number of years in the trade (Lambert). Rates of infection may be higher among male than female prostitutes in the United

States. Simon et al. (1992) reported that nearly 18 percent of the 211 male prostitutes they studied tested positive for HIV. Boles and Elifson (1994) found that 35 percent of the 224 male prostitutes in their study carried HIV and 28 percent tested positive for syphilis. Male prostitutes who identified themselves as homosexual had higher rates of HIV infection (50 percent) than those who described themselves as heterosexual (18.5 percent).

Prostitutes are a potentially high-risk group for contracting HIV because they often engage in two high-risk behaviors for exposure to HIV: having sex involving fluid exchange with multiple partners and injectable drug use. The nature of prostitutes' work, the sex trade, puts them in frequent contact with bodily fluids. Prostitutes who practice unprotected receptive anal sex are especially vulnerable to HIV infection (Karim & Ramjee, 1998). Their lifestyle commonly involves injectable drug use. Although there has been a trend for increased condom use among prostitutes, it is by no means consistent and universal. Many prostitutes who are not injectable drug users have a regular sex partner who is. Therefore, the partner's behavior puts the prostitute at risk for HIV disease since male and female prostitutes rarely practice safer sex with their regular partners (Albert, Warner, & Hatcher, 1998).

Recognizing these problems, several programs have been implemented to reduce health risks among prostitutes and their clients. One such program, EMPOWER (Education Means Protection of Women in Recreation), was developed in Thailand to provide HIV testing, education, and health counseling. Preliminary results reveal that this and other programs are effective in reducing rates of STDs, including HIV, among prostitutes (Hanenberg & Rojanapithayakorn, 1998).

Prostitution in Perspective

Sociologists and feminists have emphasized the gender inequality that is evident in prostitution. Prostitution primarily benefits men, both customers and pimps. Customers obtain sexual enjoyment from prostitutes who, in turn, financially support their pimps. Those women who are most likely to enter the trade are the economically disadvantaged, with limited education and skills, and commonly having a background of abuse (L. Bell, 1987; Shaver, 2005). They apparently enter prostitution because they believe they have few viable resources in society other than their sexuality.

Prostitution is never really accepted in any modern society. Prostitutes generally are held at the lowest ranks of the social ladder. Even in societies where prostitution is legalized, it is "not an expression of society's acceptance of prostitution but instead epitomizes a policy of isolation and stigma toward the prostitute" (Hobson, 1987, p. 233). In other words, prostitution policies and regulations in tolerant societies represent subtle attempts to control or segregate prostitutes from this perspective. In a fair, egalitarian society, many acceptable options would be available for disadvantaged women and rarely would they select such a deviant occupation. Hobson noted that

> [a] society that institutionalizes prostitution as a work option for the poor makes a statement about its position on inequality. One can see this in the policy toward prostitution in countries like Korea, and until recently, the Philippines. The governments have sought to legitimize prostitution as work, even elevated it to a patriotic endeavor, since sex commerce has brought in foreign tourism and reduced the national debt. (p. 235)

Within the feminist movement, there is disagreement over whether prostitution is degrading to women or an acceptable choice for independent women. Feminists have debated whether the prostitute is the "quintessential oppressed woman or the quintessential liberated woman" (Tong, 1984). As Shaver (2005) noted, categorizing the sex trade as either a career or as an exploitation reflects this ongoing debate. It is also evident in the labels applied to sex trade workers, who are "bad girls" in sharp contrast to "good girls," a carryover of the Victorian dichotomized view of women. Exotic dancers seem to view the transactions with customers as mutual exploitation. As one dancer put it, "It's really double exploitation as far as I can see. The female is exploiting the male for money; selling her sexual magnetism for money. The male is exploiting the woman because he is debasing her..." (H. Bell et al., 1998, p. 362). The majority of feminists though have argued that women would not choose a deviant role such as prostitute if they were offered better alternatives. With the proper education, economic opportunities, and positive self-concept, women would be free to select any career, and it seems unlikely that many would opt for such degrading socially rejected roles as prostitute, topless dancer, or actress in sexually explicit films (Bell, 1987).

From the perspective of evolutionary psychology, prostitution and all forms of commercial sex can be understood based on two simultaneous factors—men's inherent desire for casual sex and for sexual variety, and the willingness of some women, either by choice or out of economic desperation, to exchange sexual services for material resources (Buss, 1999). Men, whether viewing pornography or visiting a prostitute, are seeking sexual variety with minimal investment. On the other hand, women who sell sexual favors are motivated by financial remuneration. As Buss noted, "[S]ome women choose prostitution because it provides a quick and lucrative source of income and hence may be seen as a desirable alternative to a nine-to-five job or a demanding husband" (pp. 341–342). Prostitutes, like other women who pursue sex without commitment, are controversial because they compete with other women for men's resources by exploiting men's desires for casual sex. In other words, "prostitutes may siphon off resources that might otherwise go to a man's wife or children" (Buss, p. 342).

From any perspective, the sex trade is flourishing and will continue to do so despite efforts to regulate or eliminate it (Bullough & Bullough, 1995). Clearly, commercial sex, in all its forms, represents one of the most controversial aspects of human sexuality.

NOTE

1. Most drag queens are *not* prostitutes.

REFERENCES

Adams, R. (1987). The role of prostitution in AIDS and other STDs. *Medical Aspects of Human Sexuality, 21*, 27–33.

Albert, A. E., Warner, D. L., & Hatcher, R. A. (1998). Facilitating condom use with clients during commercial sex in Nevada's legal brothels. *American Journal of Public Health, 88*, 643–647.

Bell, H., Sloan, L., & Stickland, C. (1998). Exploiter or exploited: Topless dancers reflect on their experiences. *Affilia: Journal of Women and Social Work, 13*, 352–369.

Bell, L. (Ed.). (1987). *Good girls/bad girls: Sex trade workers and feminists face to face.* Toronto: Women's Press.

Berstein, E. (2001). The meaning of purchase: Desire, demand and the commerce of sex. *Ethnography, 2*, 389–420.

Birnbaum, J. (1993, August). Heidi does Hollywood. *Time*, pp. 56–57.

Bishop, R., & Robinson, L. S. (1998). *Night market: Sexual cultures and the Thai economic miracle.* London: Routledge.

Boles, J., & Elifson, K. W. (1994). Sexual identity and HIV: The male prostitute. *Journal of Sex Research, 31*, 39–46.

Boyle, C., & Noonan, S. (1987). Gender neutrality, prostitution, and pornography. In L. Bell (Ed.), *Good girls/bad girls: Sex trade workers and feminists face to face* (pp. 34–37). Toronto: Women's Press.

Buckingham, R. W., Meister, E., & Webb, N. (2004). Condom use among the female sex worker population in Thailand. *International Journal of STD and AIDS, 15*, 210–211.

Bullough, B., & Bullough, V. L. (1995). Female prostitution: Current research and changing interpretations. *Annual Review of Sex Research, 7*, 158–180.

Bullough, V. L., & Bullough, B. (1977). *Sin, sickness, and sanity: A history of sexual attitudes.* New York: Garland.

Bullough, V. L., & Bullough, B. (1978). *Prostitution: An illustrated social history.* New York: Crown.

Buss, D. M. (1999). *Evolutionary psychology: The new science of the mind.* Needham Heights, MA: Allyn & Bacon.

Campagna, D. S., & Poffenberger, D. L. (1988). *The sexual trafficking of children: An investigation of the child sex trade.* Dover, MA: Auburn House.

Cordelier, J. (1976/1978). *"The life": Memoirs of a French hooker* (H. Matthews, Trans.). New York: Viking Press.

Cusick, L. (2005). Youth prostitution: A literature review. *Child Abuse Review, 11,* 230–251.

de Zalduondo, B. O. (1991). Prostitution viewed cross-culturally: Toward re-contextualized sex work in AIDS intervention research. *Journal of Sex Research, 28,* 223–248.

Dressel, P. L., & Petersen, D. (1982). Becoming a male stripper: Recruitment, socialization, and ideological development. *Work and Occupation, 9,* 387–406.

Earls, C. M., & David, H. (1989). Male and female prostitution: A review. *Annals of Sex Research, 2,* 5–28.

Edgley, C. (1989). Commercial sex: Pornography, prostitution, and advertising. In K. McKinney & S. Sprecher (Eds.), *Human sexuality: The societal and interpersonal context* (pp. 370–424). Norwood, NJ: Ablex.

Enck, G. E., & Preston, J. D. (1988). Counterfeit intimacy: A dramaturgical analysis of an erotic performance. *Deviant Behavior, 9,* 369–381.

Estes, R. J., & Weiner, N. A. (2001). *The commercial sexual exploitation of children in the U.S., Canada, and Mexico.* Philadelphia: University of Philadelphia Press.

Freund, M., Lee, N., & Leonard, T. (1991). Sexual behavior of clients with street prostitutes in Camden, NJ. *Journal of Sex Research, 28,* 579–591.

Freund, M., Leonard, T. L., & Lee, N. (1989). Sexual behavior of resident street prostitutes with their clients in Camden, NJ. *Journal of Sex Research, 26,* 460–478.

Fullilove, M. T., Lown, E. A., & Fullilove, R. E. (1992). Crack 'hos and skeezers: Traumatic experiences of women crack users. *Journal of Sex Research, 29,* 275–287.

Goode, E. (1990). *Deviant behavior* (3rd ed.). Englewood Cliffs, NJ: Prentice-Hall.

Gray, J. A., Dore, G. J., Li, U. M., Supawitkul, S., Effler, P., & Kaldor, J. M. (1997). HIV-1 infection among female commercial sex workers in rural Thailand. *AIDS, 11,* 89–94.

Greenwald, H. (1970). *The call girl.* New York: Ballantine Books.

Guy, D. J. (1991). *Sex and danger in Buenos Aires: Prostitution, family, and nation in Argentina.* Lincoln: University of Nebraska.

Hanenberg, R., & Rojanapithayakorn, W. (1998). Changes in prostitution and the AIDS epidemic in Thailand. *AIDS Care, 10,* 69–80.

Heyl, B. S. (1979). *The madam as entrepreneur: Career management in house of prostitution.* New York: Transaction.

Hobson, B. M. (1987). *Uneasy virtue: The politics of prostitution and the American reform tradition.* New York: Basic Books.

Høigård, C., & Finstad, L. (1986/1992). *Backstreets: Prostitution, money, and love* (K. Hanson, N. Sipe, & B. Wilson, Trans.). University Park: Pennsylvania State University Press.

Hunt, M. (1974). *Sexual behavior in the 1970s.* New York: Dell Books.

Jaget, C. (1980). *Prostitutes—Our life.* Bristol, UK: Falling Wall Press.

Janus, S. S., & Janus, C. L. (1993). *The Janus Report on sexual behavior*. New York: Wiley.

Karim, S. S. A., & Ramjee, G. (1998). Anal sex and HIV transmission in women. *American Journal of Public Health, 88*, 1265–1267.

Kelly, L. (2002). *Journeys of jeopardy: A review of research on trafficking in women and children in Europe*. Geneva, Switzerland: IOM Migration Research Series.

Kinsey, A. C., Pomeroy, W. B., & Martin, C. E. (1948). *Sexual behavior in the human male*. Philadelphia: Saunders.

Kramer, L. A., & Berg, E. C. (2003). A survival analysis of timing of entry into prostitution: The differential impact of race, educational level, and childhood/adolescence risk factors. *Sociological Inquiry, 73*, 511–528.

Lambert, B. (1988, September 20). AIDS among prostitutes not as prevalent as believed, studies show. *New York Times*, p. D9.

Laumann, E. O., Gagnon, J. H., Michael, R. T., & Michaels, S. (1994). *The social organization of sexuality: Sexual practices in the United States*. Chicago: University of Chicago Press.

Lewis, J. (1998). Lap dancing: Personal and legal implications for exotic dancers. In J. Elias, V. L. Bullough, V. Elias, & G. Brewer (Eds.), *Prostitution: On whores, hustlers, and johns* (pp. 377–391). Amherst, NY: Prometheus Books.

Manderson, L. (1992). Public sex performances in Patpong and explorations of the edges of imagination. *Journal of Sex Research, 29*, 451–475.

McAnulty, R. D., Satterwhite, R., & Gullick, E. (1995, March). *Topless dancers: Personality and background*. Paper presented at the meeting of the Southeastern Psychological Association, Savannah, GA.

McCaghy, C. H., & Hou, C. (1994). Family affiliation and prostitution in a cultural context: Career onsets of Taiwanese Prostitutes. *Archives of Sexual Behavior, 23*, 251–266.

Monto, M. A. (2001). Prostitution and fellatio. *Journal of Sex Research, 38*, 140–145.

Monto, M. A. (2004). Female prostitution, customers, and violence. *Violence against Women, 10*, 160–188.

Monto, M. A. (2005). A comparison of male customers of female street prostitutes with national samples of men. *International Journal of Offender Therapy and Comparative Criminology, 49*, 505–529.

Morais, R. C. (1999, June 14). Porn goes public. *Forbes, 163*, 214–221.

Nadon, S. M., Koverola, C., & Schludermann, E. H. (1998). Antecedents to prostitution: Childhood victimization. *Journal of Interpersonal Violence, 13*, 201–221.

Pitts, M. K., Smith, A. M. A., Grierson, J., O'Brien, M., & Misson, S. (2004). Who pays for sex and why? An analysis of social and motivational factors associated with male clients of sex workers. *Archives of Sexual Behavior, 33*, 353–358.

Pleak, R. R., & Meyer-Bahlburg, H. F. L. (1990). Sexual behavior and AIDS knowledge of young male prostitutes in Manhattan. *Journal of Sex Research, 27*, 557–587.

Potterat, J. J., Rothenberg, R. B., & Muth, S. Q. (1998). Pathways to prostitu-
    tion: The chronology of sexual and drug abuse milestones. *Journal of Sex
    Research, 35,* 333–341.
Potterat, J. J., Woodhouse, D. E., Muth, J. B., & Muth, S. Q. (1990). Estimating
    the prevalence and career longevity of prostitute women. *Journal of Sex
    Research, 27,* 233–243.
Rechy, J. (1963). *City of night.* New York: Grove Press.
Rotheram-Borus, M. J., Meyer-Bahlburg, H. F. L., Koopman, C., Rosario, M.,
    Exner, T. M., Henderson, R., et al. (1992). Lifetime sexual behaviors
    among runaway males and females. *Journal of Sex Research, 29,* 15–29.
Rotheram-Borus, M. J., Rosario, M., Meyer-Bahlburg, H. F. L., Koopman, C.,
    Dopkins, S. C., & Davies, M. (1994). Sexual and substance use acts of gay
    and bisexual male adolescents in New York City. *Journal of Sex Research,
    31,* 47–58.
Salutin, M. (1971). Stripper morality. *Trans-Action, 8,* 12–22.
Schlosser, E. (1997, February 10). The business of pornography. *U.S. News and
    World Report,* 40–42.
Shaver, F. M. (2005). Sex work research: Methodological and ethical challenges.
    Journal of Interpersonal Violence, 20, 296–319.
Silbert, M. H., & Pines, A. M. (1981a). Occupational hazards of street prostitutes.
    Criminal Justice and Behavior, 8, 395–399.
Silbert, M. H., & Pines, A. M. (1981b). Sexual child abuse as an antecedent to
    prostitution. *Child Abuse and Neglect, 5,* 407–411.
Simon, P. M., Morse, E. V., Osofsky, H. J., Balson, P. M., & Gaumer, H. R.
    (1992). Psychological characteristics of a sample of male street prostitutes.
    Archives of Sexual Behavior, 21, 22–44.
Simons, R., & Whitbeck, L. (1991). Sexual abuse as a precursor to prostitution
    and victimization among adolescent and adult homeless women. *Journal
    of Family Issues, 12,* 361–380.
Skipper, J. K., & McCaghy, C. H. (1970). Stripteasers: The anatomy and career
    contingencies of a deviant occupation. *Social Problems, 17,* 391–405.
Sterk, C. E., Elifson, K. W., & German, D. (2000). Female crack users and their
    sexual relationships: The role of sex-for-crack exchanges. *Journal of Sex
    Research, 37,* 354–360.
St. James, M. (1987). The reclamation of whores. In L. Bell (Ed.), *Good girls/
    bad girls: Sex trade workers and feminists face to face* (pp. 81–87). Toronto:
    Women's Press.
Swann, S. (1998). *Whose daughter's next?* Essex, UK: Barnados Publications.
Taylor, G. R. (1970). *Sex in history.* New York: Harper & Row.
Tong, R. (1984). *Women, sex, and the law.* Totowa, NJ: Rowman & Littlefield.
U.S. Department of State. (2002). *Victims of trafficking and Violence Protection
    Act 2000: Trafficking in Persons Report.* Washington, DC: Department of
    State.
West, D. J., & de Villiers, B. (1993). *Male prostitution.* New York: Haworth Press.

Williard, J. (1991). *Juvenile prostitution*. Washington, DC: National Victim Resource Center.

Willis, B. M., & Levy, B. S. (2002). Child prostitution: Global health burden, research needs, and interventions. *Lancet, 359*, 1417–1423.

Winick, C., & Kinsie, P. M. (1971). *The lively commerce: Prostitution in the United States*. Chicago: Quadrangle Books.

13

Sexual Risk-Taking: Correlates and Prevention

Virginia Gil-Rivas and Leslie Kooyman ◆

Lorena is nervously sitting in a patient room of the local health clinic waiting to receive the results of her HIV test. She is a 23-year-old Latina who just finished college. As she waits for the counselor, her mind is racing, her anxiety grows, and she thinks about the potential consequences of a sexual encounter with someone she met at a party two months ago. They had been drinking, and she ended up spending the night at his apartment having sex without a condom. Lorena had been taking birth control pills, so she was not concerned about pregnancy. He was very fit and played sports, so she assumed he was healthy and disease free. A couple of weeks after this incident, a girlfriend called Lorena to let her know that the guy she had sex with was rumored to have slept with men as well. Lorena did not think much of this news, until her friend cautioned her about the possibility of HIV infection. She had some education about HIV, had read news articles, but she never perceived herself to be at risk.

This scenario illustrates some of the potential undesirable consequences associated with risky sexual behaviors. Sexual risk-taking contributes to the spread of sexually transmitted diseases (STDs), human immunodeficiency virus (HIV) infection, and unintended pregnancy. Risky sexual behaviors include engaging in unprotected sexual activity, having multiple or casual sexual partners, using alcohol or drugs before or during sex, and the inability or failure to discuss risky sexual behaviors prior to engaging in sexual activities (Centers for Disease Control and Prevention [CDC], 2002; Cooper, 2002).

Sexual risk-taking occurs within a social context and is influenced by a variety of individual and contextual factors such as characteristics of the individual (e.g., age, gender), aspects of close interpersonal relationships (e.g., power, conflict), attitudes, beliefs, individual and cultural norms, and social and economic conditions (DiClemente, Wingood, Vermund, & Stewart, 1999; Halperin et al., 2004).

In this chapter, we begin by presenting a brief review of the potential health and social consequences associated with sexual risk-taking. Then we summarize the empirical evidence on individual and contextual factors that independently and jointly have been found to predict risk taking among various groups. We continue with a description of successful STD and HIV prevention and intervention efforts aimed at reducing sexual risk-taking. We conclude by offering suggestions for research, prevention intervention, and health policy.

HEALTH CONSEQUENCES OF SEXUAL RISK-TAKING

Sexually transmitted diseases are one of the major health concerns in the United States with an estimated annual medical cost of $15.5 billion (CDC, 2004c). Recent estimates by the CDC indicate that 19 million Americans become infected every year, and nearly half of those infected (46.7 percent) are adolescents and young adults (Weinstock, Berman, & Cates, 2004). These estimates also revealed that women, ethnic minority groups, and men who have sex with men (MSM) are particularly vulnerable to STD infections (CDC, 2004c).

Approximately twenty-five diseases are primarily transmitted through sexual contact (CDC, 2001c). Not including infection with HIV, the most common STDs in the United States are chlamydia, gonorrhea, syphilis, genital herpes, and human papillomavirus (HPV). Of these diseases, chlamydia, gonorrhea, syphilis, and HIV/AIDS are closely monitored due to their significant impact on the health of the American population. Chlamydia and gonorrhea are particularly common among women, younger individuals (15–24 years old), and African Americans (CDC, 2001c). These bacterial infections are frequently asymptomatic and can only be detected through testing. If untreated, these infections can result in pelvic inflammatory disease (PID), lead to ectopic pregnancy (pregnancies occurring outside the uterus), undesirable pregnancy outcomes (e.g., eye disease and pneumonia in infants), and permanent infertility for both men and women (CDC, 2001b, 2004a). Moreover, chlamydia infections place women at a greater risk for contracting HIV if exposed to the virus (CDC, 2001a).

Syphilis is a curable sexually transmitted bacterial infection that can also be transmitted to the fetus during pregnancy or childbirth. Infection rates are higher among African Americans, Hispanics, women aged 20–24 years, and men aged 35–39 years (CDC, 2004a). In the late stage of the disease, infected individuals develop cardiovascular and neurological diseases (e.g., loss of motor coordination, paralysis), blindness, and may eventually die (American Social Health Association, 2005; CDC, 2001c). Furthermore, individuals with syphilis sores are two to five times more likely to contract HIV compared to those without this condition.

Approximately 40,000 individuals contract HIV every year in the United States (CDC, 2004a), and about 1,039,000 to 1,185,000 were living with HIV/AIDS by the end of 2003 (Glynn & Rhodes, 2005). The highest rates of infection in 2003 occurred among MSM, followed by infections among adolescents and adults through heterosexual contact. Racial minority groups have been disproportionately impacted by HIV/AIDS, accounting for about 68 percent of all HIV/AIDS diagnoses in 2003 (CDC, 2004c). Worldwide, an estimated 39.4 million people were living with HIV/AIDS, and 4.9 million became infected by the end of 2004 (United Nations Program on HIV/AIDS/ World Health Organization, 2004).

HIV is transmitted primarily through sexual contact (exchange of semen, blood, or vaginal fluids) and blood-to-blood contact (e.g., needle sharing). Although the virus may not produce symptoms years after infection, it can be transmitted to others during this time. Over time, HIV destroys immune cells (CD4 and T cells) and, eventually, symptoms of infection appear. If untreated or undiagnosed, the immune system will be gradually damaged and the individual's ability to fight infections seriously compromised, leading to the diagnosis of acquired immunodeficiency syndrome (AIDS) and eventual death. Although there is no cure for AIDS, improvements in HIV/AIDS treatment have resulted in a growing number of persons living longer, healthier, and more productive lives (CDC, 2003). Unfortunately, approximately 25–40 percent of those infected continue to engage in sexual risk-taking, increasing the likelihood of HIV transmission or reinfection (Kalichman et al., 2001).

Despite these potential health consequences associated with sexual risk-taking, and the public health efforts to increase awareness of these risks, rates of STD and HIV infection remain extremely high among the U.S. population. In the next section, we provide a brief review of individual and contextual factors that independently and jointly contribute to sexual risk-taking.

INDIVIDUAL FACTORS ASSOCIATED WITH SEXUAL RISK BEHAVIORS

Although sexual risk-taking occurs at all stages of the lifespan, it is during adolescence and young adulthood that sexual activities are typically initiated and sexual risk behaviors emerge (Tubman, Windle, & Windle, 1996). During adolescence, individuals undergo rapid biological, cognitive, and social changes that contribute to risk-taking behavior in general, and sexual risk-taking in particular (Kelley, Schochet, & Landry, 2004). At the biological level, these changes include physical development and sexual maturation. Among girls, signs of maturation appear between 8 and 10 years of age, while among boys, signs of maturation appear between 9 and 16 years of age (Kaplowitz, Oberfield, et al., 1999). By the time adolescents enter high school, a good proportion of them would have had sexual intercourse. The most recent Youth Risk Behavior Surveillance data showed that 46.7 percent of ninth to twelfth graders in the United States had engaged in sexual intercourse, and 14.4 percent of those who were sexually active reported having more than four sex partners during their lifetime. Moreover, among those who were sexually active within the previous three months (34.3 percent), only 63 percent reported using a condom and 17 percent reported that they or their partner had used birth control during the last sexual intercourse (Grunbaum et al., 2004).

While sexual activity during adolescence is not necessarily problematic, an early sexual debut (intercourse before age 16) is associated with a greater likelihood of engaging in risky behaviors such as using alcohol and drugs (Dick, Rose, Viken, & Kaprio, 2000), having unprotected sex (Lynch, Krantz, Russell, Hornberger, & Van Ness, 2000), and having multiple sex partners (Capaldi, Stoolmiller, Clark, & Owen, 2002).

Some of the characteristics of romantic relationships during adolescence may also increase the likelihood of sexual risk-taking. These relationships are frequently short-lived and are frequently described as warm, caring, and committed (Miller, Christopherson, & King, 1993). Thus, adolescents tend to have multiple sex partners in a relatively short period of time and tend to view condom use as unnecessary in these committed but brief relationships (Bauman & Berman, 2005). Moreover, an age difference among partners also appears to contribute to sexual risk-taking. Females who are involved with older males are more likely to engage in unprotected intercourse, to have sex while under the influence of alcohol or drugs, to experience sexual coercion by their partner, and to have unintended pregnancies (Gowen, Feldman, Díaz, & Yisrael, 2004), compared to those with similar-age partners.

Several factors have been hypothesized to play an important role in adolescents' risk taking (Annie E. Casey Foundation, 1999). Their strong desire to seek novel situations and their need for higher levels of stimulation compared to older individuals may contribute to these behaviors. In fact, the need for experimentation is an important component of identity development during adolescence and young adulthood. These factors, coupled with adolescents' difficulties regulating their behavior and evaluating potential costs and benefits in situations involving emotional arousal, contribute to risk taking in general (Steinberg, 2004) and sexual risk-taking in particular.

Alcohol and Substance Use

Risk-taking behaviors seldom occur in isolation (Jessor, 1991); in fact, sexual risk-taking frequently co-occurs with the use of alcohol and drugs

(McKirnan, Ostrow, & Hope, 1996; Zweig, Lindberg, & McGinley, 2001). At a global level, heavy and frequent alcohol use is associated with a greater likelihood of having multiple sex partners and unprotected intercourse (Cooper, 2002; Stall & Purcell, 2000). For example, in a national study of adolescents and young adults, Santelli, Brener, Lowry, Bhatt, and Zabin (1998) found that heavier alcohol use was associated with having a greater number of sexual partners. However, situation studies (studies that examine the co-occurrence of alcohol use and sexual risk-taking on particular occasions) have not found a consistent association between alcohol use and sexual risk-taking. In particular, alcohol use is not predictive of the frequency of unprotected intercourse, suggesting that although these behaviors co-occur, alcohol does not play a causal role.

Several explanations for the association between alcohol use and sexual risk-taking have been offered. Some researchers have suggested that alcohol has the ability to reduce sexual inhibitions through its impairing effects on individuals' ability to think about potential negative consequences. Thus, under the influence of alcohol, individuals mainly focus on their sexual arousal and have a limited ability to focus on the more distant consequences associated with these behaviors (Steele & Josephs, 1990). Others have suggested that this association is not the result of the pharmacological effects of alcohol, but rather the result of individuals' beliefs about alcohol's ability to increase their sexual arousal and reduce inhibitions. Therefore, individuals are likely to drink in anticipation of sexual encounters, or in response to specific situations, and then behave according to those expectations (George, Stoner, Norris, Lopez, & Lehman, 2000; Lang, 1985). To date, the empirical evidence has provided some support for both of these explanations. Specifically, the effect of alcohol on sexual risk-taking appears to vary depending on the strength of coexisting inhibiting forces (e.g., perceived costs and benefits) and disinhibiting forces (arousal). Simultaneously, individuals' alcohol expectancies play a role in promoting alcohol use in sexual situations or in anticipation of these situations, leading to sexual risk-taking (Cooper, 2002; George et al., 2000). For example, a recent study by Vanable et al. (2004) concluded that the social context, specifically, sex with a casual partner, predicted both alcohol consumption and sexual risk-taking. The authors concluded that their findings might be explained by both the impairing effects of alcohol intoxication and by individuals' expectations of increased arousal and disinhibition in situations that are viewed as desirable but would be avoided while sober.

As in the case of alcohol, the relationship between drug use and sexual risk-taking is complex. At a global level, drug use before or during sex is associated with having multiple sex partners, trading sex for drugs or money, and weak peer norms for condom use. However, it is unclear whether this association is causal or holds with all types of sex partners (Stall & Purcell, 2000) or situations. In fact, several factors might explain this association. Among some groups, exchanging sex for drugs is common, and in these situations, individuals are less likely to practice safe sex (Windle, 1997). Some drugs can have a significant impact on sexual behavior. For example, amphetamine and crack cocaine users frequently report that these drugs increase their levels of sexual desire, sexual stamina, and reduce sexual inhibitions (Ross & Williams, 2001). In some circumstances, these drugs are used "strategically" to achieve these effects, particularly in situations or settings that promote sexual risk-taking behaviors (e.g., bars, dance clubs, parties) (Green, 2003). In sum, these findings suggest that the use of alcohol and drugs may not play a causal role in sexual risk-taking; rather, it appears that other individual (e.g., personality, beliefs), contextual (e.g., partner type, social setting), and social factors (e.g., relationship type and quality) may explain their co-occurrence (Ross & Williams, 2001; Weinhardt & Carey, 2000).

Personality

Sensation seeking (the tendency to seek novelty and excitement and the willingness to take risks in order to have these experiences), and impulsivity (the tendency to act without planning or deliberation) (Zuckerman, 1994) have been found to be associated with several risky behaviors, including smoking, alcohol and drug use, and sexual risk-taking (Zuckerman & Kuhlman, 2000). For example, a recent quantitative review by Hoyle, Fejfar, and Miller (2000), of fifty-three studies of college and high-risk populations (e.g., MSM), concluded that these two personality characteristics predicted a variety of sexual risk behaviors, including frequent unprotected sexual intercourse, sex with strangers, multiple sexual partners, and having sex while intoxicated. Sensation seeking appears to contribute to sexual risk-taking in the following ways: (1) by interfering with individuals' ability to engage in safe sex in the "heat of the moment" (Bancroft et al., 2003; Pinkerton & Abramson, 1995), and (2) causing individuals who are high in sensation-seeking to report low levels of perceived risk after engaging in these behaviors (Zuckerman, 1979).

The empirical evidence also suggests that personality characteristics interact with other individual and situational factors to predict sexual risk-taking (Hoyle et al., 2000). More recently, researchers have focused on identifying factors that might clarify the nature of these associations. For example, Kalichman, Cain, Zwebebm, and Geoff (2003) found that sensation seeking was directly associated with higher expectations of increased sexual arousal and disinhibition while under the influence of alcohol. In turn, these expectations were associated with alcohol use in sexual situations and with unprotected intercourse with nonprimary sex partners. Thus, it is possible that personality plays a role in sexual risk-taking through its impact on individuals' expectations, beliefs, attitudes, and norms.

Cognitive Factors

Several theoretical perspectives, such as the theories of reasoned action (Ajzen & Fishbein, 1977) and planned behavior (Ajzen, 1991), have proposed that individuals' intentions to engage in a particular behavior predict future behavior. These intentions are the result of attitudes (i.e., a positive versus a negative evaluation of a behavior), subjective norms (individuals' perceptions of what others approve of), and perceived behavioral control (ease or difficulty associated with engaging in that behavior). A recent meta-analysis of forty-two studies of predictors of condom use provided support for these theories. As expected, individuals' intentions to use condoms were explained by their attitudes about condom use, subjective norms, and perceived behavioral control (Albarracin, Johnson, Fishbein, & Muellerleile, 2001). However, the strength of these associations differed by gender, age, ethnic background, and education. Specifically, behavioral control had a stronger association with actual condom use among younger, less educated, and ethnic minority groups (Albarracin, Kumkale, & Johnson, 2004). Likewise, the association between intentions and perceived behavioral control was stronger among women, younger individuals, and ethnic minorities. Subjective norms and intentions had a stronger association with condom use among youths, males, and individuals with higher levels of education. More recently, a study by Halkitis, Wilton, Parsons, and Hoff (2004) examined the role of beliefs about HIV noninfection (e.g., the effectiveness of current medical treatment) in risky sexual behaviors among MSM. The findings indicated that those individuals who used drugs and believed that medical treatment advances have reduced the risk of contracting HIV were more likely to report engaging in unprotected anal intercourse with casual partners.

Self-efficacy—individuals' belief that they have the ability to exercise control over their behavior and the demands associated with particular situations (Bandura, 1994)—has been found to be an important predictor of individuals' intentions to engage in safe sex practices. In general, higher levels of self-efficacy regarding one's ability to negotiate safe sex with a partner, prevent HIV/AIDS infection, and refuse unprotected sex predict the frequency of condom use (Parson, Halkitis, Bimbi, & Borkowski, 2000; Polacsek, Calentano, O'Campo, & Santelli, 1999). The strength of this relationship appears to vary by gender, such that the perceived ability to negotiate safer sex is a stronger predictor of protected sexual intercourse among women compared to men (LoConte, O'Leary, & Labouvie, 1997; Longshore, Stein, Kowalewski, & Anglin, 1998).

The brief review presented above suggests that although intentions, expectations, and beliefs are important predictors of sexual risk-taking, other factors may influence the magnitude of this association. In fact, many studies examining the association between cognitive factors and sexual risk-taking have been criticized on various grounds. First, these studies assume that an individual's decision to engage in sexual risk-taking behaviors is based on informed and rational decision-making processes. However, the evidence suggests that many decisions about sexual risk-taking are made in the "heat of the moment" (Gold, 2000). Second, the extent to which cognitive factors play a significant role in sexual risk-taking might be influenced by social norms regarding sexual risk behaviors and power inequalities in relationships (Amaro, 1995). Finally, the characteristics of a relationship, such as level of commitment and love, may influence individuals' intentions, expectations, and attitudes about specific sexual practices (Bauman & Berman, 2005). Below, we present a selective overview of social and contextual factors associated with sexual risk-taking.

CONTEXTUAL FACTORS ASSOCIATED WITH SEXUAL RISK BEHAVIORS

Aspects of the social context such as characteristics of dyadic relationships (e.g., closeness), gender roles, family and peer influences, group and social norms, and environmental factors (e.g., poverty) play an important role in predicting sexual risk behaviors.

Characteristics of Dyadic Relationships

Sexual risk-taking is strongly influenced by individuals' feelings toward a particular partner (Kelly & Kalichman, 1995). For example, in the context of committed heterosexual (Lansky, Thomas, & Earp, 1998) or homosexual (Hays, Kegeles, & Coates, 1997) relationships, individuals are more likely to view condoms as unnecessary. This attitude toward condom use might be explained, at least in part, by the meaning given to unprotected intercourse in this context. For many couples, the exchange of body fluids is viewed as a sign of greater intimacy and commitment (Odets, 1994; Sobo, 1995). Thus, a request for condom use might be interpreted as mistrust, a lack of commitment to the relationships, an indication of infidelity, or a lack of concern for the pleasure of one's partner (O'Leary, 2000). Unfortunately, the epidemiological evidence suggests that individuals in long-term committed relationships frequently engage in sexual encounters outside of their primary relationship. In the United States (Adimora et al., 2002) and other nations (UNAIDS/WHO, 2004), a good proportion of both single males and those in committed relationships report having concurrent sexual relationships (relationships that overlap over time), increasing the likelihood of the rapid spread of STDs or HIV infections. In some cultures, the acceptance and the greater frequency of concurrent sexual relationships among males might be greater, placing their partners, particularly women, at a greater risk for becoming infected with an STD or HIV by their primary partner (UNAIDS/WHO, 2004; Wingood & DiClemente, 1998).

In addition to one's feelings toward a sexual partner, the extent to which couples are able to discuss STD/HIV concerns, the use of condoms, and their views about sexual risk behaviors play an important role in predicting sexual risk-taking (DiClemente & Wingood, 1995). For example, among young MSM, Molitor, Facer, and Ruiz (1999) found that individuals' ability to discuss safe sex with their partners predicted the frequency of unprotected anal intercourse.

Gender Roles

Gender roles also play an important role in predicting sexual risk behaviors, behavioral choices, and the ability to initiate and maintain behavioral changes. Among women, the tendency to place a greater emphasis on maintaining harmony and connectedness and providing support in their relationships (Simon, 1995) contributes to their tendency to put their partners' needs above their desire to protect themselves from STD/HIV infection (Misovich, Fisher, & Fisher, 1997). In fact, women frequently avoid making requests to use condoms if they expect that such requests will lead to conflict or violence (Wingood & DiClemente, 1998). Cultural beliefs about women's sexual roles and behavior also act as barriers for women's ability to negotiate safe sex practices with their partners (Gomez & Marin, 1996; St. Lawrence et al., 1998). For example, traditional gender roles assign women less decision-making power, interfering with their ability to make decisions that go against their partners' wishes (Amaro, 1995). These power inequalities also contribute to women's vulnerability to violence within their intimate relationships (Amaro). Among college women, nearly one-third report having been pressured or forced to engage in sexual activities (Muehlenhard, Goggins, Jones, & Satterfield, 1991). Women with a history of sexual victimization are more likely to experience further victimization, to report a history of STDs (El-Bassel, Gilbert, Rajah, Foleno, & Fyre, 2000), and to be at a greater risk for HIV infection (Garcia-Moreno & Watts, 2000) compared to women without such histories. Thus, the amount of power women hold in relationships is an important predictor of both the frequency of condom use and exposure to sexual coercion (Pulerwitz, Gortmaker, & DeJong, 2000). These findings suggest that women's intentions to avoid risky behaviors, and their knowledge and skills about how to prevent HIV/STD infection, might not be the strongest predictors of sexual risk-taking. Rather, women's behaviors are greatly determined by their partners' attitudes and behaviors about safe sex practices (Logan, Cole, & Leukefeld, 2002).

Power inequalities and sexual coercion do not occur only among women; in fact, a study conducted by Kalichman and Rompa (1995) found that 29 percent of gay and bisexual males had experienced sexual coercion involving attempted or completed unprotected anal intercourse. Men with a history of victimization are also more likely to avoid talking with their partners about the use of condoms for fear of the potential consequences (Kalichman et al., 2001). These findings suggest that aspects of close interpersonal relationships are important contributors to sexual risk-taking and STD/HIV infection.

Social Influences

Outside of the dyadic relationship, members of one's social network play an important role in predicting sexual behaviors. Among adolescents, aspects of the parent-adolescent relationship are associated with the age of sexual initiation and sexual risk-taking. Specifically, greater parental warmth and acceptance (Markham et al., 2003), more frequent parent-adolescent discussions about sex and sexual risk-taking (Hutchinson, Jemmott, Jemmott, Braverman, & Fong, 2003; Miller, Forehand, & Kotchick, 2000), and parental knowledge of teen's activities (Huebner & Howell, 2003; Luster & Small, 1994) predict adolescents' decision to delay the initiation of sexual activity, greater use of condoms and contraceptives, and fewer sexual partners. Peers also play an important role in predicting sexual behaviors and sexual risk-taking (K. S. Miller et al., 2000). For example, adolescents' perceptions of their peers' attitudes toward risky behaviors in general (e.g., alcohol and drug use) and norms regarding sexual intercourse and condom use (Kinsman, Romer, Furstenberg, & Schwarz, 1998) are associated with the initiation of sexual activity and the frequency of condom (K. S. Miller et al., 2000) and birth control use (Vesely et al., 2004), even after accounting for individual characteristics (e.g., gender) and parental influences. Similarly, among adults, individuals' perceptions of group norms for condom use are important predictors of intentions to use condoms (Boyd & Wandersman, 1991) and the frequency of unprotected sexual intercourse (Hart, Peterson, Community Intervention Trial for Youth Study Team, 2004). For example, among women (Sikkema et al., 2000) and gay men (Kegeles, Hays, & Coates, 1996), individuals' beliefs about the attitudes toward safer sex held by members of their community and social groups are important predictors of the frequency of condom use.

Environmental Influences

Poverty has been shown to be associated with a variety of health indicators such as health status, physical functioning, and mortality (Kawachi & Berkman, 2000). Several factors associated with poverty, such as violent behavior, substance use, and the exchange of sex for money, drugs, or goods may also contribute to sexual risk-taking and higher rates of STD/HIV infections (Miles-Doan, 1998). Individuals living in poverty frequently experience high levels of stress, greater exposure to community violence (Catalano, 2004), limited access to health services, and might be overwhelmed by the tasks associated with meeting their basic needs for food, shelter, and safety. Thus, under these conditions, individuals may place less emphasis on avoiding sexual risk practices (Logan et al., 2002).

As suggested by the aforementioned review, various individual, social, and contextual factors contribute to sexual risk-taking. Several prevention intervention strategies have been developed with the goal of modifying these factors and promoting behavior change among various populations. In the next section, we provide a brief summary of successful prevention interventions and describe their key characteristics.

PREVENTION INTERVENTIONS

Primary prevention interventions are aimed at modifying behavioral, cognitive, social, and environmental factors that have been shown to be associated with sexual risk-taking and STD/HIV infection. These interventions have been largely guided by health behavior theories (e.g., health belief model, social cognitive theory) that propose that individuals' intentions, beliefs, and expectations are important predictors of sexual risk-taking and behavior change (Logan et al., 2002). During the past decade, researchers have tailored interventions based on these models to address specific developmental, cultural, social, and situational factors that influence individuals' ability to initiate and maintain behavioral changes (Kelly & Kalichman, 2002).

Prevention intervention approaches can be directed to the individual and to the community (Coates, 1990). Successful prevention interventions aimed at the individual involve face-to-face counseling and group sessions. In general, these programs are based on the social cognitive and reasoned action theories and include the following components: risk-reduction education, activities aimed at encouraging behavioral change and positive attitudes toward safe sex practices, and exercises to increase safe sex communication and negotiation and assertiveness skills. Typically, these interventions involve several group or individual sessions that are provided in community- or clinic-based programs (Kelly & Kalichman, 2002). Small group meetings are thought to provide an opportunity for individuals to interact with peers who support safe sex strategies and who can help them increase their sense of self-efficacy (DiClemente et al., 1999). Overall, interventions aimed at the individual have been shown to reduce the frequency of unprotected intercourse and increase condom use. However, individuals may not always be motivated to participate in multiple session programs that require a considerable time commitment on their part. Several brief interventions modeled after these multiple-session programs have been developed; unfortunately, these interventions have been shown to have minimal effects on sexual risk-taking (Kelly & Kalichman, 2002).

Community-level prevention interventions seek to reduce sexual risk-taking by changing norms and practices within an entire target population. These interventions frequently focus on leaders or popular individuals within a particular community with the goal of promoting changes in beliefs and attitudes toward safe sex practices across existing social networks. These efforts are often implemented in settings frequented by members of the target population, such as bars, barbershops, grocery stores, and restaurants (Kelly & Kalichman, 2002; Ross & Williams, 2002).

Below, we present a summary of the common elements of successful individual- and community-level prevention interventions targeted at specific populations at high risk for STD/HIV infection.

Adolescents

Prevention intervention programs for adolescents are typically delivered in schools, clinics, and community settings (Pedlow & Carey, 2003). School-based interventions are implemented as part of the school curricula and are provided to a broad range of students. The materials covered in these interventions range from abstinence-only messages, STD/HIV education, to the discussion of safe sex practices (Kirby, 2001). The Safer Choices program is an example of a school-based prevention intervention that has shown some promising results. The intervention was implemented in ten schools and was delivered by a teacher and peer leaders. High school students participated in ten sessions that involved role-playing activities, groups, and exercises aimed at building skills. These activities targeted both individual (i.e., attitudes) and social (i.e., parent-adolescent communication) factors that have been shown to influence sexual risk-taking. This program also included student homework that required parental involvement. Seven months after the intervention, students who participated in this program were less likely to engage in un-protected intercourse, more likely to report condom use during their last intercourse, and reported fewer barriers to condom use compared to those who received only AIDS education (Coyle et al., 1999). Although some school-based programs have shown some success, these programs cannot reach out-of-school adolescents who are typically at high risk for STD/HIV infection.

Community-based prevention programs for adolescents are better able to reach high-risk populations. For example, Rotheram-Borus, Feldman, Rosario, and Dunne (1994) conducted a prevention intervention program with runaway homeless adolescents that involved multiple (more than fifteen) face-to-face individual sessions led by skilled trainers. The intervention included HIV/AIDS education, coping skills training, activities aimed at reducing barriers for safe sex, and the provision of medical and health care services. Adolescents who participated in the intervention reported increases in condom use and fewer sex partners at the six months and twelve months follow-ups, compared to those who received only counseling.

Several common key characteristics of successful prevention intervention programs for youths have been identified. The critical components are (1) a focus on reducing one or more sexual risk-taking behaviors, (2) use of health behavior theories to develop the interventions, (3) consistent focus on one clear message about abstaining from sexual activity and/or using condoms, (4) provision of education about how to avoid risky situations and the use of effective prevention methods, (5) provision of modeling and practice of communication or negotiation skills, and (6) inclusion of activities that focus on social and media influences on sexual behavior (DiClemente et al., 1999; Kirby, 2001).

Women

Successful prevention interventions for women are frequently guided by the principles of social cognitive theory (Bandura, 1994), and include skills training in condom use, safe sex communication and negotiation, and gender-related factors (i.e., power imbalances) that influence sexual risk-taking (DiClemente et al., 1999). These prevention intervention programs have been implemented in community and clinic settings and are frequently peer led.

Kelly et al. (1994) conducted a clinic-based intervention with inner-city African American women. The five-session intervention focused on HIV/AIDS education, addressed individual attitudes toward safe sex, and provided activities aimed at identifying and handling barriers for condom use. Women who participated in this intervention reported greater use of condoms and fewer episodes of unprotected intercourse three months postintervention, compared to those women in a control condition. In addition, women also reported improvements in their ability to negotiate condom use and safe sex practices with their partners.

A community-level intervention for women was implemented by Sikkema et al. (2000). This intervention was delivered in nine low-income housing communities in five different cities. First, the investigators offered workshops on HIV risk reduction. These workshops were followed by ongoing conversations, social events, and community activities led by women who had been identified as popular among their neighbors. Nine other low-income communities served as a comparison group; these communities received AIDS education materials and condoms as part of the intervention. One year after the intervention, women in the communities that received the intervention reported a greater decline in the percentage of unprotected intercourse episodes and increases in condom use, compared to women in the control condition.

Overall, these interventions have had moderate success. In particular, it is unclear to what extent they have resulted in changes in sexual risk-taking in the context of primary committed relationships, the main route of STD/HIV infection among women (Logan et al., 2002; O'Leary, 2000).

Men Who Have Sex with Men

Historically, gay men and MSM have been impacted by HIV longer than any other population. Although significant reductions in infection rates have been reported in recent years, MSM continue to have the highest rate of HIV infection in the United States (CDC, 2004a). Thus, a large number of prevention intervention programs have been developed to address the factors associated with sexual risk-taking in this population. An example of a successful individual-level intervention for MSM is the National Institute of Mental Health Multisite HIV Prevention Trial Group (1998), a program that was implemented in STD and health clinics in seven U.S. cities. This intervention involved small-group sessions that used teaching, group discussion, role-play and practice exercises, and activities aimed at creating attitude changes and helping individuals set behavioral goals. Those men who participated in these sessions were more likely to use condoms and less likely to report an STD infection twelve months after the intervention, compared to those who received only one AIDS education session.

Kelly et al. (1991, 1992, 1997) developed a series of community-level interventions to reduce sexual risk behaviors among gay men at high risk for HIV infection. These interventions were based on the diffusion of innovation theory (Rogers, 1983), which proposes that new behavior patterns in a population can be initiated by targeting key opinion leaders. Key opinion leaders were trained on how to influence others' views about AIDS-related risks, how to recommend sex-related risk reduction strategies, and how to endorse the benefits and norms associated with safe sex. These interventions resulted in significant declines in sexual risk-taking among residents of the targeted communities.

In general, successful prevention intervention programs for MSM are guided by theoretical perspectives that emphasize the role of cognitive and attitudinal factors, intentions for behavior change, self-efficacy beliefs, and social norms in predicting sexual risk-taking behaviors. In addition, researchers have become increasingly aware of the importance of modifying these interventions to respond to changes in attitudes about safe sex. For example, in recent years, increases in rates of sexual risk-taking among MSM have been reported (CDC, 2000). These increases appear to be explained at least in part by improvements in the efficacy of HIV/AIDS treatment (Halkitis et al., 2004) and "safer sex burnout" among young MSM (Rofes, 1998).

CONCLUSION AND FUTURE DIRECTIONS

As suggested by this review, individual, social, and environmental factors act independently or jointly to influence sexual risk-taking. Moreover, the relative importance of these factors may vary by age, gender, cultural background, relationship characteristics, and socioeconomic conditions. Although the literature suggests that prevention intervention efforts have been successful at reducing sexual risk-taking, these interventions are not equally effective for all populations. These efforts need to be tailored to address the specific needs of each population (DiClemente et al., 1999) and the meaning given by the individual or the community to these behaviors (Ostrow, 2000). Moreover, changes in treatment, social attitudes, and socioeconomic conditions may impact the extent to which these interventions will be effective in the future.

Overall, several key characteristics of successful prevention intervention programs have been identified: the interventions (1) are based on theoretical models and address the interplay between attitudes, beliefs, expectations, behaviors, and environmental influences; (2) are designed with an understanding of the contextual and behavioral factors influencing sexual risk-taking and behavior change; (3) focus on specific sexual risk-taking behaviors (e.g., unprotected anal intercourse, condom use); (4) provide education regarding STD/HIV infection and safe sex practices; (5) provide modeling and training in sexual communication, negotiation, and assertiveness skills; and (6) address the role of situation factors and social and peer norms in sexual risk-taking (DiClemente et al., 1999; Kelly & Kalichman, 2002).

Despite the advances made in prevention intervention research and the declines in rates of STD/HIV infections, these conditions continue to exert an enormous toll on the health and well-being of people in the United States (CDC, 2004b). Thus, it is crucial to implement empirically based interventions that address the needs of vulnerable populations. Moreover, a greater emphasis should be placed on designing interventions that support the maintenance of behavioral change over time (Auerbach & Coates, 2000).

REFERENCES

Adimora, A. A., Schoenbach, V. J., Bonas, D., Martinson, F. E. A., Donaldson, K. H., & Stancil, T. R. (2002). Concurrent partnerships among women in the United States. *Epidemiology, 14,* 155–160.

Ajzen, I. (1991). The theory of planned behavior. *Organizational Behavior and Human Decision Processes, 50,* 179–211.

Ajzen, I., & Fishbein, M. (1977). Attitude-behavior relations: A theoretical analysis and review of empirical research. *Psychological Bulletin, 84,* 888–918.

Albarracin, D., Johnson, B. T., Fishbein, M., & Muellerleile, P. A. (2001). Theories of reasoned action and planned behavior as models of condom use: A meta-analysis. *Psychological Bulletin, 127*(1), 142–161.

Albarracin, D., Kumkale, G. T., & Johnson, B. T. (2004). Influences of social power and normative support on condom use decisions: A research synthesis. *AIDS Care, 16*(6), 700–723.

Amaro, H. (1995). Considering women's realities in HIV prevention. *American Psychologist, 50*(6), 437–447.

American Social Health Association. (2005). *Facts and answers about STDs.* Research Triangle Park, NC: Author. Retrieved July 31, 2005, from www.ashastd.org/stdfaqs/syphilis.html

Annie E. Casey Foundation. (1999). *When teens have sex: Issues and trends*—A Kids Count special report. Baltimore: Author. Retrieved July 9, 2005, from www.aecf.org/kidscount/teen/foreword.htm

Auerbach, J. D., & Coates, T. J. (2000). HIV prevention research: Accomplishments and challenges for the third decade of AIDS. *American Journal of Public Health, 90*, 1029–1032.

Bancroft, J., Janssen, E., Strong, D., Carnes, L., Vukadinovic, Z., & Long, J. S. (2003). Sexual risk-taking in gay men: The relevance of sexual arousability, mood and sensation seeking. *Archives of Sexual Behavior, 32*(6), 555–572.

Bandura, A. (1994). Social cognitive theory and exercise of control over HIV infection. In R. J. DiClemente & J. Peterson (Eds.), *Preventing AIDS: Theories and methods of behavioral interventions* (pp. 25–60). New York: Plenum Press.

Bauman, L. J., & Berman, R. (2005). Adolescent relationships and condom use: Trust, love and commitment. *AIDS and Behavior, 9*(2), 211–222.

Boyd, B., & Wandersman, A. (1991). Predicting undergraduate condom use with Fishbein and Ajzen and the Triandis attitude behavior models: Implications for public health interventions. *Journal of Applied Social Psychology, 21*, 1810–1830.

Capaldi, D. M., Stoolmiller, M., Clark, S., & Owen, L. D. (2002). Heterosexual risk behaviors in at-risk young men from early adolescence to young adulthood: Prevalence, prediction, and association with STD contraction. *Developmental Psychology, 38*(3), 394–406.

Catalano, S. M. (2004). *Criminal victimization 2003*. Washington, DC: U.S. Department of Justice. Retrieved September 16, 2005, from www.ojp.usdoj.gov/bjs/pub/pdf/cv03.pdf

Centers for Disease Control and Prevention (2000). *Consultation on recent trends in STD and HIV morbidity and risk behaviors among MSM: Meeting report, October 2000.* Atlanta, GA: U.S. Department of Health and Human Services.

Centers for Disease Control and Prevention. (2001a). *Strategic plan for HIV prevention through 2005.* Retrieved July 6, 2005, from www.cdc.gov/nchstp/od/hiv_plan/default.htm

Centers for Disease Control and Prevention. (2001b). *Taking action to combat increases in STDs and HIV risk among men who have sex with men.* Atlanta, GA: U.S. Department of Health and Human Services. Retrieved July 6, 2005, from www.cdc.gov/nchstp/od/news/92288_AED_CDC_report–0427c.htm

Centers for Disease Control and Prevention. (2001c). *Tracking the hidden epidemics: Trends in STDs in the United States.* Atlanta, GA: U.S. Department of Health and Human Services. Retrieved July 6, 2005, from www.cdc.gov/nchstp/dstd/disease_info.htm

Centers for Disease Control and Prevention. (2002). Trends in sexual risk behaviors among high school students—United States, 1991–2001. *Morbidity and Mortality Weekly Report, 51*(38), 856–859.

Centers for Disease Control and Prevention. (2003). Advancing HIV prevention: New strategies for a changing epidemic—United States, 2003. *Morbidity and Mortality Weekly Report, 52*(15), 329–332.

Centers for Disease Control and Prevention. (2004a). *HIV/AIDS Surveillance Report, 2003.* Atlanta, GA: U.S. Department of Health and Human Services. Retrieved March 16, 2005, from www.cdc.gov/hiv/stats/2003surveillancereport.pdf

Centers for Disease Control and Prevention. (2004b). *HIV prevention in the third decade: Activities of CDC's Division of HIV/AIDS Prevention.* Retrieved September 16, 2005, from www.cdc.gov/hiv/HIV_3rdDecade/default.htm

Centers for Disease Control and Prevention. (2004c). *Sexually Transmitted Disease Surveillance, 2003.* Atlanta, GA: U.S. Department of Health and Human Services. Retrieved June 27, 2005, from www.cdc.gov/std/stats/toc2003.htm

Coates, T. J. (1990). Strategies for modifying sexual behavior for primary and secondary prevention of HIV disease. *Journal of Consulting and Clinical Psychology, 58,* 57–69.

Cooper, M. L. (2002). Alcohol use and risky sexual behavior among college students and youth: Evaluating the evidence. *Journal of Studies on Alcohol, 62*(Suppl. 14), 101–117.

Coyle, K., Basen-Engquist, K., Kirby, D., Parcel, G., Banspach, S., Harrist, R., et al. (1999). Short-term impact of safer choices: A multicomponent, school-based HIV, other STD, and pregnancy prevention program. *Journal of School Health, 69,* 181–188.

Dick, D. M., Rose, R. J., Viken, R. J., & Kaprio, J. (2000). Pubertal timing and substance use: Associations between and within families across late adolescence. *Developmental Psychology, 36*(2), 180–189.

DiClemente, R. J., & Wingood, G. M. (1995). A randomized controlled trial of an HIV sexual risk-reduction intervention for young African-American women. *Journal of the American Medical Association, 274*(16), 1271–1276.

DiClemente, R. J., Wingood, G. M., Vermund, S. H., & Stewart, K. E. (1999). Prevention of HIV/AIDS. In J. M. Raczynski & R. J. DiClemente (Eds.), *Handbook of health promotion and disease prevention* (pp. 371–394). New York: Kluwer Academic.

El-Bassel, N., Gilbert, L., Rajah, V., Foleno, A., & Frye, V. (2000). Fear and violence: Raising the HIV stakes. *AIDS Education and Prevention, 12,* 154–170.

Garcia-Moreno, C., & Watts, C. (2000). Violence against women: Its importance for HIV/AIDS. *AIDS, 14*(Suppl. 3), S235–S265.

George, W. H., Stoner, S. A., Norris, J., Lopez, P. A., & Lehman, G. I. (2000). Alcohol expectancies and sexuality: A self-fulfilling prophecy analysis of dyadic perceptions and behavior. *Journal of Studies on Alcohol, 61,* 168–176.

Glynn, M., & Rhodes, P. (2005, June). *Estimated HIV prevalence in the United States at the end of 2003.* National HIV Prevention Conference, Atlanta, GA.

Gold, R. S. (2000). AIDS education for gay men: Towards a more cognitive approach. *AIDS Care, 12,* 267–272.

Gomez, C., & Marin, B. (1996). Gender, culture, and power: Barriers to HIV-prevention strategies for women. *Journal of Sex Research, 33,* 355–362.

Gowen, L. K., Feldman, S. S., Díaz, R., & Yisrael, D. S. (2004). A comparison of the sexual behaviors and attitudes of adolescent girls with older vs. similar-aged boyfriends. *Journal of Youth and Adolescence, 33*(2), 167–175.

Green, A. I. (2003). "Chem friendly": The institutional basis of "club drug" use in a sample of urban gay men. *Deviant Behavior, 24,* 427–447.

Grunbaum, J. A., Kann, L., Kinchen, S., Roos, J., Hawkins, J., Lowry, R., et al. (2004). Youth risk behavior surveillance—United States, 2003. *Morbidity and Mortality Weekly Report, 53,* SS-2.

Halkitis, P. N., Wilton, L., Parsons, J. T., & Hoff, C. (2004). Correlates of sexual risk—taking behavior among HIV seropositive gay men in concordant primary partner relationships. *Psychology, Health and Medicine, 9*(1), 99–113.

Halperin, D. T., Steiner, M. J., Cassell, M. M., Green, E. C., Hearst, N., Kirby, D., et al. (2004). The time has come for common ground on preventing sexual transmission of HIV. *Lancet, 364,* 1913–1915.

Hart, T., Peterson, J. L., & the Community Intervention Trial for Youth Study Team. (2004). Predictors of risky sexual behavior among young African-American men who have sex with men. *American Journal of Public Health, 94*(7), 1122–1123.

Hays, R. B., Kegeles, S. M., & Coates, T. J. (1997). Unprotected sex and HIV risk-taking among young gay men within boyfriend relationships. *AIDS Education and Prevention, 9,* 314–329.

Hoyle, R. H., Fejfar, M. C., & Miller, J. D. (2000). Personality and sexual risk taking: A quantitative review. *Journal of Personality, 68*(6), 1203–1231.

Huebner, A. J., & Howell, L. W. (2003). Examining the relationship between adolescent sexual risk-taking and perceptions of monitoring, communication, and parenting styles. *Journal of Adolescent Health, 33*(2), 71–78.

Hutchinson, M. K., Jemmott, J. B., Jemmott, L. S., Braverman, P., & Fong, G. T. (2003). The role of mother–daughter sexual risk communication in reducing sexual risk behaviors among urban adolescent females: A prospective study. *Journal of Adolescent Health, 33,* 98–107.

Jessor, R. (1991). Risk behavior in adolescence: A psychosocial framework for understanding and action. *Journal of Adolescent Health, 12*(8), 597–605.

Kalichman, S. C., Benotsch, E., Rompa, D., Gore-Felton, C., Austin, J., Webster, L., et al. (2001). Unwanted sexual experiences and sexual risk in gay and bisexual men: Associations among revictimization, substance use, and psychiatric symptoms. *Journal of Sex Research, 38*(1), 1–9.

Kalichman, S. C., Cain, D., Zwebebm, A., & Geoff, S. (2003). Sensation seeking, alcohol use and sexual risk behaviors among men receiving services at a clinic for sexually transmitted infections. *Quarterly Journal of Studies on Alcohol, 64*(4), 564–569.

Kalichman, S. C., & Rompa, D. (1995). Sexually coerced and noncoerced gay and bisexual men: Factors relevant to risk for human immunodeficiency virus (HIV) infection. *Journal of Sex Research, 32,* 45–50.

Kaplowitz, P. B., Oberfield, S. E., & Drug and Therapeutics and Executive Committees of the Lawson Wilkins Pediatric Endocrine Society. (1999).

Reexamination of the age limit for defining when puberty is precocious in girls in the United States: Implications for evaluation and treatment. *Pediatrics, 104,* 936–941.

Kawachi, I., & Berkman, L. F. (2000). Social cohesion, social capital, and health. In L. F. Berkman & I. Kawachi (Ed.), *Social epidemiology* (pp. 174–190). New York: Oxford University Press.

Kegeles, S. M., Hays, R. B., & Coates, T. J. (1996). The Mpowerment Project: A community-level HIV prevention intervention for young gay men. *American Journal of Public Health, 86*(8), 1129–1136.

Kelley, A. E., Schochet, T., & Landry, C. F. (2004). Risk taking and novelty seeking in adolescence: Introduction to Part I. *Annals of the New York Academy of Sciences, 1021,* 27–32.

Kelly, J. A., & Kalichman, S. C. (1995). Increased attention to human sexuality can improve HIV-AIDS prevention efforts: Key research issues and directions. *Journal of Consulting and Clinical Psychology, 63*(6), 907–918.

Kelly, J. A., & Kalichman, S. C. (2002). Behavioral research in HIV/AIDS primary and secondary prevention: Recent advances and future directions. *Journal of Consulting and Clinical Psychology, 70*(3), 626–639.

Kelly, J. A., Murphy, D. A., Sikkema, K. J., McAuliffe, T. L., Roffman, R. A., Solomon, L. J., et al. (1997). Randomized, controlled, community-level HIV prevention intervention for sexual risk behavior among homosexual men in U.S. cities. *Lancet, 35,* 1500–1504.

Kelly, J. A., Murphy, D. A., Washington, C. D., Wilson, T. S., Koob, J. J., Davis, D. R., et al. (1994). The effects of HIV/AIDS intervention groups for high-risk women in urban clinics. *American Journal of Public Health, 84,* 1918–1922.

Kelly, J. A., St. Lawrence, J. S., Diaz, Y. E., Stevenson, L. Y., Hauth, A. C., Brasfield, T. L., et al. (1991). HIV risk behavior reaction following intervention with key opinion leaders of population: An experimental analysis. *American Journal of Public Health, 81,* 168–171.

Kelly, J. A., St. Lawrence, J. S., Stevenson, L. Y., Hauth, A. C., Kalichman, S. C., Diaz, Y. E., et al. (1992). Community AIDS/HIV risk reduction: The effects of endorsements by popular people in three cities. *American Journal of Public Health, 82*(11), 1483–1489.

Kinsman, S. B., Romer, D., Furstenberg, F. F., & Schwarz, D. F. (1998). Early sexual initiation: The role of peer norms. *Pediatrics, 102*(5), 1185–1192.

Kirby, D. (2001). *Emerging answers: Research findings on programs to reduce teen pregnancy (Summary).* Washington, DC: National Campaign to Prevent Teen Pregnancy. Retrieved July 10, 2005, from www.teenpregnancy.org/resources/data/report_summaries/emerging_answers/default.asp

Lang, A. R. (1985). The psychology of drinking and human sexuality. *Journal of Drug Issues, 15,* 273–289.

Lansky, A., Thomas, J. C., & Earp, J. A. (1998). Partner-specific sexual behaviors among persons with both main and other partners. *Family Planning Perspectives, 30*(2), 93–96.

LoConte, J., O'Leary, A., & Labouvie, E. (1997). Psychosocial correlates of HIV-related sexual behavior in an inner-city STD clinic. *Psychology and Health, 12*, 589–601.

Logan, T. K., Cole, J., & Leukefeld, C. (2002). Women, sex, and HIV: Social and contextual factors, meta-analysis of published interventions, and implications for practice and research. *Psychological Bulletin, 128*, 851–885.

Longshore, D., Stein, J. A., Kowalewski, M., & Anglin, M. D. (1998). Psychosocial antecedents of unprotected sex by drug-using men and women. *AIDS and Behavior, 2*(4), 293–306.

Luster, T., & Small, S. A. (1994). Factors associated with sexual risk-taking behaviors among adolescents. *Journal of Marriage and the Family, 56*, 622–632.

Lynch, D., Krantz, S., Russell, J., Hornberger, L., & Van Ness, C. (2000). HIV infection: A retrospective analysis of adolescent high-risk behaviors. *Journal of Pediatric Health Care, 14*, 20–25.

Markham, C. M., Tortolero, S. R., Escobar-Chavez, S. L., Parcel, G. S., Harrist, R., & Addy, R. C. (2003). Family connectedness and sexual risk-taking among urban youth attending alternative high schools. *Perspectives on Sexual and Reproductive Health, 35*(4), 174–179.

McKirnan, D. J., Ostrow, D. G., & Hope, B. (1996). Sex, drugs and escape: A psychological model of HIV-risk sexual behaviors. *AIDS Care, 8*, 655–669.

Miles-Doan, R. (1998). Violence between spouses and intimates: Does neighborhood matter? *Social Forces, 77*(2), 623–645.

Miller, B. C., Christopherson, C. R., & King, P. K. (1993). Sexual behavior in adolescence. In T. P. Gullotta, G. R. Adams, & R. Montemayor (Eds.), *Adolescent sexuality* (pp. 57–76). Newbury Park, CA: Sage.

Miller, K. S., Forehand, R., & Kotchick, B. A. (2000). Adolescent sexual behavior in two ethnic minority groups: A multisystem perspective. *Adolescence, 35*(138), 313–333.

Misovich, S., Fisher, J., & Fisher, W. (1997). Close relationships and elevated HIV risk behavior: Evidence and possible underlying psychological processes. *Review of General Psychology, 1*, 72–107.

Molitor, F., Facer, M., & Ruiz, J. D. (1999). Safer sex communication and unsafe sexual behavior among young men who have sex with men in California. *Archives of Sexual Behavior, 28*(4), 335–343.

Muehlenhard, C. L., Goggins, M., Jones, J., & Satterfield, A. (1991). Date rape and sexual coercion in close relationships. In K. McKinney & S. Sprecher (Eds.), *Sexuality in close relationships* (pp. 155–175). Hillsdale, NJ: Lawrence Erlbaum.

National Institute of Mental Health Multisite HIV Prevention Trial Group. (1998). The NIMH Multisite HIV prevention trial: Reducing HIV sexual risk behavior. *Science, 280*, 1889–1894.

Odets, W. (1994). AIDS education and harm reduction for gay men: Psychological approaches for the 21st century. *AIDS and Public Policy Journal, 9*, 1–18.

O'Leary, A. (2000). Women at risk for HIV from a primary partner: Balancing risk and intimacy. *Annual Review of Sex Research, 11*, 191–234.

Ostrow, D. G. (2000). The role of drugs in the sexual lives of men who have sex with men: Continuing barriers to researching this question. *AIDS and Behavior, 4*(2), 205–219.

Parson, J. T., Halkitis, P. N., Bimbi, D., & Borkowski, T. (2000). Perceptions of the benefits and costs associated with condom use and unprotected sex among late adolescent college students. *Journal of Adolescence, 23*, 377–391.

Pedlow, C. T., & Carey, M. P. (2003). HIV sexual risk-reduction interventions for youth: A review and methodological critique of randomized controlled trials. *Behavior Modification, 27*(2), 135–190.

Pinkerton, S. D., & Abramson, P. R. (1995). Decision making and personality factors in sexual risk-taking for HIV/AIDS: A theoretical integration. *Personality and Individual Differences, 19*(5), 713–723.

Polacsek, M., Calentano, D. D., O'Campo, P., & Santelli, J. (1999). Correlates of condom use stage of change: Implications for intervention. *AIDS Education and Prevention, 11*, 38–52.

Pulerwitz, J., Gortmaker, S., & DeJong, W. (2000). Measuring sexual relationship power in HIV/STD research. *Sex Roles, 42*, 637–660.

Rofes, E. (1998). *Dry bones breathe: Gay men creating post-AIDS identities and cultures.* Binghamton, NY: Harrington Press.

Rogers, E. M. (1983). *Diffusion of innovations.* New York: Free Press.

Ross, M. W., & Williams, M. L. (2001). Sexual behavior and illicit drug use. *Annual Review of Sex Research, 12*, 290–310.

Ross, M. W., & Williams, M. L. (2002). Effective targeted and community HIV/STD prevention programs. *Journal of Sex Research, 39*(1), 58–62.

Rotheram-Borus, M. J., Feldman, J., Rosario, M., & Dunne, E. (1994). Preventing HIV among runaways: Victims and victimization. In R. J. DiClemente & J. Peterson (Eds.), *Preventing AIDS: Theories and methods of behavioral interventions* (pp. 175–188). New York: Plenum Press.

Santelli, J. S., Brener, N. D., Lowry, R., Bhatt, A., & Zabin, L. S. (1998). Multiple sexual partners among U.S. adolescents and young adults. *Family Planning Perspectives, 30*(6), 271–275.

Sikkema, K. J., Kelly, J. A., Winett, R. A., Solomon, L. J., Cargill, V. A., Roffman, R. A., et al. (2000). Outcomes of a randomized community-level HIV prevention intervention for women living in 18 low-income housing developments. *American Journal of Public Health, 90*, 57–63.

Simon, R. (1995). Gender, multiple roles, role meaning, and mental health. *Journal of Health and Social Behavior, 36*, 182–194.

Sobo, E. (1995). Women and AIDS in the United States. In E. Sobo (Ed.), *Choosing unsafe sex: AIDS-risk denial among disadvantaged inner city women* (pp. 9–24). Philadelphia: University of Pennsylvania Press.

Stall, R. D., & Purcell, D. W. (2000). Intertwining epidemics: A review of research on substance use among men who have sex with men and its connection to the AIDS epidemic. *AIDS and Behavior, 4*, 181–192.

Steele, C. M., & Josephs, R. A. (1990). Alcohol myopia: Its prized and dangerous effects. *American Psychologist, 45*, 921–933.

Steinberg, L. (2004). Risk taking in adolescence: What changes, and why? *Annals of the New York Academy of Sciences, 1021,* 51–58.

St. Lawrence, J., Eldridge, G., Reitman, D., Little, C., Shelby, M., & Brasfield, T. (1998). Factors influencing condom use among African American women: Implications for risk reduction interventions. *American Journal of Community Psychology, 26,* 7–28.

Tubman, J. G., Windle, M., & Windle, R. C. (1996). Cumulative sexual intercourse patterns among middle adolescents: Problem behavior precursors and concurrent health risk behaviors. *Journal of Adolescent Health, 18,* 182–191.

United Nations Program on HIV/AIDS/World Health Organization. (2004). *AIDS epidemic update: 2004.* Geneva, Switzerland: Author. Retrieved July 8, 2005, from www.unaids.org/wad2004/report_pdf.html

Vanable, P. A., McKirnan, D. J., Buchbinder, S. P., Bartholow, B. N., Douglas, J. M., et al. (2004). Alcohol use and high-risk sexual behavior among men who have sex with men: The effects of consumption level and partner type. *Health Psychology, 23*(5), 525–532.

Vesely, S. K., Wyatt, V. H., Oman, R. F., Aspy, C. B., Kegler, M. C., Rodine, S., et al. (2004). The potential protective effects of youth assets from adolescent sexual risk behaviors. *Journal of Adolescent Health, 34,* 356–365.

Weinhardt, L. S., & Carey, M. P. (2000). Does alcohol lead to sexual risk behavior? Findings from event-level research. *Annual Review of Sex Research, 11,* 125–157.

Weinstock, H., Berman, S., & Cates, W. (2004). Sexually transmitted diseases among American youth: Incidence and prevalence estimates, 2000. *Perspectives on Sexual and Reproductive Health, 36*(1), 6–10.

Windle, M. (1997). The trading of sex for money or drugs, sexually transmitted diseases (STDs), and HIV-related risk behaviors among multisubstance using alcohol inpatients. *Drug and Alcohol Dependence, 49,* 33–38.

Wingood, G., & DiClemente, R. (1998). Relationship characteristics associated with noncondom use among young adult African-American women: Implications for HIV prevention. *Journal of Black Psychology, 19,* 190–203.

Zuckerman, M. (1979). Sensation seeking and risk taking. In C. E. Izard (Ed.), *Emotions in personality and psychopathology* (pp. 163–197). New York: Plenum Press.

Zuckerman, M. (1994). Impulsive unsocialized sensation seeking: The biological foundations of basic dimension of personality. In J. E. Bates & T. D. Wachs (Eds.), *Temperament: Individual differences at the interface of biology and behavior* (pp. 219–258). Washington, DC: American Psychological Association.

Zuckerman, M., & Kuhlman, D. M. (2000). Personality and risk-taking: Common biosocial factors. *Journal of Personality, 68*(6), 999–1029.

Zweig, J. M., Lindberg, L. D., & McGinley, K. A. (2001). Adolescent health risk profiles: The co-occurrence of health risks among females and males. *Journal of Youth and Adolescence, 30*(6), 707–728.

14

Erotic Plasticity: Nature, Culture, Gender, and Sexuality

Roy F. Baumeister and Tyler Stillman ◆

Erotic plasticity is defined as the degree to which the sex drive is shaped by social, cultural, and situational factors. High plasticity means that the sex drive is highly amenable to such influences, whereas low plasticity suggests indifference or even immunity to such sources of influence.

All theories of sex strike some sort of balance between the influence of social and cultural factors and the influence of natural, biological factors. For example, the question of whether homosexuality is the result of biological influences (such as a gay gene) or social and cultural ones (such as having a clinging, intrusive mother) has come up over and over in every generation of theory, and there is still no definite answer. Most modern experts now accept that both types of causes play some role, so that any major sphere of sexual behavior reflects some combination of natural and cultural or social causes. Even so, the various theories differ widely as to how much of each is important. Some theories heavily emphasize the influence of innate, genetic, hormonal, and other biological factors, whereas others concede only a preliminary and minimal role to those and focus mainly on social, cultural, and situational factors as decisive.

In that context, the degree of erotic plasticity reflects the degree to which culture should be emphasized over nature. If erotic plasticity is high, then nature is not all that important, and most of the variation in human behavior can be attributed to cultural and other social factors. If it is low, then behavior follows straight from genes and hormones, and the influence of culture is at best a peripheral factor. The question of plasticity thus lies at the heart of one of the most far-reaching and bitter debates in the field of sexuality theory. To be sure, it is possible to state the issue in a less antagonistic manner: high plasticity can be considered an adaptation by which nature makes creatures better able to adjust and change in response to meaningful experience.

The most discussed application of this concept concerns the possibility of gender differences. An article by Baumeister (2000) contended that a basic, fundamental difference is that female sexuality has higher erotic plasticity than male sexuality. In relative terms, this means that women's sexual responses and feelings are more affected by social, cultural, and situational factors, whereas male sexuality is relatively more shaped by genetic, hormonal, and other biological factors. The bulk of this article will focus on the question of gender differences in erotic plasticity.

Assuming that plasticity is not a strictly constant quantity, there is no single answer to the great and hotly debated question of nature versus nurture in sexuality. For some people, the sex drive would be a relatively fixed biological fact, whereas for others it would be subject to considerable influence from the social environment.

Value judgments also introduce a dimension of sensitive problems into debates about sexual behavior. We concur with the view that erotic plasticity is not an inherently evaluative dimension, in the sense that it is not clearly or a priori better to have high versus low plasticity. There might be some ways in which high or low plasticity is better, but these largely cancel each other out, and for the most part it is not clearly better to be one or the other. However, the difference can be hugely influential on behavior, and failure to appreciate its importance can introduce deeply divisive or even offensive misunderstandings.

Ultimately, it may emerge that some individuals have higher erotic plasticity than others. At present, there is no published scale available to assess these differences, but some researchers have begun discussions about creating one, and it is possible that after this work is published, a trait scale may become available.

GENDER DIFFERENCES IN EROTIC PLASTICITY

At present, the best established difference in erotic plasticity is between men and women. The evidence for this will be summarized in the next section. Women have higher erotic plasticity than men. This statement means that female sexuality will be more influenced by, and more variable in response to, social, cultural, and situational factors, as compared to male sexuality. The term "plasticity" is thus used only in the biological sense of being amenable to environmental influence and change. The second meaning of plasticity, as in artificiality or falseness, is not implied in any sense and is not relevant to gender differences in sex drive.

A gender difference in erotic plasticity would lead to a group of other gender differences in sexual behavior, not to mention potentially making it harder for men and women to achieve an intuitive understanding of one another. Self-knowledge in the sexual realm would be more difficult for women than for men to achieve, insofar as women would be seeking to gain knowledge about a moving target, unlike men (see Vanwesenbeeck, Bekker, & van Lenning, 1998). Women would generally show greater change in response to different social and cultural demands, and, indeed, adapting to new sexual rules or otherwise new contingencies should be easier for women than for men. In contrast, the greater plasticity might make women more gullible and susceptible to influence, and ultimately it might become easier to convince a woman than a man to engage in some sexual activity toward which the person was initially disinclined. In adjusting to marriage or other long-term relationships, women should be more willing than men to compromise in the sexual domain. Sexual decision-making ultimately should be more difficult and complex for women than for men, insofar as men can assume that their responses and feelings are relatively constant, and so they do not need to consider much about the specific circumstances in order to make a decision, whereas for a woman the nuances of meaning in the current situation may prove powerfully decisive.

There would also be implications for sex therapy. To be sure, one must recognize that each individual is unique, and the special needs or problems of each individual must be recognized and understood before prescribing treatment. Still, by and large, there should be a general pattern such that different kinds of therapy will be differentially effective by gender. For women, sexual response depends on social and cultural factors, such as meaning, and so a sex therapist would typically need to understand the subjective meanings and interpretations, along with their emotional implications, in order to treat sexual problems. For men, in contrast, sex is more of a physical and biological phenomenon, and so physiological treatments may be recommended as the first option in many cases. Hormonal treatments and other physiological interventions should generally be more effective with men, whereas women may need "talking cure," insight-oriented interventions. In plainer terms, many men's sexual problems will respond to purely physical treatments such as Viagra, but we should not expect sex therapy for women to be quite as physical or as simple.

Evidence and Applications

This section will cover some of the phenomena that have been cited as relevant to the gender difference in erotic plasticity. The differences can be invoked as evidence for the thesis that women have higher erotic plasticity than men. It can also be seen as surveying the range of phenomena that will be different for men versus women as a result of women's greater plasticity.

Do People Change over Time?

The first set of applications is based on comparing people with themselves across time. High plasticity makes people prone to change as they encounter new or different circumstances. If men are relatively low in erotic plasticity, then their sexual patterns should remain essentially the same across their adult life, whereas the higher plasticity of women would make them more prone to change their sexual patterns and preferences as they move through different phases of adult life.

A first pattern, involving fluctuations in the total amount of sexual activity, was noted in the original Kinsey reports (Kinsey, Pomeroy, & Martin, 1948; Kinsey, Pomeroy, Martin, & Gebhard, 1953). Kinsey and his colleagues noted a pattern in women's sexual histories that was almost entirely absent in men's. What they called "total outlet"—the sum of all orgasms per week from any and all modes of stimulation—fluctuated much more widely among women than among men. Thus, a woman might have a happy, busy, and energetic sex life with one partner, but upon losing that partner she might eschew all sexual activity for some months, then resume with a new partner. In contrast, if a man lost his main partner, he would typically make up the deficit with masturbation, casual partners, prostitutes, or other sources. These wide fluctuations in total sexual activity indicate a degree of plasticity that is much more common among women than among men.

Converging evidence comes from studies of long-term sexual adjustment in marriage and through the aging process. Husbands and wives typically agree that wives make more sexual adjustments than husbands in adapting to marriage (Ard, 1977). Studies of the impact of aging on sex typically show a broad reduction in total sex, reflecting an apparent waning of sexual interest as one grows old. One study that searched for exceptions did find some instances in which people had acquired new sexual interests or activities by age 60 that they had not had in their twenties, but these were mainly among women (Adams & Turner, 1985). Thus, a man's sexual tastes seem to emerge early in life and remain fairly constant, whereas some women acquire new sexual interests at various points in adulthood, consistent with the view that women have higher erotic plasticity.

Changes in sexual orientation provide some of the most interesting (from both theoretical and practical perspectives) applications of erotic plasticity. People with low plasticity should presumably be quite fixed and unchanging in their category of desired sex partners, whereas higher plasticity would bring an openness to new partners. Multiple findings and studies suggest that women have higher plasticity in this regard. For example, lesbians are more likely than gay males to have had heterosexual sex (Bart, 1993; Bell & Weinberg, 1978; Goode & Haber, 1977; Kinsey et al., 1948; Kinsey et al., 1953; Kitzinger & Wilkinson, 1995; Laumann, Gagnon, Michael, & Michaels, 1994; McCauley & Ehrhardt, 1980; Rosario et al., 1996; Savin-Williams, 1990; Schäfer, 1976;

Whisman, 1996), and they are also more likely to have heterosexual relationships even after having been exclusively gay for years (Rust, 1992). Circumstances that promote sexual experimentation, such as swinging (i.e., mate-swapping) parties, seem to induce a fair number of heterosexual women but hardly any heterosexual men to experiment with same-gender sex (Fang, 1976; O'Neill & O'Neill, 1970; Smith & Smith, 1970). Likewise, some evidence suggests that there is more consensual same-gender activity in women's than in men's prisons, and women seem to make the transition much more smoothly and easily from an exclusively heterosexual orientation prior to their imprisonment, to homosexual while in prison, and then back to heterosexual upon release from prison than do men (Gagnon & Simon, 1968; Giallombardo, 1966; Ward & Kassebaum, 1965). All of this supports the view of greater plasticity in sexual orientation among women.

Impact of Social and Cultural Factors

A second way to search for evidence about plasticity is to consider specific sociocultural variables and see how much effect they have. If women have higher plasticity than men, then social and cultural factors should generally produce bigger effects on women than on men.

Education and religion are two of the most powerful and important socializing influences in most cultures. The National Health and Social Life Survey (NHSLS) (Laumann et al., 1994) is widely regarded as the methodologically best large-scale survey about sexual behavior in the United States, and it provided extensive data on how education and religion were linked to sex. Almost invariably, it found both variables to have larger effects on women's than on men's sexuality, consistent with the view that women have higher erotic plasticity. Thus, the most educated women differed from the least educated women on multiple dimensions, including oral sex, anal sex, liking for different sexual activities, use of contraception, and same-gender activity, whereas the corresponding differences for men were smaller or not significant. Likewise, the most religious women's sex lives were notably different from those of the least religious, whereas the most and least religious men were largely similar. As variables, religion and education complement each other in a methodologically helpful manner, because higher religiosity tends to be associated with less sexual activity, whereas higher education tends to be associated with more. Thus, two powerful social institutions that pull in opposite directions both seem to have more impact on women than on men.

Other studies have likewise found religion and education to affect women more than men (Adams & Turner, 1985; Harrison, Bennett, Globetti, & Alsikafi, 1974; Reiss, 1967; Wilson, 1975). Sex education also seems to change women's attitudes and behaviors more than men's (Weis, Rabinowitz, & Ruckstuhl, 1992). These findings do not appear to be explainable as floor or ceiling effects, and thus point toward a difference in plasticity.

The recent expansion of research on cultural differences in psychology will likely result in an accelerated accumulation of knowledge about how sex differs across cultures. Although the amount of information available on such issues has been small, the weight of evidence does seem to show greater cross-cultural variability in women's sexuality than in men's. Studies comparing different cultures typically find that women differ more across those cultural boundaries than do men (e.g., Christensen & Carpenter, 1962). One large and systematic compilation of results from nearly 200 cultures found significantly greater variation in sexual behavior among female than male adolescents (Barry & Schlegel, 1984).

Plasticity can be seen not just in the simple fact of cultural variation but also in acculturation. That is, when a person moves from one culture to another, does the person adopt the values and practices of the new culture or retain the habits and tendencies taught in the old one? An extensive study of Latino immigrants to Detroit found that women's sexuality was closely linked to the process of learning and internalizing the new culture, whereas for men, the links between acculturation and sex were weak (Ford & Norris, 1993).

Education, religion, and culture are large, powerful forces, and one can complement them by examining the smaller and more proximal sources of social influence, namely, peer groups and parents. There again, the available evidence supports the conclusion of higher plasticity among women and girls than among men and boys. Peer groups have been shown to have a significantly greater impact on young women than on young men, at least in the sexual arena (Mirande, 1968; Sack, Keller, & Hinkle, 1984). To be sure, some correlational findings could be taken to mean that people choose their peer groups to match their sexual preferences. But other studies have ruled out this alternative explanation by tracking people over time and showing that it is the peer group at time 1 that predicts sexual behavior at time 2, rather than the reverse (Billy & Udry, 1985). In plainer terms, it is not that a girl who loses her virginity then reshuffles her peer group by dumping her virgin friends and acquiring new, nonvirgin friends; rather, having nonvirgin friends increases the likelihood that she will lose her own virginity.

The greater influence of the female peer group finds converging evidence in studies that look at parental influence. A variety of findings suggest that parents have more impact on their daughters' sexuality than on their sons' (Miller & Moore, 1990; Newcomer & Udry, 1987). Parental attitudes, behaviors, and teachings seem to have greater effects on females than on males (Thornton & Camburn, 1987).

Parents are not subject to being chosen or dropped on the basis of personal inclinations, so studies of parents are not vulnerable to the alternative explanation on the basis that sexual wishes are the cause rather than the effect, but there are other issues. In particular, it is plausible that parents try harder to influence their daughters than their sons. Still, some of the parental impact studies do not reflect differential exertion. For example, parental divorce appears to have a stronger effect on the daughter's subsequent sex life (e.g., toward starting earlier and having more partners) than the son's, and it is fair to assume that almost no divorces are motivated by the goal of making the daughter more promiscuous.

The question whether sexual orientation is chosen or not has been debated at some length and with some political and religious bias (e.g., is it fair to reproach people as sinful for feeling ways they cannot help). One creative and novel approach has been to ask people whether they feel they had some choice as to whether be homosexual or heterosexual. Having choice is one sign of plasticity, insofar as one must be capable of more than one possible orientation in order to be able to choose from them. Only a minority of people claim to feel that their sexual orientation was a matter of choice, but this minority is almost entirely female (Rosenbluth, 1997; Whisman, 1996). Indeed, gay males are more likely than gay females to express the wish that they could change to a heterosexual orientation, but apparently most men feel that this is impossible.

Another approach to assessing social and cultural influences is to consider the environmental factors and compare them against genetic influences. Stronger effects of genes indicate low plasticity. Although the information base for this sort of comparison is limited, there are several findings suggesting that genetic influences on sexuality are stronger among males than among females. One finding is that male identical twins are more likely than other pairs to have begun having sex at the same age (though the finding is limited to more modern times, after the sexual revolution, probably because of limited opportunities available to males before this) (Dunne et al., 1997). Female identical twins are less likely to start having sex at the same age, which implies that the onset of sexual behavior has a stronger genetic component among males than among females (and therefore, conversely, the onset of sexual behavior is more shaped by social and situational factors among females than among males).

The issue of genetic influences on homosexuality has attracted considerable research attention. Most studies find stronger evidence of some genetic input among males than among females. In particular, the preliminary finding of a possible "gay gene" was based solely on a male sample, and no such claim has been made regarding females. A review by Bailey and Pillard (1995) concluded that either male homosexuality is more genetically determined than female homosexuality, or the state of evidence remains inadequate to draw a conclusion. At the time, they favored the latter (more cautious) position, but we suspect that in time the former conclusion will be confirmed. Recent work by Lippa (2003) further supports a greater biological contribution to homosexuality in men than in women. In a study of more than 2,000 participants, he found that the ratio of index to ring-finger lengths differed in males and females. Men typically have a lower index to ring-finger ratio than do females. Homosexual and heterosexual men also showed different ratios. Homosexual men had higher, more typically feminine ratios. However, finger-length ratios were not related to sexual orientation in women, which suggests a lesser biological contribution to sexual orientation in women than in men.

The pattern of sexual identification in a gay and a lesbian sample is also instructive. Savin-Williams and Diamond (2000) found that women generally self-identify as lesbians first, and then engage in same-sex sexual activity. The pattern was reversed in men. They generally labeled themselves as gay after seeking sexual encounters with other men. Assuming that biology is less involved in self-labeling than it is in the pursuit of sex, this pattern points to the primacy of biology in male sexuality in contrast to the primacy of meaningful self-definition in women.

Given the sensitive political nature of the issue, we hasten to clarify our position. It would be reckless to conclude that sexual orientation is entirely dictated by genes or environment in anyone. Even identical twins, who share exactly the same genes, do not always end up with the same sexual orientation. Most likely, some combination of genetic predisposition, social influences, and formative experiences (see Bem, 1996) contribute to sexual orientation in both genders. Our point is merely that the direct contribution of genes is probably stronger in males, whereas the greater plasticity of females leaves more room for the social environment to shape sexual orientation—perhaps repeatedly.

Indeed, plasticity may underlie some of the startling new findings about sexual orientation in women. Diamond (2000) has noted the stereotype that people merely try to pass as heterosexual because of social and cultural pressures, but once a woman engages in lesbian sex, she may discover that it is her true nature and hence will not go back. Contrary to this, Diamond's longitudinal sample has provided ample cases of women who initially identify as heterosexual, then have a serious lesbian relationship, and when that ends have their next relationship with a man. The person, rather than the person's gender, was apparently the crucial determinant of whom the woman would love and sexually desire. The ability to be satisfied in a sexual relationship with someone of either gender is itself an indication of relatively high plasticity. In a recent follow-up study, Diamond (2003) found that 27 percent of lesbian or bisexual women had changed their sexual identities over a five-year period. Half of these women gave up any identity label, and half had reclaimed heterosexuality. Those who relinquished their lesbian or bisexual identities were similar to those who had maintained it in their sexual identity development. Consistent with the erotic plasticity hypothesis, the crucial factor in altering their identity appears to have been a shift in those they found sexually desirable.

Attitude-Behavior Consistency

A third way that erotic plasticity manifests itself is in low correlations between general attitudes and specific behaviors. If plasticity is low, then the person's general attitudes are likely to predict what he will feel and want (and presumably do) in most situations. In contrast, if plasticity is high, then the person will find that her behavior depends on specific aspects of the situation, and her general attitudes will not apply all the time. High plasticity means that social and situational factors are influential, in which case, behavior is less consistent.

A variety of evidence confirms that attitude-behavior consistency is lower, at least in the sexual realm, among women than among men. Many researchers have confirmed that girls and women are more likely than boys and men to engage in sexual behaviors of which they do not approve, and, indeed, they may continue doing them despite their own ongoing disapproval (Antonovsky, Shoham, Kavenocki, Modan, & Lancet, 1978; Christensen & Carpenter, 1962). These inconsistencies ranged from adolescent girls who were having intercourse despite advocating abstinence, to adult women who disapproved of casual sex but engaged in it anyway (Croake & James, 1973; Herold & Mewhinney, 1993). A variation on this inconsistency is having sex when one does not desire to have it. Although both men and women in committed relationships periodically report engaging in sex when they did not feel desire (usually because they wanted to please a partner), women report this more frequently than men (Beck, Bozman, & Qualtrough, 1991).

Most people advocate using condoms, especially when having sex for the first time or with a partner one does not know well. But many people act contrary to this, by having sex without condoms or other protection under those circumstances. Still, some work suggests that the gap is larger for women than for men (Herold & Mewhinney, 1993). This is ironic because most people believe that condoms detract from male sexual pleasure more than from that of female, so one might have predicted the opposite result. Plasticity can, however, explain the greater gap for women.

Many people disapprove of extramarital sexual activity or extradyadic sexual activity (e.g., sex outside of a committed relationship) but engage in it anyway. Such inconsistency appears to be higher among women. Hansen (1987) showed that attitudes toward extramarital sex predicted actual behavior fairly closely for men but not for women. Thus, many women may regard extradyadic sex as desirable and exciting yet never engage in it, while others may disapprove of it but do it anyway.

Similar findings emerged regarding same-sex activity. The NHSLS (Laumann et al., 1994) asked respondents whether they liked the idea of having sex with a member of their own gender and whether they had done so during the past year. For males, these questions were very highly correlated, but for women there was much less connection. Thus, again, many women liked the idea but never did it, whereas others disliked the idea but had done it anyway. Specific and situational factors presumably overrode the general attitudes, consistent with high plasticity.

Attitudes about sexuality are conducive to making specific predictions about behavior. One would expect behavior to correspond to the attitude. However, there are other dispositional variables that do not lend themselves to a priori predictions about sexual behavior. Attachment style is one such variable that appears to affect sexuality. In a sample of nearly 800 participants, Bogaert and Sadava (2002) found that adult attachment style covaries with sexual behavior, and it does so disproportionably in women. Infidelity was related significantly to an anxious attachment style in women, and not in men. Recent condom use was related to both secure and anxious attachment styles in women, but not in men. Age of first intercourse was also related to both secure and anxious attachment in women, and, again, not in men. There were no behavioral variables (although some dispositional variables) that were significantly correlated to attachment style in men, with the exception of attachment.

It is plausible that some of the behaviors (i.e., early intercourse) may have influenced attachment style, so we do not cite this as evidence that female sexuality is necessarily dictated by attachment style. However, it does appear safe to conclude that attachment is a social/situational factor that is more closely tied to female sexuality than to male sexuality. As the scale tips toward a relatively greater social influence in women, it points to a relatively greater role of biology in men.

Differential Arousal in the Laboratory

This broad pattern of gender differences in erotic plasticity should also be observable when tested empirically in the laboratory. Indeed, objective physiological measurements of sexual arousal also indicate that women display greater variability in the stimuli that sexually arouse them than do men. By monitoring penile circumference fluctuations (via plethysmograph) and vaginal vasocongestion (by photoplethysmograph), level of arousal can be directly monitored. Using this technique, researchers have shown that women are aroused by a greater variety of erotic images than are men (Chivers, Rieger, Latty, & Bailey, 2004). Regardless of sexual orientation, men reacted physiologically to seeing sexual acts performed by the gender of their preference: homosexual men were aroused by watching male–male sex, while heterosexual men were aroused by watching female–female sex. Women did not display this same pattern of arousal. Lesbian and heterosexual women were aroused as a result of seeing both male–male and female–female sexual acts.

Clearly, the instrumentation needed to measure vaginal vasocongestion differs from what is needed to measure penile circumference fluctuations, which presents a potential limit to interpretability. The gender differences in arousal plausibly could have been because vaginal vasocongestion is only capable of measuring diffuse sexual arousal, not the gender-of-preference-specific arousal found in men. Chivers et al. (2004) employed a clever solution. Using the same instrumentation employed in the genetic female sample, they tested male-to-female transsexuals. Results indicated that transsexuals who preferred men were aroused by male–male images, while those who preferred women were aroused by the female-female stimulus. Thus, male-to-female transsexuals showed the same preference-specific physiological reactions as did heterosexual and homosexual males, and did so using instrumentation that did not detect this pattern in females.

Subjective measures of arousal also were consistent with greater plasticity in women. Women indicated that they were aroused by a greater variety of stimuli than were men. However, women's subjective ratings of arousal showed a much weaker correspondence with physiological arousal than did men's. Although this finding does not necessarily follow a priori from the plasticity hypothesis, it is relevant, particularly in light of evolutionary theories of sexuality.

Species propagation cannot occur without a high degree of male arousal, but it can occur without a commensurate degree of female arousal. Therefore, sexual initiation would have been wasteful if the male were not physiologically prepared for penetration. Thus, it would be efficient that the traditional initiator, the male, be more consciously aware of preparedness for mating than the female. The seeming disconnect between women's conscious awareness of arousal and actual physiological arousal is likely to result in a degree of uncertainty about actual physiological arousal. This uncertainty in females may have made them more receptive to male initiation, regardless of their actual arousal. If a female who is somewhat less aroused than her male counterpart is unaware of this fact, she is more likely to consent to mating than if she were aware of it. Therefore, if a degree of uncertainty is indeed related to greater receptivity, the disconnect between consciousness and physical arousal, and the resulting uncertainty, may help explain the pattern of broader sexual receptivity (plasticity) in women.

A classical conditioning study found this same pattern of gender-based differences in erotic plasticity (Hoffmann, Janssen, & Turner, 2004). Researchers paired a picture of an abdomen with an erotic film clip for both male and female participants. Heterosexual male participants were shown a female abdomen, and heterosexual female participants were shown a male abdomen. Both genders became sexually conditioned to the abdomen. That is, repeated pairings demonstrated an increase over baseline in genital arousal when participants were presented with the abdomen. However, when the stimulus paired with the erotic film clip was both sexually irrelevant and presented subliminally, a disparity emerged. Women showed a significant increase in genital sexual arousal when the erotic film was paired with a gun, while men did not show a commensurate increase. This is consistent with the female sex drive as changeable.

Any Exceptions?

A determined search for counterexamples yielded only a handful of suggestive findings. For instance, not all evidence points in the direction of greater biological contributions in sexual orientation for men than for women. A study investigating the relationship between fingerprint patterns and handedness found a significant relationship between handedness and sexual orientation in women, but not in men (Mustanski, Bailey, & Kaspar, 2002). Fingerprint patterns were unrelated to orientation in both genders. The aforementioned difference in finger-length ratios is a natural point of comparison to this finding. Finger-length ratios are more compelling evidence of biology than is handedness because handedness is subject to social factors, and finger lengths are not. A study investigating shifting handedness trends in Japan found some evidence that men's hand preferences are more malleable than women's (Iwasaki, Kaiho, & Iseki, 1995). This might account for the lack of relationship between handedness and sexual orientation in men.

The most instructive counterexamples of erotic plasticity point toward childhood. For example, males are more likely than females to acquire sexual paraphilias (sexual arousal to atypical stimuli, e.g., nonhuman objects or unconsenting humans), and although the origins of these are poorly understood, most evidence points to some kind of childhood experience that creates the unusual sexual desire. In adulthood, paraphilias have low plasticity and are quite difficult to change or erase.

There is also some evidence that childhood sexual abuse has more severe and long-lasting effects on boys than on girls. A follow-up to the NHSLS found that people who had suffered sexual abuse as children were more likely to have sexual health problems as adults if they were men rather than women (Laumann, Paik, & Rosen, 1999).

Such findings suggest that there may be a phase of plasticity in male sexual development, but it is apparently in childhood. Once the boy reaches puberty, the pattern of sexual tastes and preferences is largely set (though the person may not discover all these until some time later, especially if he regards his desires as socially unacceptable). In contrast, female sexuality may continue to develop and change throughout adulthood. This may help women recover from events of childhood, and, as such, would be one clear benefit of plasticity for some people.

Some research with animals confirms the conclusion of a brief phase of plasticity during male childhood, although cross-species generalizations about sex must be made very cautiously. An experimental study by Kendrick, Haupt, Hinton, Broad, and Skinner (2001) swapped baby sheep and goats at birth, so that each was raised by the other species. The adults were allowed access to both species, and their mating preferences were observed. Consistent with high plasticity, the females copulated with the other species. The males exhibited low plasticity but in a most curious manner: they would only mate with their adoptive species, and not their own true species. This indicates that the male sexual preferences were shaped during childhood and remained fixed during adulthood, even though those preferences were such that they would prevent offspring.

Why the Difference?

The evidence for the gender difference in erotic plasticity is abundant and consistent, but the reason for the difference is far less clear. Several possible explanations could be proposed:

Differential power provides one line of explanation. Because women have generally had less physical strength and less political power than men, they may have had to be more flexible. Lacking power to get what they want, they would instead benefit from accommodating themselves to external influences. This line of argument would predict that women would generally have higher plasticity in most social behaviors.

An intriguing explanation could be developed from the so-called gate-keeper role of female sexuality. The idea here is that men want sex earlier and with more partners, and so it is up to the woman to decide when and whether sex happens. In practice, most women will start out saying no to most sexual invitations, but at some point the woman may change her vote to yes, and at that point sex happens. The close linkage of sex to changing one's decision could require or foster a broader flexibility that could be manifested in erotic plasticity. This line of argument would be specific to sex.

The third explanation invokes strength of motivation. It is plausible that milder drives are more amenable to civilizing influences. Nearly all signs indicate that men have more frequent and intense sexual desires than women (for review, see Baumeister, Catanese, & Vohs, 2001), and women's plasticity might derive from the milder drive. This line of argument would apply wherever there are gender (or other group) differences in strength of motivation.

More research is needed before we can establish which of these explanations is correct. At present, the evidence seems to favor the last one. The relevant test case would be some motivation that is more frequent and intense among women than among men: would then men have higher plasticity? By most accounts, the desire to create and nurture children is stronger among women than among men. Moreover, and crucially, the father role appears to be much more variable across cultural and historical boundaries than the mother role (e.g., Fukuyama, 1999). In other words, when women's desire is stronger, it is also marked by less plasticity, and so this lends plausibility to the argument that the difference in sexual drive is linked to the difference in erotic plasticity.

CONCLUSION

Erotic plasticity makes the sex drive malleable and enables cultural and situational factors to shape and alter it, not least by use of meanings. Plainly, many animals in nature have satisfactory, efficacious sex without any influence of culturally constructed or individually interpreted meanings. Yet, just as plainly, many human sexual responses depend heavily and sometimes crucially on meaning. The great variety of human sexual response is partly attributable to the plasticity that is prepared by nature and activated by cultural meanings.

A substantial body of evidence indicates that female sexuality has higher plasticity, and is therefore more open to social and cultural influences, than male sexuality. The reason for the gender difference in plasticity is not established with anywhere near the certainty that the fact of the difference is, but at present the best guess is that it is linked to the mildness versus intensity of the desire. High erotic plasticity is not necessarily better or worse than low, but it has wide-ranging implications, including ease of self-knowledge, ease of adaptation to new demands and circumstances, capacity for change across the lifespan, and optimal type of therapeutic intervention. Future work is needed to extend and verify the implications of gender differences in plasticity as well as to establish its basic causes. Future work is also desirable to map out dimensions other than gender that can promote differential plasticity.

REFERENCES

Adams, C. G., & Turner, B. F. (1985). Reported change in sexuality from young adulthood to old age. *Journal of Sex Research, 21*, 126–141.

Antonovsky, H. F., Shoham, I., Kavenocki, S., Modan, B., & Lancet, M. (1978). Sexual attitude-behavior discrepancy among Israeli adolescent girls. *Journal of Sex Research, 14*, 260–272.

Ard, B. N. (1977). Sex in lasting marriages: A longitudinal study. *Journal of Sex Research, 13*, 274–285.

Bailey, J. M., & Pillard, R. C. (1995). Genetics of human sexual orientation. *Annual Review of Sex Research, 6*, 126–150.

Barry, H., & Schlegel, A. (1984). Measurements of adolescent sexual behavior in the standard sample of societies. *Ethnology, 23*, 315–329.

Bart, P. B. (1993). Protean women: The liquidity of female sexuality and the tenaciousness of lesbian identity. In S. Wilkinson & C. Kitzinger (Eds.), *Heterosexuality: Feminism and psychology reader* (pp. 246–252). London: Sage.

Baumeister, R. F. (2000). Gender differences in erotic plasticity: The female sex drive as socially flexible and responsive. *Psychological Bulletin, 126*, 347–374.

Baumeister, R. F., Catanese, K. R., & Vohs, K. D. (2001). Is there a gender difference in strength of sex drive? Theoretical views, conceptual distinctions, and a review of relevant evidence. *Personality and Social Psychology Review, 5*, 242–273.

Beck, J. G., Bozman, A. W., & Qualtrough, T. (1991). The experience of sexual desire: Psychological correlates in a college sample. *Journal of Sex Research, 28*, 443–456.

Bell, A. P., & Weinberg, M. S. (1978). *Homosexualities: A study of diversity among men and women.* New York: Simon and Schuster.

Bem, D. J. (1996). Exotic becomes erotic: A developmental theory of sexual orientation. *Psychological Review, 103*, 320–335.

Billy, J. O. G., & Udry, J. R. (1985). Patterns of adolescent friendship and effects on sexual behavior. *Social Psychology Quarterly, 48*, 27–41.

Bogaert, A. F., & Sadava, S. (2002). Attachment style and sexual behavior. *Personal Relationships, 9*, 191–204.

Chivers, M. L., Rieger, G., Latty, E., & Bailey, J. M. (2004). A sex difference in the specificity of sexual arousal. *Psychological Science, 15*, 736–744.

Christensen, H. T., & Carpenter, G. R. (1962). Value-behavior discrepancies regarding premarital coitus in three Western cultures. *American Sociological Review, 27*, 66–74.

Croake, J. W., & James, B. (1973). A four-year comparison of premarital sexual attitudes. *Journal of Sex Research, 9*, 91–96.

Diamond, L. M. (2000). Sexual identity, attractions, and behavior among young sexual-minority women over a two-year period. *Developmental Psychology, 36*, 241–250.

Diamond, L. M. (2003). Was it a phase? Young women's relinquishment of lesbian/bisexual identities over a 5-year period. *Journal of Personality and Social Psychology, 84*, 352–364.

Dunne, M. P., Martin, N. G., Statham, D. J., Slutske, W. S., Dinwiddie, S. H., Bucholz, K. K., et al. (1997). Genetic and environmental contributions to variance in age at first sexual intercourse. *Psychological Science, 8*, 211–216.

Fang, B. (1976). Swinging: In retrospect. *Journal of Sex Research, 12*, 220–237.

Ford, K., & Norris, A. E. (1993). Urban Hispanic adolescents and young adults: Relationship of acculturation to sexual behavior. *Journal of Sex Research, 30*, 316–323.

Fukuyama, F. (1999). *The great disruption: Human nature and the reconstitution of social order.* New York: Free Press.

Gagnon, J. H., & Simon, W. (1968). The social meaning of prison homosexuality. *Federal Probation, 32*, 28–29.

Giallombardo, R. (1966). *Society of women: A study of a women's prison.* New York: Wiley.

Goode, E., & Haber, L. (1977). Sexual correlates of homosexual experience: An exploratory study of college women. *Journal of Sex Research, 13*, 12–21.

Hansen, G. L. (1987). Extradyadic relations during courtship. *Journal of Sex Research, 23*, 382–390.

Harrison, D. A., Bennett, W. H., Globetti, G., & Alsikafi, M. (1974). Premarital sexual standards of rural youth. *Journal of Sex Research, 10*, 266–277.

Herold, E. S., & Mewhinney, D.-M. K. (1993). Gender differences in casual sex and AIDS prevention: A survey of dating bars. *Journal of Sex Research, 30*, 36–42.

Hoffmann, H., Janssen, E., & Turner, S. (2004). Classical conditioning of sexual arousal in women and men: Effects of varying awareness and biological relevance of the CS. *Archives of Sexual Behavior, 33*, 43–53.

Iwasaki, S., Kaiho, T., & Iseki, K. (1995). Handedness trends across age groups in a Japanese sample of 2316. *Perceptual & Motor Skills, 80,* 979–994.

Kendrick, K. M., Haupt, M. A., Hinton, M. R., Broad, K. D., & Skinner J. D. (2001). Sex differences in the influence of mothers on the socio-sexual preferences of their offspring. *Hormones and Behaviour, 40,* 322–338.

Kinsey, A. C., Pomeroy, W. B., & Martin, C. E. (1948). *Sexual behavior in the human male.* Philadelphia: Saunders.

Kinsey, A. C., Pomeroy, W. B., Martin, C. E., & Gebhard, P. H. (1953). *Sexual behavior in the human female.* Philadelphia: Saunders.

Kitzinger, C., & Wilkinson, S. (1995). Transitions from heterosexuality to lesbianism: The discursive production of lesbian identities. *Developmental Psychology, 31,* 95–104.

Laumann, E. O., Gagnon, J. H., Michael, R. T., & Michaels, S. (1994). *The social organization of sexuality: Sexual practices in the United States.* Chicago: University of Chicago Press.

Laumann, E. O., Paik, A., & Rosen, R. C. (1999). Sexual dysfunction in the United States: Prevalence and predictors. *Journal of the American Medical Association, 281,* 537–544.

Lippa, R. A. (2003). Handedness, sexual orientation, and gender-related personality traits in men and women. *Archives of Sexual Behavior, 32,* 103–114.

McCauley, E. A., & Ehrhardt, A. A. (1980). Sexual behavior in female transsexuals and lesbians. *Journal of Sex Research, 16,* 202–211.

Miller, B. C., & Moore, K. A. (1990). Adolescent sexual behavior, pregnancy, and parenting: Research through the 1980s. *Journal of Marriage and the Family, 52,* 1025–1044.

Mirande, A. M. (1968). Reference group theory and adolescent sexual behavior. *Journal of Marriage and the Family, 30,* 572–577.

Mustanski, B. S., Bailey, J. M., & Kaspar, S. (2002). Dermato-glyphics, handedness, sex and sexual orientation. *Archives of Sexual Behavior, 31,* 113–122.

Newcomer, S., & Udry, J. R. (1987). Parental marital status effects on adolescent sexual behavior. *Journal of Marriage and the Family, 49,* 235–240.

O'Neill, G. C., & O'Neill, N. (1970). Patterns in group sexual activity. *Journal of Sex Research, 6,* 101–112.

Reiss, I. L. (1967). *The social context of premarital sexual permissiveness.* New York: Holt, Rinehart, & Winston.

Rosario, M., Meyer-Bahlburg, H. F. L., Hunter, J., Exner, T. M., Gwadz, M., & Keller, A. M. (1996). The psychosexual development of urban lesbian, gay, and bisexual youths. *Journal of Sex Research, 33,* 113–126.

Rosenbluth, S. (1997). Is sexual orientation a matter of choice? *Psychology of Women Quarterly, 21,* 595–610.

Rust, P. C. (1992). The politics of sexual identity: Sexual attraction and behavior among lesbian and bisexual women. *Social Problems, 39,* 366–386.

Sack, A. R., Keller, J. F., & Hinkle, D. E. (1984). Premarital sexual intercourse: A test of the effects of peer group, religiosity, and sexual guilt. *Journal of Sex Research, 20,* 168–185.

Savin-Williams, R. C. (1990). *Gay and lesbian youth: Expressions of identity.* New York: Hemisphere.

Savin-Williams, R. C., & Diamond, L. M. (2000). Sexual identity trajectories among sexual-minority youths: Gender comparisons. *Archives of Sexual Behavior, 29,* 419–440.

Schäfer, S. (1976). Sexual and social problems of lesbians. *Journal of Sex Research, 12,* 50–69.

Smith, J. R., & Smith, L. G. (1970). Co-marital sex and the sexual freedom movement. *Journal of Sex Research, 6,* 131–142.

Thornton, A., & Camburn, D. (1987). The influence of the family on premarital attitudes and behavior. *Demography, 24,* 323–340.

Vanwesenbeeck, I., Bekker, M., & van Lenning, A. (1998). Gender attitudes, sexual meanings, and interactional patterns in heterosexual encounters among college students in the Netherlands. *Journal of Sex Research, 35,* 317–327.

Ward, D. A., & Kassebaum, G. G. (1965). *Women's prison: Sex and social structure.* Chicago: Aldine.

Weis, D., Rabinowitz, B., & Ruckstuhl, M. F. (1992). Individual changes in sexual attitudes and behavior within college-level human sexuality courses. *Journal of Sex Research, 29,* 43–59.

Whisman, V. (1996). *Queer by choice.* New York: Routledge.

Wilson, W. C. (1975). The distribution of selected sexual attitudes and behaviors among the adult population of the United States. *Journal of Sex Research, 11,* 46–64.

Index

About the Editors
and Contributors

M. MICHELE BURNETTE holds a doctorate in clinical psychology and a Master's of Public Health in epidemiology. Dr. Burnette was formerly a psychology professor at Western Michigan University, during which time she taught courses in human sexuality and conducted research on sexual function and health. She has also taught at the community college level and at the University of Pittsburgh. She is currently in private practice in Columbia, South Carolina, where she specializes in therapy for sexual problems. She has coauthored two textbooks with Richard D. McAnulty, *Human Sexuality: Making Healthy Decisions* (2004) and *Fundamentals in Human Sexuality: Making Healthy Decisions* (2003). She is also coeditor of this set.

RICHARD D. McANULTY is an associate professor of psychology at the University of North Carolina at Charlotte. He earned his Ph.D. in clinical psychology from the University of Georgia under the late Henry E. Adams. His research interests broadly encompass human sexuality and its problems. His books include *The Psychology of Sexual Orientation, Behavior, and Identity: A Handbook*, edited with Louis Diamant (Greenwood Press, 1994), and *Human Sexuality: Making Healthy Decisions* (2004), with Michele Burnette. He has served on the board of several journals, including the *Journal of Sex Research*.

ROY F. BAUMEISTER is the Eppes Eminent Professor of Psychology at Florida State University. He has over 300 research publications on topics that include self and identity, self-control, the need to belong and interpersonal rejection, sexuality, aggression, and violence. His books include *The Cultural Animal: Human Nature, Meaning, and Social Life; The Social Dimension of Sex; Evil: Inside Human Violence and Cruelty;* and *Meanings of Life.*

LAINA Y. BAY-CHENG is assistant professor of social work at the University at Buffalo—SUNY, where she studies the confluence of gender and sexual socialization during adolescence. Her scholarship includes critical studies of sexuality education—both in schools and online—as well as empowerment practice with early adolescent girls. Current research considers the relational contexts of adolescent women's sexual experiences including issues of power, consent, and desire.

DAN BROWN, Ph.D., is professor of communication and associate dean of the College of Arts and Sciences at East Tennessee State University. His publications deal with growth trends in media, content and uses of pornography, learning and media, effects of television on family values, entertainment features in children's educational television, humor in mass media and college teaching, and enjoyment of televised sports.

VERN L. BULLOUGH is a State University of New York Distinguished Professor Emeritus. His current research focuses on sex and gender issues. Among other honors, he has been given the Alfred Kinsey Award and the John MoneyAward for his research in human sexuality, and he received an honorary D.Sci. degree from SUNY at the Buffalo State College convocation in 2004. He is the author, coauthor, or editor of more than fifty books, has contributed chapters to more than 100 other books, and has published more than 100 refereed articles. He is a fellow of the Society for the Scientific Study of Sex and of the American Academy of Nursing. He is also a laureate in the International Academy of Humanism. He was a founder of the Center for Sex Research at California State University, Northridge (now called the Center for Sex and Gender Studies). He has lectured and presented in most of the fifty states and in thirty-five foreign countries.

C. NATHAN DEWALL is a graduate student in social psychology at Florida State University. His primary area of interest is self and identity, and he has published several papers related to the emotional, cognitive, and behavioral consequences of social exclusion. He has also published papers on topics related to attitudes and persuasion, and prejudice and stereotyping.

VIRGINIA GIL-RIVAS received her doctorate degree in psychology and social behavior at the University of California, Irvine, with a dual emphasis on health and developmental psychology. She is currently an associate professor of psychology at the University of North Carolina, Charlotte. She previously worked as the director of several federally funded research projects at the University of California, Los Angeles—Integrated Substance Abuse Programs. Her research interests include studying the long-term psychosocial effects of traumatic events on adolescents and adults, such as behavioral difficulties, depression, anxiety disorders, and substance use. In addition, her work has focused on examining factors associated with the initiation and maintenance of healthy behavior change, and evaluation of prevention and treatment interventions among diverse populations.

MICHAEL R. KAUTH, Ph.D., is codirector of the Department of Veterans Affairs (VA) South Central Mental Illness Research, Education and Clinical Center (MIRECC). He is also assistant clinical professor at the Tulane University School of Medicine and the Louisiana State University School of Medicine. He has written several chapters and articles on sexual orientation and sexuality and is the author of *True Nature: A Theory of Sexual Attraction* (2000).

RYAN P. KILMER is associate professor of psychology at the University of North Carolina at Charlotte. A child clinical-community psychologist, his interests center around children and families and factors influencing the development of children at risk for emotional, behavioral, or academic difficulties, particularly child risk and resilience (i.e., effective coping and adaptation in the face of major life stress); the use of evaluation research to guide system change, program refinement, and service delivery; and clinical assessment. His primary current research effort is an NIMH-funded project examining risk and resilience among the siblings of children with severe emotional disturbances. He has also been actively involved in efforts to improve services for children and families served through local mental health systems.

LESLIE KOOYMAN, M.A., is currently pursuing a doctorate in counseling at the University of North Carolina at Charlotte. He has worked in HIV/AIDS for the past twenty years as the founding director of the community-based AIDS service organization in the Charlotte region. His work includes developing and managing both care and prevention services for people living with HIV disease. He has also maintained a counseling and consulting practice assisting individuals and communities in addressing HIV/AIDS issues.

LINWOOD J. LEWIS is assistant professor of psychology at Sarah Lawrence College, as well as an adjunct assistant professor of medical psychology (in sociomedical sciences and psychiatry) at Columbia University. His research interests range from the development of sexuality in ethnic minority adolescents and adults, to the negotiation of HIV within families, to the effects of culture and social context on conceptualization of genetic health and illness. He is a member of the International Academy of Sex Research, the National Society of Genetic Counselors, and the American Psychological Association.

JON K. MANER is an assistant professor of psychology at Florida State University. He received his Ph.D. in 2003 from Arizona State University. Dr. Maner's research focuses on applying evolutionary principles to explore the links between human motivation and social cognition. He has published several papers on the psychology of human mating and was awarded the 2005 Postdoctoral Research Award by the Human Behavior and Evolution Society for his work on mating-related cognition.

TAMAR MURACHVER (Ph.D., University of California, San Diego) is a senior lecturer in psychology at the University of Otago, New Zealand. Her research and teaching focus on language, thought, and child development. Her research interests include the interplay between language and memory, how language is used to create and maintain social categories (such as gender and ethnicity), and how opportunities to communicate help children learn about the thoughts and feelings of others.

CHARLENE RAPSEY is a doctoral and clinical psychology student at the University of Otago, New Zealand. Her research interests involve interventions promoting adolescent well-being, with a focus on sexuality. She has had the privilege of working directly with adolescents as a teacher and in community settings.

ARIANA SHAHINFAR is a developmental psychologist and adjunct faculty member at the University of North Carolina at Charlotte. Her research interests include understanding the impact of growing up in high-risk communities on the social and emotional development of children and adolescents. She is currently involved in developing ways in which to support the psychological health of at-risk families and communities by strengthening parent-infant attachments. Among other honors, she was the recipient of the American Psychological Association's Distinguished Dissertation Award for her research on the correlates of community violence exposure among preschool-aged children.

THOMASINA H. SHARPE, M.D., is a board certified family physician who is the medical director of the University of South Alabama Student Health Center. She has published and lectured widely on topics of adolescent, geriatric, and adult sexuality as well as gender issues in genital and clitoral hood piercing. A former assistant professor of family medicine at the University of South Alabama College of Medicine, Dr. Sharpe still lectures undergraduate, graduate, medical, and physician assistant students on a variety of medical and sexual topics. She is a graduate of the University of South Alabama College of Medicine and completed her residency training in family medicine at East Tennessee State University. Dr. Sharpe is currently studying the clinical and cultural significance of aesthetic trends in genital adornment in adolescent and college women.

TOM W. SMITH is an internationally recognized expert in survey research specializing in the study of social change and survey methodology. Since 1980 he has been coprincipal investigator of the National Data Program for the Social Sciences and director of its General Social Survey. He is also cofounder and former secretary general (1997–2003) of the International Social Survey Program, the largest cross-national collaboration in the social sciences. Smith has taught at Purdue University, Northwestern University, the University of Chicago, and Tel Aviv University. He was awarded the 1994 Worcester Prize by the World Association for Public Opinion Research (WAPOR) for the best article on public opinion, the 2000 and 2003 Innovators Award of the American Association for Public Opinion Research (AAPOR), and the 2002 AAPOR Award for Exceptionally Distinguished Achievement.

TYLER STILLMAN is a Ph.D. student in social psychology at Florida State University. He has a master's degree in psychology from Brigham Young University. He is researching self-control, close relationships, and the value of consciousness with his academic advisors Roy Baumeister and Dianne Tice.

MICHAEL WIEDERMAN is an associate professor of psychology at Columbia College, a small, all-women's college in Columbia, South Carolina. He is currently the book review editor for the *Journal of Sex Research* and serves on the editorial boards of *Body Image* and the *Journal of Psychology and Human Sexuality*. Wiederman authored *Understanding Sexuality Research* (2001) and coedited *The Handbook for Conducting Research on Human Sexuality* (2001). More recently, Wiederman founded Mindful Publications, LLC, to promote dissemination of psychology to the general public.